# An Introduction to
# Forensic
# DNA
# Analysis

Credits for contributed photos:

Figures 6-10, 7-12, 9-14, 9-16, 9-18; courtesy of *Roche Molecular Systems*
Figure 7-17; courtesy of *TECAN, Austria*
Figure 7-18; courtesy of *Perkin-Elmer/Applied Biosystems Division*
Figure 7-19; courtesy of *Molecular Dynamics*
SIDEBAR 3; courtesy of *Dr. Edward Blake*
SIDEBAR 4; courtesy of *Armed Forces DNA Identification Laboratory* (previously published
    in Nature Genetics Vol. 12 pg 417)
SIDEBAR 5; courtesy of *Palm Beach County Sheriff's Office Crime Laboratory*
SIDEBAR 10; courtesy of *District Attorney's office, Orlando, FL*


Illustrations (including cover) and Photography: Norah Rudin, PhD.




Slide and print sets from the illustrations and photos in this book are available directly from
the authors. Please contact:

NR BIOCOM
11780 San Pablo Avenue
Suite 4C, Box 225
El Cerrito, CA  94530-1750

FAX: (510) 236-1601
e. mail: nrbiocom@uclink4.berkeley.edu

# An Introduction to
# Forensic
# DNA
# Analysis

## Keith Inman, M. Crim.
Senior Criminalist, California Department of Justice DNA Laboratory
Instructor, University of California at Berkeley Extension

## Norah Rudin, Ph.D.
Forensic DNA Consultant, Richmond, California
Science and Technical Writer
Instructor, University of California at Berkeley Extension

**CRC Press**
**Boca Raton   New York**

| | |
|---|---|
| Publisher: | Robert B. Stern |
| Project Editor: | Helen Linna |
| Marketing Manager: | Greg Daurelle |
| Direct Marketing Manager: | Bill Boone |
| Cover design: | Denise Craig |
| PrePress: | Kevin Luong |

**Library of Congress Cataloging-in-Publication Data**

Inman, Keith
    An introduction to forensic DNA analysis/ Keith Inman and Norah Rudin
        p.  cm.
    Includes bibliographical references and index.
    ISBN 0-8493-8117-7
    1. DNA fingerprinting.  I. Rudin, Norah.  II. Title.
  RA1057.55.I56 1996
  614′.1—dc21
                                                                96-38138
                                                               CIP

*Author's Note:*

Many of our readers will be familiar with the previous iteration of this work, *DNA Demystified*. Because of the addition of major sections and a change in title, the rules and regulations of the literary world do not allow us to call this work a second edition. However, *An Introduction to Forensic DNA Analysis* is, in fact, the updated and expanded version of *DNA Demystified*. We have also gratefully acquired CRC Press, Inc. as a publisher, allowing us to concentrate on the technical material.

In preparing this volume, we have incorporated numerous suggestions from our readers and colleagues. As the field progresses in sophistication, so do its consumers. With this in mind, we have greatly expanded our consideration of interpretational issues in particular. These discussions are concentrated in *Chapter 9*, but are also scattered in various other sections  With their inclusion, this book can no longer be considered "for beginners only". For those who are truly novice in DNA typing (and where were you during *Simpson* anyway?), we suggest that you simply start from the beginning and work your way through. We have instituted a paradigm, both within each chapter, and for the book as a whole, of proceeding with each concept, in order, from simpler generalizations to more complex specifics. Although additional information is included for those who are in a position to take advantage of it, the beginner will still be able to extract basic information, and simply ignore the rest until necessity or curiosity strikes.

We have added a section (*Chapter 11*) on quality control and regulation of forensic DNA typing, an area that is currently under great scrutiny. We have also added a number of case studies (*Sidebars*), both to illustrate some important concepts and to introduce some of the less pervasive techniques.  Additionally we have made a point of including a representative sampling of cases and legal decisions from across the country.

We sincerely hope that these additions will increase the usefulness of this book. As always, we welcome input from our readers.

# TABLE OF CONTENTS

**Chapter 1**
Introduction ........................................................................................................................ 1

**Chapter 2**
The Nature of Physical Evidence ..................................................................................... 3
    I.   Science and the Law ................................................................................ 3
    II.  From Identification to Individualization ............................................. 3
    III. Fingerprints and DNA ......................................................................... 6
    IV. Conventional Blood Typing ................................................................. 6

**Chapter 3**
The Collection and Preservation of Physical Evidence ................................................. 11
    I.   Contamination ...................................................................................... 12
    II.  Collection of Evidence ........................................................................ 13
    III. Preservation of Evidence .................................................................... 14
    IV. Evaluation of Evidence ....................................................................... 14
        A.  RFLP ........................................................................................... 15
        B.  PCR ............................................................................................. 15

**Chapter 4**
A Short History of DNA Typing ..................................................................................... 19

**Chapter 5**
The Scientific Basis of DNA Typing .............................................................................. 29
    I.   Why DNA? ........................................................................................... 29
    II.  An Introduction to Human Genetics ................................................. 29
        A. The physical basis of heredity ............................................... 29
        B. Alleles - variations on a theme .............................................. 31
        D. Population genetics ................................................................. 32
    III. An Introduction to the Molecular Biology of DNA ......................... 33
    IV. Two Kinds of Variation ...................................................................... 34
    V.  Enzymes, the Workhorses of the Biological World ......................... 34

**Chapter 6**
An Overview of Forensic DNA Typing Systems ........................................................... 37
    I.   RFLP Analysis ..................................................................................... 37
    II.  PCR Amplification .............................................................................. 41
        A. HLA DQa/HLA DQA1 ........................................................... 41
        B. AmpliType® PM – "polymarker" ........................................... 45
        C.  D1S80 ........................................................................................ 47
        E.  Gender ID ................................................................................. 50
        F. Mitochondrial DNA ................................................................ 50
    III. What Kinds of Samples can be Analyzed? ........................................ 52
    IV. How Much Sample Do You Need? ..................................................... 55

**Chapter 7**
Procedures for Forensic DNA Analysis .......................................................................... 59
    I.   Isolation of DNA ................................................................................. 59
        A.  Chelex extraction ...................................................................... 59
        B.  Organic extraction ..................................................................... 62

        C. Differential extraction...................................................................62
  II.   Determining Quality and Quantity of DNA.....................................63
  III.  RFLP Analysis ...................................................................................64
  IV.  PCR Amplification ............................................................................69
  V.   Analysis of PCR Product ..................................................................70
        A. Sequence Polymorphisms ...........................................................70
           1. DQa, Polymarker               70
        B. Length polymorphisms (D1S80, STRs, Gender ID)....................77
  VI.  Automated Analysis Systems..............................................................83

**Chapter 8**
Significance of Results.............................................................................87
  I.    Determination of Similarity ...............................................................87
  II.   Evaluation of results...........................................................................89
  III.  Frequency estimate calculations.........................................................90
  IV.  Population substructure.......................................................................91

**Chapter 9**
Interpretation of DNA Typing Results ...................................................101
  I.    Complicating Factors .......................................................................101
  II.   System Specific Interpretational Issues............................................104

**Chapter 10**
DNA and the Database.............................................................................133

**Chapter 11**
Quality Control and Regulation...............................................................139
  I.    Certification and Accreditation..........................................................139
  II.   TWGDAM.........................................................................................140
  III.  NRC I and II......................................................................................140
        A. NRC I ...........................................................................................141
        B. NRC II ..........................................................................................142
  IV.  Federal DNA Advisory Committee ..................................................143

**Chapter 12**
Admissibility Standards - Science on Trial in the Courtroom .................145
  I.    The Frye Standard and the Federal Rules of Evidence.....................145
        A. RFLP............................................................................................147
        B. PCR .............................................................................................150
  III.  The State of the debate.....................................................................152

**Chapter 13**
Epilogue - Moving into the Next Millennium..........................................157

**Glossary**..............................................................................................161

**Appendix A**
DNA - Some Key Phrases .......................................................................174

**Appendix B**
Slot Blot...................................................................................................176

**Appendix C**
Yield Gel..................................................................................................177

**Appendix D**
Digest Gel.................................................................................................178

**Appendix E**
Product Gel...............................................................................................179

**Appendix F**
Chromosomal Location of Some Forensic Loci......................................180

**Appendix G**
Sample Frequency Calculation................................................................181

**Appendix H**
Guidelines for a Quality Assurance Program for DNA Analysis............187

**Appendix I**
NRC I and NRC II Recommendations.....................................................211

**Appendix J**
State Statutes and Legislation Regarding the Admissibility of DNA Evidence...............220

**Appendix K**
Statutes and Legislation Regarding Mandatory Submission of Blood Samples for DNA
Identification............................................................................................221

**Appendix L**
Summary of DNA Decisions...................................................................223

**Appendix M**
Reported Court Decisions on Forensic DNA Evidence..........................224

**Appendix N**
Amicus Brief Presented to the Supreme Court of the State of California by the California
Association of Criminalists.....................................................................239

**Appendix O**
Forensic Science Internet Resources......................................................245

**Index**..................................................................................................247

# TABLE OF CASE HISTORIES (SIDEBARS)

SIDEBAR 1
To Catch a Cougar.................................................................................21

SIDEBAR 2
The Bungled Burglary (or, the burglar that couldn't) ...............................................39

SIDEBAR 3
Quintanilla ......................................................................................42

SIDEBAR 4
The Czar's Bones (or, what difference a base pair?)................................................52

SIDEBAR 5
A Case of Victim's Evidence (or, one bled and the other pled)......................................73

SIDEBAR 6
Minisatellite Variable Repeat Analysis (MVR).......................................................79

SIDEBAR 7
The Simpson Saga...............................................................................117

SIDEBAR 8
The Case of the Disappearing Sperm (or, whose type is it anyway?)..............................122

SIDEBAR 9
The Botanical Witness (or, what the seed pod saw)................................................134

SIDEBAR 10
A Cold Hit in Minnesota (or, the database in winter)..............................................136

SIDEBAR 11
The First RFLP Case (State of Florida v. Tommy Lee Andrews) ..................................152

# About the Authors

**Keith Inman** holds a B.S. and M. Crim., both from the University of California at Berkeley. He is also a Diplomate of the American Board of Criminalistics. In his professional career he has been employed as a criminalist by the Orange County Sheriff's Department, the Los Angeles County Sheriff's Department, the Los Angeles County Chief Medical Examiner-Coroner and the Oakland Police Department. He was in private practice for six years at Forensic Science Services of CA Inc., a private crime laboratory which undertook both prosecution and defense work. Mr. Inman is currently employed as a criminalist by the California Department of Justice DNA Laboratory.

**Norah Rudin** holds a B.A. from Pomona College and a Ph.D. in genetics and molecular biology from Brandeis University. After completing a post-doctoral fellowship at Lawrence Berkeley Laboratory, she worked for three years as a full-time consultant for the California Department of Justice DNA laboratory. Dr. Rudin currently divides her time between consulting and writing about topics in forensic science and biology in general.

Dr. Rudin and Mr. Inman also teach a variety of courses encompassing both DNA and Forensic Science in general.

# Acknowledgments

We would, first of all, like to thank Bob Stern for giving us the opportunity to write for CRC Press. Our project editor, Helen Linna, was remarkably thorough and patient in coordinating the production of this book. We are also indebted to all the unnamed, behind the scenes folks in the production and marketing departments of CRC. Paul Keim and Bill Clayton graciously shared their expertise and knowledge for *The Botanical Witness* Sidebar and Jeff Ashton provided the autorad as well as historical corrections for *The First DNA Case* Sidebar. Ed Blake gave us more information than we could possibly use, including all the photographs for the *Quintanilla* Sidebar. Cecelia Crouse gave us the *Case of Victim's Evidence* Sidebar, including the photo. She also reviewed the book in its entirety and challenged us to rethink certain points. Rebecca Reynolds sifted through stacks of PCR photos to find the ones that we needed to demonstrate certain concepts, and also reviewed related portions of the book. We are grateful to Martin Buoncristiani and Lance Gima, who provided expert review and commentary on portions of the manuscript. Clay Strange, formerly of the APRI, and Renee Kostick and Matthew Lynch, currently of the APRI, graciously provided all the material for the legal appendices. Jim McFadden and Amy Lewis provided technical support for the computer programs we used to prepare this book, as well as general encouragement. Gerri and Howard Levine gave us the enlarger "on permanent loan" which was used to print all the photos. Last, but certainly not least, we would like to thank each other for the support and encouragement necessary to survive the late nights and weekends needed to complete this project.

*Whenever you have excluded the impossible,*
*whatever remains, however improbable,*
*must be the truth -*

*Sir Arthur Conan Doyle*
*The Adventures of Sherlock Holmes*
*"The Adventure of the Beryl Coronet"*

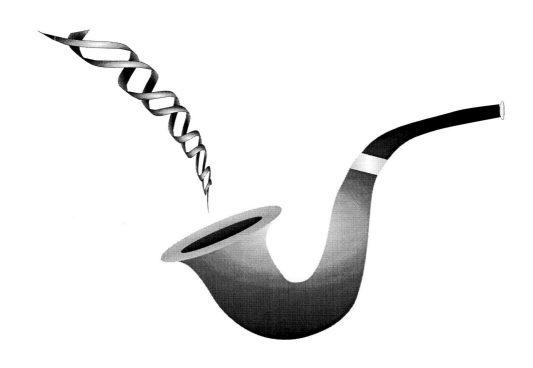

# Chapter 1

## INTRODUCTION

The newest tool for personal identification has gained its biggest and brightest spotlight yet in the shadow of a football legend accused of a brutal double murder. DNA analysis, which claims roots in classical genetics, biochemistry and molecular biology has, from its origins, found itself in an unlikely arena, a court of law. How can judges and juries, generally people with no specific scientific training, hope to comprehend the minutiae of molecular biology and population genetics, subjects which have only recently emerged from the ivory tower of academia?

Our intention in the following pages is to translate science into English, so that the layperson can gain an insight into how the process works, from sample collection to interpretation of results. Key to the understanding of any analytical technique is a keen appreciation of its advantages and limitations. These concepts, even more than any specifics performed in the laboratory, aid in a determination of the appropriate application and interpretation of any test. By definition, any science becomes somewhat less precise when simplified. We have tried to write for the person who is being introduced to DNA for the first time. To this end, we aim to clarify general principles; the exceptions that occur in every field are best left to a more advanced treatise.

The potential power of DNA typing has served to highlight issues of certification of laboratory personnel and accreditation of laboratories. Not only DNA, but all of forensic science has come under public scrutiny and the demand to show competence and adherence to proper procedures. As the underlying science becomes recognized by the legal community as generally accepted, these issues come to the front as weapons with which to refute evidence in any particular case. Appropriately, the forensic community has instituted peer-administered programs for initial and on-going testing of both analysts and laboratories.

The statistical interpretation of DNA typing results, specifically in the context of population genetics, has been the least understood and, therefore by definition, the most hotly debated issue of recent admissibility hearings. The perceived incomprehensibility of the subject, fueled by the views of, what some feel, have been only a few outspoken individuals, has led to a recalcitrance of the judicial system to accept DNA typing. In the light of additional data, as well as additional comprehension, this issue appears on its way toward becoming resolved.

Legal decisions pertaining to the admissibility of DNA are both numerous, and sometimes difficult to obtain in a timely fashion. This is particularly true of unpublished decisions. We have compiled such information as was available to us so that general trends might be noted, but the listings should not be regarded as definitive or comprehensive.

As with all current technology, the future of DNA typing lies in the direction of automation and miniaturization. The unique aspect of forensics, however, is that each case is different. The previous history and current state of any sample must be considered when making decisions regarding the handling and analysis of samples, and this process of assessment continues throughout the analysis. These are not decisions that any analyst will willingly give up to a machine. Computer technology will be invaluable in the processing and management of large numbers of similar samples, such as those used in making a database.  Computers will also continue to be used as an aid in the evaluation, statistical analysis and storage of data.  We do not foresee the day, however, when the computer will take the stand, swear an oath "to tell the truth, and nothing but the truth, so help you God", and render an opinion that "this sample came from that person".

# Chapter 2

## THE NATURE OF PHYSICAL EVIDENCE

### I. SCIENCE AND THE LAW

The application of science to the legal arena is fundamentally one of reconstruction, that is, trying to assist in determining what happened, where it happened, when it happened, and who was involved. It is not concerned with, and cannot determine, why something (the motivation) happened. When science is applied in this way, the adjective "forensic" is added, which means that it is suitable for a law court. Forensic analysis is performed on evidence to assist the court in establishing physical facts so that criminal or civil disputes may be resolved. The legal question determines the direction of scientific inquiry. It is the job of the forensic scientist to translate the legal inquest into an appropriate scientific question, and to advise the judiciary on the capabilities and limitations of current techniques.

In forensic science the laws of natural science are considered in making a determination about the state of a piece of **physical evidence** at the time of collection. Using the scientific method, deductions are made about how the evidence came to be in that state. These deductions then limit the events that may or may not have taken place in connection with said evidence. The law defines elements of a crime; science contributes information to assist in determining whether an element is present or absent.

The reconstruction aspect of the scientific contribution must be emphasized. Science used in court does not establish guilt or innocence (which are properly the province of the judge and jury); rather, forensic science contributes information about what may have happened and who may have been involved. It does not assert whether the action was legal or illegal. The primary way in which reconstruction occurs is by establishing **associations**; a bullet is associated with a weapon, a fingerprint associated with a person, a shoeprint associated with a shoe, etc.

By its very nature, physical evidence is **circumstantial**; it provides clues to a particular course of events, but does so only indirectly. It is up to the forensic scientist, and ultimately the court, to use inference and deduction to interpret the physical facts.

### II. FROM IDENTIFICATION TO INDIVIDUALIZATION

In forensic science, there are two principle concepts by which associations between items are made; these are known as **identification** and **individualization**.

An item is identified when it can be placed into a class of items with similar characteristics. For example, firearms are classified according to their caliber and rifling characteristics and shoes are classified according to their size and tread pattern. Any physical item will have a large number of **class characteristics** that make it what it is, and these may vary depending on what part of the item is of interest and on what scale it is examined.

Forensic scientists have classified a number of items that are routinely encountered in criminal investigations, and have developed tests based on those traits that, in their testing, have proven to be useful in identifying an item as belonging to a particular class. For example, hairs are routinely found in crimes of violence. Analysts have found that examining some of the microscopic characteristics will assist in identifying it as a hair, as opposed to a fiber, and will also serve to place it in the category of human hair, as opposed to an animal hair.

One of the key parts of this understanding of class characteristics as identifying an item is that there are many other items with similar characteristics in the world. For example, there are usually many millions of shoes that have a particular size and tread pattern in existence at any one time. This means that measuring and describing class characteristics of a track found at a crime scene will only serve to say that it is one tennis shoe of many millions in the U.S. This still, however, serves to eliminate many other kinds of footwear as being responsible for the evidence shoeprint, and narrows the search and comparison considerably.

An item is individualized when it can be described in such a way that no other item in the universe is like it, even items identified as being similar. Individualization relies on the acquisition of traits that are so rare, either alone or in combination with other traits, that it is unreasonable to think of them being duplicated by chance alone.

A consideration of snowflakes serves as a useful illustration. It is estimated that there have been about $3 \times 10^{31}$ snowflakes (that's a 3 with 31 zeros behind it, or 30,000,000,000,000,000,000,000,000,000,000) produced in the 130 million years since the Jurassic period. The number of water molecules in a typical snowflake is about $1 \times 10^{15}$ (that's a 1 with 15 zeros behind it, or 100,000,000,000,000). This number of molecules can be arranged in $(10^{15})^{10^{15}}$ ways. This number is virtually impossible to imagine. It is so astronomically larger than the number of snowflakes that have ever existed that it is unreasonable to believe that any one arrangement has occurred more that once. When a characteristic (or characteristics) of an item can be described in such a fashion, it is believed to be unique, with no duplicate on earth. It has then been individualized.

A key element considered in determining whether a trait is a class or an individualizing characteristic is the origin of the trait. Those traits created by a controlled process become class characteristics. Examples include rifling characteristics of a weapon, the tread pattern on a shoe, cocaine from a coca plant, and the blood group of a person. The first two examples result from the repetitive nature of manufacturing; the last two are biological products, under genetic control (see Figure 2-1). When objects or substances are the product of a repetitive process under some direction or control, class characteristics result.

When forensic scientists look at new evidence for ways of identifying it, they look to those traits that are under some known control. Frequently these traits are so obvious that they are hard to articulate. For instance, a fiber is first described as long and thin, and we describe it so quickly in our minds that it is hard to reconstruct why or how we arrive at the conclusion that it is a fiber. But it is easily distinguished from a cement truck, if for no other reason than scale and shape. Class characteristics may include millions of similar items, or only two.

Individualizing traits are those created by random acts and are therefore not predictable or controlled. Traits acquired by shoes after they are on someone's foot, such as nail holes, cuts, or embedded glass fragments, qualify as individualizing characteristics. Similarly, the microscopic variations on weapon barrels that occur during manufacture, but that are not controlled because they are so small, impart individualizing characteristics to bullets fired through them. Fingerprints arise as a result of a random process during a certain stage of gestation. Because of the number of different combinations of types of traits and spatial configurations possible on a finger, it is accepted that no two fingerprints are the same.

The theory that makes these concepts of identification and individualization applicable in the context of criminal and civil litigation is one attributed to Edmund Locard in the early 20th century. He proposed that when two objects come in contact, traces from one will be transferred from one to the other, and in both directions. These traces may not always be detectable (since detection depends on the sensitivity of the method employed), but are always present. This is known as the Locard Transfer Theory, and serves as the linchpin of all forensic examinations.

The value of physical evidence lies in the ability of the forensic scientist to measure traits in evidence left at a scene and compare them to traits found in reference materials. If the traits are found to be similar, then an association of varying strength has been created between the evidence and reference item. For example, codeine removed from a suspect's shirt (the crime scene) is compared to a reference sample of codeine in the laboratory's library, and concordance of key chemical traits confirms the identification of the material as codeine. Note that this doesn't, in and of itself, prove a crime. For example, if the codeine is found on a transient in the street without a prescription, a crime has been committed. If on the other hand, the codeine is found in the shirt of pharmacist, and his other pocket has a prescription for it to be delivered to a patient, nothing illegal has occurred, even though the physical evidence finding is the same.

In sum then, **transfer theory** allows for the comparison of **identifying** and **individualizing** traits between two objects, and the rendering of a conclusion with regard to the strength of an **association** between the two.

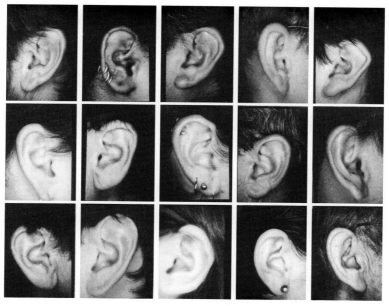

**Figure 2-1. Ears - a trait which probably approaches individuality.**

## FINGERPRINTS AND DNA

Because most people are familiar with dermatoglyphic fingerprints and are convinced of their individuality, it is useful to compare and contrast them to what were originally called "DNA fingerprints", a term that is, in fact, a misnomer. Dermatoglyphic fingerprints were described as an individualizing characteristic towards the end of the last century. Originally, their understanding and use was developed empirically, without reference to the specific genetic basis of the underlying patterns. Empirical examinations comprising tens of thousands of prints led examiners to conclude that no two that were examined were alike.

It has been thought for some time that the genetic contribution to a fingerprint, such as ridge count, is determined by not one, but several genes. In forensic applications, minutiae in the fingerprint patterns are analyzed. The minutiae result from a combination of genetic and non-genetic events during embryonic development; thus even identical twins are distinguishable. This supports the earlier empirical conclusion that the fingerprint patterns of each human being are unique. These conclusions have been further confirmed through the use of more sophisticated methods of statistical analysis and computer databasing.

The original "DNA fingerprinting" method, developed by Alec Jeffreys, examined many locations in the DNA of a genome at once. The result was a multi-banded pattern whose complexity suggested a fingerprint, and was probably unique to each individual. Because of the complexity of the system, however, it was decided that the examination of one genetic location (**locus**) at a time would provide a more comprehensible result, and would better allow for the numerical estimation of the significance of similar genetic patterns. This method, called DNA typing or DNA profiling, was also more amenable to the examination of mixed samples, since the number of bands expected from one person (1 or 2) was known.

In dermatoglyphic fingerprints, it is possible to obtain all of the information from all 10 fingerpads; thus there are no missing pieces of information. This was not true even of "DNA fingerprinting", and is certainly not the case in current DNA typing methods. If we could easily obtain information about all 3 billion genetic units, DNA typing could be compared more directly with dermatoglyphic fingerprints. Because only a small portion, perhaps 1 millionth, of the 3 billion units of human DNA are even available for examination by current methods, the result is better compared to a partial print. Similar to a partial print, however, it may not be necessary to have all of this information to be convinced of the individuality of a DNA profile. Just as a certain number of points of comparison have been deemed necessary in order to declare that two fingerprints originated from the same finger, it has been suggested that some number (9 has been discussed) of highly polymorphic DNA loci may be sufficient in order to declare that two samples have originated from the same source.

## IV. CONVENTIONAL BLOOD TYPING

Conventional blood typing is used to answer the most prevalent question about a biological sample; that is, "who could have contributed this sample?" After the discovery of the ABO blood typing groups, workers found that the differences among ABO blood group types between people could be exploited to determine who might be a donor of an evidentiary stain. As soon as it was discovered that one could exclude large percentages of the population as possible donors, genetic typing of biological fluids became a powerful technique for assisting the triers of fact in determining what might have happened at a crime scene, and in particular, who might have been involved.

The ABO blood group system was the only one used on forensic samples for a long time. But a significant breakthrough was achieved in the early 1970's when other protein and enzyme markers, which had been known to be polymorphic for a decade or more, were found to be useful for forensic evidence as well. The bulk of this work was performed by scientists in the Scotland Yard Lab in London. They found that some of the markers that had previously been used for paternity testing could also be used on bloodstains and other kinds of physiological fluid evidence found at crime scenes. In England in particular, this was beneficial since much of the crime there was and still is person-on-person. With the restriction on hand guns in that country, most of the assaults were of a personal nature, that is stabbing and beatings, where blood was shed in close proximity to the assailant. It was inevitable that the nature of the evidence would lead to the development of appropriate markers systems. The early work was performed on genetic markers well-known today, including phosphoglucomutase (PGM), erythrocyte acid phosphatase (EAP), haptoglobin and adenylate kinase (AK).

This work was brought to the U.S. through a pioneering effort of the Law Enforcement Assistance Administration (LEAA) in 1976 with the publication of a book by Brian Culliford (an examiner at Scotland Yard). In the book, outlined methods for the examination of genetic markers on bloodstained and semen-stained evidence.

The fundamental questions about conventional blood grouping and the approaches taken to analyzing blood groups are exactly the same as those used in DNA typing, and so are worth considering here. There are generally two questions that one can ask of a blood stain; the first question is "how did this stain come to be in this place?", and the second question is "whose blood is it?" The first question is properly considered a part of crime scene reconstruction, in particular, a discipline known as blood stain pattern interpretation. That will not be considered here. The second question is the one most commonly asked, and is the focus of the balance of this book.

If a blood stain is found at a crime scene, it is frequently important to know if it could be from the assailant or the victim. If a stain is found on a suspect, it is important to know if the blood could be from the victim; occasionally it is of interest to determine if a stain on the victim is from a suspect. In this way, an association is made between the crime scene evidence and suspect evidence. A biological association between the crime scene and the donor of the blood establishes that they were in contact This conclusion usually leads to the strong inference that this contact occurred during of the commission of the crime. The question then becomes: what physical properties of the evidence can be used to make a statement about the possible association between the bloodstain and a possible donor? The physical traits that can answer this question are genetic in nature. By choosing genetic traits that vary from person to person in the population, one can say that a stain could not be from a certain percentage of donors, and could be from another percentage. In addition, one can test particular individuals to determine if they have the same genetic type as the evidence; this establishes whether they are among the group of possible donors.

The classical ABO blood group system serves to illustrate the concept. There are four common ABO types; type A, type B, type AB, and type O. Further, each is known to occur with a particular frequency in any population. For example, type A occurs in about 35-40% of the Caucasian population. If a bloodstain is found at a crime scene and is typed as "A", several statements can be made about it. First, individuals who are *not* type A cannot be the source of the sample. These people are **eliminated** as the donors of the bloodstain. Second, anyone who is a type A is a possible source of the sample; they are **included** as possible donors of the stain. Third, approximately 35-40% of the Caucasian population would fall into this category of individuals included as a possible source. The significance of the typing is thus expressed as the size of any reference population that might be included as possible donors of the stain. The larger the percentage of the population that can be included, the less significant the finding is. Conversely, the less common the type is, the more likely it is that a person with the same genetic traits is the donor of the sample.

Clearly the goal of genetic typing is to reduce the frequency of the type to the smallest number possible. This is accomplished by examining more than one genetic locus (typing system). ABO is only one of numerous conventional markers that are useful for this purpose. Like ABO, these other markers have different types associated with them, and each type is present at a known frequency in any particular population. If the same bloodstain examined above is also typed in the PGM system and found to be a type 1+, then the overall significance of the findings are expressed as the frequency of ABO type A (35%) multiplied by the frequency of PGM type 1+ (19%). Another way of thinking of this is by considering what percentage of the population is ABO type A (35%), and what percentage of these type A individuals are PGM 1+ (19%). The frequency of the Caucasian population who are both ABO type A and PGM type 1+ is: 35% x 19% = 6.7%. As more markers are added, the percentage of the population who are included as possible donors becomes smaller and smaller.

Forensic DNA typing seeks to attain the same goal as conventional genetic marker systems: to reduce the number of possible donors to a minimum. The advantage of DNA in this respect is that, for the RFLP markers, between 20 and 80 types may be present at any one locus, and each type occurs with a fairly low frequency. This means that a genetic type determined by several loci in combination, each with many possible types, will be rare. Consequently, very few individuals in any population will have the types detected in an evidence item; the significance of finding someone who has those types is concordantly high. PCR markers usually have fewer types per locus than the RFLP loci, but the frequencies of these types in the population are still lower than for conventional blood typing markers. When coupled with the fact that DNA tends to be far more stable than the conventional protein and enzyme markers, DNA typing is much more powerful than conventional typing of evidentiary material.

## FURTHER REFERENCES

**Ashbaugh, D..R..,** The premises of friction ridge identification, clarity and the identification process, *Journal of Forensic Identification.* 44, 5, 499-516, 1994.

**DeForest, P., Gaensslen, R.E.., and Lee, H.,** Forensic science: An introduction to criminalistics, pp. 29-30, McGraw-Hill, 1983.

**Gaensslen, R.E.,** Sourcebook in forensic serology, immunology, and biochemistry, Washington, D.C., 1983.

**Kirk, P.,** Crime investigation, pg. 15, 2nd Ed., J. Wiley & Sons, 1974.

**Sensabaugh, G.F.,** Biochemical markers of individuality, in *Forensic Science Handbook,* Saferstein, R., ed., Prentice-Hall, Englewood Cliffs, New Jersey, 1982, 338-415.

**Stoney, D.A.,** Evaluating Associative Evidence: Choosing the relevant question, *Journal for the Forensic Science Society,* 24, 473, 1984.

**Stoney, D.A.,** What made us ever think we could individualize using statistics?, *Proceedings of the 12th IAFS Meeting,* Adelaide Australia, *Journal for the Forensic Science Society* 31,197, 1990.

**Thornton, J.,** The snowflake paradigm, letter to the editor, *Journal of Forensic Sciences,* 31, 399, 1986.

**Wilson, T.,** Automated fingerprint identification systems, *Law Enforcement Technology,* 45-48, 1986.

# Chapter 3

## THE COLLECTION AND PRESERVATION OF PHYSICAL EVIDENCE

 Before an item of evidence can be examined, it must be taken to the laboratory. This is not as trivial as it sounds. The conditions in which biological molecules exist in the body are carefully controlled and very specific. From the moment biological material is out of the body, it is in a foreign environment and changes begin to take place. DNA is packed very tightly in the chromosomes of a cell; stretched out to its full length, each chromosome might be meters long. Outside of its natural, protected environment, these long thin molecules can be very fragile. DNA is subject to degradation (breaking into smaller fragments), and that degradation can have an effect on the ability to obtain a useful result from DNA typing, particularly RFLP. The more severe the degradation, the smaller the fragments become. As the DNA fragments degrade, their average size becomes smaller than the fragment length at a particular RFLP locus. For example, fragment sizes (also expressed as **molecular weight, MW**) at a particular RFLP locus can be as large as 20,000 **base pairs (bp)**. If the average bp size of DNA in a sample that has been subjected to degradation conditions is 10,000 base pairs (10 kilobase pairs (**kb**)), then no bands will be detected above that size after analysis of that sample and the analysis may be compromised.

Factors leading to the degradation of DNA include time, temperature, humidity, light (both sunlight and UV light), and chemical or biological contamination. Various combinations of these conditions are often found together in the environment, of course. Numerous studies have been conducted to determine the effects of these conditions, which, with a few exceptions, tend to degrade the samples into smaller fragments.

An important outcome of these studies is the finding that these environmental factors will not change DNA from one type into another; in other words, an RFLP fragment size at any locus will not change from 7,000 to 4,000 bp[1], and an HLA DQα type will not change from a 1.1 into a 1.2. Rather, the degradation changes the DNA from a sample that can be typed into a sample that gives no type at all. This is an important part of the validation of any genetic typing system, for it means that the biological component of the system will not produce false positive results. In other words, because one profile cannot be changed into another, there is no danger that environmental degradation will produce a complete DNA pattern that would include someone who is not the donor of the sample. In this way the system can be described as robust. Degradation can limit the usefulness of DNA typing, but does not invalidate it.

Further, these studies have also shown that DNA is much more stable than the conventional genetic markers used in forensic examinations. While many of the conventional protein and enzyme markers degrade beyond typability in a 2-3 month period (antigenic systems are an exception), DNA under normal environmental conditions can remain stable and typable for years . This is especially true of the PCR systems, which can tolerate a large amount of degradation and still yield readable types.

---

[1] There will probably be some fragments of about 4000 bp, but they will not appear as a discrete fragment on an autorad.

A special cause for concern might be the appearance of only one allele for a particular locus in an individual instead of the more commonly seen two alleles. Is the sample from a true homozygote, or is one of two distinct alleles missing for a different reason? There might be several explanations for this phenomenon (see *Chapter 9*); one which must be considered is obviously degradation of the larger allele, but not the smaller one. This is where an assessment of the quality of a sample is key to correctly interpreting the results (see below, *Appendices B-E)*.

An important goal in collecting and preserving biological evidence is to halt any degradative process already in progress and limit any future deterioration. In general, biological processes are slowed by removing moisture and lowering the temperature. Thus the goal of the crime scene investigator is to dry a sample, and freeze it as soon as it is practical.

## I. CONTAMINATION

Just as important as preserving the biological integrity of the sample is the consideration of any contamination that might interfere in the analysis. In fact, there are different types of contamination, and the final effect on evidence, if any, varies. Non-biological contamination (e.g., dyes, soaps and other chemicals) may affect the sample by interfering in the analytical procedures (see *Chapter 9*). This type of interference typically produces an inconclusive result or no type.

Nonhuman biological contamination includes the physiological material and/or DNA from other organisms. Although cross-typing is occasionally seen in some systems, it generally does not interfere with interpretation of the final result. A particular concern is microorganismal contamination. Crime scene samples such as blood and semen provide a fertile environment for the growth of bacteria and fungi. As they grow, these microorganisms secrete biochemicals that degrade the human DNA in the sample. Even so, the DNA type will simply go away, as opposed to being magically converted into someone else's type. Partially degraded DNA must be interpreted carefully by a qualified analyst; if the sample is known to be of poor quality, and the possibility exists that part of a pattern has been obscured, a conclusion of "inconclusive" may be the safest bet (see *Chapter 9*).

The most significant type of contamination is that from a human source. In this sense, contamination is defined as the inadvertent addition of an individual's physiological material/DNA during or after collection of the sample as evidence. It is important to differentiate between a "mixed sample" and a "contaminated sample". A mixed sample is one that contains DNA from more than one individual, where the mixing occurred before or during the commission of the crime. A contaminated sample is one where the material was deposited during collection, preservation, handling or analysis.

Among the considerations in determining whether a second DNA type would even be detected is the type of testing involved. For instance, PCR-type testing, where the DNA in the sample is copied millions of times over, is inherently a more sensitive technique than RFLP. This also makes a PCR test more likely to detect traces of a second type, whatever the source.

Although great care should be taken as a matter of routine, it is really not that easy to interject extraneous human material into a sample. Contrary to what some might have us believe, DNA does not float around randomly in the air, and cells that may be sloughed off or ejected out of a person are relatively few in number and may not contain any consequential DNA. This is not to suggest that precautions not be taken, but to put the matter in some perspective.

Once the sample is dried, refrigerated and in the laboratory, the potential for contamination is mostly from other samples undergoing processing at the same time. This is where the training, qualifications of the analyst and quality control of the laboratory come into play. Safeguards are set up not only to guard against contamination from other lab samples, but just as importantly, to detect contaminated samples, should they occur.

The biggest real concern that would actually result in an incorrect DNA type, as opposed to no type, is a sample switch by the analyst. Education, training and good laboratory practice are the best weapons against sample mix-ups.

## II. COLLECTION OF EVIDENCE

There are two main methods of collecting a sample for subsequent analysis in the lab. These are: 1) collecting the stained item directly; or 2) removing the stain onto a more suitable or easier to handle substrate.

The first method is preferred, since it does not risk loss by manipulation. Simply, one picks up the item, packages it in some suitable manner, and transports it to lab for proper preservation until analysis. This is most appropriate for items like clothing, or any other item that might fit into a box or bag. The removal is left to the actual analyst, who is in a much better position to evaluate and correctly process the sample.

The second method is to remove the biological material to a better substrate (e.g., transferring a stain on asphalt to a cotton swatch). This involves either scraping the sample with a clean (sterile) scalpel or pair of forceps, or re-hydrating the stain with water or a chemical buffer, and soaking it onto a clean cotton cloth substrate (see Figure 3-1). Scraping does not re-hydrate the sample, and so does not introduce moisture and contribute to degradation. However, it does risk loss of sample by failing to remove all of the material, or by inadvertent loss during the scraping process (e.g., the stain may fly off into space from the mere touch of the scalpel). Rehydrating and soaking onto a cloth substrate tends to minimize loss and makes the stain easier to work with in the lab. However, it does introduce moisture, which must be removed as soon as possible. The moisture is removed by drying the stain, usually by placing it into a container such as an open test tube, that allows the cloth to dry quickly. If the sample is allowed to remain wet for any length of time, then the degradative processes discussed above may start to take effect.

All of these methods have their uses, and the choice of any particular method is a matter of judgment and experience of the crime scene investigator, whether it is a detective, technician, or forensic scientist. All work well when performed properly.

A standard practice when collecting evidence (Figure 3-1) is to collect one or more unstained samples from an area adjacent to the obvious stain or physiological fluid. The purpose of this exercise is to determine what was on the substrate (the object or surface upon which evidence is found) before the evidence was ever deposited. This sample serves as a control for biological material already present on substrates such as bed sheets and panty crotches and may allow for the subtraction of extraneous genetic types from the final profile (see Chapter 9). Additionally, it functions as a control for evidence collection and handling procedures. If sloppy technique is used, for instance not changing gloves when appropriate, and contamination is incurred that later shows up as a type after analysis, the substrate control may show this same type.

a                                                          b

**Figure 3-1. Evidence Collection.** One way to collect a dried bloodstain on a hard substrate, such as a window or floor, is to wick up the stain onto a small piece of cotton fabric moistened with sterile distilled water. The swatch (a), now  containing the evidentiary material, is transported to the laboratory in a clean test tube (b).

### III.  PRESERVATION OF EVIDENCE

Once a sample has been collected, it must be dried (or remain dry) to maintain its typability. It should also be stored frozen, although for DNA this is less important than for the conventional protein and enzyme systems. It should not be subjected to fluctuations in either temperature or humidity. Most laboratories will have dedicated freezers for evidence storage.

### IV.  EVALUATION OF EVIDENCE

Before an evidence item is analyzed for DNA type, presumptive tests are sometimes performed to establish the type of biological material that is present. It would be wasteful to run a full spectrum of DNA tests only to find no result because ketchup or shoe polish was being analyzed. Presumptive color tests for various fluids such as blood, semen, or saliva may be performed at the scene before a sample is collected, or in the laboratory.

Once the identification of a sample as a particular biological substance is established, either by testing or history, preliminary tests are conducted to establish the "**state of the DNA**" contained in the sample. It is possible to run tests that will reveal the quality of the DNA (how much degradation is present) in an item of evidence, how much total DNA is present, and how much of the total DNA is human. A yield gel (Appendix C) will tell how much total DNA is present, and will also show how much degradation has occurred. The quantitation of the human component of the total DNA present can be achieved via a method known as a slot blot (Appendix B). An evaluation of the "**state of the DNA**" is crucial in making decisions about what might be accomplished with any particular sample, for example, whether RFLP is possible, or whether a PCR method might be more suitable.

## A. RFLP

RFLP testing requires a minimum amount of DNA of relatively **high molecular weight (HMW)**. HMW DNA means DNA with an average fragment size of about 20,000-25,000 bp (20-23 **kilobase pairs, kb**). In other words, degradation cannot have fragmented the DNA to an average size much smaller than this. Thus when reference is made to high molecular weight DNA, it is with regard to how much degradation has taken place, and whether this would permit or preclude an RFLP analysis. As stated above, if DNA that has been severely degraded is typed using an RFLP technique, there is a danger that high molecular weight bands for any one locus might be missed. For instance, a 2-banded pattern might erroneously be typed as a 1-banded pattern, or larger bands from a second contributor to the sample might be missed. Absent knowledge of the amount of degradation in a sample from a yield gel, this might lead to a false exclusion.

In addition, a minimum amount of DNA is needed to successfully perform an RFLP analysis. This minimum amount is somewhat lab dependent, and also varies with the probe labeling method (radioactive or chemiluminescent) but tends to be in the 10 to 50 ng range. In other words, there must be 10-50 ng of high molecular weight human DNA in order to have a reasonable expectation of an RFLP result, although this does not categorically preclude a typable result with less. The yield gel and slot blot results assist in determining whether an extracted DNA sample meets these criteria.

## B. PCR

Most PCR systems require much smaller stretches of intact (non-degraded) DNA than does RFLP. Fragments as small as few hundred base pairs may yield a successful PCR result in some systems. The main advantage of PCR systems, however, is their sensitivity. For some systems, samples containing as little as 0.2 to 0.5 ng (on the order of 100 times less material than RFLP) can be successfully typed. This is the equivalent of a few hundred sperm (out of the hundreds of millions in a normal ejaculate) or a blood droplet the size of a large pinhead.

Besides the amount of human DNA and its quality, the presence of contaminants may also enter into the evaluation of the evidence. Everything from the material on which a stain is deposited (*e.g.*, leaves, soil, blue jeans, glass) to chemicals added before, during, or after the deposition of the stain (*e.g.*, oils, spermicides, bleach, soap, soda) may affect the ability to extract or otherwise analyze the sample. There are usually several different methods that can be employed to optimize the yield and quality of the DNA extracted; knowing the history of the sample will help in deciding which path to follow.

*Example 1*

Blue denim is known to contain dyes that combine with DNA and inhibit both restriction digestion in an RFLP analysis and amplification in the PCR. A method has been developed that will remove many of these dyes and allow for full analysis. Thus an analyst presented with stains on blue jean material will consider the need to perform this clean-up procedure.

*Example 2*

Soil is known to contain many microorganisms, and evidence collected from this substrate will become severely degraded and replete with nonhuman DNA in a short period of time. An analyst faced with evidence of this type will want to know how much human and nonhuman DNA is present, as well as how much degradation has occurred to the human

DNA. In most cases, regardless of how large the stain is, the analyst will be forced to use a PCR method because the DNA will be too degraded to permit an RFLP analysis.

The collection and preservation of evidence plays an important role in determining the success of DNA analysis. Careless handling that does not halt normal biological processes of degradation may compromise the laboratory's ability to perform certain tests. Drying samples and placing them into cold storage as soon as possible after collection is the best way to ensure that no further harm is done to a sample than has already occurred as a result of being shed during a crime.

──────── *FURTHER REFERENCES* ────────────────────────────────

**Akane, A., Matsubara, K., Nakamura, H., Takahashi, S., Kimura, K.,** Identification of the heme compound copurified with deoxyribonucleic acid (DNA) from bloodstains, a major inhibitor of polymerase chain reaction (PCR) amplification, *Journal of Forensic Sciences*, 39, 2, 362-72, 1994.

**Baechtel, F.S., Presley, K.W., Smerick, J.B.,** D1S80 typing of DNA from simulated forensic specimens, *Journal of Forensic Sciences*, 40, 4, 536-45, 1995 .

**Barnett, P.D., Blake, E.T., Super-Mihalovich, J., Harmor, G., Rawlinson, L., Wraxall, B.,** Discussion of "Effects of presumptive test reagents on the ability to obtain restriction fragment length polymorphism (RFLP) patterns from human blood and semen stains", *Journal of Forensic Sciences*, 37, 2, 69-70, 1992.

**Comey, C.T., Budowle, B., Adams, D.E., Baumstark, A.L., Lindsey, J.A., Presley, L.A.,** PCR amplification and typing of the HLA DQ alpha gene in forensic samples, *Journal of Forensic Sciences*, 38, 2, 239-49, 1993.

**Cosso, S., Reynolds, R.,** Validation of the AmpliFLP D1S80 PCR Amplification Kit for forensic casework analysis according to TWGDAM guidelines, *Journal of Forensic Sciences*, 40, 3, 424-34, 1995.

**Cotton, R.W., Forman, L., Word, C.J.,** Research on DNA typing validated in the literature, *American Journal of Human Genetics*, 49, 4, 898-903, 1991.

**Crouse, C.A., Schumm, J.,** Investigation of species specificity using nine PCR-based human STR systems, *Journal of Forensic Sciences*, 40, 6, 952-6, 1995.

**Culliford, B.J.,** *The Examination and Typing of Blood Stains in the Crime Laboratory*, U.S. Government Printing Office, Washington, D.C., 1971.

**Duewer, D.L., Currie, L. A., Reeder, D.J., Leigh, S.D., Liu, H.K., Mudd, J.L.,** Interlaboratory comparison of autoradiographic DNA profiling measurements, 2, Measurement uncertainty and its propagation, *Analytical Chemistry*, 67, 7, 1220-31, 1995.

**Fildes, N., Reynolds, R.,** Consistency and reproducibility of AmpliType PM results between seven laboratories: field trial results, *Journal of Forensic Sciences*, 40, 2, 279-86, 1995.

**Hochmeister, M.N., Budowle, B., Borer, U.V., Dirnhofer, R.,** Effects of nonoxinol-9 on the ability to obtain DNA profiles from postcoital vaginal swabs, *Journal of Forensic Sciences*, 38, 2, 442-7, 1993.

**Kimpton, C., Gill, P., D'Aloja, E., Andersen, J.F., Bar, W., Holgersson, S., Jacobsen, S., Johnsson, V., Kloosterman, A. D., Lareu, M. V., et al.,** Report on the second EDNAP collaborative STR exercise, European DNA Profiling Group, *Forensic Science International*, 71, 2, 137-52, 1995.

**Laber, T.L., Giese, S.A., Iverson, J.T., Liberty, J.A.,** Validation studies on the forensic analysis of restriction fragment length polymorphism (RFLP) on LE agarose gels without ethidium bromide: effects of contaminants, sunlight, and the electrophoresis of varying quantities of deoxyribonucleic acid (DNA). *Journal of Forensic Sciences*, 39(3), 707-30, 1994.

**McNally, L., Shaler, R.C., Giusti, A.,** *et al.,* The effects of environment and substrata on deoxyribonucleic acid (DNA) isolated from human bloodstains exposed to ultraviolet light, heat, humidity, and soil contamination, *Journal of Forensic Sciences*, 32, 5, 1070-1077, 1989.

**Presley, L.A., Baumstark, A.L., Dixon A.,** The effects of specific latent fingerprint and questioned document examinations on the amplification and typing of the HLA DQ alpha gene region in forensic casework, *Journal of Forensic Sciences*, 38, 5, 1028-36, 1993.

**Roy, R., Reynolds, R.,** AmpliType PM and HLA DQ alpha typing from pap smear, semen smear, and postcoital slides, *Journal of Forensic Sciences*, 40, 2, 266-9, 1995.

**Schneider, P.M. Fimmers, R., Woodroffe, S., Werrett, D. ., Bar, W., Brinkmann, B., Eriksen, B., Jones, S., Kloosterman, A.D., Mevag, B.,** *et al.,* Report of a European collaborative exercise comparing DNA typing results using a single locus VNTR probe, *Forensic Science International*, 49, 1, 1-15, 1991.

**Schwartz, T.R., Schwartz, E.A., Mieszerski, L., McNally, L., Kobilinsky, L.,** Characterization of deoxyribonucleic acid (DNA) obtained from teeth subjected to various environmental conditions, *Journal of Forensic Sciences*, 36, 4, 979-90, 1991.

**Shipp, E., Roelofs, R., Togneri, E., Wright, R., Atkinson, D., Henry B.,** Effects of argon laser light, alternate source light, and cyanoacrylate fuming on DNA typing of human bloodstains, *Journal of Forensic Sciences*, 38(1), 184-91, 1993.

**Walsh, D.J., Corey, A.C., Cotton, R.W., Forman, L., Herrin, G.L. Jr., Word, C.J., Garner, D. D.,** Isolation of deoxyribonucleic acid (DNA) from saliva and forensic science samples containing saliva, *Journal of Forensic Sciences*, 37, 2, 387-95, 1992.

**Waye, J.S., Fourney, R.M.,** Agarose gel electrophoresis of linear genomic DNA in the presence of ethidium bromide: band shifting and implications for forensic identity testing, *Applied and Theoretical Electrophoresis*, 1, 4, 193-6, 1990.

**Waye, J.S., Michaud D., Bowen J.H., Fourney R.M.,** Sensitive and specific quantification of human genomic deoxyribonucleic acid (DNA) in forensic science specimens: casework examples, *Journal of Forensic Sciences*, 36, 4, 1198-203, 1991.

**Webb, M.B., Williams, N.J., Sutton, M.D.,** Microbial DNA challenge studies of variable number tandem repeat (VNTR) probes used for DNA profiling analysis, *Journal of Forensic Sciences*, 5, 1172-5, 1993.

**Wilson, R.B., Ferrara, J.L., Baum, H.J., Shaler, R.C.,** Guidelines for internal validation of the HLA DQ alpha DNA typing system, *Forensic Science International*, 66, 1, 9-22, 1994.

# Chapter 4

## A SHORT HISTORY OF DNA TYPING

 In 1944 Oswald Avery defined the role of the cellular component known as **DNA (deoxyribonucleic acid)** as the vehicle of generational transference of heritable traits. In 1953, James Watson and Francis Crick elucidated the structure of the DNA molecule as a **double helix**. In science, as in art, form follows function; the very nature of the molecule provided an explanation for its unique properties, including the ability to propagate itself faithfully from generation to generation.[2] In 1980, David Botstein and coworkers were the first to exploit the small variations found between people at the genetic level as genetic landmarks to construct a human gene map. The particular type of variation they used is called **Restriction Fragment Length Polymorphism** or **RFLP.**

In 1984, while searching for disease markers in DNA, Alec Jeffreys discovered a unique application of RFLP technology to the science of personal identification. His method, which he termed a **"DNA fingerprint"**, has been modified and adopted by crime laboratories for general use in the U.S. today. Scientists generally agree that a more descriptive and inclusive term for the process, as currently applied, is **DNA typing** or **DNA profiling**. In 1986, the **polymerase chain reaction (PCR)** was invented by Kary Mullis, who received a portion of the Nobel prize in chemistry for his discovery. PCR, more than any other scientific advance, since perhaps the elucidation of the structure of DNA, has changed the face of molecular biology. RFLP and PCR technology together form the cornerstone of forensic DNA typing.

It should be noted that DNA analysis, in general, has a much broader usage and longer history than just identification of crime scene samples. As mentioned above, an initial and ongoing application is the search for genes implicated in disease. Due to the efforts, in large part, of the **human genome project**, all of the information contained in the human genetic code is rapidly being deciphered and catalogued. This has already led to the identification of genes involved in diseases such as Huntington's, cystic fibrosis, muscular dystrophy and various genetically-influenced cancers. One specific application is in monitoring of bone marrow transplants in leukemia patients. In this application, DNA typing is more rapid and less error-prone than other blood-typing methods; when the blood of the patient shows the donor's pattern, the transplant has succeeded. In addition to improved diagnosis and drug therapies, actual gene replacement is already in clinical trials for some of these diseases.

Immigration and paternity disputes were among the first legal arenas in which DNA typing was used. Families have been reunited, both in the U.S. and abroad, when DNA tests proved the identity of a child or sibling. Paternity cases which have traditionally relied on conventional blood typing now have the option of being resolved by an even more specific DNA test. Singer Michael Jackson was cleared in a paternity case when DNA typing showed another man to be the father.

Knowledge of the way DNA is inherited in a family can give valuable clues about the identity of missing persons. Biological remains, for instance, may be identified by typing

---

[2]Interestingly, the dimensions of a DNA helix, as measured across the width of the helix, and between each turn, assume the proportions of the golden mean, a classic proportion found throughout nature and widely exploited in art.

potential parents and/or siblings and determining the probability of a close genetic relationship between them and the deceased. Similarly, a child abducted at a very young age might be reunited with his or her biological parents based on the outcome of comparative DNA testing.

Through DNA testing methods, the Armed Forces DNA Identification Laboratory (AFDIL) has identified the remains of 15 Vietnam War veterans two decades after they died in combat. A program has recently been initiated to routinely collect and store samples from all members of the armed forces, much in the same way fingerprints have been collected for decades. DNA typing systems are invaluable in the identification of bodies and body parts from mass disasters. After the Waco disaster, which involved badly charred remains, numerous bodies were identified and linked as families by the use of PCR DNA typing methods. The DNA in this situation was minimal and badly degraded; this is a good example of the value of the PCR in examining otherwise intractable samples. One of the more creative uses of PCR DNA typing was in the conviction of one of the men accused in the World Trade Center Bombing. Minute amounts of DNA in the saliva used to lick an envelope showed the same type as the defendant.

Because of its relative stability as compared to other biological molecules, DNA, and in particular a certain type of DNA, mitochondrial DNA, has become an important tool in the study of anthropology and ancient history. At the University of Minnesota-Duluth researchers performed DNA tests on lung tissue from a 1,100-year-old mummified Chiribaya Indian, and found an exact match with the DNA of the tuberculosis bacterium. This exonerates Christopher Columbus of the charge of introducing the deadly tuberculosis strain to the New World. The study of Egyptian mummies and other ancient remains by DNA typing have already revealed much about historical migration patterns and contributed to our still limited understanding of human evolution. One recent body of work helped resolve several questions about the Russian royal family, including positive identification of the burial remains of Czar Nicholas II, and the elimination of an "Anastasia" impostor (see *Sidebar 4)*. And of course, the dinosaur park on a remote island off the coast of Costa Rica is in progress.

Animal geneticists are typing DNA in endangered species, such as cheetahs and whales, to track migration and breeding patterns. This information may be used in captive breeding programs to increase genetic diversity in anticipation of reintroducing the animals in the wild. Another interesting application was the use of DNA testing in solving the 1994 killing of a jogger by a mountain lion in California. Inroads have also been made into poaching when carcasses and steaks have been matched to biological evidence found at the original location of an animal. The ability to extract and type DNA from bone means that illegal ivory can be tracked, as well as other horns and tusks that tend to be prized in some cultures.

The first forensic use of DNA took place in England and made use of Alec Jeffrey's original method of "DNA fingerprinting". In conjunction with police investigation, the Home Office was able to identify Colin Pitchfork as responsible for the murders of two young girls in the English Midlands. Significantly, an innocent suspect was the first accused murderer to be freed based on DNA evidence. One of the novelties of this case was that every male between the ages of 13 and 34 (almost 4000 men) residing in three nearby villages was required to donate a blood sample for analysis. The details of this case are chronicled in the book "The Blooding" by Joseph Wambaugh.

In the United States, private companies were the first to analyze DNA samples for forensic use. Both federal (FBI) and state forensic laboratories were close on their heels. Most states, as well as many counties and cities, now boast their own forensic DNA labs. DNA testing for identification is, in fact, now ubiquitous around the world. International forensic DNA conferences are held regularly and provide a forum for scientific exchange. Due in part to the increased scrutiny DNA labs, as well as forensic labs in general, have implemented a process of peer review, self-regulation and accreditation.

Since DNA testing was first introduced in the U.S. in 1986, it has been used in over 24,000 cases. Of interest are FBI reports that fully 1/3 of all suspects in rape cases are released before trial because DNA evidence exonerates them. Although this number may be a bit exaggerated due to the routine submission and testing of unlikely suspects (such as the standard testing of boyfriends), it is still indicative of the power of DNA analysis to free innocent men accused of a crime. As discussed further in *Chapter 8*, the exclusion of a suspect by DNA is absolute; there is no question of a statistical probability. Numerous wrongly convicted men continue to be freed from prison after old evidence is re-tested using the newer DNA techniques. The Innocence Project at Yeshiva University, run by Barry Sheck (a member of O.J. Simpson's defense team) has been a key player in this effort.

It is worth noting here that, with the exception of the use of DNA to link a suspect to the scene of a crime, none of the other uses of DNA typing detailed above has been seriously contested by the legal or scientific communities.

## SIDEBAR 1

### To Catch a Cougar
### (or, written in blood)

On December 10, 1994 a nude female body was discovered at Cuyamaca Rancho State Park in San Diego County, California. The head had been scalped and the body bore numerous puncture wounds. Because of the nude condition of the body, and the apparent violence of the attack, the incident was initially treated as a homicide. However scalping is also consistent with a mountain lion attack. Along the path created by a set of drag marks were strewn various items of bloody clothing. At the end was the body, exhibiting wounds clearly indicative of feline claws and teeth.

Since cougars generally return to the site of a kill to collect their bounty at a later time, the body was removed as soon as the on-site investigation was completed and replaced by a fresh deer carcass tagged with a radio transmitter. Within the hour, the deer had been moved. Tracking hounds were used to tree an adult male mountain lion , which was subsequently shot in the chest (so as not to disturb potential evidence around the mouth or in the stomach) and killed. The head and all four paws were bagged.

The victim was immediately identified; however, it was still necessary to confirm that the correct cat had been destroyed. The carcass was autopsied at the California Department of Fish and Game Wildlife Forensic Laboratory, and various items of evidence were submitted to the California Department of Justice Forensic DNA Laboratory for human DNA testing. The items included: bloody fur from the front paw, a claw from the left rear paw, fur from the lip area, and a portion of the stomach contents containing what appeared to be a large piece of human scalp tissue with hair still attached. A reference blood sample from the victim was also submitted for comparison.

A section of the scalp, as well as the bloody front paw fur, were extracted using the organic method (see *Chapter 7*). When checked on a yield gel (see *Chapter 7, Appendix C*), the paw fur sample (lane 9) appeared to contain a huge amount of DNA, and the scalp (lane 11), none. The samples on the extreme right are the victim's reference (lane 13) and a positive control (lane 14). In an innovative move by the analyst, the yield gel was subjected to a small scale Southern blotting, and probed with the same human-specific probe usually used for slot blot quantitation (see *Chapter 7, Appendix B*). As expected, no signal was evident for the scalp tissue, but neither was there any evidence of human DNA on the bloody paw fur. This suggested that the DNA recovered was either bacterial, or the cat's own blood.

The other two samples, the claw and lip hair, had been judged to probably contain DNA only of sufficient quality and quantity for PCR DQα typing, so were extracted using the Chelex method (see *Chapter 7*). The samples were amplified and a small portion was run on a product gel (*Chapter 7, Appendix E*) to check for successful amplification. Only the lip hair sample showed any PCR amplification product and even that was quite faint. It was, however, enough to show a type of 4,4 on a strip, the same type as the victim.

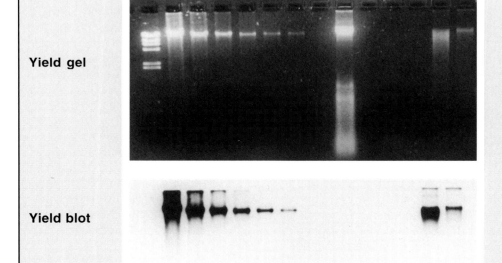

**Yield gel**

**Yield blot**

**DQα typing strips.**

evidence – lip hair

victim's reference

──── *FURTHER REFERENCES*────────────────────────────

## Science and Medicine:

**Arnheim, N., Erlich, H.,** Polymerase chain reaction strategy, *Annual Review of Biochemistry*, 61, 131-56, 1992.

**Avery, O.T., MacLeod, C.M., and McCarty, M.,** Studies on the chemical nature of the substance inducing transformation of Pneumococcal types. *Journal of Experimental Medicine* 79, 137-158, 1944.

**Botstein, D., White, R.L., and Skolnick, M.,** *et al.*, Construction of a genetic linkage map in man using restriction fragment length polymorphisms, *American Journal of Human Genetics*, 32, 314-331, 1980.

**Davies, K., Williamson, B,.** Gene therapy begins (editorial), *British Medical Journal*, 306(6893), 1625, 1993.

**Erlich, H.A., Gelfand, D., Sninsky, J.J.,** Recent advances in the polymerase chain reaction, *Science*, 252, 5013, 1643-51, 1991.

**Erlich, H.A., Arnheim, N.,** Genetic analysis using the polymerase chain reaction, *Annual Review of Genetics*, 26, 479-506, 1992.

**Gill, P., Jeffreys, A.J., and Werrett, D.J.,** Forensic application of DNA fingerprints. *Nature*, 318, 577-579, 1985.

**Jeffreys, A.J., Wilson, V., and Thein, S.L.,** *et al..* Individual specific "fingerprints" of human DNA, *Nature*, 316, 76-79, 1985.

**Lenstra, J.A.,** The applications of the polymerase chain reaction in the life sciences, *Cellular and Molecular Biology*, 41, 5, 603-14, 1995.

**Mullis, K.B, Faloona, F., Scharf, S. J., Saiki, R.K., Horn, G.T., and Erlich, H.A.,** Specific enzymatic amplification of DNA in vitro: the polymerase chain reaction, *Cold Spring Harbor Symp. Quant. Biol.*, 51, 263-273, 1986.

**Rich, D.P.,** *et al.*, Development and analysis of recombinant adenoviruses for gene therapy of cystic fibrosis, *Human Gene Therapy*, 4, 461, 1993.

**Watson, J.D., and Crick, F.H.C.,** A structure for deoxyribose nucleic acid, *Nature*, 171, 737-738, 1952.

## Science News and Reports:

**Bishop, J.E.,** The gene hunters; muscular dystrophy yields up secrets to genetic probes; teams of scientists raced to find a major cause, can now hope for a cure; next, replacing dystrophin, *Wall Street Journal*, 1988.

**Chase, M.,** DNA injection in gene therapy is called success, (University of California at San Francisco scientists report success with direct injection of DNA in the treatment of cystic fibrosis), *Wall Street Journal*, July 9, 1993.

**Moore, A.H.,** Genetics: The money rush is on, *Fortune*, May 30, 1994.

**U.S. Congress, Office of Technology Assessment.** Mapping Our Genes - Genome Projects: How Big, How Fast? OTA-BA-373, Washington, DC, 1988.

## Scientific Forensic Articles:

**Alford, R.L., Caskey, C.T.,** DNA analysis in forensics, disease and animal/plant identification, *Current Opinion in Biotechnology*, 5, 1, 29-33, 1994 .

**Allard, J.E.,** Murder in south London: a novel use of DNA profiling. *Journal of the Forensic Science Society,* Jan-Mar, 32, 1, 49-58, 1992.

**Boles, T.C., Snow, C.C., Stover E.,** Forensic DNA testing on skeletal remains from mass graves: a pilot project in Guatemala. *Journal of Forensic Sciences,* 3, 349-55, 1995.

**Blackett, R.S., Keim, P.,** Big game species identification by deoxyribonucleic acid (DNA) probes, *Journal of Forensic Sciences,* 37, 2, 590-6, 1992.

**Brauner P., Gallili, N.,** A condom — the critical link in a rape, *Journal of Forensic Sciences,* 5, 1233-6, 1993 .

**Brinkmann, B., Rand, S., Bajanowski, T.,** Forensic identification of urine samples, *International Journal of Legal Medicine,* 105,1, 59-61, 1992.

**Brown, T.A., Brown, K. A.,** Ancient DNA: using molecular biology to explore the past. *Bioessays,* 16, 10, 719-26, 1994 .

**Clayton T.M., Whitaker J.P., and Maguire C.N.,** Identification of bodies from the scene of a mass disaster using DNA amplification of short tandem repeat (STR) loci, *Forensic Science International,* 76, 1, 7-15, 1995.

**Corach, D., Sala, A., Penacino, G., Sotelo, A.,** Mass disasters: rapid molecular screening of human remains by means of short tandem repeats typing, *Electrophoresis,* 9, 1617-23, 1995.

**Costello, J., Zugibe, F.T.,** Identification of a homicide victim by a Casio data bank watch, *Journal of Forensic Sciences,* 39, 4, 1117-9, 1994 .

**Debenham, P.G.,** DNA typing. Heteroplasmy and the Tsar, *Nature,* 380, 6574, 484-5, 1996.

**Fisher, D.L., Holland, M. M., Mitchell, L., Sledzik, P.S., Wilcox, A.W., Wadhams, M., and Weedn, V.W.,** Extraction, evaluation, and amplification of DNA from decalcified and undecalcified United States Civil War bone, *Journal of Forensic Sciences,* 38, 1, 60-8, 1993.

**Gill, P., Kimpton, C., Aliston-Greiner R., Sullivan, K., Stoneking, M., Melton, T., Nott, J., Barritt, S., Roby, R., Holland, M.,** *et al.,* Establishing the identity of Anna Anderson Manahan, *Nature Genetics,* 9, 1, 9-10, 1995.

**Gill, P., Ivanov, P.L., Kimpton, C., Piercy, R., Benson, N., Tully, G., Evett, I., Hagelberg, E., and Sullivan K.,** Identification of the remains of the Romanov family by DNA analysis. *Nature Genetics,* 6(2), 130, 1994.

**Guglich, E.A., Wilson, P.J., and White, B.N.,** Forensic application of repetitive DNA markers to the species identification of animal tissues. *Journal of Forensic Science,* 39(2), 353-61, 1994.

**Hagelberg, E., Gray, I.C., and Jeffreys, A.J.,** Identification of the skeletal remains of a murder victim by DNA analysis, *Nature,* 352, 6334, 427-9, 1991.

**Haglund, W.D., Reay, D.T., and Tepper, S.L.,** Identification of decomposed human remains by deoxyribonucleic acid (DNA) profiling, *Journal of Forensic Sciences,* 3, 724-9, 1990.

**Hochmeister, M.N., Budowle, B., Borer, U.V., Rudin, O., Bohnert, M., and Dirnhofer, R.,** Confirmation of the identity of human skeletal remains using Multiplex PCR Amplification and Typing Kits, *Journal of Forensic Sciences,* 40, 4, 701-5, 1995.

**Jeffreys, A.J., Allen, M. J., Hagelberg, E., and Sonnberg, A.,** Identification of the skeletal remains of Josef Mengele by DNA analysis, *Forensic Science International,* 56, 1, 65-76, 1992

**Jeffreys, A.J., Brookfield, J.F.Y., and Semeonoff, R.,** Positive identification of an immigration test case using human DNA fingerprints, *Nature,* 317:818-819, 1986.

**Lee, H.C., Ruano, G., Pagliaro, E. M., Berka, K.M., Gaensslen, R.E.,** DNA analysis in human bone and other specimens of forensic interest: PCR typing and testing, *Journal of the Forensic Science Society,* 2, 213-6, 1991.

**Morton, N.E.,** DNA forensic science 1995, *European Journal of Human Genetics,* 3, 2, 139-44, 1995.

**Murray, B.W., McClymont, R.A., Strobeck, C.,** Forensic identification of ungulate species using restriction digests of PCR-amplified mitochondrial DNA, *Journal of Forensic Sciences*, 40, 6, 943-51, 1995.

**Sajantila, A., Strom, M., Budowle, B., Karhunen, P.J., Peltonen, L.,** The polymerase chain reaction and post-mortem forensic identity testing: application of amplified D1S80 and HLA DQ alpha loci to the identification of fire victims, *Forensic Science International*, 51, 1, 23-34, 1991.

**Sensabaugh, G.F.,** Forensic application of the polymerase chain reaction, *Journal of the Forensic Science Society*, 31, 2, 201-4, 1991.

**Sullivan, K.M.,** Forensic applications of DNA fingerprinting, *Molecular Biotechnology*, 1, 1, 13-27, 1994.

**Sweet, D.J., Sweet, C.H.,** DNA analysis of dental pulp to link incinerated remains of homicide victim to crime scene, *Journal of Forensic Sciences*, 40, 2, 310-4, 1995.

**Weedn, V.W., Roby, R.K.,** Forensic DNA testing. *Archives of Pathology and Laboratory Medicine*, 117, 5, 486-91, 1993.

**Wegel, J.G. Jr., Herrin, G. Jr.,** Deduction of the order of sexual assaults by DNA analysis of two condoms, *Journal of Forensic Sciences*, 39, 3, 844-6, 1994 .

**Whitaker, J.P., Clayton, T.M., Urquhart, A.J., Millican, E.S., Downes, T.J., Kimpton, C.P., Gill, P.,** Short tandem repeat typing of bodies from a mass disaster: high success rate and characteristic amplification patterns in highly degraded samples, *Biotechniques*, 18, 4, 670-7, 1995.

**Zhang, Y.P., Ryder, O.A.,** Phylogenetic relationships of bears (the Ursidae) inferred from mitochondrial DNA sequences, *Molecular Phylogenetics and Evolution*, 3, 4, 351-9, 1994.

## Forensic News Articles:

Anastasia claimant a fraud, *Reuter*, Oct. 5, 1994.

**Beardsley, T.,** DNA fingerprinting reconsidered (again), *Scientific American*, 267, 1, 26, 1992.

**Biederman, P.W.,** In the genes; sabertooth a relative of modern-day big cats, DNA tests show, (Findings in article by George T. Jefferson, Dennis A. Gilbert), *Los Angeles Times*, 111, Oct. 29, 1992.

**Bishop, J.E.,** DNA testing emerges from courtroom to detect whales killed unlawfully, *Wall Street Journal*, Sept. 9, 1994.

**Bishop, J.E.,** Strands of time; a geneticist's work on DNA bears fruit for anthropologists; variations in fragments hint some American natives may hail from Polynesia; the controversy over Eve, *Wall Street Journal*, Nov. 10, 1993.

**Broune, M.W.,** DNA experts expect to identify massacre victims, (Drs. Michael M. Baden and Dragan Primorac will examine bodies found in mass grave in Bosnia and Herzegovina by Croatian officials), *New York Times*, v143, 1994.

**Brown, D.,** Anthropology: looking at DNA to date migration, (researching genetic interrelatedness of tribes through DNA variations), *Washington Post*, v117, 1994.

Clue in DNA and isotopes help identify ivory origin, (An effort to help regulate the trade in elephant ivory), *New York Times*, v139, 1990.

**Dean, C.,** DNA tests may help solve whale mystery; scientists investigate the failure of a species to reproduce, *New York Times*, v138, 1988.

DNA identifies murder victim buried 8 years, *Los Angeles Times*, v110, August 5, 1991.

DNA test shows Virginia woman wasn't Anastasia, *Reuter*, Oct. 4, 1994.

**Erickson, D.,** Do DNA fingerprints protect the innocent?, *Scientific American*, 265(2), 18, 1991.

**Franklin-Barbajosa, C., Menzel, P.,** The New Science of Identity, *National Geographic*, 115, 1992.

**Hua, T., Reza, H.G. and Romney, L.,** New suspect charged as man held 17 years is freed; crime: DNA test points investigators to an ex-Marine already in custody. Police link him to six slayings, (Kevin Lee Green freed; Gerald Parker charged), *Los Angeles Times*, v115, 1996.

**Hunt, L.,** DNA used to identify murder victim, (DNA fingerprinting identifies British girl), *Washington Post*, v114, 1991.

**King, P.H.,** Killing of Jogger Barbara Schoener by Mountain Lion shocks Residents of Cool California, *Los Angeles Times*, v113, 1994.

**Kolata, G.,** Call it the DNA bug, (DNA extracted from 120 million-year-old weevil preserved in amber), *New York Times*, v142, 1993.

**Leary, W.E.,** Genetic record to be kept on members of military, (DNA samples to be obtained from all American service members for purpose of identifying future casualties of war) *New York Times*, v141, 1992.

**Monroe, L.R.,** Day of the condor? Genetic 'fingerprinting' may help save endangered birds, *Los Angeles Times* v107, 1988.

**Neufeld, P.J., Colman, N.,** When science takes the witness stand, *Scientific American*, 262, 5, 46-53, 1990.

**Okie, S.,** Gene hunters set sights on evolution; tracking Kenya's big game for their DNA. (scientists Pieter W. Kat and Peter Arctander collect tissue samples from living specimens to construct genetic portraits), *Washington Post* v116, 1993.

**Okie, S.,** Genetics: clues to birds' behavior. *Washington Post* 112, 1989.

**Pyle, A., Colvin, R.L.,** DNA test links couple, dead baby, (Patty Chavez case alleging that her baby was switched in the hospital) *Los Angeles Times* v110, 1991.

**Rensberger, B.,** 8,000-year-old genetic link found; Florida bog may reveal Indians' kinship to vanished people, *Washington Post*, v111, 1988.

**Rensberger, B.,** A mummy's revelation: TB came to new world before Columbus (University of Minnesota research may have found DNA from tuberculosis bacterium in mummified woman who died 1,040 years ago, exonerating Christopher Columbus), *Washington Post*, v117, 1994.

**Rensberger, B.,** Mummy's DNA preserves a link to ancient life; 2,400-year-old tissue shows researchers new paths for deciphering the past, *Washington Post* v108, 1985.

**Rivera, C.,** Laura Bradbury death shown by DNA evidence. (3-year-old who disappeared in 1984), *Los Angeles Times*, v110, 1990.

**Robinson, E.,** Tzar Nicholas's bones identified: Two Romanovs still unaccounted for. (DNA analysis proves bones found buried in Russian forest are those of Tzar Nicholas II, his wife and three of their four daughters), *Washington Post*, v116, 1993.

**Schefter, J.,** DNA Fingerprints on trial. *Popular Science*, 60, 1994.

**Schmeck, H.M., Jr.,** DNA from mummy is almost intact. *New York Times* v134 , 1985.

**Schmeck, H.M., Jr.,** Intact genetic material extracted from ancient Egyptian mummy; feat is latest in series using DNA to examine evolution, *New York Times*, v134, 1985.

**Schwartz, J.,** Paleontology: film takes its cue from DNA clue. ('Jurassic Park' motion picture's plot premise rapidly becoming fact; DNA from ancient weevil found intact), *Washington Post*, v116, 1993.

**Specter, M.,** Microbiology reunites families: long-lost children's genes match parents'. *Washington Post*, v112, 1989.

**Squires, S.,** Tracking telltale genes in America's ancient mystery. (original migration to North America) *Washington Post* v113, 1990.

**Sullivan, W.,** Archeologists find intact brains 7,000 years old still containing DNA. *New York Times*, v134, 1984.

Tests clear Jackson in paternity suit, - *Reuter*, Oct. 5, 1994.

Tests confirm that bones were last Russian czar's. (DNA tests completed on bones of Czar Nicholas II, executed in 1918 with other members of his family) *New York Times* v144, 1995.

**Thompson, L.,** Analyzing the genes of unknown soldiers; military plans program to identify remains through stored DNA samples. *Washington Post* v114 , 1991.

**Wambaugh, J.,** *The Blooding*, New York, NY; William Morrow & Co., Inc., 1989.

**Yoon, C.K.,** Forensic science. Botanical witness for the prosecution, *Science*, 260, 5110, 894-5, 1993.

## Overturned Rape Convictions:

**Terry, D.,** 3 innocent of killing go free, thanks to students and DNA, (Kenneth Adams, William Rainge and Dennis Williams under strict monitoring pending review of their murder case in Chicago, Illinois), *New York Times*, v145, 1996.

**Glaberson, W.,** Rematch for DNA in a rape case; beneficiary is now likely to challenge test's reliability, (The case of Kerry Kotler in Suffolk County, New York), *New York Times*, v145, 1996.

DNA clears man convicted of rape (Ronald Junior Cotton) *New York Times*, v144, 1995.

**Farnsworth, C.H.,** A man guilty only of being a misfit, (Guy Paul Morin, cleared of murder by DNA evidence for murder of Christine Jessup, Queensville, Ontario), *New York Times,* v144, 1995.

DNA tests free man in jail for decade, (Edward W. Honaker receives pardon after tests prove that he could not have been the rapist in 1985 case), *New York Times*, v144, 1994.

6 years later, conviction is overturned, (Leonard Callace rape case conviction overturned because DNA test was negative) *New York Times*, v142, 1992.

**Baker, P.,** Death-row inmate gets clemency, (Virginia Governor L. Douglas Wilder pardons mentally retarded Earl Washington Jr. whose guilt was questioned by new DNA evidence), *Washington Post*, v117, 1994.

DNA testing frees man jailed in rape; calling data crucial, Virginia Governor pardons a man who served 6 1/2 years. (Walter T. Snyder Jr. is pardoned by L. Douglas Wilder) *New York Times* v142, 1993.

DNA tests clear man imprisoned for 4 years, (Glen Dale Woodall, in prison for abduction and rape of two women, West Virginia), *New York Times*, v141, 1992.

DNA tests free man held 10 years for rape. (Frederick Rene Daye). *New York Times* v144, 1994.

**Foderaro, L.W.,** DNA frees convicted rapist after 9 years behind bars, (Charles Dabbs), *New York Times* v140, 1991.

**Gellman, B.,** DNA test clears man convicted of SE rape. (Washington D.C.), *Washington Post*, v113, 1990.

Genetic testing fails to prove a rape case, (Gary Dotson case), *New York Times*, v137, 1988.

**Kennedy, J.M.,** DNA test clears man convicted of rape, (Mark Bravo of Norwalk, California) *Los Angeles Times* v113, 1994.

**Kolata, G.,** DNA tests are unlocking prison cell doors, (DNA testing used to investigate cases of people who say they have been wrongly convicted; Innocence Project), *New York Times*, v143, 1994.

**Kunkel, T.,** Reasonable doubt? witnesses say Ed Honaker's a rapist. His genes say he's not. A forensic whodunit. (DNA test shows it extremely unlikely convicted rapist was guilty, he is likely to be released after 9 1/2 years in prison), *Washington Post*, v117, 1994.

**Montgomery, D.,** Prisoners play the DNA card for high stakes, (prisoners using DNA testing to prove they were wrongly convicted of crimes), *Washington Post*, v116, 1993.

Prosecutor says DNA tests may free man in rape case, (James M. Catterson) (New York Pages), *New York Times*, v142, 1992.

**Rabinovitz, J.,** Rape conviction overturned on DNA tests; the reversal comes after the man had served 11 years in prison, (Kerry Kotler), *New York Times*, v142, 1992.

**Stolberg, S.,** DNA tests clear man charged in rapes, (Richard Lee Nichols spent four months in Los Angeles County Jail), *Los Angeles Times*, v111, 1992.

**Sullivan, R.,** Semen wasn't defendants', F.B.I. expert testifies at jogger trial, (Federal Bureau of Investigation testimony that DNA analysis of semen found in Central Park jogger), *New York Times*, v139, 1990.

**Valentine, P.W.,** Jailed for murder, freed by DNA, (Kirk Bloodsworth cleared of killing Dawn Hamilton after being proven innocent by PCR DNA amplification procedure; includes related information), *Washington Post*, v116, 1993.

# Chapter 5

## THE SCIENTIFIC BASIS OF DNA TYPING

### I. WHY DNA?

 Forensic DNA analysis involves the intersection of several scientific disciplines including molecular biology, genetics and statistical analysis. In order to understand the usefulness, as well as the limitations, of DNA in the analysis of physical evidence it is important to be familiar with some basic underlying principles of these diverse disciplines. In the next two sections, we will endeavor to summarize some of the main ideas and concepts of molecular biology and genetics. Here is the disclaimer: volumes have been written about each of these subjects. We have purposefully simplified, streamlined, boiled down and in some cases ignored information in order to illustrate basic principles. By definition, information presented in this way is somewhat less precise than would be a full academic treatment. Our hope is to provide a context in which to interpret a result from a forensic laboratory.

What is the scientific basis for the use of **DNA** evidence in criminal investigation? It is an accepted fact that each individual's DNA is unique, with the exception of identical twins. It is, after all, the genetic material that contains all of the information necessary for any organism to develop and function. Approximately 99.5% of the DNA code is the same for all people. This is what makes us human beings rather than turnips or porcupines. It is only the other 0.5% (one-half per cent) that is of interest to the forensic scientists. This portion may vary greatly between individuals and may manifest itself in individual traits such as eye, hair color and blood type. More often the differences in DNA sequence do not show themselves in physical appearance, but must be investigated using special laboratory techniques.

### II. AN INTRODUCTION TO HUMAN GENETICS

Genetics is the study of heredity and variation in biological organisms. It can be considered either on an individual basis, such as the inheritance of particular traits from parent to child, or on a more global basis, such as tracking the movement of genetic markers in a population. Both concepts are integral to the use of DNA in forensic investigation.

### A. THE PHYSICAL BASIS OF HEREDITY

Let us consider first the mechanism of transmitting genetic information from one generation to the next. All living things are composed of **cells**, the smallest units of life (Figure 5-1). One cell is about 1/10 the diameter of a hair, and about 3 trillion cells are contained in the human body. Most body cells (the major exception being red blood cells) contain a smaller entity, called the **nucleus**, which is the organization center for the cell. Genetic information resides in the nucleus of the cell and is organized into physical structures called **chromosomes**. Chromosomes are generally transmitted as intact units from parent to child.

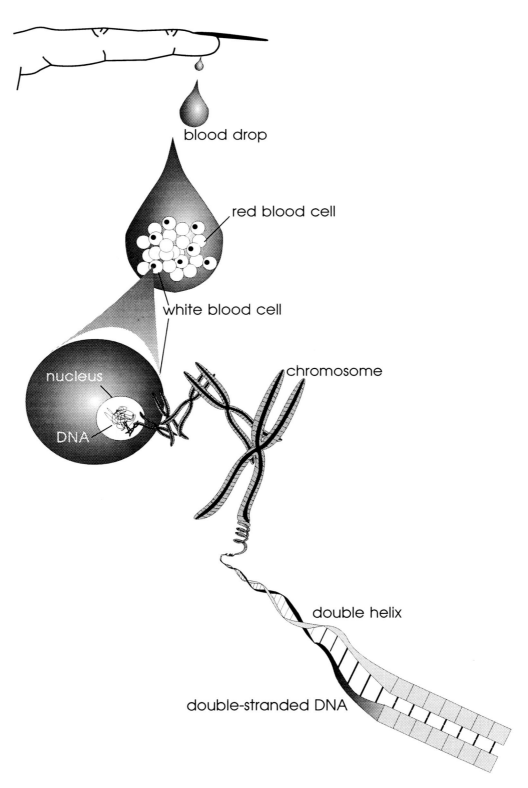

**Figure 5-1. From blood to DNA.**

Thus markers residing on the same chromosome are inherited together;[3] they exhibit **genetic linkage**. In contrast, markers on different chromosomes are generally inherited independently of one another. This principle is called **random assortment**. Markers that exhibit random assortment are not inherited together, or associated with each other in a given population, more often than might be expected by chance. Traits that show random assortment are said to be in **linkage equilibrium**. Conversely, markers that show genetic linkage, such as those close together on the same chromosome, are said to be in **linkage disequilibrium**; in a population they are associated together more often than chance would predict.

## B. ALLELES - VARIATIONS ON A THEME

Human cells contain 23 pairs of chromosomes. Each person has two copies of each chromosome; one comes from Dad, and one from Mom (Plate 1). Thus you inherit half of Dad's genetic blueprint and half of Mom's, which provides you with a full complement. As mentioned previously, small variations in an individual's DNA allow for differentiation between people. Different forms of the same gene or marker are called **alleles**. The simplest example of different alleles was observed in 1866 by Gregor Mendel, the father of modern genetics. He noticed that, for example, peas could be either green *or* yellow, wrinkled *or* round, and that he could follow these traits through many generations. Green and yellow are alternate forms (alleles) of the same gene; wrinkled and round are different alleles of another gene. ABO blood types are an example of different alleles of the same gene in humans. If the alleles at a particular location (**locus**) in the genome are the same on both chromosomes of a pair, the situation is called **homozygous**. If, on the other hand, a small difference is present at the specified locus, so that different alleles are present on each chromosome, the situation is called **heterozygous**. Differences may or may not be physically manifest. When **gametes** (eggs and sperm) are formed, each receives half the genetic complement of the parent at random (Plate 2). The chromosomes are distributed so that each gamete contains exactly one copy of each chromosome, for a total of 23. This means that if a parent is heterozygous for a particular marker, only one of the two possible alleles will be distributed to each gamete. Thus alleles of the same gene segregate away from each other. This means that you will inherit two chromosome 6's, one from each parent, and two chromosome 7's, one from each parent; you should never get both chromosome 6's or both 7's from the same parent (Plate 1). This principle is called **independent segregation**. It is a mechanism for assuring that the progeny ends up with the proper number (two) of each of the 23 chromosomes. Both independent segregation and random assortment contribute to the continuing diversification and genetic hardiness of a species.

One pair of the 23 chromosomes contains the information that determines gender. These chromosomes are given letters, rather than numbers, and are designated **X** and **Y**; males have one **X** and one **Y** chromosome (**XY**), and females have two **X** chromosomes (**XX**). Female eggs can contain only **X** chromosomes, while male sperm can contribute either an **X** or a **Y** chromosome. Therefore gender is determined by the paternal component. The information contained in the sex chromosomes is so different that they even look different visually. Gender may be determined by DNA testing, and is sometimes a useful piece of information in forensic investigation.

---

[3]This is an extreme simplification. Due to a genetic phenomenon called **crossing-over**, an exchange of material between homologous chromosomes (**recombination**) can occur quite frequently. This is particularly true for markers located far apart from each other on the same chromosome. In fact some markers that have been physically mapped to the same chromosome show no genetic linkage whatsoever. For a more in-depth discussion of this phenomenon, please refer to the references.

## C. A PROBLEM ON WHICH TO HANG YOURSELF

Let's consider a non-DNA demonstration of these principles. Suppose you have four short pieces of rope, two pieces are identical and have green and yellow stripes painted near each other; the other two are also identical to each other, and differ from the first pair in that the stripes are red and blue. Within each identical pair, tie a knot in one and not the other, to keep track of which is which. Hold the pair of green/yellow ropes in one hand and the pair of red/blue ropes in the other; the ropes are not physically connected to each other in any way. Throw the ropes in the air simultaneously and let them fall where they may. You will immediately notice two things: the green and yellow stripes on the same rope always fall very near each other because they are physically connected, as do the red and blue stripes on the other rope. They demonstrate genetic linkage. Second, consider the relationship between the ropes bearing different color stripes: how often does a particular pair of differently-colored ropes fall near each other? In one instance, the knotted ropes of different colors (and therefore the other two unknotted ropes) may be associated. The other possibility is that one knotted and one unknotted rope of each color are associated. If you perform this exercise enough times you will find there is no marked preference for any of the combinations. This is a demonstration of independent assortment; the paired association of the two different-colored ropes is determined by chance.

## D. POPULATION GENETICS

All genetic markers exhibit particular frequencies with which they are found in the population. It is well-known that ABO blood groups are found with different frequencies. In the Caucasian population, for example, the B blood type is found in approximately 10% of the people. Each allele of the markers used in DNA analysis also exhibits a particular population frequency. It is important to determine the frequency with which markers occur in order to attach a significance to any particular genetic type. If a type is found in 50% of the population, the fact that a crime scene sample and a suspect share the type is not particularly impressive. If however, that genetic type is found in only 1 out of a million people, the fact that both the sample and the suspect have that type is much more significant.

In forensic investigations, it is common to test many different markers. The most powerful way to express the overall significance of **genetic concordance** is to multiply the individual frequencies of the different markers. With each added marker, the significance of a genetic concordance increases. This calculation is only legitimate, however, if the markers in question pass certain genetic and statistical tests. The first is that the population in question be in **Hardy-Weinberg equilibrium (H-W)**.[4] This basically means that the alleles at one locus show no *a priori* correlation with each other. If they did, it could artificially increase the significance of the genetic concordance. These conditions are approached in large, random mating populations, in the absence of large changes due to migration, natural selection or gene mutation. Second, genotypes at different loci must not show correlations with each other. This is known as linkage equilibrium. One of the ways a population can deviate from Hardy-Weinberg equilibrium and/or **linkage equilibrium (LE)** is if **substructure** or **subpopulations** are present to a large degree. This might occur if small groups within a larger mixed population tend to mate mostly with each other, thus creating a relatively isolated reproductive group. Within the general population of New York city, for instance, some ethnic groups show a high rate of intra-marriage. Frequencies of alleles in such groups could deviate from those obtained by a sampling of the larger, mixed population. The chance

---

[4]This is another extreme simplification. The statistical determination of whether a real population is in Hardy-Weinberg equilibrium, the significance of the factors considered, and the implications of the conclusion, are more fully discussed elsewhere. For a full discussion of population genetics, please refer to the references.

of any two people within a subpopulation sharing genetic markers might then be different from that predicted using allele frequencies obtained from a general population survey. If the alleles in question are found at a higher frequency in the subpopulation, the significance of similar genetic patterns might be overestimated. Under any circumstances, a sampling of the population must be made in order to derive allele frequencies.

## III. AN INTRODUCTION TO THE MOLECULAR BIOLOGY OF DNA

DNA is sometimes referred to as the blueprint of life. The information for the blueprint is encoded in the four chemical building blocks of DNA, **A**denine (**A**), **T**hymine (**T**), **G**uanine (**G**), and **C**ytosine (**C**) (Plate 3). These units, called **bases**, are strung together in a linear fashion, like beads on a string. The specific sequence of the bases determines all the genetic attributes of a person. The properties of the DNA molecule are directly related to its physical structure.

DNA in nature takes the form of a double helix (Plate 3). Two ribbon-like entities are entwined around each other, and held together by cross-bars, like rungs of a ladder. Each rung is composed of two bases which have strong affinities for each other; collectively, these forces hold the DNA molecule together. Each rung of two bases is called a **base pair**. Only specific pairings between the four bases will match up and stick together. **A** always pairs with **T**, and **G** with **C**. This obligatory pairing, called **complementary base pairing**, is exploited in all DNA typing systems. When the double helix is intact, the DNA is called **double-stranded**; when the two halves of the helix come apart, either in nature, or in the test tube (*in vitro*), the DNA is called **single-stranded**.

In nature, complementary base-pairing is responsible for the ability to accurately replicate the DNA molecule, with its genetic information, and pass it on to the next generation. The double helix is unzipped by special enzymes, and new building blocks (**nucleotides**) are brought in. Each nucleotide contains one base attached to a piece of the backbone ribbon. Using each half of the original helix as a template, a second half is created, resulting in two molecules identical to the original. The order of the bases in the new strands is specified by the existing strands. Each original base captures a complementary replacement to complete the base pair. This process can be recreated *in vitro* to a limited extent, and is the basis of the **polymerase chain reaction (PCR)**, which will be discussed in more detail in a later section (Plates 4, 5).

Short segments of complementary single-stranded DNA also show a specific affinity for each other *in vitro*, defined again by the specific base sequence. Under appropriate conditions, complementary DNA fragments will find each other and stick back together. Technically this is referred to as **reannealing** or **hybridization**. In the laboratory, it is crucial that the chemical conditions for hybridization be exact. These conditions, which are determined by scientific experimentation, are called **stringency** conditions. If the stringency is too high, no hybridization will occur; if the stringency is too low, reannealing will be less than exact, and some DNA fragments might stick together even if they are not a perfect complementary match. If the sequence at a particular location in the genome is of interest, single-stranded fragments can be artificially synthesized to target that location.[5] These single-stranded fragments of known sequence are called DNA **probes**. Complementary base-pairing is essential to the detection of the genetic variations described in the next section.

---

[5]DNA probes were first created by isolating, or cloning, small pieces of genomic DNA, and replicating them using microorganisms. Today, DNA fragments of known sequence are often artificially synthesized in a laboratory.

## IV.  TWO KINDS OF VARIATION

Through scientific investigation, mostly as a by-product of disease research, standard locations in the DNA have been established where the sequence varies more than usual between people.  A molecular location is called a **locus (one locus, two loci)**.  The existence of multiple alleles of a marker at a single locus is called **polymorphism**.  When such loci exhibit extreme numbers of variants (as many as hundreds), they are called **hypervariable**.  Variations, or polymorphisms, occur either in the sequence of bases at a particular locus, or in the length of a DNA fragment between two defined endpoints.  **Sequence polymorphisms** are like different spellings for the same word in British English and American English.  When you see *analyze* spelled as *analyse*, the word and meaning are still recognizable, as well as the root culture of the word.  For example, the two double-stranded DNA fragments:

AGCTCAATCG     and     AGATCAATCG
: : : : : : : : : :             : : : : : : : : : :
TCGAGTTAGC             TCTAGTTAGC

exhibit sequence polymorphism at the third base pair from the left; the fragments are recognizable as similar, with a small variation.  **Length polymorphisms** (Plate 3) are most easily analogized to a train that can accommodate different numbers of boxcars.  The engine and caboose define the ends of the train; the total length may vary according to the number of cars attached between them at any one time.  Each boxcar contains the same small DNA sequence; the following is an example of three boxcars, or consecutive repeated DNA sequences.

AGCTCAATCG-AGCTCAATCG-AGCTCAATCG
: : : : : : : : : :   : : : : : : : : : :   : : : : : : : : : :
TCGAGTTAGC-TCGAGTTAGC-TCGAGTTAGC

In genetic terminology, the boxcars are termed **tandem repeats**.  A locus that shows variation in the number of tandem repeats is called a **variable number tandem repeat (VNTR)** locus.  A particular number of tandem repeats, for instance 35, defines a VNTR allele at that locus.  Different laboratory techniques are used to investigate the two kinds of variations.

## V.  ENZYMES, THE WORKHORSES OF THE BIOLOGICAL WORLD

It is impossible to discuss any biochemical reaction, in nature or *in vitro*, without referring to **enzymes**.  Enzymes are the biochemical workers that get the job done.  They are protein-based, and are able to catalyze the formation or breakdown of other biological components many times over.  Various enzymes in the laboratory are used for everything from breaking cells open to synthesizing DNA.  Modern molecular biology (or any biology for that matter) would not exist as such without enzymes.  When enzymes are isolated from nature, and asked to perform their function in a test tube, it is crucial to recreate their natural environment as closely as possible; otherwise they may not perform as expected.

Enzymes which catalyze the addition of components are called **polymerases**.  An example of this is *Taq* **polymerase**, which directs the addition of nucleotides in the replication of DNA.  This is the enzyme which makes PCR possible.  *Taq* polymerase possesses the unusual quality of maintaining its activity even after exposure to heat.  As we will discuss later, this attribute is critical to the PCR reaction.

**Restriction enzymes** belong to a class of enzymes that break DNA into smaller pieces. Restriction enzymes were originally conceived by nature to protect bacteria from viral invaders. They do this by recognizing specific small DNA sequences that occur in the virus, and cutting viral DNA at all the places that sequence occurs. The bacterium's own DNA is protected from being chopped to pieces by another biochemical mechanism. Molecular biologists have isolated these enzymes (there are at least hundreds of different ones) and co-opted them for their own uses. Restriction enzymes also cut human DNA with the same sequence specificity as the original intended viral DNA.

Most importantly, any restriction enzyme, under the proper conditions, *It always cuts DNA at places where a specific base sequence occurs, and no other.* For example, the restriction enzyme *Hae*III cuts a double-stranded DNA molecule at any site where the sequence **CCGG** occurs, and it always cuts between the **C** and the **G** (Plate 3). This means that any particular genome can be reproducibly cut into pieces of the same number and size. The number and size of DNA fragments will vary between the genomes of different people when polymorphisms occur. (If you think this is a word in a foreign language, stop cheating, and go back and read Section IV of this chapter.) The enzyme most often used for forensic RFLP analysis in the U.S. is called *Hae*III. In Europe, most labs use an enzyme called *Hin*fI.

──── *FURTHER REFERENCES*────────────────────────

Griffiths, A.J.F., Miller, J.H., Suzuki, D.T., Lewontin, R.C., Gelbart, W.M., *An Introduction to Genetic Analysis*, 5th ed., W.H. Freeman and Co., New York, NY, 1993.

Schleif, RF., *Genetics and Molecular Biology,* 2nd ed., Johns Hopkins University Press, Baltimore, MD, 1993.

Watson, J.D., Hopkins, N.H., Roberts, J.W., Steitz, J.A., Weiner, A.M., *Molecular Biology of the Gene*, 4th ed., The Benjamin/Cummings Pub. Co., 1987.

# Chapter 6

## AN OVERVIEW OF FORENSIC DNA TYPING SYSTEMS

### I. RFLP ANALYSIS

 The first technique that was adapted for forensic DNA analysis is called **RFLP (Restriction Fragment Length Polymorphism)**. This kind of analysis determines variation in the length of a defined DNA fragment (Plate 3). RFLP, at this writing, still provides the highest degree of discrimination per locus. If two samples originate from different sources, RFLP is the technique most likely to differentiate them. Two circumstances contribute to the huge **power of discrimination ($P_d$)** of RFLP. One is that many loci have been established for RFLP analysis; the more places you look, the greater the chance of finding a difference between two people. Forensic DNA laboratories now have access to probes for over 15 different loci. Second, forensic workers have chosen RFLP loci that have as many as hundreds of variations at each locus, increasing the chance that samples from different individuals will be differentiated.

When complete, an RFLP pattern looks like a very simple supermarket bar code (Figures 6-1, 6-2). In looking at two samples, the pattern of bars on the **autoradiograph** is compared in order to determine if they could have originated from the same source. RFLP is still the method of choice for determining whether a single sample contains DNA from more than one person. Both contributors will likely be detected clearly on the final readout. Unfortunately, the RFLP technique requires more and better quality DNA than some of the newer PCR techniques. Since forensic evidence is often old, degraded and of limited quantity, RFLP analysis is sometimes not possible.

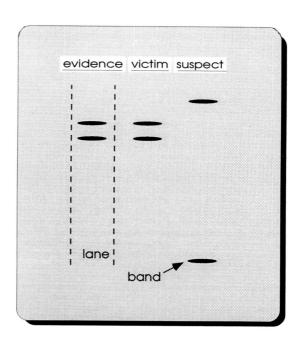

**Figure 6-1. Representation of an RFLP autorad.** Each sample is run in a lane, which is viewed vertically by convention. Each of the dark bars is called a band. All the bands in a lane come from one sample. The autorad is read by comparing the pattern of bands between different lanes.

It is important to realize that different laboratories often perform RFLP analysis with slight variations. One variation is in the enzyme, the molecular scissors used to cut the DNA. When different enzymes are used, different loci may also be analyzed, producing additional data. Even when the same locus is analyzed by different enzymes, the raw data will look dissimilar initially because different size DNA fragments are produced. However, the final result of similar or dissimilar patterns between samples will be the same, regardless of which enzyme is used. Two common enzymes used are called *Hin*fI and *Hae*III. If portions of the same samples are sent to laboratories using different enzyme systems, independent confirmation can be obtained as to the original source(s) of the samples.

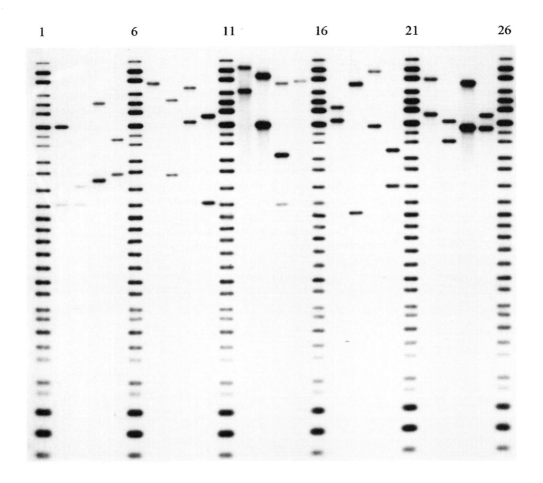

**Figure 6-2. A population autorad.** Lanes 1, 6, 11, 16, 21 and 26 contain the molecular ladder. The other lanes each contain a DNA sample from a different individual. The locus probed is D4S139.

## SIDEBAR 2

### The Bungled Burglary
### (or, the burglar that couldn't)

Once in a criminalist's lifetime there may occur a truly simple, straightforward case; what appears obvious is actually true.  Of course, it helps if the suspect confesses to a crime that was never completed.  In 1992, an aspiring burglar hurled a rock through a plate glass window in a Bank of America in Northern California.  He removed the pieces of broken glass, entered the bank through the broken window, and unsuccessfully attempted to open the locked teller drawers.  Having failed to complete his task, he fled, leaving a telltale trail of blood—straight to the Sheriff's department to "turn himself in for the burglary of the Bank of America".  Three blood swabs were collected from the scene and submitted with a sample collected from the self-indicted suspect.

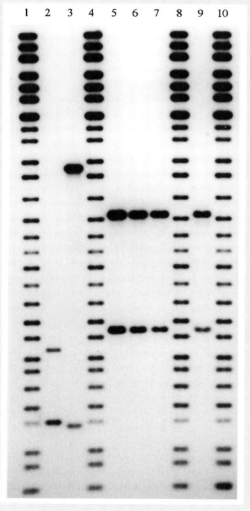

**One RFLP probing of the autorad from this case.** Lanes 1, 4, 8, and 10 contain molecular ladders.  Lane 2 contains a control sample which is used by all U.S. labs performing forensic RFLP analysis, and Lane 3 contains an intralaboratory control for which the results are known, but not to the analyst.  Lanes 5, 6, and 7 contain the three samples collected from the crime scene, and lane 9 contains the suspect's blood sample. (Portions of the molecular ladder have been cropped from this photo.)

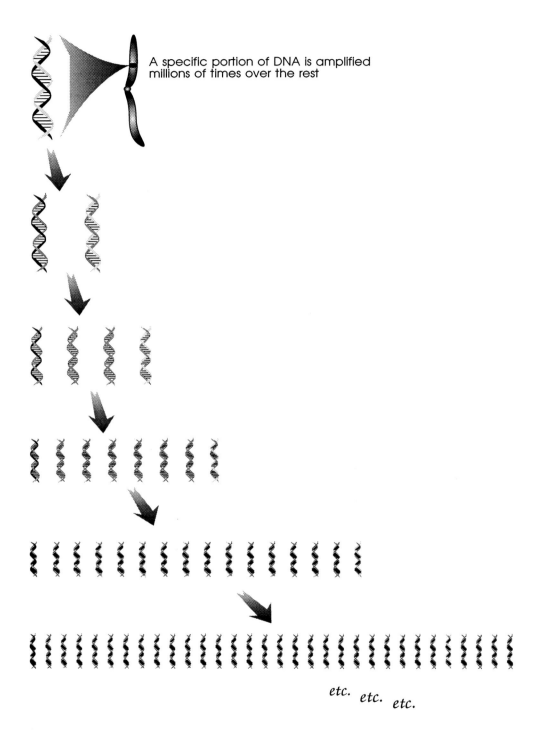

A specific portion of DNA is amplified millions of times over the rest

etc. etc. etc.

**Figure 6-3. Overview of PCR amplification.** A defined region of DNA is copied millions of times. With each round of amplification, the number of copies doubles, resulting in a theoretical geometric increase in the number of copies of that fragment over the rest.

## II. PCR AMPLIFICATION

**PCR (Polymerase Chain Reaction)** is a general technique for increasing the amount of a specific section of DNA in a sample. This is called DNA amplification. The procedure is so innovative that its inventor was awarded the Nobel prize in 1993. PCR is often referred to as molecular "Xeroxing" (Figure 6-3). It is generally designed so that only a small segment of the DNA of interest is copied, and this is accomplished with extremely high fidelity to the original. In this way, information may be gained from samples which might otherwise be refractory to analysis because of limited or degraded starting material.

The DNA samples prepared using PCR are analyzed in a variety of different ways, but currently not by RFLP analysis. The size of the DNA fragments generated by RFLP is too large for reliable and consistent amplification by current PCR methodology. Of the systems now in use for forensic analysis of PCR-amplified DNA, fewer loci have been identified and developed, and each locus tends to show less variation. Therefore, results may be obtained for a sample of limited quantity and quality, but the power of discrimination will be lower. This stands to change in the near future, due to the addition of PCR markers already on the drawing board. For the moment, however, there is less chance of showing that two samples originate from different sources with PCR than with RFLP.

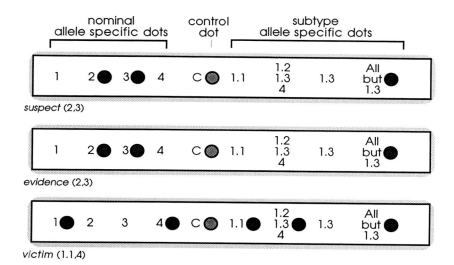

**Figure 6-4. Representation of a DQα reverse dot blot.** A total of 9 probes are present on each strip. In this case, the suspect and evidence samples show an identical pattern of dots, while the victim shows a different pattern. The C dot is a control probe that shows up regardless of **DQα** type. The dots to the left of C (1, 2, 3, and 4) give the nominal allele designations; the dots to the right of C are used to determine some of the subtypes into which the 1 allele can be subdivided. Interpretation of **DQα** results will be discussed further in *Chapter 9.*

### A. HLA DQα/HLA DQA1

The first system to become available for forensic analysis of PCR-amplified DNA is called **HLA DQα**. This is the historical name of the locus which is analyzed and is still used to refer to the original typing format for this system. The type of variation present at this locus resides in the DNA sequence. Some of the bases in this 242 bp region show differences between people. This variation is detected using specially designed molecular **probes**, synthetic fragments of DNA designed to be complementary to, and thus target, particular subregions within this locus. These probes detect six common DQα alleles which, in combination, determine 21 possible genotypes. Since only one locus with limited variability is analyzed in this system, the $P_d$ is not as high as for RFLP. The chief advantages of HLA DQα are the ability to investigate very small samples and the rapidity of analysis. The final results are seen as a series of blue dots on a paper-like strip (Figures 6-5). A comparison of the pattern of the dots between typing strips indicates whether two samples may have originated from the same source. (see Figure 6-4, 6-5)

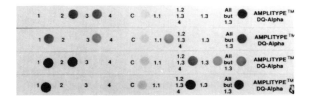

Figure 6-5. A DQα reverse dot blot. To the left are 4 typing strips, each representing a different individual.

Due to a reorganization, and renaming of the gene cluster of which DQ is part, by the genetics community, the DQα locus is now referred to as **DQA1**. DQA1 also designates an improved forensic typing system for this locus, in which the 4 allele, as well as the 1 allele can now be divided into subtypes. This results in a total of 42 detectable types, increasing the $P_d$ slightly (see Figures 6-6, 6-7). DQα now refers only to the original typing system in which the 4 alleles are not subtyped. DQA1 properly refers to the locus itself and the newer typing system which provides for subtyping of the 4 allele. Throughout this book, when we use the term DQα, we are referring to the original kit still produced by Perkin-Elmer. When the designation DQA1 is used, we refer to the new format of the test that includes the subtyping of the 4 allele, currently only available when purchased with the polymarker kit.

---

## SIDEBAR 3

### Quintanilla

In the spring and summer of 1987, two women on the San Francisco peninsula were abducted and brutally sexually assaulted. Because both the descriptions and MOs appeared quite similar, the police suspected that these assaults might be related. A separate police artist sketch was prepared according to the description of her assailant given by each victim (Panel A). Both described a young Hispanic male, thin and approximately 5'6" to 5'8" tall.

(A)

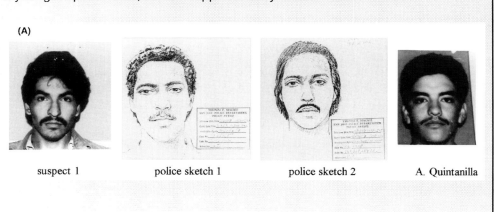

suspect 1                police sketch 1                police sketch 2                A. Quintanilla

One victim (victim 1) was able to identify an individual from a photo line-up as her attacker. She subsequently identified him both in a live lineup, and at a preliminary hearing. A photo of this suspect is shown on the far left of the police sketches above. Conventional serological typing of the sexual assault evidence was uninformative with respect to the semen donor's types. The defendant was eager to have the recently developed forensic DNA testing performed on this evidence. With approval from the prosecution, Dr. Edward Blake was retained by the defense to perform the work. Dr. Blake had been working closely with Cetus Corporation in the development of the DQα marker system using the Polymerase Chain Reaction (PCR).

Dr. Blake performed the analysis using an early version of this typing system (Panel B). The typing process at that time consisted of fixing the amplified product to strips, and then hybridizing the strips with sequence specific oligonucleotide (SSO) probes. The color reaction initially used a dye that turned red, so red dots (reproduced here in B/W) indicated a positive reaction. Subtypes were determined from separate reactions using radioactively labeled probes (not shown).

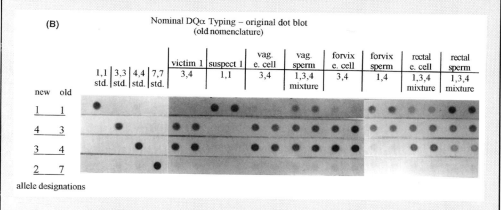

**(B)**
Nominal DQα Typing – original dot blot
(old nomenclature)

allele designations

The semen donor associated with victim 1 was reported as a 1.1,3 in the nomenclature in use at that time. This type is equivalent to a 1.1,4 in current nomenclature. A sample from the defendant was analyzed using the same system and found to be either a type 1.2,1.3, or a 1.3,1.3 (It was not possible to distinguish between the two.) In either case, the defendant identified by the victim was eliminated as the donor of the semen sample. In an act of courage and conviction, the district attorney did not challenge this new test, but dismissed charges against this suspect.

Dr. Blake subsequently also typed evidence from victim 2 (Panel C). By this time, the DQα typing system had progressed to the reverse dot blot format. In a reverse dot blot, the probes are fixed to a single strip and amplified product is hybridized to them. Current nomenclature had been established, but the red dye was still in use. The semen evidence from victim 2 also showed a type 1.1,4, linking the two sexual assaults.

Two years after the first attack, Armando Quintanilla was arrested for an attempted assault at virtually the same location in Mountain View as the first victim had reported. A photograph of Quintanilla is shown on the right of the police sketches above. Detectives felt that the similar MO, the close locations of all three attacks, and the resemblance of Quintanilla to the physical descriptions from the first assaults warranted further investigation. They submitted a reference sample from Quintanilla to Dr. Blake for testing. Quintanilla was typed as a 1.1,4 (Panel D) and therefore included as a possible donor of the semen samples in all three cases. RFLP analysis was also attempted on some of the sexual assault evidence, but the results were inconclusive.

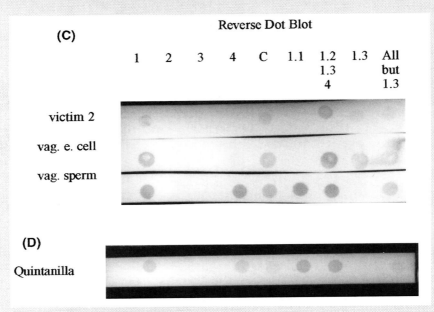

Finally, a second item of evidence from victim 1 was analyzed using the present day reverse dot blot format with pre-printed strips (Panel E). By this time the dye had been changed to a blue color (reproduced here in B/W). This item was also from a type 1.1,4 individual. A DQα type 1.1,4 was reported as occurring in approximately 7% of the Mexican-American population. Based on the totality of the evidence, a jury convicted Armando Quintanilla of numerous felonies. He was sentenced to 99 years plus life.

**(E)**    Final form of Manufacturer's Reverse Dot Blot DQα Typing Strips

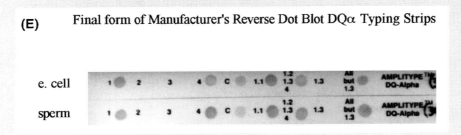

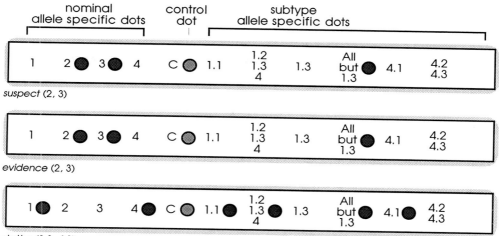

**Figure 6-6. Representation of a DQA1 reverse dot blot.** A total of 11 probes are present on each strip. In this case, the suspect and evidence samples show an identical pattern of dots, while the victim shows a different pattern. The C dot is a control probe that shows up regardless of DQα type. The dots to the left of C (1, 2, 3, and 4) give the nominal allele designations; the dots to the right of C are used to determine some of the subtypes into which the 1 and 4 alleles can be subdivided. The DQA1 system is able to distinguish the 4.1 subtype from the nominal 4 allele, an improvement over the DQα system. Interpretation of DQA1 results will be discussed further in *Chapter 9*.

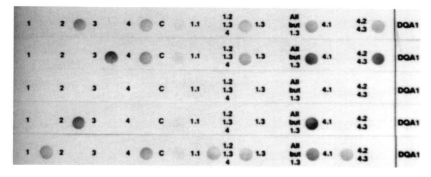

**Figure 6-7. A DQA1 reverse dot blot.** Above are 5 typing strips, each representing a different individual.

## B. AMPLITYPE® PM[6] – "POLYMARKER"

The AmpliType® PM system, commonly known as **polymarker,** is just an expansion of the technique used in HLA DQα analysis. The trick was to increase the power of discrimination ($P_d$), while retaining all the advantages of PCR. A system was developed in which several markers at different loci are analyzed at the same time. Although each of the five additional markers (Figures 6-8, 6-9) do not contain as much individual variation as HLA DQα (only 2 or 3 alleles at each), the combined result, along with that from HLA DQA1, increases the power of the test considerably. The $P_d$ of polymarker is on the order of 1 in 200. So, theoretically, for every 200 comparisons between 2 people chosen at random, about 199 pairs would have different PM types; 1 pair would have the same type. The addition of DQA1 increases the power of discrimination to 1 in 2000 comparisons. A disadvantage of

---

[6]Amplitype® is a registered trademark of Roche Molecular Systems Inc.

this test is that it is often more difficult to interpret the results from samples containing DNA from more than one contributor. As in HLA DQα analysis, the final results are seen as a series of blue dots, and a comparison of the pattern of the dots between typing strips indicates whether two samples may have originated from the same source.

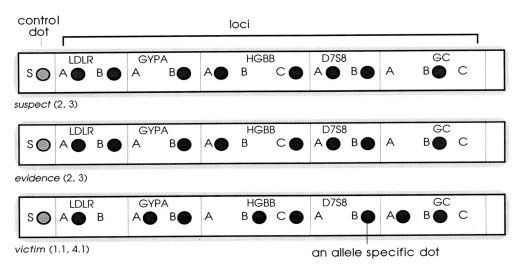

**Figure 6-8. Representation of a polymarker reverse dot blot.** A total of 13 probes are present on each strip. In this case, the suspect and evidence samples show an identical pattern of dots, while the victim shows a different pattern. The S dot is a control probe that shows up regardless of polymarker type – it is equivalent to the C dot in DQα and DQA1. The 5 typing loci have either 2 or 3 possible alleles each. Interpretation of polymarker strips is discussed more fully in *Chapter 9*.

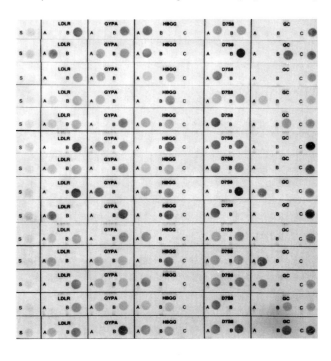

**Figure 6-9. A polymarker reverse dot blot.** To the left are 14 typing strips, each representing a different individual.

## C. D1S80

One of the more recent PCR systems to come on line in forensic laboratories is called **D1S80** (see Figure 6-10). D1S80 refers to the locus in the DNA that is being investigated. Like RFLP, the variation present at this locus is in the length of a defined DNA fragment as determined by the number of tandem repeats (a VNTR). However, because of its relatively smaller size, this fragment is amenable to amplification by PCR. In the forensic science literature, systems of this nature are called **Amplified Fragment Length Polymorphisms** (**AMP-FLPs, AFLPs, or AMFLPs**). Each repeat unit in D1S80 is 16 bp long, except for the first repeat, which is 14 bp. The number of repeats varies from about 14 to 41, producing DNA fragments in the range of hundreds of base pairs, about an order of magnitude smaller than the fragments normally analyzed in RFLP typing. Thus D1S80 analysis combines the advantages inherent in any PCR system (specifically the ability to analyze samples of limited quantity and quality) with the greater variation generally seen in length-based systems. Again, because only one locus is analyzed in this system, the power of discrimination is not as high as RFLP. Also, the D1S80 locus in particular contains two alleles that are common among many people in some racial groups. If one of these two alleles is present in the samples being analyzed, the significance of the test result may be reduced.

In RFLP analysis, all of the DNA is processed, and the regions of interest are detected with molecular probes. In D1S80 analysis, the regions defined by the PCR amplification are effectively purified before the DNA is analyzed. Thus no special probes are needed to visualize the final result. This is like buying a package of 1-inch nails which are preselected for you instead of buying a package of assorted nails and having to fish out the ones you need for your fence. D1S80 loci are detected as **discrete alleles** and thus can be compared directly to a standard ruler made up of all possible alleles (**allelic ladder**) which is run on the same gel. The DNA is commonly detected using a silver stain, and the final result looks much like the simplified supermarket bar-code often used to describe RFLP. The D1S80 locus is also amenable to the automated detection and analysis techniques described later in this chapter, although the laboratories that can afford such automated systems tend to use them to run more powerful systems, such as STRs.

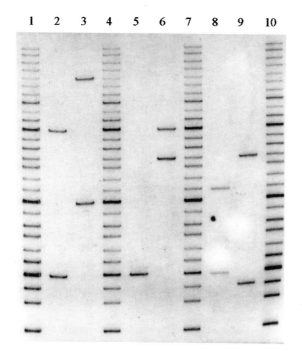

**Figure 6-10. A D1S80 Silver-stained gel.** Lanes 1, 4, 7 and 10 contain the allelic ladder to which all questioned samples are compared. Lanes 2, 3, 5, 6, 8 and 9 each contain a sample from a single individual. All except lane 5 are heterozygotes, so the variant alleles present on the two chromosomes each produce a band. The sample in lane 5 is a homozygote — the alleles on the two chromosomes are the same size and are represented by a single band.

## D. STRs

**Short Tandem Repeats (STRs)** are similar to the D1S80 system described above, except that the repeat units are shorter. The loci chosen for forensic use generally have a tandem repeat unit of 3 or 4 bp and may be repeated from a few to dozens of times. The number of alleles present in the population varies from about 5 to 20, depending on the locus. Like D1S80, STR loci are detected as discrete alleles and thus can be compared directly to an allelic ladder run on the same gel, simplifying comparison and analysis. Including flanking sequences amplified by the primers, the size of the DNA fragments produced by amplification of STR loci tends to be in the range of hundreds of base pairs, rather than the thousands of base pairs found in RFLP fragments. This makes STRs an ideal choice for degraded DNA. Although each locus is only moderately polymorphic (i.e., fewer alleles are found), many such loci exist and can be utilized simultaneously. In this respect, the system is similar to RFLP. In fact, PCR amplification of several different loci is often performed simultaneously in the same tube (**multiplexing**), producing a savings of time, materials, and most important, sample. Since the human genome contains an almost unlimited choice of STR loci, it is possible to choose those in which the distribution of STR alleles in any given population tends to be reasonably well distributed, another advantage over the D1S80 system.

Like D1S80, STR loci may be detected and analyzed manually using a silver stain (Figure 6-11). Alternatively, several systems have been developed where fluorescence is used to detect the bands, either during or after the separation (Figure 6-12). Fluorescence is amenable to automated detection, greatly facilitating subsequent analysis and storage of data. There are also several technical advantages to the use of fluorescent detection of STR loci. The disadvantage is expense, as sophisticated equipment is necessary for the process. Both manual and automated systems are currently in use around the country, and evidence analyzed with STRs is just starting to be introduced into the courts.

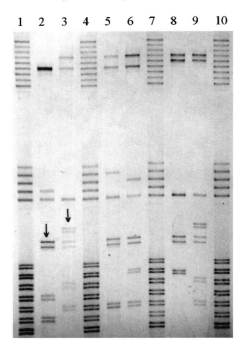

**Figure 6-11. An STR Silver-stained gel.** Lanes 1, 4, 7 and 10 each contain a mix of the allelic ladders to which all questioned samples are compared. In this case, three loci have been analyzed simultaneously; thus three distinct sets of non-overlapping bands are present in each vertical ladder lane. Lanes 2, 3, 5, 6, 8 and 9 each contain samples from a single individual. Each band is compared directly to one in the ladder lane, thus establishing the allele present in the sample. Note that all bands appear as doublets in the lower part of the gel – the reason for this is discussed in *Chapter 9*. In addition to the three multiplexed STR loci, the Gender ID locus has been added to this system. In each sample lane (but not in the ladder lanes), either one or two doublets (see arrows) are present in the vertical space between the middle and bottom sets of STR allelic ladder bands. One doublet indicates a female (lane 2); a pair of doublets indicates a male (lane 3).

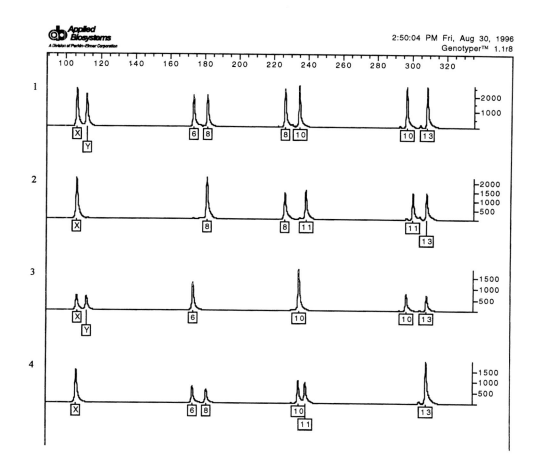

**Figure 6-12. An STR triplex amplified with fluorescently labeled primers and detected by a dynamic detection automated sequencer.** In this case, none of the three STR loci amplified have overlapping alleles, so the same green fluorescent primer was used to label all of them. The data are reproduced here in black and white. The final results of the electrophoretic run are viewed as a computer-generated histogram. Each peak is derived directly from one allele ( which corresponds to one band). Each corresponding vertical gel lane (see e.g. Plate 8) is represented as a horizontal panel; the top of the gel (larger fragments) is on the left, and the bottom (smaller fragments) is on the right. The location of the peak is directly proportional to the migration distance, and the area under the peak is directly proportional to the intensity of the signal. The computer software compares the bands (peaks) in a sample to a known molecular ladder, run in the same lane, and automatically calls the alleles present. The samples in this study are from a father (lane 1), mother (lane 2), son (lane 3) and daughter (lane 4). Note that each child shows a different combination of the parental alleles. Both males show both an X and a Y band at the gender identification locus (far left), and both females, only an X band.

## E. GENDER ID

It is often useful to know if male or female components are present in a forensic sample. The **amelogenin** locus, which is coincidentally the gene for tooth pulp, shows a length variation between the sexes (Figure 6-13). One region (left side) of the female form of the gene contains a small deletion (6 bp) in non-essential DNA and produces a shorter product when amplified by PCR. When this region is analyzed, a female with two X chromosomes will show one band. A male with both an X and a Y chromosome will show two bands, one the same size as the female and one slightly larger. In some systems the larger region (right side) of the chromosome is analyzed, producing a slightly different result; a male still produces two bands, but the smaller one is from the Y chromosome. An advantage of this system over previous loci used for gender differentiation is that both the male and female forms of the gene are detected and can be compared. Analysis of this locus is often appended to another PCR system, such as DQα or a multiplex STR system. No additional sample need be expended to make this determination, which in and of itself might eliminate only 50% of the population. Several different primer sets are commercially available, and the analyst may choose that which best fits the needs of a particular case or sample.

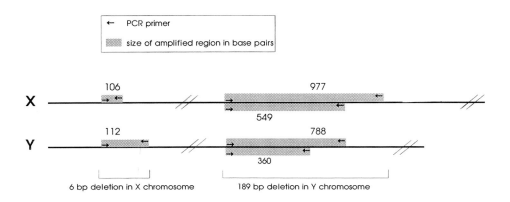

**Figure 6-13. Structure of the amelogenin locus.** Two different regions and various PCR primer sets are used in forensic gender identification (gender ID, GI). Two different pairs of fragments, suitable for analysis on agarose gels, may be produced from the region containing a 189 bp deletion in males. A pair of fragments encompassing the regions containing a 6 bp deletion in females are much smaller and suitable for analysis on polyacrylamide gels in conjunction with STR systems.

## F. MITOCHONDRIAL DNA

The vast majority of the genetic material in the human genome[7] resides in the nucleus of each cell, and all of the genetic typing systems and procedures described so far make use of loci found in **nuclear DNA**. Some additional bits of genetic material exist, however, and are contained in other small subcellular compartments called **cell organelles**. One of these is the **mitochondrion** (pl. mitochondria), in which some of the processes of cellular respiration take place.

---

[7]All life on the earth is divided into two categories. Prokaryotic organisms, such as bacteria, are very simple and don't contain subcellular organelles, such as a nucleus or mitochondrion. Eukaryotic organisms, including animals and plants, are more complex and compartmentalize their functions, including sequestering the main portion of their genome in a nucleus . Other of their organelles, such as mitochondria, also contain small bits of DNA. Mitochondria are the site of oxidative respiration in eukaryotic cells and are thought to have been evolutionarily acquired as endosymbiotic bacteria, hence the presence of residual DNA.

Mitochondria in human cells contain an autonomous circle of DNA which codes for some of these functions. The mitochondrial genome is about 16.5 kb and, of interest to forensic scientists, contains a noncoding hypervariable control region. In particular, there are two segments within this 1,100 bp control region (Figure 6-14), also called the **D-loop**, that tend to mutate with an extremely high frequency, at least 5 to 10 times that of nuclear DNA. This high mutation rate makes the region attractive for use in individual identification. It has been estimated that **mitochondrial DNA (mtDNA)** may vary between about 1% to 2.3% between unrelated individuals. That is, on average, about 1 or 2 nucleotides out of every 100 is different. In other words, mtDNA sequences are highly variable between unrelated individuals.

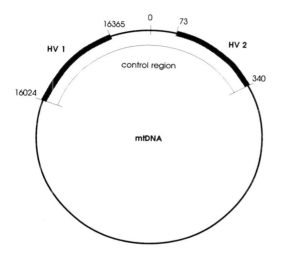

**Figure 6-14. Locations of the two hypervariable regions on the mitochondrial DNA circle.**

Another unique quality of mitochondrial DNA is its inheritance pattern. As discussed in *Chapter 5*, nuclear DNA is inherited in equal parts from both parents. Due to the technicalities of fertilization,[8] genetic material from mitochondria is inherited only from the egg cell of the mother; thus mtDNA is said to exhibit **maternal inheritance.**[9] Therefore the mtDNA type of an individual cannot be heterozygous, or exhibit two different types. A genetic element that lacks a homologous counterpart in the genome may be described as **hemizygous**; mtDNA is also sometimes referred to as **monoclonal**. This is a useful quality in tracking families and populations and also belies any possibility of new variations arising from chromosomal recombination.[10] All new variations are gained by mutation. In practical

---

[8]In most higher organisms, the egg cell is much larger that the sperm cell which fertilizes it. Consequently, the new individual acquires all cell organelles from the female parent. Additionally, mitochondria in a sperm cell are carried in a region between the head and the tail. Because only the nucleus-containing head actually enters the egg cell, the tail, including its mitochondria is not incorporated into the new zygote.

[9]As detection has been improved, some experiments in mice have shown that about 1 in 10,000 times, some mtDNA from the father may make it into the offspring. This is not a practical concern, as such a small amount will not be detected using standard procedures.

[10]Chromosomal recombination in the nuclear genome takes place during meiosis, the process by which gametes (eggs and sperm) are formed. During this process, genetic alleles which originally came from either parent are mixed up and rearranged. Since mtDNA is inherited only from the mother, this has no possibility of happening, and mtDNA is inherited faithfully.

terms, all copies of the mtDNA sequences within an individual are normally identical, as they are between maternal relatives.

Last, but not least, mtDNA is present in hundreds to thousands of copies per cell. Because of its relatively small size in comparison to nuclear chromosomes and numerous multiple copies it is often the last typable DNA present in a small, old or badly treated sample. If no results are obtained with any other system, often the mtDNA can be typed. Researchers have even been successful in typing mtDNA embedded in the dead cells of hair shafts, as well as in bones and teeth. However, because mtDNA constitutes only a single locus and presents some technical challenges, mitochondrial DNA in forensic investigation is best reserved for cases where nuclear DNA analysis has failed due to minimal quality or quantity. At present, only a few forensic DNA laboratories in the country have mtDNA analysis capabilities.

The complete 16,569 nucleotide sequence of human mtDNA has been established for a reference individual. For the moment, all comparisons are made to this reference called the *Anderson sequence*.

## III. WHAT KINDS OF SAMPLES CAN BE ANALYZED?

The DNA in a cell is contained in a small region called the nucleus. Almost all body fluids and organs have cells with nuclei. Common examples include blood, semen, saliva and hair roots. Although the red cells in blood do not contain nuclei, white cells do, so blood is easily typed for DNA. The cells in the outside layer of skin contain few or no nuclei, and as a consequence, make it difficult or impossible to contaminate an object by mere casual handling. In order to type hair, it is generally necessary to obtain samples which include a root. Hair shafts and nail clippings are not generally typable by current methods. Excretions, such as urine, feces and perspiration may or may not contain enough nucleated cells for DNA analysis, depending on the individual circumstance. Most internal organs, as well as bone, may be analyzed using DNA.

---

### SIDEBAR 4

### The Czar's Bones
### (or, what difference a base pair?)

Whose bones are buried in a multiple grave in Yekaterinburg, Russia? In 1991 the Soviet government ordered the excavation of a shallow pit that was rumored to hold the remains of the Romanovs, the Russian Imperial family executed in 1918 by the Bolsheviks. Six months after the shooting, a Russian investigator, Nicholas Sokolov, recovered some scraps of physical evidence from the probable grave site, including several fingers and bottles of congealed fat, but apparently no bodies; he concluded that they had been burnt to ashes. In April 1989, Russian film maker Geli Ryabov announced that he knew where the Romanovs were buried. Working from photographs and the Kremlin report of Yakov Yurovsky, the executioners' leader, he and geologist Alexander Avdonin had located the grave ten years earlier, five miles from the site investigated by Sokolov. They had opened the grave and exhumed three skulls, only to return them to the ground the following year. Skeletal reconstruction, dental records, and computer projection and superimposition of their facial images were consistent with the remains being those of Czar Nicholas II, his wife Alexandra, and three of their children, along with three servants and the family doctor. There was some disagreement between the Russian scientists and an American team led by William Maples as to the identity of the two missing bodies. Although both agreed that the Czarevich, Alexei, accounted for one, the Russians thought that the missing female was grand duchess Marie, while Maples insisted that it was Anastasia.

In September, 1992, Pavel Ivanov carried samples to England to have them tested at the British Forensic Science Service lab by Peter Gill and Kevin Sullivan. Genetic typing of several STR loci confirmed the relationship among the five family members and determined the sex of each individual. Mitochondrial DNA typing was then employed in order to confirm that the family was indeed the Romanovs. DNA from the bones was compared to samples obtained from known living relatives in the direct matrilineal line of descent. Mitochondrial D-loop sequences from Czarina Alexandra and her three daughters were identical to that of Prince Philip, husband of England's Queen Elizabeth II. His maternal grandmother was Czarina Alexandra's sister, so all inherited their mtDNA from the mother of both Alexandra and her sister.

The results concerning the Czar himself, however, were highly convincing and essentially conclusive, but not consummate. When mtDNA from his purported bones was analyzed, a rare anomaly called a **heteroplasmy** surfaced. This means that at one base position two different bases were found; the sequencing consistently showed both a **C** and at **T** at that point, indicating the presence of two variant populations of mtDNA in the same person. Since the mitochondrial genome is inherited only from one parent, the mother, normally only one type is present in a person, making this situation highly unusual. Two of the Czar's maternally-linked living relatives, including Countess Xenia Cheremetiff-Sfiri, the great-granddaughter of the Czar's sister, and the Duke of Fife, showed only a **T** at that point in the sequence. (The Czar's nephew, Tikhon Kulikovsky, refused to cooperate.) Researchers were "98.5%" sure that the bones belonged to the Czar, but the evidence was not absolute. The experiments were repeated by Erika Hagelberg of Cambridge University and Mary-Claire King of the University of California at Berkeley, providing independent confirmation that the heteroplasmy was not due to contamination or experimental error. Finally, the Russian authorities authorized the exhumation of Czar Nicholas II's brother, the Grand Duke of Russia, Georgij Romanov, who died of tuberculosis in 1899. Ivanov took these samples to Victor Weedn at the Armed Forces DNA Identification Laboratory (AFDIL) DNA Identification Laboratory. Weedn's group not only confirmed the heteroplasmy in Nicholas, but found a mixture of C and T at position 16169 of the mitochondrial genome of Georgij Romanov. The Grand Duke showed exactly the same heteroplasmy as his brother, confirming the identity of the remains as Czar Nicholas II, as well as solving a scientific riddle. Both brothers must have inherited their unusual mtDNA sequences from their mutual mother, and the rareness of this variation leaves virtually no doubt as to the identity of the Czar's bones.

A mystery still remains, however, regarding the fate of the two younger Romanov children whose bodies were not found with the others in the grave. There have been numerous contestants for the titles of Grand Duchess Anastasia and Czarevich Alexei. Alexei was a known hemophiliac, unlikely to have survived the violent attack on his family. The most infamous claimant to the identity of Anastasia was the late Anna Anderson, who died in Charlottesville, Virginia in 1984. Using hair samples saved by her husband, and stored in books, scientists showed that her mtDNA sequences failed to match those of her purported mother, the Czarina Alexandra. They showed instead that she was maternally related to a German man called Carl Maucher; Maucher's great-aunt, Franzisca Schanzkowska, disappeared in Berlin at about the same time as Anderson surfaced there. The mystery of Anastasia, youngest daughter of Czar Nicholas II, will no doubt continue to perplex researchers and inspire books and movies, for decades to come.

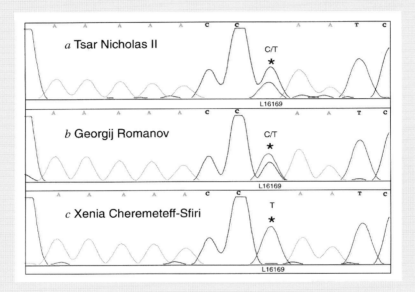

(The original 4-color data printout has been reproduced here in black and white)

**References**:

Anastasia claimant a fraud, *Reuter*, Oct. 5, 1994.

**Debenham, P. G.**, DNA typing. heteroplasmy and the Tsar, *Nature*, 380, 6574, 484-4, 1996.

DNA test shows Virginia woman wasn't Anastasia, *Reuter*, Oct. 4, 1994.

**Editorial**, Romanovs fine closure in DNA, *Nature Genetics*, 12, 417-420, 1996.

**Gill, P., Ivanov, P. L., Kimpton, C., et al.**, Identification of the remains of the Romanov Family by DNA analysis, *Nature Genetics*, 6, 2, 130-5, 1994.

**Gill, P., Kimpton, C., Aliston-Greiner, R., et al.**, Establishing the identity of Anna Anderson Manahan, *Nature Genetics*, 9, 1, 9-10, 1995.

**Glausiusz, J.**, Royal D-loops, *Discover*, Jan., 1994.

**Ivanov, P. L., Wadhams, M. J., Roby, R. K., et al.**, Mitochondrial DNA sequence heteroplasmy in the Grand Duke of Russia Georgij Romanov establishes the authenticity of the remains of Tsar Nicholas II, *Nature Genetics*, 12, 417-420, 1996.

### IV.  HOW MUCH SAMPLE DO YOU NEED?

The amount of sample needed to obtain a conclusive result in any particular typing system varies greatly on a case-by-case basis.  Environmental and historical factors, which are discussed at great length in other sections of this document, influence to a large extent the quality and quantity of DNA present in a forensic sample.  For instance, a quarter size blood stain which has been sitting on a rock in the Sahara desert for ten years will yield significantly less tractable DNA than the same size stain which has, yesterday, been deposited on a cotton swatch in a laboratory and immediately frozen.  However some generalizations may be made, assuming the sample is relatively fresh and unadulterated.  RFLP techniques require more DNA (as well as DNA of better quality) than PCR-based techniques because only the amount of DNA originally extracted from the sample can be tested.  Because the PCR technique amplifies the DNA over the amount originally obtained, less is needed to start with.  A fresh, dime-size blood stain will generally yield sufficient DNA for a strong RFLP analysis; only 1/10-1/100 of this stain might be needed to obtain a conclusive result for a PCR-based system (Figure 6-15).  All other things being equal, less semen than blood is needed to obtain an equivalent type.  This is because the concentration of sperm cells in semen is higher than white blood cells in blood.  Other types of samples may vary accordingly, depending on the density of nucleated cells per sample.

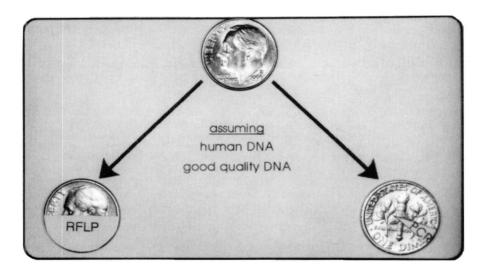

**Figure 6-15. How Much Do You Need?**  In general, a PCR test may be conducted with 1/10 to 1/100 the amount of sample needed for an RFLP test.

——— *FURTHER REFERENCES*———

**Budowle, B., Waye, J.S., Shutler, G.G., Baechtel, F.S.,** *Hae* III--a suitable restriction endonuclease for restriction fragment length polymorphism analysis of biological evidence samples, *Journal of Forensic Sciences*, 35, 3, 530-6, 1990.

**Caskey, C.T., Hammond, H.,** DNA-based Identification: Disease and Criminals, in *DNA Technology and Forensic Science*, J. Ballantyne, G. Sensabaugh, and J. Witkoski, Eds., Cold Spring Harbor Laboratory Press, Cold Spring Harbor, NY, 1989.

**Edwards, A., Hammond, H.A., Jin, L., Caskey, C.T., Chakraborty, R.,** Genetic variation at five trimeric and tetrameric tandem repeat loci in four human population groups, *Genomics*, 12,2, 241-53, 1992.

**Erlich, H.A., Gelfland, D., Sninsky, J.J.,** Recent advances in the polymerase chain reaction. *Science*, 252, 643-1651, 1991.

**Erlich, H.A.,** HLA DQ alpha typing of forensic specimens, *Forensic Science International*, 53, 2, 227-8, 1992.

**Erlich, H.A., Ed.,** *PCR Technology: Principles and applications for DNA Amplification*, Stockton Press, New York, NY, 1989.

**Fisher, D.L., Holland, M. M., Mitchell, L., Sledzik, P.S., Wilcox, A.W., Wadhams, M., Weedn, V.W.,** Extraction, evaluation, and amplification of DNA from decalcified and undecalcified United States Civil War bone. *Journal of Forensic Sciences*, 38, 1, 60-8, 1993.

**Fregeau, C.J., Fourney, R. M.,** DNA typing with fluorescently tagged short tandem repeats: a sensitive and accurate approach to human identification, *Biotechniques*, 15(1),100-19, 1993.

*Genetic Witness: forensic uses of DNA tests*, U.S. Congress, Office of Technology Assessment, OTA-BA-438, Washington, DC, 1990.

**Gill, P., Kimpton, C.P., Urquhart, A., Oldroyd, N., Millican, E.S., Watson, S.K., Downes, T. J.,** Automated short tandem repeat (STR) analysis in forensic casework--a strategy for the future, *Electrophoresis*, 16, 9, 1543-52, 1995.

**Hammond, H.A., Jin, L., Zhong, Y., Caskey, C.T., Chakraborty, R.,** Evaluation of 13 short tandem repeat loci for use in personal identification applications, *American Journal of Human Genetics*, 55,1,175-89, 1994.

**Holland, M.M., Fisher, D.L., Lee, D.A., Bryson, C.K., Weedn, V.W.,** Short tandem repeat loci: application to forensic and human remains identification, *Exs*, 67, 267-74, 1993.

**Jeffreys, A.J., Wilson, V., and Thein, S.L.,** Individual specific "Fingerprints" of Human DNA, *Nature*, 316, 76-79, 1985.

**Jeffreys, A. J., Wong, Z., Wilson, V., *et al.*,** Applications of multilocus and single-locus minisatellite DNA probes in forensic medicine, in *DNA Technology and Forensic Science*, J. Ballantyne, G. Sensebaugh, and J. Witkowski, Eds., Cold Spring Harbor Laboratory Press, Cold Spring Harbor, NY, 1989.

**Kasai, K., Nakamura, Y., White, R.,** Amplification of a variable number of tandem repeats (VNTR) Locus (pMCT118) by the polymerase chain reaction (PCR) and its application to forensic science, *Journal of Forensic Sciences*, 35, 1196-1200, 1990.

**Kawasaki, E., Saiki, R., Erlich, H.,** Genetic analysis using polymerase chain reaction-amplified DNA and immobilized oligonucleotide probes: reverse dot-blot typing, *Methods in Enzymology*, 218, 369-81, 1993.

**Kimpton, C., Fisher D., Watson, S., Adams, M., Urquhart, A. ,Lygo, J., Gill, P.,** Evaluation of an automated DNA profiling system employing multiplex amplification of four tetrameric STR loci, *International Journal of Legal Medicine*, 106, 6, 302-11, 1994.

**Kimpton, C., Fisher, D., Watson, S., Adams, M., Urquhart, A., Lygo, J., Gill, P.,** Evaluation of an automated DNA profiling system employing multiplex amplification of four tetrameric STR loci, *International Journal of Legal Medicine*, 106, 6, 302-11, 1994.

**Kloosterman, A.D., Budowle, B., Daselaar P.,** PCR-amplification and detection of the human D1S80 VNTR locus, amplification conditions, population genetics and application in forensic analysis, *International Journal of Legal Medicine*, 105, 5, 257-64, 1993.

**Lygo, J. E., Johnson P.E., Holdaway, D.J., Woodroffe, S., Whitaker, J.P., Clayton, T. M., Kimpton, C. P., Gill, P.,** The validation of short tandem repeat (STR) loci for use in forensic casework, *International Journal of Legal Medicine*, 107, 2, 77-89, 1994.

**Lygo, J.E. Johnson, P.E. Holdaway D.J. Woodroffe, S., Whitaker, J.P., Clayton, T. M. Kimpton, C. P., Gill, P.,** The validation of short tandem repeat (STR) loci for use in forensic casework, *International Journal of Legal Medicine*, 107, 2, 77-89, 1994.

**Moller, A., Wiegand, P., Gruschow, C., Seuchter, S. A., Baur, M.P., Brinkmann, B.,** Population data and forensic efficiency values for the STR systems HumVWA, HumMBP and HumFABP, *International Journal of Legal Medicine*, 106, 4, 183-9, 1994.

**Mullis, K.B., Faloona, F., Scharf, S.J., Saiki, R.K., Horn, G. T., and Erlich, H.A.,** Specific enzymatic amplification of DNA in vitro: the polymerase chain reaction, *Cold Spring Harbor Symp. Quant. Biol.* 51, 263-273, 1986.

**Mullis, K.B., Faloona F.,** Specific Synthesis of DNA *in vitro* via a polymerase catalyzed chain reaction, *Methods in Enzymology*, 155, 335-350, 1987.

**Naito, E., Dewa, K., Yamanouchi, H., Kominami, R.,** Sex typing of forensic DNA samples using male- and female-specific probes, *Journal of Forensic Sciences*, 39, 4,1009-17, 1994.

**Nakamura, Y., Leppert, M., O'Connell, P., et al.,** Variable number of tandem repeat (VNTR) markers for human gene mapping, *Science*, 237, 1616-1622, 1987.

**National Research Council,** *DNA Technology in Forensic Science*, National Academy Press, Washington D.C., 1992.

**Reynolds, R., Sensebaugh, G., Blake, E.,** Analysis of genetic markers in forensic DNA samples using the polymerase chain reaction, *Analytical Chemistry*, 63,1, 2-15, 1991.

**Robertson, J. M., Sgueglia, J. B., Badger, C. A., Juston, A. C., Ballantyne, J.,** Forensic applications of a rapid, sensitive, and precise multiplex off lysis of the four short tandem repeat loci HUMVWF31/A, HUMTH01, HUMF13A1, and HUMFES/FPS, *Electrophoresis*, 16, 9, 1568-76, 1995.

**Urquhart, A., Kimpton, C. P., Downes, T. J., Gill, P.,** Variation in short tandem repeat sequences--a survey of twelve microsatellite loci for use as forensic identification markers, *International Journal of Legal Medicine*, 107, 1, 13-20, 1994.

**Urquhart, A., Oldroyd, N. J., Kimpton, C. P., Gill, P.,** Highly discriminating heptaplex short tandem repeat PCR system for forensic identification, *Biotechniques*, 18, 1, 116-8, 120-1, 1995.

**Walsh, P. S. Erlich, H. A., Higuchi, R.,** Preferential PCR amplification of alleles: mechanisms and solutions, *PCR Methods and Applications*, 1, 4, 241-50, 1992.

**Walsh, P.S., Fildes, N., Louie, A.S., Higuchi, R.,** Report of the blind trial of the Cetus AmpliType HLA DQ alpha forensic deoxyribonucleic acid (DNA) amplification and typing kit, *Journal of Forensic Sciences*, 36, 5,1551-6, 1991.

# Chapter 7

## PROCEDURES FOR FORENSIC DNA ANALYSIS

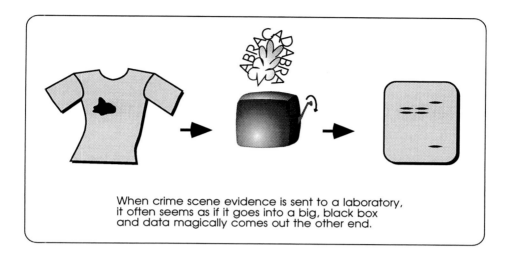

When crime scene evidence is sent to a laboratory, it often seems as if it goes into a big, black box and data magically comes out the other end.

## I. ISOLATION OF DNA

Before any type of testing can be performed, DNA must be isolated from the rest of the cellular components, as well as from any non-biological material which might be present (see Figures 7-1, 7-2). This operation must be performed carefully and thoroughly; any residual material may hamper subsequent analysis in two ways. First, the different enzymes that act on the DNA during the test procedure require specific environments to work efficiently and properly; the material that nature designed them to work on is DNA, and they work best when no foreign material is present. Second, some extraneous substances cause DNA to degrade, or fall apart. This may continue to happen, even during analysis, until the substance is removed. It is always preferable to clean the DNA from any possible harmful materials as expeditiously and as thoroughly as possible.

The isolation or extraction procedure varies somewhat according to the type of biological evidence present (e.g., blood, semen, saliva, hair etc.), the amount of evidence (which influences the type of test that is subsequently performed), and the kinds of cells which are present. These determinations are made by the visual inspection, microscopic examination, and presumptive tests discussed previously.

### A. CHELEX EXTRACTION

Sometimes, if only the most minute sample is present, for instance a speck of barely visible blood, a method called **Chelex extraction** is employed. This consists of boiling the sample in a solution containing minute beads of a chemical called **Chelex**. The boiling breaks open the cells, releasing the DNA, and the Chelex binds up most other extraneous materials which might interfere in subsequent analysis. The Chelex beads are removed, along

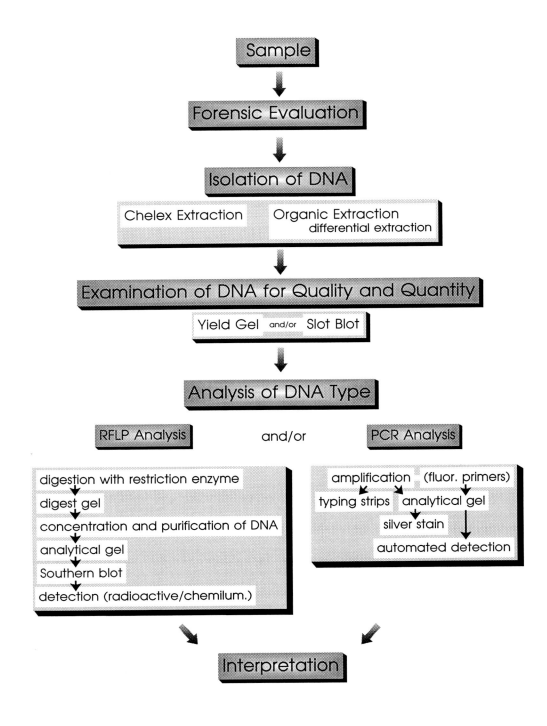

**Figure 7-1. Flow chart for forensic DNA typing.**

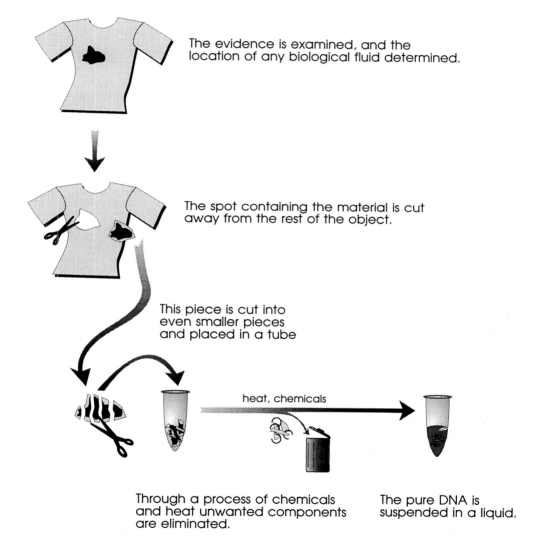

The evidence is examined, and the location of any biological fluid determined.

The spot containing the material is cut away from the rest of the object.

This piece is cut into even smaller pieces and placed in a tube

heat, chemicals

Through a process of chemicals and heat unwanted components are eliminated.

The pure DNA is suspended in a liquid.

**Figure 7-2. Flow chart for organic extraction of DNA.**

with most other non-DNA components, leaving the DNA behind.  Since this extraction technique breaks apart the two strands of the DNA double helix, it is generally reserved for very small samples where only PCR analysis is anticipated.  DNA must be double-stranded in order to perform RFLP analysis, but PCR may be performed on either single-stranded or double-stranded DNA.

## B. ORGANIC EXTRACTION

In most other situations, a general method called **organic extraction** (Figure 7-2) is usually employed.  The organic extraction method is more likely to maintain the DNA in large pieces, and cleans the DNA more thoroughly than does Chelex extraction.  The presence or absence of sperm, either alone, or along with other types of cells, directs which variation of the organic extraction procedure might be performed.  Sperm cells are harder to break open than, for instance, blood, saliva or vaginal cells, and require extra chemicals.  As will be discussed later, this fact is put to good use when mixed samples, such as a vaginal swab from a rape case, are analyzed.

If no sperm cells are either noted microscopically, or suspected from the nature of the case, a simple organic extraction is performed.  In this procedure (Figure 7-2), the sample (a piece of fabric for example) is cut into small pieces and soaked in a warm solution to gently release cells from the substrate on which they are deposited.  Using another chemical mix, and mild heat the cells are broken open, releasing the DNA.  The DNA is then isolated from any other components by the use of various organic solvents.  It is from this step that the name "organic extraction" is derived.  The DNA is further purified and concentrated using special filters, or by precipitation, producing an extract suitable for use in either PCR or RFLP analysis.

## C. DIFFERENTIAL EXTRACTION

A special situation involves samples in which sperm are present along with other types of cells, often of vaginal origin.  Many cells found in forensic evidence fall into a category called **epithelial cells** or **e. cells**.  This includes, saliva, skin, buccal, and vaginal cells, as well as those found in urine and feces.  The different properties of epithelial cells from sperm cells are exploited in order to separate them from each other before any DNA is isolated.  This simplifies the final interpretation, as the victim's and suspect's types may be analyzed and compared separately.

The type of procedure used to isolate DNA from a mixed sample of sperm and e. cells is called a **differential extraction**; it is a variation of the organic extraction procedure.  The cells (including both e. cells and sperm) are first removed from the substrate by soaking in a gentle solution. The sample is incubated in one set of chemicals which specifically break open (lyse) only the e. cells.  The liquid containing them (called the **e. cell fraction**) is then removed to a separate tube (see Figure 7-3).  The DNA from the e. cell fraction is extracted using the normal organic extraction procedure.  The sperm cells are treated with some extra chemicals to help remove them from the substrate and also break them open; this is called the **sperm fraction**.  Once DNA is released from the sperm cells, it goes through the same organic extraction procedure as all other samples.

Due to the nature of the sample, separation of the e. cell DNA and sperm DNA may not always be complete.  For instance, if the sample is in poor condition, some sperm cells may have already popped open, releasing their DNA prematurely.  Since the method of separation depends on initially intact sperm cells, some of this free sperm DNA may show up in the final e. cell fraction.  Alternatively, in a mix of many e. cells and just a few sperm, some e. cell

DNA may persist among the sperm and may be detected in the final sperm fraction. The interpretation of such results is discussed in *Chapter 9*.

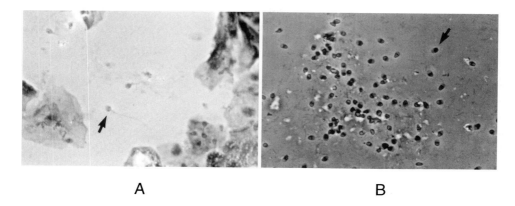

A                                                            B

**Figure 7-3. Photomicrographs of a differential extraction.** Panel A shows a sexual assault sample before differential extraction. The very large irregular objects are epithelial cells (e. cells) from the female and the minuscule round objects are sperm, some with tails still attached. In panel B, the e. cells have been lysed, leaving a concentrated sample of sperm heads. The photographs were taken using phase contrast at 400X magnification. The photograph was enlarged an additional 5X.

## II. DETERMINING QUALITY AND QUANTITY OF DNA

Before any analysis proceeds, it is imperative to determine not only how much DNA is present, but how much of it is human and how broken up it is (**degraded**). DNA remaining in relatively large pieces is said to be of **high molecular weight (HMW)**. For RFLP analysis, the quality of the final analytical result depends, in part, on using the same amount of HMW human DNA for each sample. This is referred to as "balancing the samples". Quantitative information is also necessary in order to calculate how much restriction enzyme to add to each reaction, another critical determination in assuring a high quality result. In tests beginning with PCR amplification, a long average length of the starting fragments is less important (although they must still be larger than the region determined by the primers), but quantity is critical. In particular, the addition of too much sample to a reaction is as undesirable as having too little. Specific tests are performed to define these parameters before proceeding with any analysis.

The method of this assessment is determined by both the size and quality of the original sample, as well as the method of DNA extraction. If the analyst suspects that the DNA obtained may be very limited and/or degraded, a small portion is removed and assessed on a **slot blot** (Figure 7-4, *Appendix B*). If the Chelex method of extraction has been employed, leaving the DNA in single-stranded form, it can only be assessed on a slot blot. If from an initial assessment of the sample, the analyst is reasonably confident of obtaining sufficient DNA, a **yield gel** is used for quantitation (Figure 7-5, *Appendix C*). A yield gel requires double-stranded DNA in higher quantity for a result to be obtained. If it can be used, however, more information regarding the state of degradation of the sample can be acquired. A slot blot, used together with a yield gel holds the additional advantage of providing information as to what percentage of the DNA is of human origin, as opposed to of bacterial origin. Sometimes a **Southern blot** (see *Section III*) is performed on the yield gel, and the membrane is **probed** with the same human-specific probe used for the slot blot (see *Appendix*

*B*); this method also provides an assessment of the proportion of human DNA in a sample. Depending on the particulars of a case, and what specific information the analyst deems useful, any of these methods might be employed. Occasionally, the original sample is so minuscule that it is deemed more prudent to proceed with a PCR-type analysis and back-calculate afterwards how much DNA might have been present.

| stnd. 1 | | smpl. | smpl. | | smpl. |
|---------|---|-------|-------|---|-------|
| stnd. 2 | | smpl. | smpl. | | smpl. |
| stnd. 3 | | smpl. | | | smpl. |
| stnd. 4 | | smpl. | | | smpl. |
| stnd. 5 | | smpl. | | | smpl. |
| stnd. 6 | | smpl. | | | smpl. |
| cntrl. | | | | | |

**Figure 7-4. A slot blot.** The first column contains the quantitation standards in decreasing concentration from top to bottom. The lowermost slot contains a positive control for which the quantity of DNA is known. The other lanes contain the evidence and reference samples, as well as controls for other parts of the procedure, such as extraction and handling. The concentration of an unknown sample is obtained by comparing it to the standards. Computer analysis can be used to obtain accurate results and to interpolate between standards. *stnd.* - quantitation standard; *cntrl.* - positive control sample; *smpl.* - sample

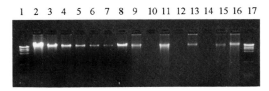

1  2  3  4  5  6  7  8  9  10 11 12 13 14 15 16 17

**Figure 7-5. A Yield Gel.** Lanes 1 and 17 contains a molecular ladder used to judge how far the gel has run. Lanes 2 to 7 contain HMW quantitation standards in decreasing concentration from left to right. Lane 8 contains the same control sample used in the slot blot (see above). The samples to be quantitated appear in lanes 9, 11, 13, 15 and 16. Computerized analysis may also be used to supplement visual interpretation of the results.

Another method that is beginning to be used by well-funded labs, both for analysis and quantitation, is **capillary electrophoresis.** Capillary electrophoresis can be used to determine with great accuracy and sensitivity the sizes of DNA fragments in extremely minute samples, but, like a yield gel, does not distinguish human DNA from any other (see Figure 7-20).

### III. RFLP ANALYSIS

As described previously, RFLP analysis measures the size of the DNA fragments produced by **restriction enzymes.** The decision to proceed with RFLP analysis is made only after it is determined that the sample contains sufficient HMW human DNA for this type of analysis to be successful. The amounts of DNA, restriction enzyme, and other components are carefully calculated then combined in a small tube, which is incubated in a warm bath overnight (Figure 7-6a, step 1). It is important that all specified sites are cut, so that no artificially large pieces are left. When some sites are left uncut, the sample is said to be **partially digested.** This is determined by removing a small portion of the sample and comparing it to uncut (undigested) and completely digested standard samples of DNA on a **digest gel** (Figure 7-7, *Appendix D*). If digestion is not complete, certain steps of the extraction procedure may be repeated in an attempt to purify the sample of any inhibitors that might prevent the restriction enzyme from working properly. The sample is then subjected to another dose of enzyme. When it is determined that the reaction is in fact complete, and no "**partials**" remain, the analyst proceeds to the next step of separating the pieces according to size. At this point, all that is visible is a colorless liquid in a colorless tube.

A blue dye is added to the solution containing the cut (digested) DNA, and each sample is loaded into its own pre-formed indentation in a slab of gel-like material called **agarose** (Figure 7-6a, step 2). Agarose is a substance extracted from sea kelp, and is, in fact, just a more purified version of those "agar-agar" plates used to grow nasty-smelling things in biology 101. An electric field is then applied to the agarose gel (Figure 7-6a, step 3). Since DNA carries an overall negative (–) charge, all of the DNA fragments will start to migrate towards the positive (+) pole. The set-up is conveniently arranged so that the positive (+) end of the electric field is at the opposite end of the gel from where the DNA is loaded.

An essential element of the process is that the gel material used to make up the slab is full of microscopic holes through which the DNA fragments pass on their way to the other end (Figure 7-6a, Plate 3). Since it is easier for the smaller fragments to fit through these pores, they migrate faster, and are the first to reach the bottom of the gel; the larger fragments migrate more slowly, and lag towards the origin. At the end of the overnight run, the DNA sample originally loaded into each well has formed an array of fragments from largest to smallest in a lane leading to the end of the gel.

At this point, the DNA is still invisible to the naked eye. Sometimes the gel is soaked in a dye, called **ethidium bromide**, which binds to DNA and makes it temporarily visible under ultra-violet light (Figure 7-8). Under these conditions, the DNA fragments appear as a smear, since the dye exposes all the DNA fragments and cannot distinguish between them. This confirms that the samples were loaded in the gel, and that the gel has run as expected.

In order to detect the specific polymorphic fragments of interest, the DNA must be transferred to a solid support. The gel is soaked in a chemical which causes the two strands of the DNA double helix to separate into single strands. A piece of nylon membrane is laid on top of the gel and a layer of absorbent material on top of that. The absorbent material draws up liquid from the gel and the DNA fragments along with it. This is the same idea as using a sponge to soak up a wet stain. When the single stranded DNA fragments hit the nylon membrane, they stick and are permanently transferred to it. This procedure is called **Southern blotting** (Figure 7-6a, step 4).

In order to detect DNA originating from designated locations in the genome, short fragments of DNA, called probes, are labeled with a radioactive or chemiluminescent tag. These probes are designed to match the places in the genome that are well-characterized as highly polymorphic. Under the right conditions, DNA strands that match will reunite into a double-stranded form. Any probe fragments that haven't bound specifically are washed away so as not to interfere with a clean signal. This process is called **hybridization** (Figure 7-6b, step 1). The labeled fragments signal where they have hybridized and this signal is recorded on a sheet of X-ray film (Figure 7-6b, step 3). The pattern recorded on the X-ray film is the image that has been likened to a simplified supermarket barcode (Figure 7-9). Each piece of exposed film is called an **autorad**, short for autoradiogram or autoradiograph. Although this terminology is inaccurate for the newer chemiluminescent probes, it has been grandfathered into the system since the result looks identical. Some refer to chemiluminescent results as lumigraphs, or simply films. Generally two bands are detected in each sample lane (Figure 7-6b, step 4). This is because a different allele is usually inherited from each parent (heterozygous).

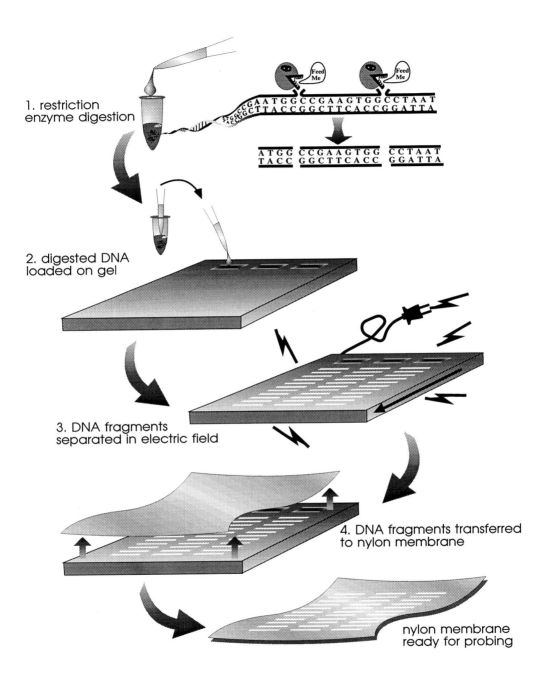

**Figure 7-6a. Restriction enzyme digestion and Southern blotting.**

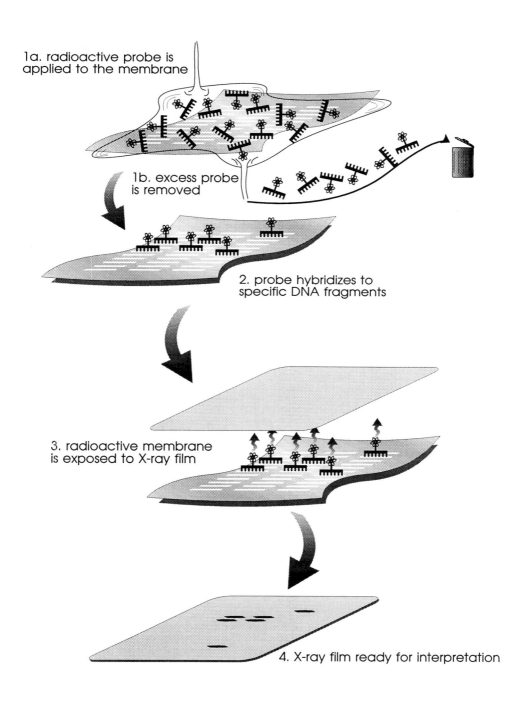

1a. radioactive probe is applied to the membrane

1b. excess probe is removed

2. probe hybridizes to specific DNA fragments

3. radioactive membrane is exposed to X-ray film

4. X-ray film ready for interpretation

**Figure 7-6b. Probing and detection.**

In the loci chosen for forensic use, different numbers of repeat units are often present between the two cuts of the restriction enzyme producing DNA fragments of different sizes (Plate 3). If a person is homozygous for a particular locus (that is, they have inherited the same length allele from both parents), only one band will be detected on the autorad. What we have described here is the detection of one locus, or location in the genome. In forensic DNA analysis, as many as 5 or 6 loci are commonly analyzed, so 10 to 12 bands are ultimately detected, 1 or 2 bands at a time, in each lane. Each probe detects a different locus.

Once the information from probe number 1 is recorded, it is removed (**stripped**) and the nylon membrane is exposed to the next probe in the series. After probe number 2 has been detected and recorded, the process is repeated for every additional probe. The exposed films, or autorads, from each particular probe provide a permanent record of the results of the analysis. The band locations are compared from lane to lane in order to identify any similar patterns. Samples which look visually similar are then subjected to computer imaging and analysis. In order to aid in this analysis, an artificially constructed molecular ruler is run on each gel; the computer then has an objective internal standard from which to calculate band (fragment) sizes. A sample for which the results are known is also run on each gel in order to monitor whether the system is working as expected. In the U.S. this standard sample is taken from an immortal cell line and is known as **K562**. If two samples are suspected to have originated from the same source, a calculation is also performed in order to estimate how often the type occurs in the population. This subject is discussed more fully in *Chapter 8*.

**Figure 7-7. A digest gel.** Lane 1 and 10 contain a molecular ladder, lane 2 contains a known undigested sample, and lane 3 contains a known digested sample. The rest of the lanes contain, in this case, completely digested samples.

**Figure 7-8. A stained analytical gel.** Samples on an agarose gel after electrophoresis and staining with ethidium bromide. The genomic DNA samples in lanes 2, 3, 5, 6, 7, and 9 show as streaks, since ethidium bromide stains all DNA and the entire genome's worth is visualized.

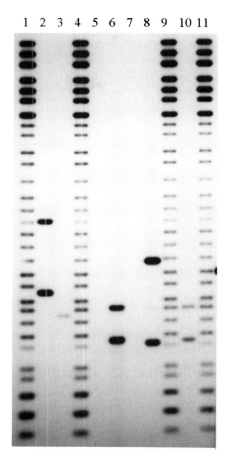

**Figure 7-9. An RFLP autorad.** The locus probed is D2S44. Lanes 1, 4, 9 and 11 contain molecular ladders. Lanes 5 and 7 contain no sample. The pattern of bands in lanes 6 and 10 appear indistinguishable. All other samples show different patterns both from these two and from each other.

## IV.  PCR AMPLIFICATION

PCR amplification is often performed on samples that are deemed too minuscule or highly degraded to give a reliable RFLP result.  The process, which faithfully replicates a defined segment of DNA millions of times, is dependent on the enzyme *Taq* polymerase.  In contrast to the restriction enzymes discussed previously, this enzyme doesn't cut DNA into pieces, but rather duplicates it.  An essential feature of this particular enzyme is that it can survive high temperatures and still keep working.  As will be seen, this is key to the "chain reaction" used to replicate the DNA.

DNA from either extraction method (Chelex or organic) is appropriate for PCR.  Three main steps make up any amplification procedure, and are repeated dozens of times (Plate 4).

1.  **Denaturation.**  The first step is to separate the two strands of the DNA double helix (denaturation), so each can be used as a template for synthesis of a new strand.  As discussed previously (*Chapters 5 and 6*), the sequence of bases added to make a single strand of DNA into a double strand is determined entirely by the previously existing strand.  Denaturation is accomplished by subjecting the DNA to fairly high heat, necessitating the heat-stable *Taq* enzyme.

2.  **Annealing**. Step two involves the annealing of **DNA primers**. Primers, like the probes used in RFLP, are short synthetic pieces of DNA that match defined locations by complementary base pairing. In this case they are called **primers** because they mark the starting location of the synthesis of new DNA and prime the reaction. Two different primers define the endpoint of a particular segment that is to be amplified, one at each end.

3.  **Extension**. In step three, the raw materials of DNA (single bases) are hooked together by *Taq* polymerase to create new DNA strands. The chemical form in which a base is added to DNA is called a **nucleotide**. The location and order are exactly defined by the original strands of DNA and the primers. If the next base on a beginning template of DNA is an **A**, it will only pair with a **T**, so the enzyme pulls a free **T** from the raw materials and adds it to the growing end of the new strand. In this way the new strand is manufactured, base by base, with a sequence complementary to the beginning template. At the end of the first cycle of PCR, the segment of interest has been duplicated.

The three steps are repeated over and over again (Plate 5), each time doubling the number of copies of DNA and resulting in millions of copies identical to the original. This is why the process is often called molecular Xeroxing. At this point, the sample is a colorless liquid in a colorless tube.

Sometimes a **product gel** (*Appendix E*) is run using a small portion of the sample in order to check that the PCR reaction has been successful. If the *Taq* polymerase enzyme has been inhibited for any reason, no amplification will occur. This would be evidenced by the failure to detect bands on a product gel. This situation would most often preclude obtaining a final typing result. If no PCR product is detected, certain steps of the extraction procedure may be repeated in an attempt to purify the samples of any inhibitors that might prevent the enzyme from working properly. Alternatively, other techniques may be used to overcome the inhibition without further purification of the sample. Another amplification run may then be attempted.

## V.  ANALYSIS OF PCR PRODUCT

Depending on the type of polymorphism being investigated, the product of PCR reactions, henceforth called "**PCR product**" is analyzed in one of two ways. Sequence polymorphisms are detected using a hybridization procedure, or sometimes, by direct sequence analysis. Length polymorphisms are most commonly detected using various procedures similar to the gel used in RFLP analysis.

## A. SEQUENCE POLYMORPHISMS
### 1. DQα/A1, Polymarker
We have mentioned the phenomenon of complementary base pairing. Under the appropriate conditions, only those single strands that match *exactly* will hybridize. If only one or a few bases are different, the two strands will fail to attach to each other. This is the scientific basis for the detection of sequence polymorphisms. A nylon strip, to which DNA probes have been attached, is challenged with the PCR product (Figure 7-10). The strips are commercially available, and contain specific DNA sequences originating from the same locus

in the genome as the DNA which has been amplified by PCR. When the probes are attached to the typing strip, the format is known as a **reverse dot blot**. Each probe is a specific sequence of DNA that defines an allele (Figure 7-11). These types of probes are known as **sequence specific oligonucleotides (SSO)**. They are sometimes also referred to in the forensic science literature as **allele specific probes (ASO)**, although this is technically incorrect. The SSO probes on the strip define a finite number of variations (types) seen in that particular region. The type of the sample is revealed by the hybridization of the amplified DNA to a specific immobilized probe on the strip.

At this point, the strip is still white with invisible dots of attached probe. When DNA segments are amplified for subsequent analysis of sequence polymorphisms, the primers used in the reaction are labeled with a biological tag called **biotin.** After all the PCR product has bound to the probe strip, any excess unbound PCR product is removed, and a **streptavidin/horseradish peroxidase conjugate** is applied and binds tightly to the biotin (Figure 7-10). The biotin molecule has a very strong affinity for the protein **streptavidin** and the streptavidin is chemically linked to the enzyme **horseradish peroxidase (HRP)**. Upon the addition of a colorless substrate (tetra-methyl-benzidine (TMB)), the HRP releases a blue color in the presence of hydrogen peroxide. Hydrogen peroxide is then supplied and dots to which DNA has stuck, via the rest of the long chain of reagents, turn blue (Figure 7-10). The pattern of dots corresponds to the alleles present in the sample (Figure 7-11). These are the famous "blue dots" which have freed a number of convicts from jail. Both the HLA DQα locus and the loci in the polymarker tests, including DQA1, are analyzed in this fashion (Figures 7-11, 7-12, 7-13). The results are recorded and saved using standard photographic techniques. The strips themselves are normally discarded, since the blue color is unstable when exposed to light.

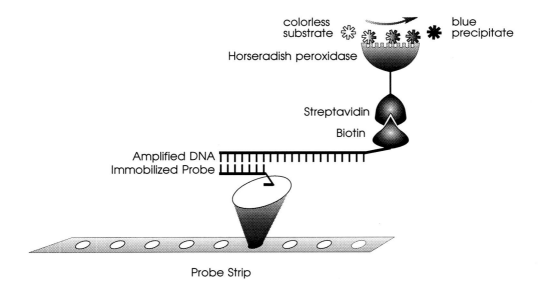

**Figure 7- 10. Detection of PCR product on a reverse dot blot.**

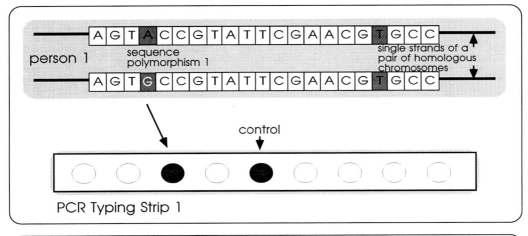

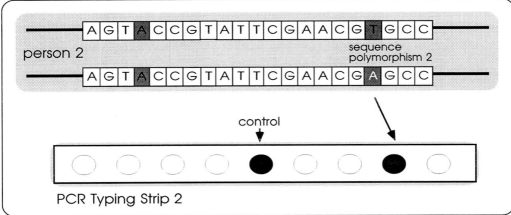

**Figure 7-11. Sequence Polymorphisms**. For each person, a pair of homologous chromosomes is represented; only one strand of the original double-stranded molecule is depicted. The typing procedure is designed to detect differences on only one of the two DNA strands.

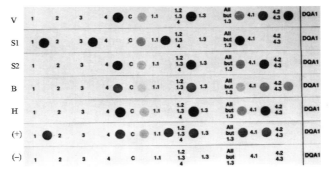

**Figure 7-12. A DQA1 reverse dot blot** In this previously adjudicated case used in develpoment of the DQA1 typing system, a victim (V), two evidence samples of blood and hair (B and H), and two suspects (S1 and S2) were typed. The blood shows the same pattern of dots as the victim, and the hair as suspect 2. Suspect 1 is excluded from contributing any of the evidence. The bottom two strips are a positive typing control (+) and a negative typing control (−), respectively. These DQA1 strips demonstrate the value of adding the 4.1 and 4.2/4.3 probes. Without these subtyping probes, samples V, S2, B and H cannot be distinguished. For more about reading the numeric types from DQA1 strips, please see *Chapter 9*.

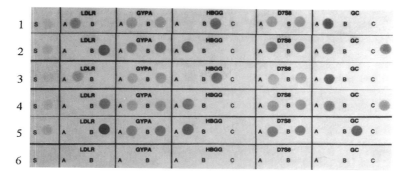

**Figure 7-13. A polymarker reverse dot blot.** Strips 1 and 3 show the same composite type, as do strips 2 and 4. Strips 5 and 6 are positive and negative typing controls, respectively.

Future reverse dot blots will have bars stretching the width of the strip instead of dots. Color contained in a line or bar is easier to compare visually, and also amenable to the computerized scanning, detection and storage techniques which are under development.

## SIDEBAR 5

### A Case of Victim's Evidence
### (or, one bled and the other pled)

The year was 1995, the location, an otherwise non-descript furniture moving company in Palm Beach County, Florida. That morning, the owner of the establishment noticed that one of his usually punctual employees failed to arrive for work at the usual hour. The owner contacted the man's sister, and when she offered no explanation for her brother's absence, immediately reported his absence to the authorities. A police search was instigated, and a few days later the mystery was solved in a most unfortunate way. The employee's body was found stuffed into the trunk of a van which had been abandoned in a local hotel parking lot. As soon as foul play was suspected, an investigation had been launched to uncover a suspect. Almost concurrently with the discovery of the body, a suspect was uncovered. As is common in brutal murders, the assailant was an acquaintance of the victim; in this case he had apparently already threatened the deceased regarding an overdue loan.

A search of the suspect's apartment revealed bloodstains on his bedspread, carpet, and a tennis shoe. The evidence was collected for DNA analysis, and blood samples were also obtained from the suspect and his roommate for comparison. The reference samples from the victim, suspect, and the roommate, as well as the bloodstains found in the apartment were analyzed in ten PCR-based marker systems. Specifically, they included the polymarker loci (LDLR, GYPA, HBGG, D7S8, GC), along with DQA1, and an STR triplex (CSF1PO, TPOX, THO1) along with the gender identification locus, amelogenin (see *Chapters 6 and 7*). The evidentiary stains from the carpet and the tennis shoe produced clear DNA profiles which were both the same. They were also indistinguishable from that of the victim. Both the suspect and the roommate were excluded from having contributed those bloodstains. No evidence was found, either physical or otherwise, to link the roommate to the crime.  The suspect pled to first degree murder.

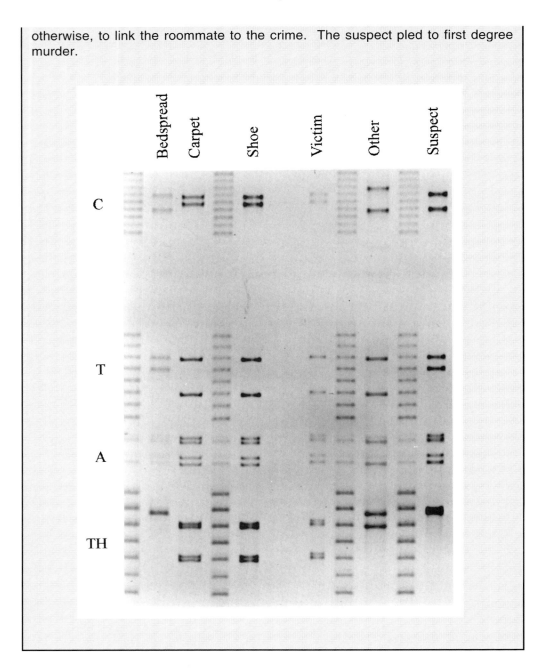

## 2. Mitochondrial DNA

A number of analysis and detection systems for the polymorphisms found in mitochondrial DNA are currently in use or development.  The variations exhibited in the two hypervariable regions are generally point mutations, although small deletions and insertions may also occur.  One general method involves direct DNA sequencing.  The second method relies on the same sequence-specific hybridization technology as the DQα/A1 and polymarker systems.  We first address mtDNA sequencing.

The most basic and comprehensive method of comparing DNA fragments is to obtain the complete nucleotide sequence of each. This method is not practical for use on most genomic samples, especially at loci selected for high variability. Because most people are heterozygous at the loci chosen for forensic analysis, two variant alleles may be present at the locus in question, and there is no way to sort out the two different sequences that would be obtained from this scenario. At this point, DNA sequencing is also time-consuming, cumbersome and technically challenging. The disadvantages usually outweigh its advantages, and it is not, at present, the method of choice for use on most forensic samples. The mtDNA locus is currently the only marker system in the forensic venue to be analyzed by direct DNA sequencing. Because the region is small, defined, and by nature only a single allele is normally present in an individual, this is at least theoretically possible.

DNA sequencing may be performed in a "manual" or "automated" fashion. The automated portion is, in actuality, only invoked at the detection step of the analysis, thus "semi-automated" might be a more accurate term. The reactions and analysis steps performed up to that point are essentially the same for both methods and are a variation on the traditional Sanger sequencing method that has been in common use in molecular biology for two decades.

The Sanger method is predicated on the use of **base analogues**—nucleotides which look enough like the real thing to be incorporated into a growing strand of DNA *in vitro*, but which, once incorporated, terminate the synthesis. These analogues are called **dideoxynucleotides**, often referred to as **dideoxys** for short. The regular nucleotides that make up DNA are, more specifically, **deoxynucleotides** and we shall use the terms here interchangeably. As in PCR, a specific oligonucleotide primer is annealed to a predetermined site on the DNA strand to be sequenced; unlike PCR, the segments to be copied are only defined by a primer on the starting end. In the presence of DNA polymerase and added nucleotides, the primer is extended, using the existing strand as a template for synthesis of a complementary DNA strand.

The dideoxys are utilized as follows (Figure 7-14). Four different tubes of reactions are prepared for each segment of DNA to be sequenced, each containing a different one of the four possible dideoxynucleotides. For instance, in one reaction, a portion of the normal adenine (**A**) deoxynucleotide is replaced by the equivalent **A** dideoxy. Every so often, and in a random fashion, an **A** dideoxynucleotide will be incorporated instead of an **A** deoxynucleotide, terminating the growing chain, and marking the position of an **A**. By the end of the reaction, the tube will contain a mixture of fragments, all terminated at **A**s, and marking the position of all the **A**s in that sequence. The remaining three tubes will contain finished reactions marking the position of the **G**s, **T**s and **C**s, respectively. In a variation using PCR technology, called **cycle sequencing**, the reactions are repeated many times, greatly increasing the amount of product, and therefore the sensitivity and ease of detection. It is also common to preamplify a defined region using standard PCR procedures before attempting any sequencing reactions.

In manual sequencing, one of the normal deoxynucleotides is radioactively or chemiluminescently labeled, so all fragments may be visualized. The fragments are separated by electrophoresis through a polyacrylamide gel and each of the reactions is run in a different lane, resulting in four side-by-side ladders from which the sequence can be read simply by following them sequentially up the gel (Figure 7-14).

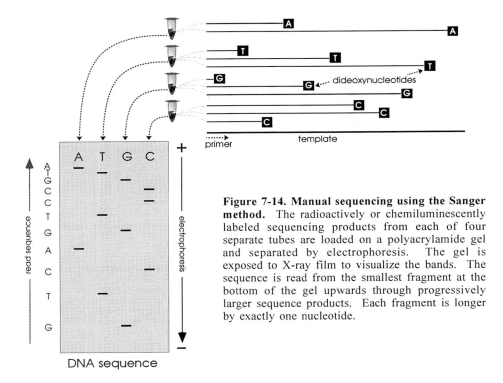

**Figure 7-14. Manual sequencing using the Sanger method.** The radioactively or chemiluminescently labeled sequencing products from each of four separate tubes are loaded on a polyacrylamide gel and separated by electrophoresis. The gel is exposed to X-ray film to visualize the bands. The sequence is read from the smallest fragment at the bottom of the gel upwards through progressively larger sequence products. Each fragment is longer by exactly one nucleotide.

Automated sequencing exploits fluorescent-based detection of the sequencing products (and depends on a very complicated and expensive piece of equipment! (Figures 7-18, 7-19). Fluorescent tags in four different colors, one for each reaction, are incorporated into the sequencing reactions, and the sequencing products are loaded into a gel which is contained within a special detection instrument. Real-time laser-detection of the color-specific fragments allows the reactions to be combined into one lane, saving time and materials. The data from each sequencing run is routed to a computer file for analysis, storage, and eventually comparison. Because each fragment is detected as it passes a preset location in the gel during the electrophoresis, the resolving power of the instrument is greater than using the manual method, and longer stretches of sequence can be read from a single run. The final output is usually shown as a series of overlapping colored peaks (Plate 6), each of which is correlated to a termination point which marks the location of a specific base. Fluorescence-based automated detection technology may also be used with several other of the genetic marker systems used in forensics, in particular the shorter amplified length polymorphisms such as STRs.

The regions of the mitochondrial genome to be sequenced have not yet been standardized between labs. This may also not be necessary, as the sequences to be compared can simply be designated for each case.

A completely different approach to the analysis of the mtDNA hypervariable regions involves the identification of mutational hot spots and the creation of a set of defined probes for these sites. This type of test, based on the same technology as the DQα/A1 and polymarker tests described earlier, has been developed by Roche Molecular Systems, and is in the beta-testing stage as we go to press. mtDNA probe strips contain a total of sixteen immobilized probes which distinguish variants in five sections of **hypervariable region II (HVII)** for a total of about 200 possible types. The strip also contains a positive control probe to a nonpolymorphic region. A defined region of HVII is amplified and allowed to interact with the strip.  Where a particular sequence complimentary to the immobilized probe occurs, hybridization will take place, and the area (now a line rather than a dot) will turn blue. An individual type is read by noting the presence and location of blue lines in each region of the strip which correspond to the defined alleles in each section of HVII.  Because it is presented in a digital format, this set-up is ideal for computerized detection, analysis, storage and comparison.  Although less total information is obtained than with direct sequencing, the ease of use, and lack of necessity to purchase additional expensive equipment, are large pluses. As with all technologies, this format presents several interpretational issues.  We will reserve discussion about these issues until the systen has had a chance to be optimized and is in general use.

## B. LENGTH POLYMORPHISMS (D1S80, STRS, GENDER ID)

PCR can be used to amplify some length polymorphisms.  This is a much simpler process than RFLP analysis because the DNA of interest has already been amplified many times over the rest and for all practical purposes is the only DNA present.  The procedures for all three marker systems discussed are similar.  The PCR product is loaded into a gel, similar to that used for RFLP, but made out of a different substance called **polyacrylamide.** This gel material is more appropriate for analyzing the smaller size PCR products than the agarose used for RFLP.  The gel is run in a similar fashion to that described previously, and the PCR fragments are separated by length (Plate 7).  The bands may be stained directly, and since no extraneous DNA is present; the secondary detection method of probing and hybridization used in RFLP is no longer needed to detect the amplified fragments.  In manual detection, a silver stain is used to visualize the separated DNA bands (Figure 7-15), and the gel is then dried to be kept as a permanent record.

The pattern of bands obtained by this method is visually compared between samples, as well as to a molecular ladder consisting of examples of most or all alleles known to exist at each locus.  Just as in RFLP analysis, each locus will produce one or two bands representing the alleles present.  STRs, in particular, show a higher incidence of homozygotes (1 banded patterns) since the system is less polymorphic.  If several loci are amplified in the same tube, they are consequently run in the same lane.  A lane containing the products from three loci may contain from 3 to 6 bands, depending on whether the person is homozygous (1 band) or heterozygous (2 bands) at each locus.  This assumes that the original sample came from only one person; otherwise more bands are possible.  Each locus has its own allelic ladder for comparison, and a multiplex system intended for manual analysis is ideally constructed so that the alleles from each locus do not overlap.  The gender locus, having only two possible alleles, one male and one female, is often appended to an STR multiplex system.

There is a trend towards fluorescent detection and automated analysis of STR systems, in particular.  At least two variations on this theme may be encountered.  In the first method, the acrylamide gel is run as for manual analysis, but the gel is read by a computerized laser detection system instead of by eye (Figures 7-16, 7-19).  The information is stored in the computer, and a printout may also be obtained.  In the second method, a laser beam detects the fluorescent bands as they are running through the gel (Plate 8, Figure 7-18).  Data is stored and analyzed in much the same way.  It is not clear yet which, if either, automated system will become standard in forensic laboratories.  In both cases, a fluorescent tag is incorporated into the PCR product during amplification.

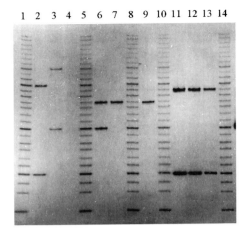

**Figure 7-15. A D1S80 silver stained gel.** Lanes 1, 5, 8, 10 and 14 contain the allelic ladders for direct comparison to sample alleles. Lanes 2, 3, 6, 7, 9, 11, 12 and 13 each contain a sample from one individual. The samples in lanes 7 and 9 are homozygous and show the same D1S80 allele. The samples in lanes 11, 12 and 13 are heterozygous and show the same alleles.

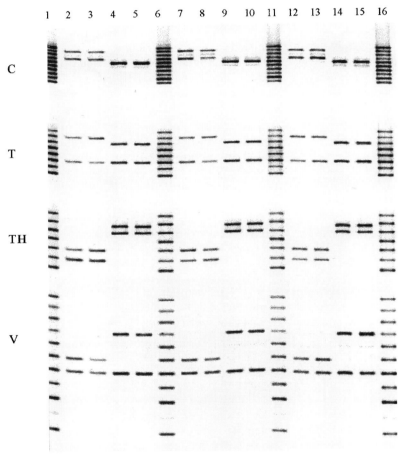

**Figure 7-16. STRs and Gender ID.** An STR quadraplex (CSFPO1, TPOX, THO1 and VWF) run on the Hitachi FMBIO 100 fluorescent scanner. One PCR primer of each pair is labeled with a fluorescent primer. The gel is run on a bench apparatus and dried and imaged statistically. The allelic ladders are located in lanes 1, 6, 11 and 16. The samples in lanes 2, 3, 7, 8, 12 and 13 are all from one individual. The samples in lanes 4, 5, 9, 10, 14 and 15 are all from another individual.

One major advantage of fluorescent detection is that only one of the two denatured strands from each DNA duplex is visualized. Because the resolution power of the gel system is so high, each strand of complementary DNA may run slightly differently because of their complementary nucleotide sequences. For fluorescent detection, only the primer complementary to one strand is tagged, thus eliminating any confusion resulting from reading doublets at each allele. Additionally, the use of multiple colored fluorescent tags allows the combination of STR loci in which the lengths of some alleles overlap. These systems can be run in the same gel lane, and still be clearly distinguished by color. In the case of automated detection, special sizing standards of yet a different color are run in the same lane as each sample, obviating the need for allelic ladders for each locus. In-lane sizing standards mean that the computer will calculate the size of a particular band against a ruler that has been subjected to exactly the same electrophoretic micro-environment as the sample, rendering extremely accurate results.

## SIDEBAR 6

### Minisatellite Variable Repeat Analysis (MVR)

In 1990, yet another tool for the analysis of polymorphisms in DNA was unveiled by Alec Jeffreys (who developed the original RFLP typing system). This system combines the advantages afforded by PCR amplification of sequence-variant alleles with the detection of discrete lengths of DNA. Each locus is a VNTR (variable number tandem repeat), consisting of hundreds of tandem repeats; however, the primary polymorphism lies in the sequence of each repeat. The first locus to be developed, D1S8 (MS32) was first analyzed by RFLP. Within the 19 bp sequence of each repeat, one bp in particular shows hypervariability. As it so happens, this results in the presence or absence of an *Hae*III restriction enzyme cut site. Because each of the hundreds of repeats may show either variant, the sequence of which is completely independent of that on the homologous chromosome, the number of possible alleles in the population is huge. It is in fact much higher than any other single-locus system. Additionally, the information so far suggests that the alleles are relatively evenly distributed in the population.

Analysis of the D1S8 variation was easily transferred to PCR technology by designing primers specific to the two alternate sequence variants. A third primer, the same for each pair, is designed to bind just outside the repeat region, in invariant flanking DNA. The presence of a specific sequence in any particular repeat is then evidenced as fragments of DNA corresponding to the length between the flanking primer and the location of the repeat within the array. In the PCR reaction, the repeat-sequence specific primers will bind to all of their complementary repeat units, thus their locations will be represented as an array of sequentially sized PCR product fragments. The fragments are separated by electrophoresis on an agarose gel and detected by Southern blotting and hybridization to chemiluminescent probes. An important point is that the reaction for each of the two sequence-specific primers is carried out in a separate tube, and they are loaded in adjacent lanes. Some work has also been done towards labeling the variant primers with different colored fluorescent tags, and using an automated laser-detection system, thus negating the need for separate reactions and gel lanes.

The allele on each chromosome is read as a binary code marking the repeats in sequence as to the presence or absence of one of the two designated primer binding sites. Occasionally, neither primer binds, giving a null allele. Null alleles are also produced at the 5' end of the gene, where one allele typically runs out of repeats before the other. In a diploid genome, such as in humans, the full code is a compilation of the binary code read for each chromosome, resulting in a ternary code with six possible variations labeled 1 through 6. The system stands to become even more powerful as more MVR-type loci are developed. Since the results produce a digital code, MVR analysis is a natural for computerized detection, analysis, storage and comparison. Additionally, this confers immunity to electrophoretic distortions such as band shifts and negates any requirement for gel system standardization. Because the alleles are discrete sequence polymorphisms, they can be determined precisely eliminating any imprecision associated with band sizing. MVR has been grossly underutilized in forensic analysis, in part because it was introduced relatively late in the decision-making process of choosing standard systems, and also because although scientifically elegant, it is intellectually somewhat challenging.

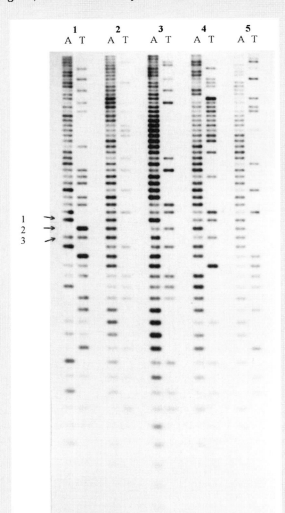

**An MVR autorad.** Each pair of lanes represents one individual, and is read together as a type. The five samples on this gel each shows a different MVR type.

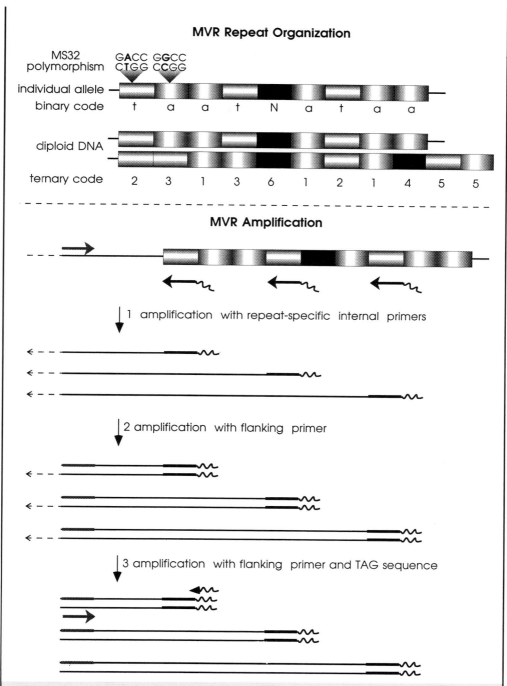

**SIDEBAR 6.  MVR analysis – amplification.** In the first round of PCR (step 1), sequence-specific primers, which are present in low concentration, bind to a small number of repeats per molecule.  In the second round of PCR (step 2), these molecules are truncated by amplification from the invariant flanking primer, producing a representative set of fragments.  In subsequent rounds (step 3), the existing set of PCR-defined fragments are amplified equally, and to a high degree, using high concentrations of the invariant flanking primer, along with a fourth primer which binds to a non-repeat-specific TAG introduced on the end of each sequence-specific primer.

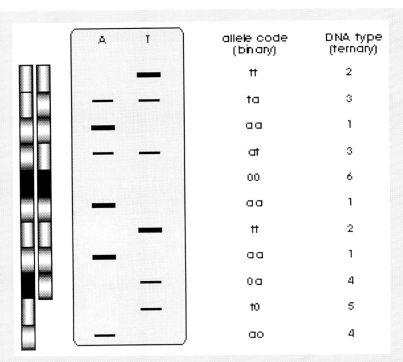

| allele code (binary) | DNA type (ternary) |
|---|---|
| tt | 2 |
| ta | 3 |
| aa | 1 |
| at | 3 |
| 00 | 6 |
| aa | 1 |
| tt | 2 |
| aa | 1 |
| 0a | 4 |
| t0 | 5 |
| ao | 4 |

**SIDEBAR 6. MVR detection and analysis.** At each repeat position, 6 different states are possible: (1) two As, (2) two Ts, (3) one A and one T, (4) one A and one null, (5) one T and one null, (6) two nulls. Two of the same repeat variants are seen as a double intensity band.

## References:

**Hopkins, B., Williams, N.J., Webb, M.B., Debenham, P.G., Jeffreys, A. J.,** The use of minisatellite variant repeat-polymerase chain reaction (MVR-PCR) to determine the source of saliva on a used postage stamp, *Journal of Forensic Sciences*, 39(2), 526-31, 1994.

**Jeffreys, A.J., MacLeod, A., Tamaki, K., Neil, D.L., Monckton, D. G.,** Minisatellite repeat coding as a digital approach to DNA typing, *Nature*, 354(6350), 204-9, 1991.

**Jeffreys, A.J., Monckton, D.G., Tamaki, K., Neil, D.L., Armour, J. A., MacLeod, A., Collick, A., Allen, M., Jobling, M.,** Minisatellite variant repeat mapping: application to DNA typing and mutation analysis, *Exs*, 67, 125-39, 1993.

**Monckton, D.G., Tamaki, K., MacLeod, A., Neil, D.L., Jeffreys, A. J.,** Allele-specific MVR-PCR analysis at minisatellite D1S8, *Human Molecular Genetics*, 2, 5, 513-9, 1993.

**Neil, D.L., Jeffreys, A.J.,** Digital DNA typing at a second hypervariable locus by minisatellite variant repeat mapping, *Human Molecular Genetics*, Aug, 2(8), 1129-35, 1993.

**Tamaki, K., Huang, X. L., Yamamoto, T., Uchihi, R., Nozawa, H., Katsumata, Y.,** Applications of minisatellite variant repeat (MVR) mapping for maternal identification from remains of an infant and placenta, *Journal of Forensic Sciences*, 40, 4, 695-700, 1995.

**Tamaki, K., Monckton, D. G., MacLeod, A., Allen, M., Jeffreys, A. J.,** Four-state MVR-PCR: increased discrimination of digital DNA typing by simultaneous analysis of two polymorphic sites within minisatellite variant repeats at D1S8, *Human Molecular Genetics*, 2, 10, 1629-32, 1993.

PCR: increased discrimination of digital DNA typing by simultaneous analysis of two polymorphic sites within minisatellite variant repeats at D1S8, *Human Molecular Genetics*, Oct., 2, 10, 1629-32, 1993.

**Yamamoto, T., Tamaki, K., Kojima, T., Uchihi, R., Katsumata, Y., Jeffrey, A. J.,** DNA typing of the D1S8 (MS32) locus by rapid detection minisatellite variant repeat (MVR) mapping using polymerase chain reaction (PCR) assay, *Forensic Science International*, 66, 1, 69-75, 1994 .

**Yamamoto, T., Tamaki, K., Kojima, T., Uchihi, R., Katsumata Y.,** Potential forensic applications of minisatellite variant repeat (MVR) mapping using the polymerase chain reaction (PCR) at D1S8, *Journal of Forensic Sciences*, 39(3), 743-50, 1994.

## VI. AUTOMATED ANALYSIS SYSTEMS

The word "robot" was invented in 1920 by the Czech playwright Karel Capek to describe the slave-type creatures in his play R.U.R. Since that time, the word has come to be applied to any manufactured device, usually envisaged as humanoid in shape (although it doesn't have to be), and made of metal (though again, it doesn't have to be) which is capable of doing work ordinarily done by human beings. The word "robotics" was coined by Isaac Azimov in his book "I Robot", a book which inspired the first invention of a working robot by George C. Devol, Jr. in 1954.[11]

Automation of DNA typing is a goal for those labs that desire a greater throughput of case material, or which have large numbers of samples that require the same repetitive handling procedures. Instruments exist that can perform many of these tasks, and efforts have been underway to take advantage of the capabilities of various kinds of instrumental robots.

The typing process can be perceived as a series of steps that may be relatively independent of each other. These steps include extraction of DNA, digestion with a restriction enzyme, electrophoresis, PCR set-up and amplification, detection, and typing. Each has different requirements for handling, setup, and quality control. The efforts to automate have focused on one or a few steps; no work has yet been done to automate the process from sample preparation to typing.

Examples of automation include semi-automated development of reverse dot blot strips for typing systems such as DQα/A1 and polymarker (Figure 7-17), automated detection of bands during electrophoresis using fluorescence technology (Figures 7-18, 7-19, 7-20), an extraction and restriction digestion robot (Figure 7-21), and determination of band sizes and genotypes using computer assisted imaging techniques. The thermal cycler itself is an automated system for controlling the time and temperature cycles necessary for PCR amplification of DNA.

Technologies currently under development in other areas of molecular biology include DNA-on-a-chip (similar to computer chips, with hundreds of DNA sequences on a small wafer), small scale PCR, where microscopic drops of DNA are amplified and typed in

---

[11] Asimov, I., *Asimov's Chronology of Science and Discovery*. Harper Collins, 1994.

minutes rather than hours, sequencing by hybridization, a variation of the DNA on a chip technology, and automated differential extractions, where the separation of sperm from epithelial cells in rape cases is accomplished with little human manipulation.

These possibilities carry a danger. As robots and computers take over the mundane tasks of DNA typing, it is tempting to allow the reproducibility of the nonhuman aspect to usurp the importance of trained judgment in the evaluation of results and rendering of opinions. Regardless of the ever more technical evolution of the field, there will always be the need for a person to sit in front of a jury and say in plain English what was done, and what the results mean in that particular case.

**Figure 7-17. The TECAN Profiblot** In forensic science, this instrument is used to semi-automate the typing of reverse dot blot strips, such as DQα and AmpliType® PM+DQA1.

**Figure 7-18. The Perkin-Elmer Applied Biosystems Division 377 DNA sequencer.** In forensic science, this instrument is used in automated analysis of length polymorphisms, primarily STRs, and for mitochondrial DNA sequence analysis. It detects fluorescently labeled fragments with a laser as they run past a predetermined point.

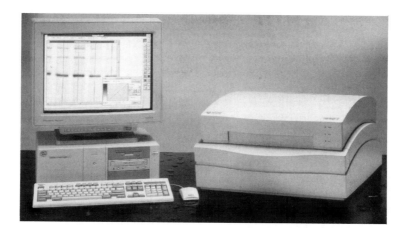

FlourImager® is a trademark of Molecular Dynamics

**Figure 7-19. The Molecular Dynamics FluorImager®.** In forensic science, this instrument is used for fluorescent detection of length polymorphisms, such as STRs. It detects fragment in a static mode, after the gel run has been completed.

**Figure 7-20. The Perkin Elmer Capillary Electrophoresis Unit.** In forensic science, this instrument is in development for use in the automated analysis of extremely minute amounts of DNA. It detects fluorescently labeled fragments with a laser as they run past a predetermined point.

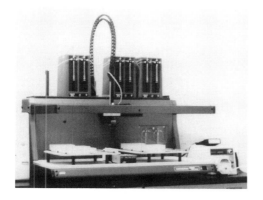

**Figure 7-21. The extraction robot.** In forensic science, this instrument is used in the automated extraction of DNA from database samples.

———— *FURTHER  REFERENCES*————

**Akane, A., Seki, S., Shiono, H., Nakamura, H., Hasegawa, M., Kagawa, M., Matsubara, K., Nakahori, Y., Nagafuchi, S., Nakagome, Y.,** Sex determination of forensic samples by dual PCR amplification of an X-Y homologous gene, *Forensic Science International*, 52, 2, 143-8, 1992.

**Blake, E., Mihalovic, J., Higuchi, R., Walsh, P. S., Erlich, H.,** Polymerase chain reaction (PCR) amplification and human leukocyte antigen (HLA)-DQ alpha oligonucleotide typing on biological evidence samples: casework experience, *Journal of Forensic Sciences*, 37, 3, 700-26, 1992.

**Budowle, B., Baechtel F. S., Comey, C. T., Giusti, A. M., Klevan, L.,** Simple protocols for typing forensic biological evidence: chemiluminescent detection for human DNA quantitation and restriction fragment length polymorphism (RFLP) analyses and manual typing of polymerase chain reaction (PCR) amplified polymorphisms, *Electrophoresis*, 16, 9, 1559-67, 1995.

**Budowle, B., Chakraborty, R., Guisti, A.,** *et al.*, Analysis of the VNTR locus (D1S80) by the PCR followed by high-resolution PAGE, *American Journal of Human Genetics*, 48, 137-144, 1991.

**Budowle, B., Waye, J. S., Shutler, G. G., Baechtel, F. S.,** *Hae* III--a suitable restriction endonuclease for restriction fragment length polymorphism analysis of biological evidence samples, *Journal of Forensic Sciences*, 35, 3, 530-6, 1990.

**Crouse, C. A., Vincek., V, Caraballo, B. K.,** Analysis and interpretation of the HLA DQ alpha "1.1 weak-signal" observed during the PCR-based typing method, *Journal of Forensic Sciences*, 39, 1, 41-51, 1994.

**Erlich, H. A., Ed.,** *PCR Technology: Principles and Applications for DNA Amplification*, Stockton Press, New York, 1989.

**Fregeau, C. J., Fourney, R. M.,** DNA typing with fluorescently tagged short tandem repeats: a sensitive and accurate approach to human identification. *Biotechniques*, 15(1):100-19, 1993.

**Ginther, C., Issel-Tarver, L., King, M. C.,** Identifying individuals by sequencing mitochondrial DNA from teeth, *Nature Genetics*, 2, 2, 135-8, 1992.

**Kawasaki, E., Saiki, R., Erlich, H.,** Genetic analysis using polymerase chain reaction-amplified DNA and immobilized oligonucleotide probes: reverse dot-blot typing. *Methods in Enzymology*, 218, 369-81, 1993.

**Klevan, L., Horton, L., Carlson, D. P., Eisenberg, A. J.,** Chemiluminescent detection of DNA probes in forensic analysis, *Electrophoresis*, 16, 9, 1553-8, 1995.

**Kloosterman, A. D., Budowle, B., Daselaar, P.,** PCR-amplification and detection of the human D1S80 VNTR locus, amplification conditions, population genetics and application in forensic analysis, *International Journal of Legal Medicine*, 105, 5, 257-64, 1993.

Perkin-Elmer AmpliType[TM] User Guide, Version 2.

**Southern, E.M.,** Detection of specific sequences among DNA fragments separated by gel electrophoresis, *Journalof Molecular Biology*, 98, 03-527, 1975.

**Sullivan, K. M., Hopgood, R., Gill, P.,** Identification of human remains by amplification and automated sequencing of mitochondrial DNA, *International Journal of Legal Medicine*, 105, 2, 83-6, 1992.

**Walsh, P. S., Metzger, D. A., Higuchi, R.,** Chelex 100 as a medium for simple extraction of DNA for PCR-based typing from forensic material, *Biotechniques*, 10, 4, 506-13, 1991.

# Chapter 8

## SIGNIFICANCE OF RESULTS

 The entire purpose of DNA typing is to test the hypothesis that a particular person is the source of an item of biological evidence. An attempt is made to ascertain whether an association exists between an evidence sample and a reference sample taken from an individual (*Chapter 2*). The evidence sample (a biological fluid or tissue) and reference (typically a blood sample) are subjected to a battery of DNA tests. Upon completion, the analyst is able to render a determination as to the genetic similarity of the samples. Three conclusions are possible.

1) The types are different and therefore must have originated from different sources (**exclusion**). This conclusion is absolute and requires no further analysis or discussion.

2) It is not possible to be sure, based on the results of the test, whether the samples have similar DNA types (**inconclusive**). This might occur for a variety of reasons including degradation, contamination, or failure of some aspect of the protocol (e.g., inhibition of restriction enzyme). Various parts of the analysis might then be repeated with the same or a different sample, in an attempt to obtain a more conclusive result. One way of thinking about an inconclusive result is that there is no more information after the analysis than before; it is as if the analysis had never been performed.

3) The types are similar, and could have originated from the same source.

If the samples are determined to be similar, the question becomes: What is the significance of this similarity? The rest of this chapter will be spent discussing the basis of some of the concepts used in reaching a conclusion of similarity, and determining its significance.

## I. DETERMINATION OF SIMILARITY

Frequently the word "match" is used to describe the genetic similarity between the evidence and reference samples. Scientists reserve a very narrow meaning for the word "match", and it is quite different than the connotation usually attributed to the word by non-scientists. Scientists are careful to limit the term match to mean that no significant differences were observed between the two samples in the particular test(s) conducted. It is certainly possible that two samples may be different, but that the test used has failed to reveal those differences. Since DNA tests currently sample a relatively small percentage of the entire human genome, further analyses might reveal differences that would lead to a different conclusion. In contrast, the perception of the general public is that the word match connotes an absolute "individualization". A conclusion of **genetic similarity** or **genetic concordance** merely describes the fact that no differences were seen between the two samples in the particular tests conducted. Having said that, however, the strength of DNA typing lies in its immense powers of discrimination; samples that show genetic concordance over several highly discriminating DNA loci approach, and in some cases reach, individuality.

In determining whether two samples have similar types, it is important to know the kind of marker system used. Typing systems may be divided into those detecting **continuous alleles** and those detecting **discrete alleles**.

## A. CONTINUOUS ALLELE SYSTEMS

RFLP markers are considered continuous allele systems; discrete individual types (where the exact number of repeat units can be ascertained) are not resolved by the methods used. This is in large part due to the plethora of alleles possible at one locus and their relative composition. As an example, an allele containing 99 repeats of a 10 bp repeat unit may not be distinguishable from an allele containing 100 repeats of the same 10 bp repeat unit, but may be easily distinguished from an allele of 110 repeats. Therefore, after a visual assessment, a mathematical algorithm is used to estimate the fragment sizes with the aid of a computer.

For RFLP specifically, the first evaluation involves a visual inspection of the profiles. The analyst determines, based on education, training, and experience, whether the profiles show sufficient similarity to proceed to the next step. If the profiles are obviously different, there is no need to determine the size of the fragments to confirm the dissimilarity. There may also be situations where the patterns of the bands in the two profiles, while close, do not support a conclusion of similarity. If, in the analyst's trained judgment, the patterns appear indistinguishable, the profiles are submitted to computer analysis. Figure 8-1 is a computer generated composite showing profiles in which the patterns are visually concordant with each other.

In this step a computer is used to measure the fragment length; the measurement is expressed in base pairs. The precision of the experimental measurement is considered in describing the significance of genetic similarity. The fragment length, as measured by the computer, has some experimental uncertainty associated with it. Research and experience have demonstrated that this is a function of the sample, the specific laboratory methodology and the computer measurement system. When two samples are said to "match", it is meant that, while fragments may not be *exactly* the same size, they are the same within the experimental uncertainty of the total method. When fragment lengths are compared between evidence and reference samples from the same source, small differences will be seen in the number of base pairs which the computer has calculated for a particular band. These differences are expected from method-induced variation, as well as from sample-to-sample variation. The amount of difference that can occur between two samples that are from the same source is established through individual laboratory experimentation. This results in a **match criterion**, usually expressed as a percentage of the band size. It means that measurements of two bands must be within a certain percentage of each other to be considered the same. For example, if the match criteria is ± 2.5%, the two samples must have band sizes that are within either +2.5% or -2.5% of their average.

## B. DISCRETE ALLELE SYSTEMS

In PCR systems, the markers are generally detected as discrete alleles, meaning that the method clearly differentiates the types. This is facilitated by the existence of fewer alleles at each locus and the relative ease in resolving them. The comparison may be likened to analog (continuous allele) versus digital (discrete allele) electronics. Genotypes of two samples are either the same or they are not. Ambiguity is present only for situations such as mixtures or weak samples where a complete genotype cannot be deduced.

## II.  EVALUATION OF RESULTS

Samples may show genetic similarity under three circumstances:

1) **The samples come from a common source.** This means that the evidence sample (blood stain, semen sample, saliva stain, etc.) comes from the same person who provided the reference sample.

2) **The similarity is a coincidence.** This means that the evidence sample comes from someone other than the person who provided the reference sample. The genetic similarity results from two individuals, the reference donor and the true donor, who share the same genetic profile for the particular markers examined.

3) **The similarity is an accident** (erroneous). This means that the evidence sample comes from someone other than the reference donor but that some collection/analytical/clerical error has occurred to make the evidence and reference samples appear to have the same DNA profile.

Both the analyst and the courts, as well as any innocent parties, want to know which of these three alternatives is the correct one for the case under consideration. The ultimate significance of the similarity depends on the relative strengths of each of these possible causes of concordant genetic patterns. If only one or a few individuals have the type found in the evidence, and the chance of error is small, then concordance between evidence and reference points to a strong indication of association. If, on the other hand, a large percentage of the population shares the genetic profile detected, then the significance of the genetic similarity is reduced. This situation may occur when analysis of the evidence is limited to systems with relatively poor inherent discrimination because of the state of the DNA in the sample. The quality and/or quantity may already be poor as originally collected, or the integrity of the evidence might have been compromised by poor evidence handling or analytical procedures (see *Chapters 3, 9*).

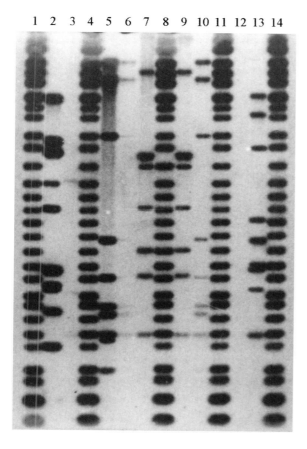

**Figure 8-1. A computer composite of the RFLP probings from five loci.** It is clear that the pattern of bands is indistinguishable between lanes 5 and 6, and also between lanes 7 and 9.

## III.  FREQUENCY ESTIMATE CALCULATIONS

Once it has been decided that there is an association (by "matching" DNA profiles) between the evidence sample and reference donor, the strength of the association becomes the next critical question.  If many individuals have this type, then the significance is minimal, because it means that there is some reasonable chance that anyone taken at random from the population (e.g., the wrong suspect chosen by the detective) will have the same type.  If, on the other hand, only a low probability exists that the types found are from someone other than the reference donor, then the association is strong.  The inference is equally strong that the reference donor is, in fact, the source of the biological evidence.

The question then becomes: What is the probability of a "match" if someone other than the reference donor is the true donor? (or what is the probability of a random match?)  The answer has typically been provided in the form of a profile frequency, that is, the number of times that this profile is seen in some reference population.  An alternate form of that question is: What is the probability of finding this profile if the reference donor were the true donor, compared to the probability of finding this profile if someone other than the reference donor were the true donor?  While this seems like a more complicated question, in fact it is a more complete statement of the first question.

In summary, the critical matter in forensic science is to measure the significance of the association between the biological evidence and the reference donor.  A common way of expressing that significance is to incorporate the frequency of the evidence profile in some form.

In simple terms, we want to express how many people might possess the profile seen in the biological evidence (see Figure 8-2).  The only way to determine this is by testing a representative number of people from a reference population and counting the number of times each genotype occurs.  For genetic marker systems with just a few alleles, it is likely that all of the genotypes will be seen several times.  In the PGM system for example, there were originally 2 alleles which together produce 3 genotypes.  If only 20 people were tested, each of these types would be seen several times.  This gives us confidence in the observed frequency of any particular type.

The problem becomes more complex with additional alleles.  To extend the PGM analogy, two additional alleles were subsequently discovered bringing the total to four, and the number of combined genotypes to ten.  A database of 20 people may now not be sufficient to detect all ten genotypes at their true representative frequencies; some might be over-represented, while others might be under-represented or missed entirely.  We may have to test 50 to 100 people to have confidence that the genotype frequencies are a true representation of the population makeup.

Consider now the hypervariable RFLP loci.  Some of these loci have 50 or more alleles, such that they can combine into approximately 1275 genotypes.  Typing enough people to find how often each of these types occurs would be a daunting task.  Further complicate the situation by considering four hypervariable loci, each with 50 alleles.  The number of allele combinations at four loci is (1275) x (1275) x (1275) x (1275), or about 2.6 trillion possible genotypes.  Testing everyone in order to obtain a fair representation of all these types is clearly impossible.  Additionally, since there are only about 5.5 billion people alive on earth at this time, most of these combinations do not even exist.

The solution to this dilemma (how to estimate frequencies when there are a large number of alleles, each at low frequency) is to invoke population genetics theory, particularly two principles called **Hardy-Weinberg equilibrium (H-W)** and **linkage equilibrium (LE)**. These principles allow for the estimation of genotypes based on individual **allele frequencies**, rather than observed **genotype frequencies**. Since the total number of alleles is much smaller than the possible combinations of those alleles into genotypes, this is clearly a much more practical proposition. The principles may be summarized as follows:

> The **Hardy-Weinberg** model states that there is a predictable relationship between allele frequencies and genotype frequencies at a single locus. This is a mathematical relationship that allows for the estimation of genotype frequencies in a population even if the genotype has not been seen in an actual population survey.

> **Linkage equilibrium** is defined as the steady-state condition of a population where the frequency of any multi-locus genotypic frequency is the product of each separate locus. This allows for the estimation of a DNA profile over several loci, even if the profile has not been seen in an actual population survey.

## IV.  POPULATION SUBSTRUCTURE

Theoretical application of the Hardy-Weinberg principle rests on several assumptions.[12] mating must be random, the mating population large, and migration negligible. However, it can be reasonably argued that mating is not random in most human populations, that some mating populations are not large, and that migration is variable among mating populations throughout the world. In fact, it is well accepted that the United States population is a mixture of people of various origins. For instance, in New York City, it is well known that neighborhoods exist of, for example, Italians, Germans, and Russians. It is also commonly accepted that people tend to mate among those with similar ancestry. This results in matings among people who are more related to each other than to people outside of their common ancestry. If a suspect comes from such a group, more people with similar DNA types may exist in this particular community than we would estimate from a survey of the general population. The phrases used to express this existence of smaller populations within a larger group include **population subgroups**, **subpopulations**, **population substructure**, and **structured populations**.

Given that the U.S. population is structured to some extent, and the assumptions for Hardy-Weinberg cannot be met, how is it possible to use these principles and arrive at useful frequency estimates? In actual fact, imperfect adherence to Hardy-Weinberg and linkage equilibrium does not invalidate the use of these principles in computing frequencies for DNA profiles. This is substantiated by both scientific theory and empirical testing.

Research has shown that the effects of substructuring are predictable. Relative to theoretical Hardy-Weinberg proportions, the effect is to increase the occurrence of homozygotes and to reduce the number of heterozygotes at a single locus. The effect on linkage equilibrium

---

[12]Strictly speaking, these assumptions are essential, but not neccessarily sufficient, and are particular to human populations.

is to increase the correlation between some loci, while decreasing the correlation between others. These deviations can be taken into account and accommodated statistically. Once sufficient data has been gathered for a specific population, departures from both Hardy-Weinberg and linkage equilibrium can be estimated. This allows for an evaluation of the extent and direction of the error that might occur if frequency estimates are calculated using HW and LE calculations.

The concern over the lack of knowledge regarding the effects of population substructure has instigated two major studies by the National Research Council (NRC) of the National Academy of Sciences. The first study, published in 1992, concluded that insufficient knowledge existed to substantiate use of the H-W and LE calculations. Several recommendations were made that resulted in an extremely conservative method of estimating the frequency of a DNA profile (termed the "**ceiling principle**"). In 1996, the second NRC report (known as NRC II) concluded that enough information had been collected since the original study to eliminate the most conservative recommendations (including the ceiling principle) as unnecessary. This second report (see *Further References*) is an excellent source for a deeper understanding of the issues and the solutions presented here.

Finally, it is imperative to emphasize that frequencies are estimated for the *evidence profile*, not the *suspect profile*. The race/ethnicity of the suspect is irrelevant when interpreting test results. It is erroneous to assume that the suspect was at the crime scene to determine if the suspect was at the crime scene! It is also not possible to evoke the race or ethnicity of a person by looking at the markers used in forensic DNA testing. Therefore, the choice of a relevant population for determining the frequency of an evidence profile is influenced by external factors and the context of the case such as eye-witness accounts or the location of the crime. In the absence of such external information, general population frequencies can be employed and racial/ethnic frequencies are used as comparisons or limits.

## A. ESTIMATING FREQUENCIES
The goal in deriving frequencies for any DNA profile is to provide an estimate that is scientifically conservative; that is, it should not overstate the significance of the association. There are several methods that forensic scientists, geneticists, and biostatisticians have devised to accomplish this goal (see *Appendix G* for an example). We describe here a generic outline of the steps used in estimating profile frequencies.

### 1. Continuous allele systems (RFLP)
*a. Population studies*
Population data is collected for different population groups (commonly Caucasian, African, American, Hispanic, and Asian), and allele sizes at particular loci are measured. Since RFLP markers are continuous allele systems, they are transformed into discrete allele systems by a method called **binning.** For any one locus, the length of the autorad is divided into size groups called **bins.** The alleles that fall between any two of these arbitrarily defined boundaries are combined into the same bin[13]. The frequency for all the alleles in a bin is derived by counting them and dividing by the total alleles in the population. A result of this is that very rare alleles that may have been undersampled in the population are assigned artificially high frequencies. Consequently, their rareness is not overstated.

---

[13]The binning system provides instructions for very specific contingencies, such as an allele situated on a bin boundary. For more information, see Budowle *et al.*, 1991.

*b. Evaluation for Hardy-Weinberg and linkage equilibrium*

The frequency of the observed alleles and genotypes within and between loci are tested for departure from Hardy-Weinberg and linkage equilibrium. Since some departure always exists, the magnitude is evaluated, and a decision is made to use or reject the frequency data.

*c. Calculate genotype frequencies*

The bands from an evidence profile are assigned to the appropriate bin(s) in the population data table. The allele frequencies derived from these bins are used to calculate the genotype frequency at any one locus using the Hardy-Weinberg equation. The calculation of homozygote frequencies must be treated differently, however. Because, in substructured populations homozygotes are more prevalent than Hardy-Weinberg would predict, a modification is used that ameliorates this effect (see *Appendix G* for an example).

*d. Multiplication of loci*

The frequencies from different loci are multiplied together under the assumption of linkage equilibrium to obtain the frequency of the complete DNA profile. This can be expressed as a percentage (y%) or as "1 in xxx", where xxx denotes some number of people (e.g., 1 in 300, or 1 in 3 million).

## 2. Discrete allele systems (all PCR systems)

*a. Population studies*

Population data is collected for different population groups (commonly Caucasian, African, American, Hispanic, and Asian), and allele frequencies at each locus of interest are calculated.

*b. Evaluation for Hardy-Weinberg and linkage equilibrium*

The frequency of the observed alleles and genotypes within and between loci are tested for departure from Hardy-Weinberg and linkage equilibrium. Since some departure always exists, the magnitude is evaluated and a decision is made to use or reject the frequency data.

*c. Calculate genotype frequencies*

The allele frequencies are used to calculate the frequency of a genotype at any one locus using Hardy-Weinberg proportions with, again, one exception. Homozygote frequencies are calculated using a correction factor (different from the one used with continuous allele data) that accounts for the effect of substructuring.

*d. Multiplication of loci (application of the product rule)*

The frequencies determined for different loci are multiplied together, under the assumption of linkage equilibrium, to obtain the frequency of the complete DNA profile. This can be expressed as a percentage (y%) or as "1 in xxx", where xxx denotes some number of people (e.g., 1 in 300, or 1 in 3 million).

## 3. Combining discrete and continuous allele systems

Provided linkage equilibrium studies have been performed between continuous and discrete allele systems, genotype frequencies can be multiplied together to obtain profile frequencies.

Different workers have formulated a variety of correction factors that ensure conservative frequency estimates. NRC II provides guidance on reasonable corrections that prevent over-estimating the significance of the concordance without seriously compromising the power of the tests.

The calculations outlined above are for random unrelated individuals. A special case exists for related individuals. Siblings potentially share more genetic material with each other than anyone else. This is because they inherit their genes from the same two people; Mom and Dad. This idea can be extended to more distant relationships such as children, grandchildren and cousins. In these relationships, some genetic material is shared, but the more distant the relationship, the fewer the genes that are held in common. For the highly variable DNA regions that are used in forensic testing, this means that even siblings are unlikely to share the same profiles when several highly variable DNA regions are analyzed. Special calculations are applied in those circumstances where relatives might be involved.

There are other workers who have tried to assess the significance of genetic concordance without using the assumptions of Hardy-Weinberg and linkage equilibrium. They rely primarily on the size of the population study. These calculations do not take advantage of population theory and tend to underestimate the significance of the concordance compared to frequency calculations.

The power of DNA testing is such that the information provided by several highly variable loci is often sufficient to convince us of the source of a sample. With sufficient data it might be concluded that two samples originate from a single common source to the exclusion of all other individuals (see Figure 8-2). We suggest that when close relatives can be eliminated (including identical twins) the appropriate quality control measures have been followed, and the conservative frequency estimates reach one thousand times the population of the earth (presently 6 billion people), individuality can be concluded.

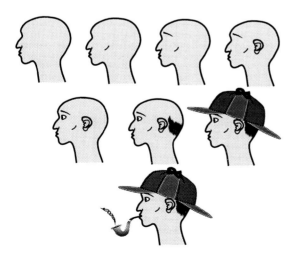

**Figure 8-2. The anatomy of a profile.** Individual features such as eyes, nose, ears, hair, and accouterments help us to differentiate one person from the next. With enough features, we can be confident in the identity of any particular person. Genetic markers work in exactly the same way; with enough loci (provided certain other conditions are met), we can have confidence in the individuality of a sample.

─── *FURTHER REFERENCES* ───────────────────

al-Nassar, K.E., Mathew, J., Thomas, N., Fatania, H.R., HLA DQ alpha allele and genotype frequencies in a native Kuwaiti population, *Forensic Science International,* 72, 1, 65-9, 1995.

Allen, M., Saldeen, T., Pettersson, U., Gyllensten, U., Genetic typing of HLA class II genes in Swedish populations: application to forensic analysis., *Journal of Forensic Sciences,* 38, 3, 554-70, 1993.

Alper, B., Meyer, E., Schurenkamp, M, Brinkmann, B., HumFES/FPS and HumF13B: Turkish and German population data, *International Journal of Legal Medicine,* 108, 2, 93-5, 1995.

Balding, D.J., Nichols, R.A., DNA profile match probability calculation: how to allow for population stratification, relatedness, database selection and single bands, *Forensic Science International,* 64, 2-3, 125-40, 1994 .

Bellamy, R.J., Inglehearn, C. F. Jalili, I.K., Jeffrey, A. J., Bhattacharya, S.S., Increased band sharing in DNA fingerprints of an inbred human population, *Human Genetics,* 87, 3, 341-7, 1991.

Brookfield, J.F., Statistical issues in DNA evidence. *Electrophoresis,* 16, 9, 1665-9, 1995.

Brookfield, J.F., The effect of relatedness on likelihood ratios and the use of conservative estimates, *Genetica,* 96, 1-2, 13-9, 1995.

Budowle, B., The effects of inbreeding on DNA profile frequency estimates using PCR-based loci, *Genetica,* 96, 1-2, 21-5, 1995.

Budowle, B., Baechtel, F.S., Smerick, J. B., Presley, K.W., Giusti, A.M., Parsons, G., Alevy, M.C., Chakraborty, R., D1S80 population data in African Americans, Caucasians, southeastern Hispanics, southwestern Hispanics, and Orientals, *Journal of Forensic Sciences,* 40, 1, 38-44, 1995.

Budowle, B., Giusti, A.M., Fixed bin frequency distributions for the VNTR locus D5S110 in general United States reference databases, *Journal of Forensic Sciences,* 40, 2, 236-8, 1995.

Budowle, B., Lindsey, J.A., DeCou, J.A., Koons, B.W., Giusti, A.M., Comey, C.T., Validation and population studies of the loci LDLR, GYPA, HBGG, D7S8, and GC (PM loci), and HLA DQ alpha using a multiplex amplification and typing procedure, *Journal of Forensic Sciences,* 40, 1, 45-54, 1995.

Budowle, B., Monson, K.L., Greater differences in forensic DNA profile frequencies estimated from racial groups than from ethnic subgroups, *Clinica Chimica Acta,* 228, 1, 3-18, 1994 .

Budowle, B., Monson, K.L., Giusti, A.M., A reassessment of frequency estimates of PvuII-generated VNTR profiles in a Finnish, an Italian, and a general U.S. Caucasian database: no evidence for ethnic subgroups affecting forensic estimates, *American Journal of Human Genetics,* 55, 3, 533-9, 1994 .

Budowle, B., Monson, K.L., Giusti, A. M., Brown, B.L., The assessment of frequency estimates of *Hae*III-generated VNTR profiles in various reference databases, *Journal of Forensic Sciences,* 39, 2, 319-52, 1994.

Budowle, B., Monson, K.L., Giusti, A.M., Brown, B.L., Evaluation of *Hinf* I-generated VNTR profile frequencies determined using various ethnic databases, *Journal of Forensic Sciences,* 39(4):988-1008, 1994.

Budowle, B., Monson K.L., The forensic significance of various reference population databases for estimating the rarity of variable number of tandem repeat (VNTR) loci profiles, *Exs,* 67, 177-91, 1993.

Budowle, B., Giusti, A.M., Waye, J.S., Baechtel, F.S., Fourney, R. M., Adams, D.E., Presley, L.A., Deadman, H.A., Monson, K.L., Fixed-bin analysis for statistical evaluation of continuous distributions of allelic data from VNTR loci, for use in forensic comparisons *American Journal of Human Genetics,* May, 48, 5, 841-55, 1991.

**Buscemi, L., Cucurachi, N., Mencarelli, R., Tagliabracci, A., Wiegand, P., Ferrara, S. D.,** PCR analysis of the short tandem repeat (STR) system HUMVWA31. Allele and genotype frequencies in an Italian population sample, *International Journal of Legal Medicine*, 107, 4, 171, 1995.

**Chakraborty, R., De Andrade, M., Daiger, S.P., Budowle, B.,** Apparent heterozygote deficiencies observed in DNA typing data and their implications in forensic applications, *Annals of Human Genetics*, 56, Pt 1, 45-57, 1992.

**Chakraborty, R., Fornage, M., Gueguen, R., Boerwinkle, E.,** Population genetics of hypervariable loci: analysis of PCR based VNTR polymorphism within a population. *Exs*, 58,127-43, 1991.

**Chakraborty, R., Jin, L.,** Heterozygote deficiency, population substructure and their implications in DNA fingerprinting, *Human Genetics*, 88(3), 267-72, 1992.

**Chakraborty, R., Jin, L., Zhong, Y., Srinivasan, M. R., Budowle, B.,** On allele frequency computation from DNA typing data, *International Journal of Legal Medicine*, 106, 2, 103, 1993.

**Chakraborty, R., Kidd, K.K.,** The utility of DNA typing in forensic work. *Science*, 254, 5039, 1735-9, 1991.

**Chakraborty, R.,** Sample size requirements for addressing the population genetic issues of forensic use of DNA typing, *Human Biology*, 642, 141-59, 1992.

**Chakraborty, R., Srinivasan, M.R., Daiger, S.P.,** Evaluation of standard error and confidence interval of estimated  multilocus genotype probabilities, and their implications in DNA forensics, *American Journal of Human Genetics*, 52, 1, 60, 1993.

**Chakraborty, R., Srinivasan, M.R., de Andrade, M.,** Intraclass and interclass correlations of allele sizes within and between loci in DNA typing data, *Genetics*, 133, 2,  411, 1993.

**Chakraborty, R., Zhong, Y., Jin, L., Budowle, B.,** Nondetectability of restriction fragments and independence of DNA fragment sizes within and between loci in RFLP typing of DNA, *American Journal of Human Genetics*, 55, 2, 391, 1994.

**Chakraborty, R., Zhong, Y.,** Statistical power of an exact test of Hardy-Weinberg proportions of genotypic data at a multiallelic locus, *Human Heredity*, 44, 1, 1, 1994 .

**Chakraborty, R., Li., Z.,** Correlation of DNA fragment sizes within loci in the presence of  non-detectable alleles, *Genetica*, 96, 1-2, 27-36, 1995.

**Chow, S.T., Tan, W.F., Yap, K.H., Ng, T.L.,** The development of DNA profiling database in an *Hae*III based RFLP system for Chinese, Malays, and Indians in Singapore, *Journal of Forensic Sciences*, 38, 4, 874, 1993.

**Clark, A.G., Hamilton, J.F., Chambers, G.K.,** Inference of population subdivision from the VNTR distributions of New Zealanders, *Genetica*, 96, 1-2, 7-49, 1995.

**Cohen, J.E.,** The ceiling principle is not always conservative in assigning genotype  frequencies for forensic DNA testing, *American Journal of Human Genetics*, 51, 5, 1165-8, 1992.

**Cohen, J.E.,** DNA fingerprinting for forensic identification: potential effects on data interpretation of subpopulation heterogeneity and band number variability, *American Journal of Human Genetics*, 46, 2, 358-68, 1990.

**Chow, S.T., Tan, W. F., Yap, K.H., Ng, T.L.,** The development of DNA profiling database in an *Hae* III based RFLP  system for Chinese, Malays, and Indians in Singapore, *Journal of Forensic Sciences*, 38, 4, 874-84, 1993.

**Chuah, S.Y., Tan, W. F., Yap, K.H. Tai, H.E., Chow, S.T.,** Analysis of the D1S80 locus by amplified fragment length polymorphism technique in the Chinese, Malays and Indians in Singapore. *Forensic Science International*, 68, 3, 169-80, 1994.

**Collins, A., Morton, N.E.,** Likelihood ratios for DNA identification. *Proceedings of the National Academy of Sciences of the United States of America*, 91, 13, 6007-11, 1994.

**D'Eustachio, P.,** Interpreting DNA fingerprints, *Nature*, 356, 6369, 483, 1992.

**Deka, R., Shriver, M.D., Yu, L.M., Ferrell, R.E. Chakraborty, R.,** Intra- and inter-population diversity at short tandem repeat loci in diverse populations of the world, *Electrophoresis*, 16, 9, 659-64, 1995.

**Deka, R., DeCroo, S., Jin, L., McGarvey, S.T., Rothhammer, F., Ferrell, R.E. Chakraborty, R.,** Population genetic characteristics of the D1S80 locus in seven human populations, *Human Genetics*, 94, 3, 252-8, 1994 .

**Devlin, B., Risch, N.,** A note on Hardy-Weinberg equilibrium of VNTR data by using the Federal Bureau of Investigation's fixed-bin method, *American Journal of Human Genetics*, 51, 3, 549-53, 1992.

**Devlin, B., Risch, N.,** Physical properties of VNTR data, and their impact on a test of allelic independence, *American Journal of Human Genetics*, 53, 2, 324-9, 1993.

**Devlin, B., Risch, N., Roeder, K.,** Comments on the statistical aspects of the NRC's report on DNA typing, *Journal of Forensic Sciences*, 39, 1, 28-40, 1994.

**Devlin, B., Risch, N., Roeder, K.,** No excess of homozygosity at loci used for DNA fingerprinting, *Science*, 249, 4975, 1416-20, 1990.

**Duncan, G.T., Noppinger, K., Carey, J., Tracey, M.,** Comparison of VNTR allele frequencies and inclusion probabilities over six populations, *Genetica*, 88, 1, 51-7, 1993.

**Edwards, A., Hammond, H.A., Jin, L., Caskey, C.T., Chakraborty, R.,** Genetic variation at five trimeric and tetrameric tandem repeat loci in four human population groups, *Genomics*, 12, 2, 241-53, 1992.

**Eriksen, B., Svensmark, O.,** Analysis of a Danish Caucasian population sample of single locus DNA-profiles: Allele frequencies, frequencies of DNA-profiles and heterozygosity, *Forensic Science International*, 59, 2, 119-29, 1993.

**Evett, I. W., Gill, P.D., Scrange, J. K., Weir, B.S.,** Establishing the robustness of short-tandem-repeat statistics for forensic applications, *American Journal of Human Genetics*, 58, 2, 398-407, 1996.

**Evett, I. W., Scranage, J., Pinchin, R.,** An illustration of the advantages of efficient statistical methods for RFLP analysis in forensic science, *American Journal of Human Genetics*, 52, 3, 498-505, 1993.

**Evett, I.W.,** Evaluating DNA profiles in a case where the defence is "it was my brother", *Journal - Forensic Science Society*, 32, 1, 5-14, 1992.

**Evett, I.W., Buffery, C., Willott, G., Stoney, D.,** A guide to interpreting single locus profiles of DNA mixtures in forensic cases, *Journal - Forensic Science Society*, 31, 1, 41-7, 1991.

**Evett, I.W., Gill, P.,** A discussion of the robustness of methods for assessing the evidential value of DNA single locus profiles in crime investigations, *Electrophoresis*, 12, 2, 226-30, 1991.

**Gasparini, P., Mandich, P., Novelli, G., Bellone, E., Sangiuolo, F., De Stefano, F., Potenza, L., Trabetti, E., Marigo, M., Pignatti, P. F., et al.,** Forensic applications of molecular genetic analysis: an Italian collaborative study on paternity testing by the determination of variable number of tandem repeat DNA polymorphisms, *Human Heredity*, 413, 174-81, 1991.

**Gill, P., Woodroffe, S., Lygo, J.E., Millican, E.S.,** Population genetics of four hypervariable loci, *International Journal of Legal Medicine,* 104, 4, 221-7, 1991.

**Hatzaki, A., Loukopoulos, D., Spiliopoulou, H., Koutselinis, A.,** A study of five variable number tandem repeat (VNTR) loci in the Greek population, *Molecular and Cellular Probes*, 9, 2, 129-33, 1995.

**Hayes, J.M., Budowle, B., Freund, M.,** Arab population data on the PCR-based loci: HLA DQA1, LDLR, GYPA, HBGG, D7S8, Gc, and D1S80, *Journal of Forensic Sciences*, 40, 5, 888-92, 1995.

**Herrin, G., Jr.,** Probability of matching RFLP patterns from unrelated individuals, *American Journal of Human Genetics*, 52, 3, 491-7, 1993.

**Herrin, G., Jr.,** A comparison of models used for calculation of RFLP pattern frequencies, *Journal of Forensic Sciences*, Nov., 37, 6, 1640-51, 1992.

**Hochmeister, M.N, Budowle, B., Borer, U.V., Dirnhofer, R.,** Swiss population data on the loci HLA DQ alpha, LDLR, GYPA, HBGG, D7S8, Gc and D1S80, *Forensic Science International*, 67, 3, 175-84, 1994

**Hochmeister, M.N., Budowle, B., Schumm, J.W., Precher, C.J., Borer, U.V., Dirnhofer, R.,** Swiss population data and forensic efficiency values on 3 tetrameric short tandem repeat loci- HUMTH01, TPOX, and CSF1PO-derived using a STR multiplex system, *International Journal of Legal Medicine*, 107, 5, 246-9, 1995.

**Hochmeister, M.N., Jung, J.M., Budowle, B., Borer, U.V., Dirnhofer, R.,** Swiss population data on three tetrameric short tandem repeat loci--VWA, HUMTHO1, and F13A1--derived using multiplex PCR and laser fluorescence detection, *International Journal of Legal Medicine*, 107, 1, 34-6, 1994.

**Hochmeister, M., Borer, U.V., Gisin, D., Baier, K., Dirnhofer, R.,** Population genetic *Hae*III/RFLP and HLA DQ-alpha data of a Caucasian population sample in *Switzerland Beitrage zur Gerichtlichen Medizin*, 50, 75-87, 1992.

**Huang, N.E., Budowle, B.,** Chinese population data on the PCR-based loci HLA DQ alpha, low-density-lipoprotein receptor, glycophorin A, hemoglobin gamma G, D7S8, and group-specific component, *Human Heredity*, 45, 1, 34-40, 1995.

**Huang, N.E., Budowle, B.,** Fixed bin population data for the VNTR loci D1S7, D2S44, D4S139, D5S110, and D17S79 in Chinese from Taiwan, *Journal of Forensic Sciences*, 40, 2, 287-90, 1995.

**Huang, N.E., Chakraborty, R., Budowle, B.,** D1S80 allele frequencies in a Chinese population, *International Journal of Legal Medicine*, 107, 3, 118-20, 1994.

**Jin , L., Chakraborty, R.,** Population structure, stepwise mutations, heterozygote deficiency and their implications in DNA forensics, *Heredity*, 74, 274-85, 1995.

**Kaye, D.H.,** The forensic debut of the NRC's DNA report: population structure, ceiling frequencies and the need for numbers, *Genetica*, 96, 1-2, 99-105, 1995.

**Kloosterman, A.D., Sjerps, M., Wust, D.,** Dutch Caucasian population data on the loci LDLR, GYPA, HBGG, D7S8, and GC, *International Journal of Legal Medicine*, 108, 1, 36-8, 1995.

**Kloosterman, A.D., Budowle, B., Riley, E.L.,** Population data of the HLA DQ alpha locus in Dutch Caucasians. Comparison with other population studies, *International Journal of Legal Medicine*, 105, 4, 233-8, 1993.

**Koh, C.L., Benjamin, D.G.,** HLA DQ alpha genotype and allele frequencies in Malays, Chinese, and Indians in the Malaysian population, *Human Heredity*, 44, 3, 150-5, 1994.

**Krane, D.E., Allen, R. W., Sawye, S.A., Petrov, D.A., Hartl, D.L.,** Genetic differences at four DNA typing loci in Finnish, Italian, and mixed Caucasian populations, *Proceedings of the National Academy of Sciences of the United States of America*, 89(22), 10583-7, 1992.

**Laber, T.L., Iverson, J.T., Liberty, J. A., Giese, S.A.,** The evaluation and implementation of match criteria for forensic analysis of DNA, *Journal of Forensic Sciences*, 40, 6, 1058-64, 1995.

**Lambert, J.A., Scranage, J.K., Evett, I.W.,** Large scale database experiments to assess the significance of matching DNA profiles, *International Journal of Legal Medicine*, 108, 1, 8-13, 1995.

**Lange, K.,** Match probabilities in racially admixed populations. *American Journal of Human Genetics*, 52, 2, 305-11, 1993.

**Lareu, M.V., Munoz, I., Pestoni, C., Rodriguez, M.S., Vide, C., Carracedo, A.,** The distribution of HLA DQA1 and D1S80 (pMCT118) alleles and genotypes in the populations of Galicia and central Portugal, *International Journal of Legal Medicine*, 106, 3, 124-8, 1993.

**Lewontin, R.C., Hartl, D.L.,** Population genetics in forensic DNA typing, *Science*, 254(5039), 1745-50, 1991.

**Lewontin, R.C.,** Which population?, *American Journal of Human Genetics*, 52(1), 205-6, 1993.

**Lin, S. J., Ko, Y. H., Wang, W.P., Lai, M. D., Lai, M. L.,** Population genetic study of selected tetranucleotide repeat DNA polymorphisms on chromosomes Y and 12, *Journal of the Formosan Medical Association*, 94, 6, 318-21, 1995.

**Lorente, J.A., Lorente, M., Budowle, B., Wilson, M.R., Villanueva, E.,** Analysis of the HUMTH01 allele frequencies in the Spanish population, *Journal of Forensic Sciences*, 39, 5, 1270-4, 1994.

**Mannucci, A., Sullivan, K. M., Ivanov, P. L., Gill, P.,** Forensic application of a rapid and quantitative DNA sex test by amplification of the X-Y homologous gene amelogenin, *International Journal of Legal Medicine*, 106, 4, 190-3, 1994.

**Menevse, S., Ulkuer, U.,** The distribution of the HLA DQ alpha alleles and genotypes in the Turkish population as determined by the use of DNA amplification and allele-specific oligonucleotides, *Science and Justice*, 35, 4, 259-62, 1995.

**Moller, A., Wiegand, P., Gruschow, C., Seuchter, S.A., Baur, M.P., Brinkmann B.,** Population data and forensic efficiency values for the STR systems HumVWA, HumMBP and HumFABP, *International Journal of Legal Medicine*, 106, 4, 183-9, 1994.

**Monson, K.L., Budowle, B.** A comparison of the fixed bin method with the floating bin and direct count methods: effect of VNTR profile frequency estimation and reference population, *Journal of Forensic Sciences*, 38(5), 1037-50, 1993.

**Morton, N.E., Collins, A., Balazs, I.,** Kinship bioassay on hypervariable loci in blacks and Caucasians, *Proceedings of the National Academy of Sciences of the United States of America*, 90(5), 1892-6, 1993.

**Monson, K.L., Moisan, J.P., Pascal, O., McSween, M., Aubert, D., Giusti, A., Budowle, B., Lavergne, L.,** Description and analysis of allele distribution for four VNTR markers in French and French Canadian populations, *Human Heredity*, 3, 135-43, 1995.

**Morton, N.E.,** Genetic structure of forensic populations, *American Journal of Human Genetics,* 55, 3, 587-8, 1994.

**Morton, N.E., Collins, A., Balazs, I.,** Kinship bioassay on hypervariable loci in blacks and Caucasians, *Proceedings of the National Academy of Sciences of the United States of America*, 90, 5, 1892-6, 1993.

**Morton, N.E.,** Genetic structure of forensic populations. *Proceedings of the National Academy of Sciences of the United States of America*, 89(7), 2556-60, 1992.

**Nellemann, L.J., Moller, A., Morling, N.,** PCR typing of DNA fragments of the short tandem repeat (STR) system HUMTH01 in Danes and Greenland Eskimos, *Forensic Science International*, 68, 1, 45-51, 1994.

**Nichols, R.A., Balding, D.J.,** Effects of population structure on DNA fingerprint analysis in forensic science, *Heredity*, Edinburgh, ( Pt 2), 297-302. 1991.

**Pandian, S.K., Kumar, S., Krishnan, M., Dharmalingam, K., Damodaran, C.,** Allele frequency distribution for the variable number of tandem repeat locus D10S28 in Tamil Nadu (south India) population, *Electrophoresis*, 16, 9, 1689-92, 1995.

**Pestoni, C, Lareu M.V, Rodriguez M.S., Munoz, I., Barros, F., Carracedo A.,** The use of the STRs HUMTH01, HUMVWA31/A, HUMF13A1, HUMFES/FPS, HUMLPL in forensic application: validation studies and population data for Galicia (NW Spain), *International Journal of Legal Medicine*, 107, 6, 283-90, 1995.

**Pfitzinger, H., Ludes, B., Kintz, P., Tracqui, A., Mangin, P.,** French Caucasian population data for HUMTH01 and HUMFES/FPS short tandem repeat (STR) systems, *Journal of Forensic Sciences*, 40, 2, 270-4, 1995.

**Risch, N.J., Devlin, B.,** On the probability of matching DNA fingerprints, *Science*, 255, 5045, 717-20, 1992.

**Sajantila, A., Budowle, B., Strom, M., Johnsson, V., Lukka, M., Peltonen, L., Ehnholm, C.,** PCR amplification of alleles at the DIS80 locus: comparison of a Finnish and a North American Caucasian population sample, and forensic casework evaluation, *American Journal of Human Genetics*, 50, 4, 816-25, 1992.

**Sajantila, A., Pacek, P., Lukka, M., Syvanen, A. C., Nokelainen, P., Sistonen, P., Peltonen, L., Budowle, B.,** A microsatellite polymorphism in the von Willebrand factor gene: comparison of allele frequencies in different population samples and  evaluation for forensic medicine, *Forensic Science International*, 68, 2, 91-102, 1994.

**Sajantila, A., Strom, M., Budowle, B., Tienari, P. J., Ehnholm, C., Peltonen, L.** Erlich, H. A., Ed., The distribution of the HLA DQ alpha alleles and genotypes in the  Finnish population as determined by the use of DNA amplification and  allele specific oligonucleotides, *International Journal of Legal Medicine*, 104, 4, 181-4, 199.

**Sharma, B.R., Thompson, M., Bolding, J.R., Zhong, Y., Jin, L., Chakraborty, R.**A., comparative study of genetic variation at five VNTR loci in three ethnic groups of Houston, Texas, *Journal of Forensic Sciences*, 40, 6, 933-42, 1995.

**Slimowitz, J.R., Cohen, J.E.,** Violations of the ceiling principle: exact conditions and statistical evidence, *American Journal of Human Genetics*, Aug, 53, 2, 314-23, 1993.

**Smith, J.C., Anwar, R., Riley, J., Jenner, D., Markham, A.F., Jeffreys, A.J.,** Highly polymorphic minisatellite sequences: allele frequencies and  mutation rates for five locus-specific probes in a Caucasian population, *Journal of the Forensic Science Society*, 30, 1, 9-32, 1990.

**Stoney, D.A.,** Reporting of highly individual genetic typing results: a practical approach, *Journal of Forensic Sciences*, 37, 2, 373-86, 1992.

**Sudbury, A.W., Marinopoulos, J., Gunn, P.,** Assessing the evidential value of DNA profiles matching without using the assumption of independent loci, *Journal - Forensic Science Society*, 33, 2, 73-82, 1993.

**Sullivan, K.M., Gill, P., Lingard, D., Lygo, J.E.,** Characterisation of HLA DQ alpha for forensic purposes, Allele and genotype frequencies in British Caucasian, Afro-Caribbean and Asian populations, *International Journal of Legal Medicine*, 105, 1, 17-20, 1992.

**Turowska, B., Sanak, M.,** D1S80 VNTR locus genotypes in population of south Poland; meta-analysis pointer to genetic disequilibrium of human populations, *Forensic Science International*, 75, 2-3, 207-16, 1995.

**Waye, J.S., Richard, M., Carmody, G., Newall, P.J.,** Allele frequency data for VNTR locus D17S79: identification of an internal *Hae*III polymorphism in the black population, *Human Mutation*, 3, 3, 248-53, 1994.

**Weir, B.S.,** Forensic population genetics and the National Research Council (NRC), *American Journal of Human Genetics*, 52, 2, 437-40, 1993.

**Weir, B.S., Hill, W.G.,** Population genetics of DNA profiles, *Journal of Forensic Science Society*, 33, 4, 218-25, 1993.

**Weir, B.S.,** Population genetics in the forensic DNA debate, *Proceedings of the National Academy of Sciences of the United States of America*, 89, 24, 11654-9, 1992.

## Chapter 9

## INTERPRETATION OF DNA TYPING RESULTS
### Warning! - for intermediate users only (or brave beginners)

 A word about this chapter. The material discussed in this chapter was not included in *DNA Demystified* for a very good reason. It is most definitely aimed at the intermediate user. We have decided to include it in this iteration both, as a result of requests from our readers, and because interpreting the results from a scientific test is the most crucial part of a criminalist's job. The estimation of the rareness of a genetic profile in the population is inconsequential if the conclusion of similarity of two samples is based on incomplete or erroneous information. In this chapter we address many of the sample-specific and system-specific issues that must be considered when drawing a conclusion based on DNA testing. Although each issue is discussed in context, and some information is necessarily repeated, we do assume that you have read and have a reasonable understanding of the previous chapters, particularly Chapters 5 to 7. Good luck!

### I. COMPLICATING FACTORS

Several factors may influence the straight-forward interpretation of any DNA typing result. These are enumerated below, along with a brief explanation of their potential effect on evaluating the meaning of the evidence.

### A. MULTIPLE CONTRIBUTORS

When more than one human individual has contributed biological material to an evidentiary sample, multiple DNA profiles are present. Mixtures are commonly found on evidence items such as vaginal swabs that contain material from the vagina as well as semen (and occasionally additional fluids such as saliva and fecal matter). In general, items of clothing with sites of accumulation, such as panty crotches and shirt armpits will continually collect secreted biological material from the orifices of the wearer. Another situation that may generate mixtures is a crime scene where multiple people are bleeding. This might include both victim and assailant or multiple victims. Since each person contributing biological material will donate on average 2 alleles per locus to the stain, multiple alleles (be they bands, dots or peaks) will be detected. In a situation where multiple contributors are suspected, it is generally not advisable to attempt to group alleles into true DNA profiles. In particular, the indiscriminate pairing of two alleles in a questioned sample, simply because they are associated in a reference sample, may be misleading, because those two alleles may have been contributed independently in the evidence sample. An exception to this caution is in order when interpreting results from sexual assault evidence, in which both the source and type of one contributor (usually the victim) are known with confidence.

### B. DIFFERENTIAL EXTRACTION

A special case exists when multiple donors are individually represented by sperm cells and epithelial cells (e. cells). This occurs in, for example, vaginal, oral or rectal sexual assault evidence. In this situation, the different types of cells from the individual contributors may be separated by means of a differential extraction (see *Chapter 7*). This separation is not always one hundred percent successful, and there may be leakage of DNA from the sperm into the e. cell fraction and e. cell DNA into the sperm fraction (Figure 9-1). This leads to patterns with more than two alleles per locus. As in the general case of multiple donors, the interpretation is complicated by the inability to confidently pair alleles with each other into profiles. One advantage, however, is that both the evidence and victim reference samples are taken directly from a known individual's body. Consequently, this pair of alleles may be easily identified in the mixed pattern and removed from further consideration.

Interpretation of the results from differential extractions is particularly problematic in samples where there are very few sperm and many e. cells. This situation usually results in low levels of recovered DNA from the sperm fraction, almost invariably leading to an analysis using PCR. Since most PCR systems currently have far less discrimination potential than a combination of RFLP loci, there is a reasonable chance that the victim and semen donor will show the same type. This leads to some agonizing over whether the type seen in the sperm fraction (which may contain some carry-over e. cell DNA from the extraction process) is from the semen donor or from the victim. A careful consideration of all of the analytical results, including a microscopic inspection of the cell debris from the various extractions, is necessary for proper interpretation of such a sample.

1 2 3 4 5 6 7 8 9

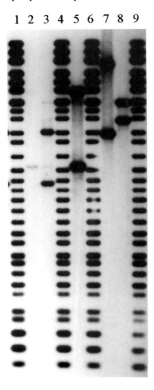

**Figure 9-1. An RFLP autorad from a sexual assault case.** Lanes 1, 4, 6, and 9 contain molecular ladders. Lane 2 contains the e. cell fraction, and Lane 3, the sperm fraction from the sexual assault sample. Lane 5 contains the victim's reference blood sample; lane 7, the suspect 's blood sample; and lane 8, a sample from the boyfriend. As expected, the e. cell fraction contains the same two bands as the victim's reference. Note the evidence of carryover from the e. cell fraction into the sperm fraction, particularly for the bottom band. Also evident in the e. cell fraction are bands in the same place as those in the boyfriend's sample. The suspect is excluded from having contributed to the sexual assault sample.

## C. DEGRADATION

When DNA is subjected to any environment outside of the body, it is not as stable as when it is inside the body. If the environmental conditions become extreme, the DNA may change it's physical and chemical properties. The environmental conditions that lead to these changes include time, temperature, humidity, light, and contamination (chemical and biological) (see *Chapter 3*). Normally these conditions will break the DNA into smaller fragments. Fragmentation of the DNA can be mild or severe depending on the particular conditions. This phenomenon is termed "degradation", and is used to describe DNA that contains smaller fragment sizes than expected. Degraded DNA may or may not affect the analysis, depending on the extent, and the DNA typing system employed. For example,

RFLP analysis detects DNA fragments between approximately 0.6 kb and 20 kb in length. If the average size of DNA fragments in a highly degraded evidence sample (say, for example, a bloodstain that was on an asphalt road in the sun for 2 or 3 days) are in the 2 to 4 kb range, then it is unlikely that any fragments larger than this would be detected, although any fragments smaller than this range would be. This circumstance immediately suggests the possibility of single-banded patterns that do not reflect the true profile of the donor, potentially leading to false exclusions or (extremely less likely) false inclusions. The level of degradation of any DNA sample can be assessed by a yield gel, a test that provides information about the average fragment size. This information can be used to predict whether RFLP analysis would likely produce a band pattern that could be interpreted with confidence, or whether another marker system that tests smaller regions of DNA would have a better chance of success.

The PCR-based tests are generally better suited for the analysis of smaller DNA fragment sizes than RFLP. The evidence example above, for example, in which the DNA had fragment sizes of 2 to 4 kb, would be perfectly suited to any of the suite of PCR tests currently available to forensic workers. In general, the longest fragments of DNA required are less than 1 kb, and in some cases they are as small as 106 bp (gender ID). This means that evidence samples subjected to extreme conditions of heat, humidity, and contamination have a high likelihood of successful typing by these methods.

## D. CONTAMINATION

An evidence sample may be contaminated in two substantially different ways. The first is characterized by the presence of some chemical or biological agent that is *inherent* to the sample or its substrate. An example of this would be the aforementioned crotch or armpit fabric. Before an evidentiary semen stain or bloodstain was ever deposited in these areas, other materials might have accumulated on the substrate. These could include biological agents such as bacteria, cells containing human DNA, and chemical contaminants such as soaps, lotions and deodorants. The second way in which a sample may become contaminated is by the accidental introduction of these same agents to the sample by inappropriate handling during collection or analysis (see *Chapter 3*). In either case, the various results of contamination are the same: inhibition of a DNA test, degradation of human DNA by bacterial enzymes, or worst-case, contamination with extraneous human DNA producing an erroneous result which points to a wrong donor or multiple contributors.

### 1. Inhibition of test

Because both the RFLP and PCR tests rely on enzymes (*Hae*III and *Taq*, respectively; see *Chapters 5, 7*) to perform properly, any agent that interferes with proper enzymatic function will potentially inhibit their ability to act on DNA. This includes a variety of commonly encountered substances, such as dyes used in clothing (particularly denim dyes), and some biological substances, in particular the red-colored heme in blood. An attempt is made to eliminate these substances during the extraction/purification phase of analysis; inhibition can be diagnosed at various points of the analysis by evaluative tests (product gel, digest gel; see *Chapter 7, Appendices C, E*), and certain operations can be repeated if deemed necessary. More extreme measures include the use of special beads that will bind dyes present in a substrate, and which can then be physically removed before any further enzymatic reaction is attempted. Enzyme inhibitors may also be neutralized during a reaction. BSA (bovine serum albumin) protein is commonly added directly to enzyme reactions, and seems to bind and disable inhibitors even while the reaction is proceeding. This is a standard molecular biological technique for optimizing enzyme reactions. Inhibition of enzymes will not always be overcome; in such cases, the typing results are negative (no type obtained).

## 2. Nonhuman DNA

By definition, all organisms contain DNA. Given that the world is a dirty place, it is not unusual to find evidence samples that contain nonhuman DNA. Examples include microorganisms (bacteria, fungi, etc.) such as would normally be found in physiological fluids and soil, as well as DNA from plants and nonhuman animals. Nonhuman DNA is not troublesome *per se*, as the DNA tests used for forensic purposes are human specific (that is, the loci used do not cross-react with other animal species). However, the presence of microorganisms that produce DNA-destroying enzymes can contribute to the degradation of human DNA. This severely affects the results by rendering an evidence sample untypable. Further, all tests rely on an accurate estimate of the amount of human DNA present in a sample in order to work optimally. This means that the analyst must calculate the amount of total DNA, as well as the amount of human DNA, present in a sample, both to intelligently choose a marker system(s) to use, and also to optimize the outcome of the analysis.

## II. SYSTEM SPECIFIC INTERPRETATIONAL ISSUES

The factors discussed in the previous section may all interact with each other to affect the DNA and potentially the resulting analysis and interpretation. Forensic DNA protocols have been tested, optimized and validated using samples that have been purposely subjected to most conceivable environmental insults and complicating factors. The effects have been categorized, and usually a diagnostic test or flag has been devised to detect their occurrence. These clues alert the analyst and assist him in both choosing the most informative analytical path to follow and in interpreting the results of the test. The following section discusses some topics relating to the reading and interpretation of specific systems, including consequences of the more common environmental conditions encountered in forensic casework.

### A. RFLP

Because the RFLP loci used in forensic DNA testing are so highly variable, most individuals inherit a different allele from each parent, producing a characteristic profile of two bands. Deviation from this expected norm may be due to normal genetic variation, or it may result from artifacts either inherent in the samples or generated by analytical conditions. In the following sections we delineate some common variations from the expected norm, and discuss their etiology and interpretational consequences.

### 1. Multi-(more than two) banded patterns

When more than two bands are seen in an RFLP profile, the key question is whether more than one individual has contributed to the profile (a mixture), or whether the extra bands are artifacts and the profile represents a single individual. The next section outlines the circumstances whereby extra bands may be observed in the absence of multiple donors.

### a. Three-banded Patterns

In certain rare genetic circumstances an individual may consistently show three bands at a particular locus (Figures 9-2, 9-3). This seems contradictory to our knowledge of chromosomes existing as pairs. Three-banded patterns occur when a point mutation occurs inside a VNTR sequence, such that a novel *Hae*III site is created. Thus a VNTR that normally would show a band size of 8 kb would be split it into two smaller bands (*e.g.*, 2 kb and 6 kb). These infrequent mutations do show Mendelian inheritance (passed faithfully to offspring) indicating a true genetic origin as opposed to a temporary biological artifact. In fact, they can be quite useful in contributing to the rareness of a particular profile.

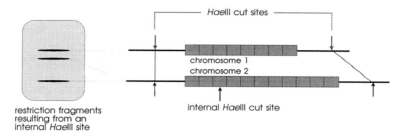

**Figure 9-2. Diagram of the molecular basis of a 3-banded pattern.**

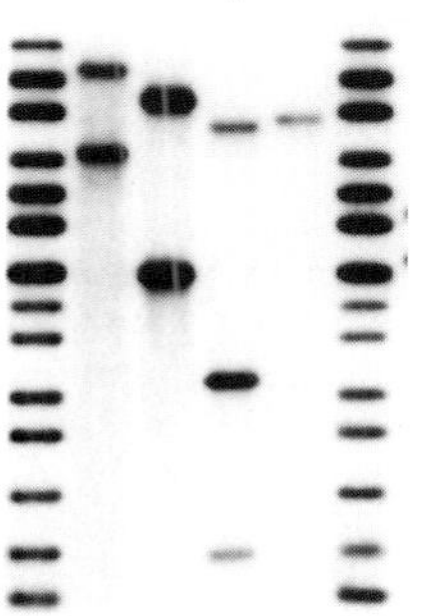

3-banded pattern

↓

**Figure 9-3. Autorad of a 3-banded pattern.** *Hae*III sites internal to a VNTR produce 3-banded patterns. They are found relatively frequently at locus D4S39. To the left is an example.

*b. Partial digestion by the restriction enzyme (partials)*

When the restriction sites along a strand of DNA are chemically blocked, or when the *Hae*III enzyme is hindered from functioning at full capacity, or is present in insufficient quantity for the amount of DNA present, some proportion of the *Hae*III sites in the genome may remain uncut (Figures 9-4, 9-5, 9-6). This means that some DNA strands will be longer than would be expected after a complete digestion. The extra length of the fragment is predictable to some extent, because the restriction sites are at fixed positions relative to the repeat sequence of interest. Thus partial digestion results in some fragments of correct size, and some slightly larger. The distance (in bp) from the sites immediately bracketing the VNTR to the next sites out in the flanking regions can be measured experimentally. The result of partial digestion is the presence of the normal bands for a DNA profile, as well as the appearance of larger DNA fragments, usually fainter in intensity than the primary (real) bands. The size of these larger fragments can be measured and compared to the predicted sizes based on the known pattern of sites progressing outward from the primary fragment. The consistent appearance of these predictable larger fragments over 2 or 3 loci is convincing evidence of partial digestion as opposed to the presence of another profile from a mixture.

Partial digestion occurs in enough forensic samples that a diagnostic test has been devised for use partway through the analysis. This is known as a "test gel", or a "restriction digest gel" (see *Chapter 7, Appendix D*). It is adequate for detecting gross failures to digest by a restriction enzyme. In the event of partial digestion, the analyst may subject the sample to additional clean-up procedures and/or adjust the reaction conditions to obtain complete digestion. It must be emphasized here that truly complete digestion almost never occurs, and that with long exposures faint partial digestion bands may often be detected   .

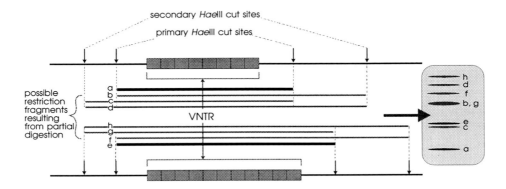

**Figure 9-4. Diagram of the molecular basis of partial digestion.**

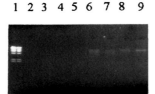

**Figure 9-5. A digest gel demonstrating incompletely digested samples.** Lane 1 contains a molecular ladder, and lane 2 is blank. Lane 3 contains a known completely digested control sample. Lanes 4 and 5 contain samples that are completely digested by the restriction enzyme as evidenced by the faintly visible, low molecular weight smears. Lanes 6 and 7 contain duplicate samples that show evidence of a substantial amount of HMW DNA, indicating incomplete digestion. Lanes 8 and 9 contain duplicate samples that both show sharp bands migrating even slightly higher than those in lanes 6 and 7. These samples are most likely completely uncut.

**Figure 9-6. An RFLP autorad demonstrating incomplete digestion.** Lanes 2 and 3 contain the undigested samples from lanes 6 and 7 in Figure 9-5, One consequence of this may be that only a faint smudge is visible at the top of the autorad or sometimes no signal at all. A more classical presentation of partially digested samples is found in lanes 5 and 6 (the samples from lanes 8 and 9 in Figure 9-5– a number of fainter bands are seen *above* the primary bands. The samples in lanes 7 and 8 (from lanes 4 and 5 in Figure 9-5) are completely digested.

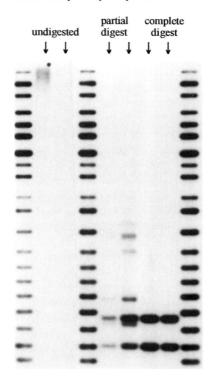

*c. Star activity*

Every enzyme requires highly specific, well-documented biochemical conditions for optimal performance. "Star activity" is the technical molecular biology term that refers to the relaxation of specificity of a restriction enzyme for the particular base sequence that defines it. For example, *Hae*III under proper conditions will cleave DNA only when it encounters the sequence **GGCC** (along with its complementary sequence **CCGG**). Under certain conditions, the enzyme will begin to recognize closely related sequences, for example, **GG*G*C**. The result of this decreased enzyme specificity is the appearance of bands smaller than the true allele (Figures 9-7, 9-8). To illustrate, let's assume the presence of a **GG*G*C** sequence internal to a VNTR locus. The enzyme would cut the normal **GGCC** sequences and additionally cut the DNA at the internal **GG*G*C** site. This would result in two bands rather than one for each allele. Each pair of star activity-generated fragments would be smaller than their primary parent band.

One of the original considerations in choosing *Hae*III for forensic work is its remarkable ability to resist "star activity". However, as experience with the enzyme has grown, star activity has, in fact, been observed under certain analytical conditions. These include conditions leading to incomplete inactivation of the enzyme after digestion, or its presence under inappropriate biochemical conditions. Star bands are sometimes even more intense than the primary bands in a profile. This may not only lead to false exclusions, but has the potential (although remote) to produce false positives as well. This is the worst possible outcome of any forensic test. Fortunately this problem is simple to both diagnose and remedy. The choice of an enzyme (*Hae*III) refractory to star activity, coupled with a protocol that avoids conditions leading to it and a diagnostic test for detecting it, serve to avoid this unwelcome prospect.

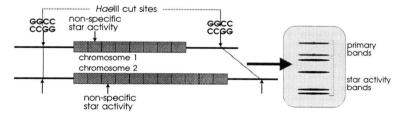

**Figure 9-7. Diagram of the molecular basis of star activity.**

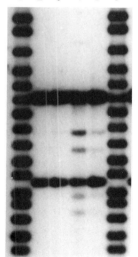

**Figure 9-8. RFLP autorad demonstrating star activity.** The samples in lanes 2 and 3 are properly digested – no evidence of extra bands is seen. The samples in lanes 3 and 4 were purposely subjected to conditions (in this case resuspending a dried DNA sample in distilled water) known to promote star activity. Extra fainter bands are seen *below* the primary bands.

*d. Incomplete stripping of probe from a previous probing*

RFLP patterns are detected by reaction with a locus-specific probe that is labeled either chemiluminescently or radioactively. At the end of the detection period, the probe is removed before the next one is applied (see *Chapter 7*). Sometimes, when the next probing in line is developed, faint bands are detected that are clearly in the same positions as those from the previous probe. This tends to be more evident with radioactive labeling. Incomplete stripping is easily diagnosed by a comparison of consecutive autorads, determining both visually and by sizing that the weak secondary bands are in the same location as those from the previous exposure.

*e. Summary of multi-banded patterns*

Multi-banded patterns may be caused by the presence of multiple donors, genetic mutation (three-banded patterns), incomplete stripping of probe from a prior hybridization, partial digestion by the restriction enzyme, or relaxed specificity of the restriction enzyme (star activity). When an analyst is attempting to differentiate between these possibilities, several tests will assist with this task. Incomplete stripping is proven by visual and sizing comparison of the current and previous autorads. Partial digestion will result in bands that are of a known increment larger than the primary bands in a profile. The persistent finding, over several loci, of bands that are predictably larger than the primary bands is sufficient to conclude that partial digestion has occurred. Star activity will result in bands of lower molecular weight than the primary profile bands. The reduction in intensity of a monomorphic (invariant) band (e.g. D7Z17), with the concomitant increase in intensity of the lower bands, is a clear indication that star activity has occurred. True genetic three-banded patterns show no evidence of partial digestion (the sizes are not consistent with partials for that locus and extra bands are not seen at other loci) and show no evidence of star activity (the monomorph has adequate intensity and there are no extra bands at other loci).

## 2. Single-banded patterns

Because the RFLP loci used in forensic DNA testing are so highly variable, most individuals inherit a different allele from each parent producing a characteristic profile of two bands. There are occasions, of course, when by chance the same allele is inherited from both parents. This offspring will show a single band on an RFLP gel at this locus, and is described as "homozygous" (an individual showing a profile of two different alleles is "heterozygous"). There are other conditions, however, that may lead to the appearance of a single band on an RFLP gel when, in fact, the individual is heterozygous. These conditions are enumerated below.

*a. Closely spaced bands*

There is a practical limit on the ability of the RFLP analytical gel to resolve two restriction fragments that are only one or a few repeat units different in length. For example, the D1S7 locus has a repeat sequence that is only 9 bp in length, yet the fragment sizes are usually in the 4 kb to 12 kb range. The analytical gel is simply not capable of discriminating between a fragment 6,200 and 6,209 bps in length. These two bands will appear as a single band giving the gross visual impression that the individual is homozygous at this locus, when, in fact, at the molecular level the person is heterozygous. Due to the physical nature of the gel, this limitation becomes more pronounced towards the top, as fragment sizes become larger and thus less well separated. This inability to detect all of the alleles in a system has given rise to the term "continuous allele system" because the boundaries between adjacent alleles are not discrete; just where one allele stops and another starts is ambiguous in the detection system. As discussed in *Chapter 8*, RFLP alleles are identified as falling into a size class as defined by externally imposed boundaries, rather than as individual alleles. It is important to emphasize that this is an artifact produced by the separation and detection technologies, not by the genetics of the organism.

### b. Bands running off the bottom of the gel

One of the criteria for selecting RFLP loci for forensic work is that the range of possible band sizes correspond to those retained by the gel during electrophoresis. The loci commonly used produce bands primarily between about 0.6 kb to 20 kb in length, but some alleles will fall outside these extremes. The larger bands generally present no problems, because they can still be seen, even if their sizes cannot be measured (see *Chapter 8*). The smaller bands, however, are much more difficult to detect. This is because they are more diffuse at the lower end of the gel, and because the smallest ones may literally (although rarely) run off the end of the gel during electrophoresis. Thus it is possible to have a profile with a detected band and an undetected band; This produces a single-banded pattern. Again, this looks like the profile of a homozygous individual when, in fact, the sample donor is heterozygous at that particular locus. Failure to detect very small alleles is also an artifact of the separation and detection technologies.

### c. Degradation

As outlined in *Chapter 3*, it is possible for DNA to be degraded to a point where an insufficient amount of DNA above a certain fragment length to produce an RFLP profile with bands in that region (Figures 9-9, 9-10, 9-11). Imagine breaking a pane of glass with a hammer. The number and size of glass fragments produced will depend on the number of blows and their intensity. One or a few blows will produce a few larger shards of approximately similar size (all of which of course are smaller than the original pane), whereas many repeated or very hard strikes will create microscopic pieces of glass (glass dust), leaving no larger pieces. Degradation of DNA (the glass pane) occurs as a result of chemical or physical damage (the hammer). The more numerous or intense the damage, the smaller the average size of the DNA becomes. When the average size becomes so small that one or both degraded ends of some of the molecules are internal to the termini defined by the restriction enzyme, the smaller fragments will be detected while the larger ones will be lost as distinct entities.

Degradation (as manifest by average fragment size) can be detected via a yield gel (*Appendix C*). This is a miniaturized version of the RFLP analytical gel where the total DNA present in an extracted sample is viewed (not just DNA from a specific locus). The average size of the DNA can be estimated by comparison to a reference ladder of molecular size standards run on the same gel. In this way an analyst can determine whether the DNA is of sufficient quality to allow a successful analysis by RFLP. If the DNA sample appears highly degraded (glass dust) or even somewhat degraded (glass shards), the analyst might elect to run a PCR system (which does not require high molecular weight (HMW) DNA), and/or temper his interpretation of RFLP results with the knowledge that some information may be missing. In particular, she would be wise not to include or exclude based on any band above the average size of the DNA. Take a situation where, due to environmental factors, the average DNA size is about 7 kb. For a heterozygous individual with an intact profile of bands at 10 kb and 4 kb, the 10 kb band will not be detected because there are no (really too few) fragments of that size, while the 4 kb band will be detected. This results in a single-banded pattern from a heterozygous individual due to an artifact inflicted by nature.

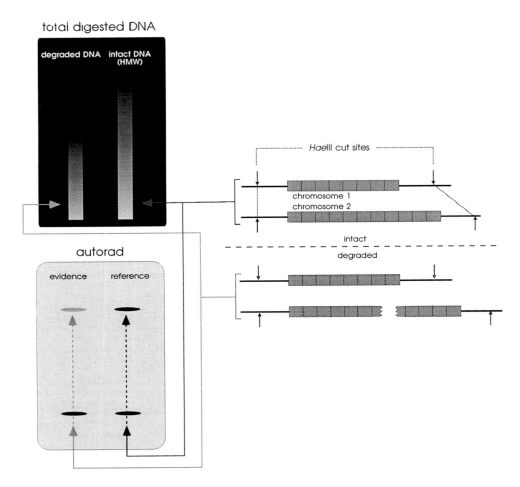

**Figure 9-9. Diagram of the molecular basis of degradation.**

1  2  3  4  5  6  7  8  9  10 11 12 13 14 15 16 17 18

**Figure 9-10. A Yield gel demonstrating degradation.** The first lane contains the molecular ladder and lanes 2 through 8, the standards and control. Lanes 9 through 18 contain DNA from DNA semen samples that have been held at 65°C for varying lengths of time. The duplicate samples in lanes 17 and 18 were heated for 1 month, and are the only samples on the gel that show any evidence of degradation. The resulting autorads are shown in Figure 9-11.

Degradation leading to single-banded patterns is normally, but not always, an issue for evidence rather than reference samples; the analyst has no control over the degradation of evidence samples prior to collection.  Reference samples, however, are normally collected specifically for genetic typing purposes, and steps should have been taken to preserve the sample by curtailing degradative processes (see *Chapter 3*).  Thus a typical situation is exemplified in a profile comparison where the reference sample shows two bands, while an evidence sample shows a single band which "matches" the lower band of the reference.  Exceptions to this general expectation might include reference samples taken from homicide victims where the body was not found immediately or that have not been collected and preserved properly by, for instance, the medical examiner.  In this sort of instance, a dried evidence stain found on a suspect's shirt, for example, might be better preserved than the reference sample from a deteriorating corpse, and the evidence would show two bands while the reference might show a single ("matching") lower band.

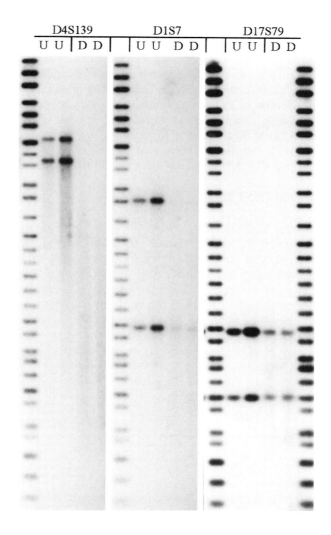

**Figure 9-11. RFLP autorads demonstrating degradation.** The same two duplicate samples were run together on a gel and the resulting membrane probed with three different probes.   Each of the three probes generally produces band sizes in different regions of the autorad.  Within each set of four, the duplicate samples on the left (from lanes 15 and 16 in Figure 9-10) were mostly undegraded, and the duplicate samples on the right (from lanes 17 and 18 in Figure 9-10) were highly degraded. At locus D4S139, the only evidence left of the degraded samples is a low molecular weight smear.  At locus D1S7, the top band in the degraded samples is completely gone, leaving an apparent single-banded pattern.   At locus D17S79, the DNA fragments left in the degraded samples are still of sufficient length to produce two clear bands. U–undegraded; D–degraded.

*d. Summary of single-banded patterns*

Four possible causes may contribute to the appearance of single-banded patterns at any RFLP locus: true homozygosity, closely-spaced bands, non-detection of one extremely small band, and degradation that destroys the larger of two alleles. In the latter three situations, a profile from a heterozygous individual appears as homozygous. The analyst in possession of this knowledge will be able to interpret the results of an analysis with the appropriate caution and scientific conservatism. The implications of single-banded patterns extend to the statistical estimation of a profile frequency, in particular the assumption of independent inheritance of the alleles. This issue is discussed in detail in *Chapter 8*.

### 3. Summary of RFLP interpretational issues

The immense diversity (the great capacity to discriminate between individuals) of these hypervariable loci that makes them so attractive for forensic work also presents analytical challenges and renders them susceptible to environmentally induced alterations. A great amount of work has been performed to determine whether these artifacts constitute fatal flaws, or merely complications that can be factored into the conclusions drawn from analytical results on a case-by-case basis. The enormous amount of validation and proficiency testing performed using RFLP systems has led to the consensus among crime labs and academic experts (with a few exceptions) that the difficulties can be adequately addressed and accounted for in most cases, and that the advantages conferred by the discrimination power of the RFLP loci can be used properly and conservatively. These analytical challenges emphasize the need for education, training and experience. The forensic scientist must draw on all these attributes to apply his best judgment to the analysis and interpretation of these special types of samples. She is required to understand the capabilities and limitations of each test, and employ that knowledge to differentiate an artifactual profile from a true profile.

### B. PCR SYSTEMS

Several methods have been devised for the detection and analysis of PCR products at specific loci. In the length-based systems, PCR products are run on a gel and read in a fashion similar to RFLP results. Other markers are based on the detection of allele-specific sequence differences, and are constructed so as to indicate that a particular sequence is either present (signal on) or absent (signal off) (Figure 9-12). This form of detection is usually in a dot or slot blot format, where each dot or slot represents one allele. Although two different alleles are often present at any particular locus, most PCR-based loci are much less polymorphic (present at a lower heterozygosity index in the population) than the hypervariable loci used in RFLP testing. Thus there is a much greater chance that the same allele will be present on both chromosomes (homozygous) than with RFLP testing.

**Figure 9-12. The "ON-OFF" signal by which reverse dot blots are interpreted.**

In the early PCR systems developed for use in forensic casework, each locus was amplified separately, followed by some form of detection. Recently, techniques have been perfected that allow for the concurrent amplification of multiple loci in one test tube (multiplexing). This expands the utility of PCR because the same amount of DNA is used to analyze three or more loci. The loci in the multiplexed sample can be analyzed simultaneously, either in the same gel lane or on the same hybridization strip. Regardless of the individual differences between systems, certain issues are common to all PCR reactions. These will be considered first followed by marker-specific issues.

## 1. General PCR considerations

### a. Mixed Samples

A sample containing DNA from two or more people creates a major concern in a PCR-based system, the possibility that all alleles initially present may not be equivalently amplified, and consequently that dot or band intensities will differ. Studies with many different marker systems have repeatedly shown that samples mixed in certain ratios will produce relatively predictable allele intensities. We also know that when the ratio of major to minor types reaches sufficient disparity, the minor type is not amplified to detectable levels. For example, samples mixed in a 1:1 ratio will show relatively equivalent allele intensities (whether detected by dot blot or electrophoretic systems). As a practical matter, when sample ratios become greater than about 1:20 to 1:50, the minor type is not detectable, and the sample does not appear as a mixture. Samples in which the types from two different sources are present in ratios closer to equivalency (about 1:20 to 1:1) will manifest the alleles from one person as more intense (darker) to some degree than the alleles from the other person. When the difference in intensity reaches a sufficiently divergent level (more than the normal variation in intensity expected with any particular system), experienced analysts may elect to call major and minor types.

### b. Amplification parameters

Each component of a PCR reaction is essential. It must be added at concentrations within predetermined limits and at the correct time for the amplification to proceed optimally. Further, the specific amplification conditions (denaturation, annealing, and extension temperatures, the length of time the reaction is held at these temperatures, and the number of amplification cycles) must be thoroughly tested during development and validation to ensure that none of the side effects outlined below occur.

### c. Preferential amplification

Preferential amplification refers to the amplification of one allele to a much greater degree than another one in the same reaction. This may result in a heterozygote (two different alleles) appearing to be a homozygote (two identical alleles). This phenomenon has also been dubbed "allelic dropout." There are several causes of preferential amplification; each will be discussed separately below.

#### i) stochastic fluctuation

With very low levels of input DNA (the DNA that is extracted from a sample and then added to the amplification reaction mixture), it is possible that the two alleles of a heterozygote will amplify unequally relative to each other during the first few rounds of PCR. This would result in the enrichment of one allele over the other at a very early stage in the process. In subsequent rounds, this situation will only be exacerbated: the enriched allele will be preferentially amplified, while the other allele will continue to lag in amplification. The end result may be detection of only one of the two alleles, leading to the erroneous conclusion that the sample comes from a homozygote rather than a heterozygote. The solution to this problem is to establish, through experimentation, a minimum amount of input DNA that will reproducibly yield a "true" result for the specific amplification conditions.

*ii*) wide variation in allele length

The *Taq* polymerse has a processivity limitation that results in shorter stretches of DNA being amplified more efficiently than longer sequences. This is of little consequence for markers based on sequence polymorphisms, such as DQα/A1 and the polymarker loci, but for PCR systems based on disparate length polymorphisms (particularly D1S80), this phenomenon must be addressed. The consequence of this processivity limitation on length polymorphisms is that under certain circumstances the longer alleles may not be consistently extended to their full length. This may result in a dearth of complete copies of the larger allele, reducing the intensity of the discrete band. The resulting  discrepancy in the comparative intensities of the bands might lead to an interpretation of the presence of a mixture or, if the band is absent altogether, reading the type as a homozygote rather than a heterozygote.

A practical solution to this problem (like many other enzymatic glitches) is the addition of a highly purified form of the enzymatically inert protein, BSA. Figure 9-19b shows the effect of BSA on normalizing the intensities of two highly disparate alleles. This type of preferential amplification is less of an issue for the STR systems. The repeat units are small and relatively few, limiting the difference in length between the smallest and largest alleles to the point where processivity of the enzyme is no longer a significant factor.

*iii*) variation in allele sequences

The nature of the chemical bonds which hold the DNA base pairs together determines that **G:C** base pairs are stronger than **A:T** base pairs, and thus require a slightly higher temperature to melt (denature) them. If one allele (of two or more present) in a PCR reaction) contains more **G:C** base pairs than average, then it may not fully denature if the denaturation temperature is a bit low. Since the amplification primers must bind to single-stranded DNA, incomplete denaturation will inhibit the primers from annealing in subsequent rounds, causing amplification of the GC-rich allele to lag (Figure 9-14). Development and validation studies have consistently indicated that one of the elements critical to the success of a PCR reaction is careful temperature control at each of the various stages.

Preferential amplification originally became an issue with the early thermal cyclers which showed some variation in the temperatures measured between wells. This resulted in incomplete denaturation of some samples prior to annealing and extension, that in turn led to the observation of preferential amplification. The solution to this problem was two-fold; the thermal cycler was both re-designed to distribute the heat more evenly between all the wells, and a protocol was developed for the calibration and testing of each instrument. In a laboratory which uses properly calibrated thermal cyclers, preferential amplification should be considered a non-issue. An additional solution that obviates this problem entirely is the careful screening and adoption of marker systems that are relatively insensitive to temperature variation. The criteria include the selection of regions exhibiting an average **GC** content, and in multiplexed systems, markers in which the base pair composition is similar between both the alternate alleles and different loci in the reaction. All of the newer PCR systems being developed for forensic use are selected to minimize the problem of preferential amplification.

*d. Heteroduplex formation*

Heteroduplex formation is the annealing of two strands of DNA that have a similar, but not exactly the same, nucleotide sequence (two perfectly complementary strands of DNA are termed homologous, and form a homoduplex). For most PCR reactions, the conditions of annealing are so stringent that this does not occur. For some very closely related sequences, however, this phenomenon can occur with some demonstrable effect on the results of the testing. Heteroduplex formation can occur when sequence polymorphisms are closely related (as in the 1.3 and 3 alleles in the DQα/A1 system) and may inhibit the amplification of a specific allele relative to another under certain conditions. In PCR-amplified fragment length polymorphisms (D1S80 and STR systems), single strands from the different alleles present in the amplification mix may mispair, giving rise to novel bands on the gel.

*e. Enzyme inhibition*

The PCR reaction relies on an enzyme (*Taq* polymerase, or one of its derivatives or cousins) for its primary function of replicating DNA. As with any enzyme, *Taq* is susceptible to difficulties in function if conditions are not optimal. The primary difficulty encountered with forensic samples is inhibition of the enzyme, a problem usually caused by the presence of some substance that has co-purified with the DNA during the extraction procedure. Three common solutions are applied to overcome inhibition of enzymatic activity. These include adding more *Taq* polymerase, reducing the amount of input DNA (effectively diluting the inhibitor), and adding the chemically inert protein BSA. Each of these methods has proven effective under various conditions; the analyst is required to use judgment and experience in deciding which may be preferred in a particular situation. The addition of BSA seems to be the most common remedy, and, in fact, some laboratories routinely add BSA to all enzyme reactions. Some amplification protocols have been validated with BSA as an integral part of the mix. The addition of an inert protein, such as BSA, to optimize enzyme reactions is a widely used method in molecular biology in general.

*f. Threshold detection control*

It is important to have some means of positively establishing whether the amplification and/or typing conditions during a particular run were sufficient to amplify and detect a predetermined minimum amount of sample. This helps in deciding whether faint or weak signals should be counted as real alleles, rather than any of the minor artifacts discussed throughout this section. Some systems (DQα/A1, polymarker) have been developed with an integral internal control that serves such a purpose. Sometimes laboratories establish and include their own threshold detection control (along with other types of controls) in other typing systems.

## 2. Sequence-based PCR marker systems

Virtually all laboratories performing forensic DNA analysis employ the commercial kits developed originally by Cetus corporation (now Roche Molecular Systems (RMS)) to type several sequence-specific loci. These markers include some of the earliest developed for forensic use, including DQα/A1 and polymarker. A similar kit to type mitochondrial markers is currently in the research and development stage. These systems are all presented in a reverse dot blot format (see *Chapter 7*), and contain all the critical materials and reagents for both the amplification and typing of samples. The types are read as a combination of "on" or "off" signals (blue dots) for each system. For the five polymarker loci, this is relatively straight forward, but for the original DQα system, and similarly for the DQA1 strip in the polymarker kit, some alleles cannot be read directly. It is important to understand both the rules which are followed to read genetic types from the strips and some of the limitations inherent in the technology. The following discussion considers system-specific examples of the general issues discussed above.

*a. DQα*

This discussion will focus on reading the original DQα typing strips. The DQA1 system available with the polymarker kit is read in a similar fashion with additional subtyping of the 4 allele. There are 6 common alleles in the DQα system; 1.1, 1.2, 1.3, 2, 3, and 4. 1, 2, 3 and 4 are termed "nominal" alleles. This system further detects variants of the 1 allele (1.1, 1.2, 1.3), termed "subtypes". All the different pairwise combination of these 6 alleles yield a total of 21 different types. Examples of heterozygous DQα types would be 1.3,2 or 3,4. Homozygotes are designated 3,3 or 1.2,1.2, for example.

One of the complicating factors inherent in this typing system is that the 1.2 allele does not have a specific probe; instead, its presence is deduced by reading a combination of probes that will react with more than one subtype. Specifically, a probe exists for the 1.1 allele, as well as a probe that reacts with the 1.3 allele. These alleles can be typed based exclusively on a positive reaction (blue dot) in the position of each of their specific probes on the strip. One of the probes has been designed to react simultaneously with the 1.2, 1.3, and 4 alleles and is labeled as such. If a sample reacts with this "trio" but not with the individual 1.1 or 1.3 probes, the 1.2 allele must then, by elimination, be present. The last difficulty to overcome is differentiating between a 1.2,1.3 and a 1.3,1.3 homozygote. This is solved by one last probe, the "All but 1.3", that reacts with every allele *except* the 1.3. Thus in a 1.2,1.3 individual, the "All but 1.3" probe will be positive, while in a 1.3 homozygote this dot will be negative.

Let's take two illustrative examples:

1) A strip showing blue dots at the nominal 1 and 4 positions must represent a sample containing some subtype of 1 and a 4 allele (Figure 9-13a). In this example, the 1.1 dot also lights up, as do the "trio" and the "All but 1.3" dots. The positive 1.1 signal indicates which 1 subtype is present. The other two dots light up superfluously due to the presence of, respectively, the 4 allele (the "trio") and both the 1.1 and 4 alleles (the "All but 1.3"). These dots are not needed to interpret this particular type. The DQα type of this sample is 1.1,4.

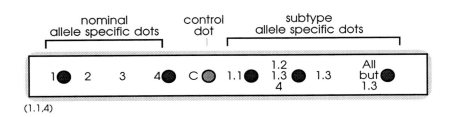

(1.1,4)

**Figure 9-13a. A DQα strip showing a type of 1.1,4.**

2) A strip showing blue dots at the nominal 1 and 3 positions must represent a sample containing some subtype of 1 and a 3 allele (Figure 9-13b). In this example, the "trio" and the "All but 1.3" dots also light up. Since no nominal 4 dot is present, we know that this is not the source of "trio" dot; the absence of a dot at the 1.3 probe indicates that the 1.3 allele is also not the source of the positive "trio" signal. Therefore, by the process of elimination, we are left with the 1.2 allele as the source of the "trio" dot. The DQα type of this individual is then 1.2,3.

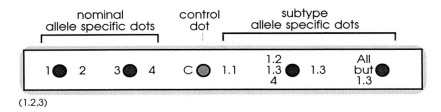

**Figure 9-13b. A DQα strip showing a type of 1.2,3.**

This typing system includes an important quality control aspect, a built-in amplification control called the "C" dot (the threshold detection control). This is a probe recognized by all of the alleles, but its sequence length and concentration are such that it is the weakest-reacting probe on the typing strip. The purpose of this control is to help the analyst determine what dots represent true alleles, and which, if any, faint or weak signals are artifactual and therefore should not be considered in interpreting the result. If the typing dots are all of greater or equal intensity to "C", the analyst can have confidence that they are genuine alleles from a contributor to the sample (assuming all of the other quality control measures are in place, such as properly calibrated thermal cyclers and correct amplification parameters). The "C" dot is also helpful as a guide in interpreting mixtures. If some dots are less than "C" as might occur in, for example a highly disparate mixture, then there is some chance that an allele has not been detected because it was present at such a low starting level that it never amplified properly. In general, if a sample is so weak that the "C" dot is not present, then the sample is considered inconclusive as to its full genotype although "alleles present" may be called.

*i*) multiple donors

Because only six alleles are detected by the DQα marker system, mixed samples often involve individuals with common alleles. Additionally, not all alleles are detected by autonomous probes, complicating the analysis. If no alleles are shared and the ratio between the amounts of the major and minor contributors is relatively large, genotypes can sometimes be identified. Specifically, mixture ratios greater than 1:5 show at least moderate differences in intensity between the major and minor contributor. The more widely disparate the ratio of the contributors, the easier it is to determine major and minor types. When it appears that more that one contributor is represented in a sample, and it is suspected that they share one or more alleles, the analyst will exercise appropriate caution in assigning genotypes and probably outline the possible genotypes that could be present to produce the result seen.

## SIDEBAR 7

### The Simpson Saga

On June 12, Nicole Brown (NB) and Ronald Goldman (RG) were brutally murdered. O.J. Simpson (OS) was charged with commission of the crime, and among the evidentiary items confiscated was his white Ford Bronco. A bloody smear on the passenger side of the center console was initially noted and sampled on June 14, 1994. At least 3 relevant forensic questions can be asked about this evidence.

1) How was the stain deposited?

2) When was the stain deposited?

3) Who may have contributed to this stain?

For the purposes of this exercise we will not attempt to address how and when the stain was deposited. We will concentrate on what the evidence can tell us about who contributed to the stain.

DNA testing was used to investigate the source(s) of the stain. Both DQα and D1S80 tests were performed on the two evidence samples collected in June 1994. From the results, it was concluded that one stain included Simpson as a donor, while excluding NB and RG. The other showed a mixture consistent with OS and RG. A larger sample was collected on September 1, 1994. It should be noted that in the intervening time period, the Bronco was burglarized. Although the items taken were themselves of no evidentiary value, the integrity of the bloodstain evidence could no longer be guaranteed. Three separate swatches were collected that more nearly covered the large area of the smear. These samples were also analyzed for DQα and D1S80. Let's examine the data from two of these swatches in detail.

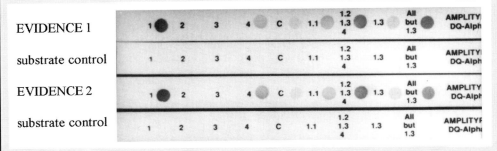

Above is a set of DQα strips showing the results from two of the later samplings, along with their substrate controls. (A substrate control is collected from an apparently clean area near an evidentiary stain. It is a way of assessing which, if any, genetic types might be present in the background.) One of the ways an analyst avoids even unconscious bias is to analyze the evidence before comparing it with the reference samples. In this case, both evidence strips show the same pattern of dots, and even the intensities are similar. In both samples, all the dots, with the exception of 2 and 3, are positive, so we can safely eliminate anyone with a 2 or 3 allele from having contributed to this sample. The next step is to note that more than two alleles are manifest. Since any normal individual has, at most, two alleles at any one genetic locus, this is a clear indication of multiple contributors.

From an examination of the nominal dots to the left of "C", we note the presence a 4 allele and a 1 allele. The 1.1 and 1.3 dots are both positive, and although the 1.3 dot is substantially lighter, both are stronger than the "C" dot. The 1.1 and 1.3 subtype, at least, are represented. Is the 1.2 allele also present?

Consider the more difficult "trio" and "all but 1.3" dots, both of which are positive and greater than "C". The "trio" dot may be positive due to the presence of the 1.2 allele, the 1.3 allele or the 4 allele individually, or any combination of them. Since we can confirm the presence of both the 4 allele and the 1.3 allele, the "trio" would be positive regardless of the presence of a 1.2 allele, and so cannot be used to determine its presence. This consequently makes the "all but 1.3" dot useless in determining, along with the "trio", the presence of a 1.2 allele. In short, from the pattern of dots on these strips, it is impossible to tell if a 1.2 allele is present in the sample or not.

At this point in the interpretation, the analyst would normally draw up a chart of alleles excluded (2, 3), those positively present (1.1, 1.3, 4), and those about which we have insufficient information to determine presence or absence (1.2). He would also list possible pairwise associations of the alleles into genotypes of the possible contributors (we will spare you this exercise). Enumeration of the types in the DQα system depends in part on compound dots which together determine a type. Because of this, the analysis of mixtures becomes a bit complex. In addition, a mixture of bloodstains is often more difficult to interpret than a sexual assault mixture, in which at least one of the contributing types (the victim's) is often known.

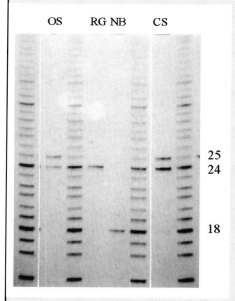

Now lets take a look at the DQα types of the three principals in this crime. OS is a 1.1,1.2, NB a 1.1,1.1 and RG, a 1.3,4. Since none of them possess a 2 or 3 allele, none are excluded on that basis from having contributed to the samples.

Both these samples were also analyzed using the D1S80 system. The advantage of D1S80 is that the interpretation of alleles present is straight forward – there are no hidden alleles. The disadvantage is that two D1S80 alleles, 18 and 24, are quite common in the population. The D1S80 results from both swatches showed bands at 18, 24 and 25. (One of them is shown below as CS). This is, again, clearly indicative of a mixture. Can genotypes be assigned? It depends on what can be assumed. If it can be assumed that there are only two donors then clearly the 24 and 25 alleles are present as a genotype based on the similar intensities of the bands as compared to the 18 band. If two or more donors are assumed, then the alleles cannot be paired into genotypes with confidence. No information is gleaned from either the DQα or D1S80 results that supports one assumption over the other.

The final interpretation might be summarized as follows:

1. More than one individual contributed to the blood samples collected from the console of the Bronco.

2. All individuals carrying the 2 and 3 DQα alleles are eliminated as contributors to the detected DNA. All others are included as possible donors.

3. Individuals included in the evaluation in step #2 are eliminated if they do not have some combination of the D1S80 18, 24, and/or 25 alleles. The remainder are included as possible donors.

The genotypes of the three reference samples each contain some combination of the DQα 1.1, 1.2, 1.3, and/or 4 alleles. Each also contains at least one of D1S80 18, 24, and/or 25 alleles. Thus none of the three principles are eliminated as possible contributors to this sample.

Another way of evaluating the results would be to examine combinations of types from the reference samples to see if any combination could produce the pattern seen in the evidence stain. The Bronco console stain(s) cannot be just a mix of NB and OS, they both lack the DQα 1.3 and 4 alleles. All other combinations are possible (NB/RG; OS/RG; NB/OS/RG). Similarly, the stain(s) cannot be a mix of only OS and RG; neither carry the D1S80 18 allele. The stain(s) also cannot be a mix of only NB and RG; neither has the D1S80 25 allele. Other combinations cannot be eliminated (NB/OS; NB/OS/RG).

Thus all pairwise combinations of the reference genotypes are eliminated by the results from either one or the other marker system. Only a mixture of all three could account for the evidentiary pattern. Therefore the stain was either contributed by a mixture of all three principles, or by 2 or more unknown individuals.

*ii*) cross-hybridization

A common occurrence noted with the DQα typing system is the appearance of weak positive signals in the 1 subtyping dots with single source samples such as reference bloods. These are usually so much less intense than the "C" dot that they are barely visible. This results from the 1 subtypes being so close in sequence that some cross-reaction occurs between, for example, amplified 1.2 product and the 1.3 typing probe on the strip. In this case, the "trio" dot will be strongly positive, while the 1.3 dot will show only a slight blue color. This is minimized (though not always completely eliminated) by calibrating the water bath used to develop the typing strips and maintaining it at the recommended temperature for typing. Some analysts will stop the development of the color (which occurs over a time period) earlier than normal to avoid development of these "cross–hybe" dots. The weak nature of these artifactual dots, and their predictable appearance with certain 1 subtypes makes this an annoying but rarely substantive problem in typing evidence samples.

*iii*) preferential amplification

Preferential amplification in the DQα/A1 system has been seen when all of the wells of the thermal cycler do not reach the same temperature and in certain mixtures where heteroduplex DNA is formed. In the early *TC* version of the Thermal Cycler from Perkin Elmer, some of the wells at the outer edges of the unit did not always reach the same temperature as the inner wells during the denaturing cycle. Thus the DNA in the tubes in those wells would fail to denature completely, particularly if it had a slightly higher GC content than average (see *Section IV*). If the DNA was still in a double-stranded form, the PCR primers would have no place to bind, and amplification of this particular allele would be inhibited. This resulted in some heterozygote samples that were erroneously typed as homozygotes (Figure 9-14). Once this problem was recognized, it was solved with a re-designed temperature block and a protocol for calibrating each well of the instrument. Since these early occurrences, there has been no reported problem with preferential amplification due to unequal well temperatures.

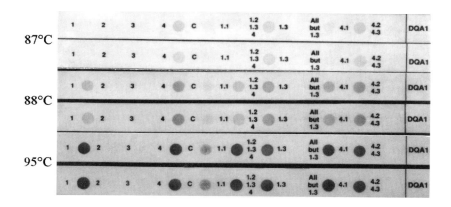

**Figure 9-14. Preferential amplification of DQA1.** The DQA1 genotype of all the samples shown above is known to be a 1.1,4.1. When the denaturation step during amplification is performed at 95°C, as specified in the manufacturer's protocol, all dots are of equal intensity. At 88°C, every dot is somewhat less intense because all the DNA is incompletely denatured The 1.1 allele (which has a greater GC content) is affected to a greater degree relative to the 4.1 allele. At 87°C, all dots are yet lighter and the 1.1 allele has completely disappeared, giving the false impression that the type is a 4.1 homozygote.

Preferential amplification due to heteroduplex formation in the DQα system requires a complex set of circumstances. These are a mixed sample, where one allele of the major type is close in sequence to one allele of the minor type combined with sample ratios in the zone of about 1:3 to 1:5 of the two contributing DNA profiles. During the latter stages of amplification under these conditions, the DNA strands present in relatively high concentration from the major allele may form a heteroduplex with the nearly homologous minor allele, preventing the primers from annealing to it. In this situation amplification of this minor allele, but not its heterozygous partner, will be inhibited. The result is an imbalance in the intensities of alleles from a single genotype. Under the worst circumstances, the two alleles will fall on either side of the "C" dot (that is, one will be greater than C, while the other will be less than C), creating confusion with regard to calling the genotypes for the minor contributor to the sample.

# SIDEBAR 8

## The Case of the Disappearing Sperm
## (or, whose type is it anyway?)

Sometime in 1992, a young woman was accosted by a man as she was getting into her car in a mall parking lot. She was sexually molested, but vaginal penetration was not even attempted. Instead, her assailant forced her to perform oral sex, and ejaculated in her mouth. The victim spit the ejaculate into a piece of facial tissue, which was subsequently recovered as evidence. The suspect quickly got out of the car and disappeared. To date, no suspects have been apprehended.

A microscopic analysis of the tissue sample revealed surprisingly few sperm. A few epithelial cells (e. cells) were noted, presumably from the inside of the victim's mouth. The samples were typed using the DQα marker system, the only PCR test validated for forensic use at that time. Unfortunately, the victims reference (not shown), the e. cell fraction (strip 1) and the sperm cell fraction (strip 3) all showed the same type, a 1.2,3 (see below). Was the assailant's type actually 1.2,3 or was the type in the sperm fraction due to leakage of e. cells into the sperm fraction? This interpretational challenge is always a possibility in instances of low sperm levels, particularly when a relatively large number of e. cells are present. In this case, the large number of e. cells were not viewed microscopically, but were evidenced by the initial α-amylase assay. The e. cells might have been missed visually because their cell membranes had already burst, leaving no visible cells, but plenty of DNA. Sperm are much more hardy and tend to survive even harsh conditions intact. Even though the sperm fraction is well-washed during separation, trace amounts of a large initial proportion of e. cell DNA might still remain. With very little sperm DNA present, one must consider both the possibility that the 1.2,3 DQα type represents the sperm contribution, or alternatively, that it is solely due to leakage from the victim's e. cells.

| | 1 | 2 | 3 | 4 | C | 1.1 | 1.2 1.3 4 | 1.3 | All but 1.3 | AMPLITYPE™ DQ-Alpha |
|---|---|---|---|---|---|---|---|---|---|---|
| e. cell fraction | ● | | ● | | | | | | ● | |
| negative control | | | | | | | | | | |
| sperm fraction | ● | | ● | | | | | | ● | |

In this case, it was decided that no conclusion could be drawn from the test results.

*b. Polymarker*

The AmpliType® PM kit, more commonly referred to as polymarker, extends the concept of the DQα sequence-specific marker by combining five additional marker systems, with 2 or 3 common alleles each, into a single amplification and typing protocol. In the most recent version, the DQA1 typing system replaces DQα, such that the 4 allele subtypes may be detected. Thus the same amount of input DNA (2 ng, for example) can be used to obtain information from multiple marker systems. The polymarker equivalent to the DQα "C" dot is the "S" dot. This is a threshold control that signals a successful amplification and typing procedure. Dot intensities above the "S" dot are considered positive, those below are considered inconclusive for calling full genotypes. If the "S" dot is not present, full genotypes may not be represented.

*i)* multiple donors

Because of the many primer sets and probes involved in the polymarker system, amplification and typing conditions (especially temperatures) are crucial in obtaining consistent results. For example, if the temperature of the water bath used to type the samples varies by less than a degree, the dot intensities within a locus will begin to change relative to each other. The LDLR (low density lipoprotein receptor) locus is particularly sensitive to temperature variation. This makes the interpretation of major and minor types in mixtures even more difficult than with a single-locus sequence variant system, such as DQα. Additionally, since each of the five additional loci in polymarker is only biallelic or triallelic, the likelihood of allele sharing between two individuals is concomitantly higher. All of these reasons contribute to a more challenging interpretation of mixtures in samples typed with the polymarker system (Figure 9-15). There is some discrepancy in the field as to the willingness of different analysts to call composite genotypes rather than single alleles from a polymarker typing that shows evidence of multiple contributors. As in DQα, an influential factor is the perceived ratios of the two putative donor profiles; the more disparate, the more confidence an analyst can have in assigning alleles to a genotype. When the mixed sample is from a sexual assault situation, where one of the donors (hence pairs of alleles) is reliably known, it may be more reasonable to combine the remaining alleles into a donor profile.

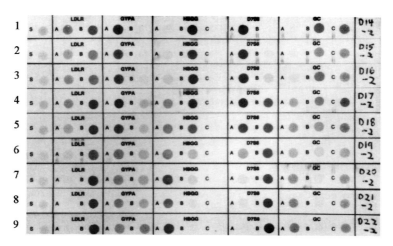

**Figure 9-15. Polymarker strips demonstrating a mixture study.** Two individual samples were typed separately (strips 1 and 9) and mixed in increasingly similar proportions, as shown in the figure, until a 50:50 mixture was reached (strip 5). These types of experiments help to establish at what proportion of a sample a minor type will become detectable.

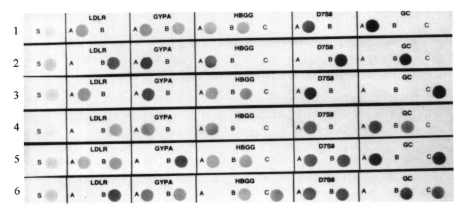

**Figure 9-16. Polymarker analysis.** Above are six typing strips, each from a different individual. The samples are from a previously adjudicated case. All the DNA samples in this demonstration run were moderately degraded. The homozygote dots are generally darker than the heterozygote dots. There is also a general trend, within each strip, of increasing intensity from left to right when comparing only homozygotes or only heterozygotes.

*ii*) degradation

The amplified regions of the polymarker loci were designed to be both relatively small and similar in length to each other. Even so, highly degraded samples will still show a gradient in dot intensities across the strip such that markers on the left of the typing strip will appear less intense than the markers on the right (Figure 9-16). The bands observed in a product gel (*Appendix E*) from the same amplification will mirror this degradation gradient, such that the higher bands will be less intense than the lower bands. Used in this way, the product gel can aid the analyst in interpreting the results. As always, caution is urged when drawing a conclusion from results which clearly approach the practical limits of a typing system.

**3. Length-based PCR marker systems**

Length-based PCR markers are similar to RFLP systems in that the polymorphism is conferred by the number of repeat units of a core sequence. D1S80 is one PCR-based VNTR locus developed for forensic use; the number of possible alleles at the D1S80 locus approaches the hypervariability of the RFLP loci. The STR loci (they are not considered VNTRs) developed for forensic use have a core repeat sequence of either three or four bases, and have far fewer repeats. While there is less variation at any one locus, their power lies in the ability to combine them (multiplexing). It is with STRs that the greatest advances have been made in DNA typing, both in approaching the discrimination capabilities of the RFLP loci and in automating the process.

*a. D1S80*

The D1S80 core repeat sequence is 16 bp in length, and most alleles contain between 14 and 41 repeat units. The type is called from the number of repeat units. For example, an individual with alleles containing, respectively, 18 repeats and 24 repeats would be called an "18,24". As with most VNTRs, there is some degeneracy within the repeat unit sequence. This means that some repeat units embody slight variations in base pair composition. This sequence degeneracy has little or no effect on the length of the allele and is not detected in the type of analysis used. Amplified D1S80 product is analyzed by electrophoresis on an acrylamide gel, where the alleles containing different numbers of repeat units can be separated completely from one another. The type is determined by comparison to a standard containing many alleles, commonly referred to as an allelic ladder  A D1S80 allelic ladder is commercially available and contains a representative of each allele from 14 through 41, except for 15, which is quite rare in most populations. Occasionally, alleles greater than 41 are encountered (Figure 9-17). Since the allelic ladder doesn't contain any standards for comparison above 41, the exact allele cannot be determined in this system, and they are classed together as ">41" (read "greater than 41"). Two D1S80 alleles are very common, namely 18 and 24 (see Figure 9-18). The other alleles are fairly evenly distributed in the population.

D1S80 is a discrete allele system for the variation detected, namely the number of repeat units. Sequence-based subtypes are certainly present due to the degeneracy of the repeat units but these are not considered in the analysis of this system. It should be noted that this is not unique to D1S80; RFLP alleles certainly contain sequence variants that are not detected. Even in conventional protein typing systems, the tests were constructed to detect a certain set of polymorphisms with the knowledge that further variation (subtypes) was most likely present and not considered.

*i*) preferential amplification of shorter alleles

The wide variation in allele sizes makes D1S80 particularly susceptible to preferential amplification. Figure 9-19 shows a study in which increasingly smaller amounts of sample containing two alleles of very different length have been amplified. In all instances, the larger allele (top band) is much weaker in intensity than the lower allele (Figure 9-19a). This becomes particularly pronounced at 30 ng of input DNA, which is albeit a ridiculously large amount of sample to use for a PCR test. However, a case sample exhibiting this phenomenon could, based on the intensity differences, be easily misinterpreted as a mixture. This limitation is overcome by addition of the apparently ubiquitous fix for all enzyme reactions, BSA to the amplification cocktail. Figure 9-19b shows the same samples after amplification with BSA; the intensities of the bands are much more balanced.

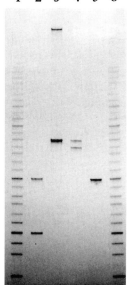

**Figure 9-17. D1S80 gel showing a ">41" allele.** Lane 3 contains a sample with an allele greater than the top band (41) of the allelic ladders (lanes 1, 6).

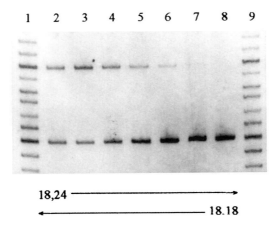

**Figure 9-18. D1S80 silver-stained gel demonstrating a mixture.** DNA from two individuals with D1S80 types of, respectively, 18,24 (lane 2) and 18,18, (lane 8), were mixed in increasingly similar concentrations, as shown in the figure. Lane 4 contains an equal mixture of both types. Obviously caution and experience is required in interpreting the results of D1S80 typing–because of the intensity differences conferred on the bands by the proportions of the two alleles present in the mixture (three 18s and one 24), this sample could be mistaken for a degraded sample from a single individual. The top half of the photo, containing the rest of the ladder bands, has been cropped for this illustration.

*ii*) degradation

Another consequence of the wide range in D1S80 allele sizes is the potential for misinterpretation of typing results from degraded DNA. As in RFLP, degradation might result in the loss of a larger allele while leaving a smaller one intact Consequently, a heterozygote might appear to be a homozygote.

*iii*) heteroduplex formation

The inhibition of amplification *per se* by heteroduplex formation is not a concern for D1S80. However, heteroduplex formation may produce artifactual bands due to molecular interactions which occur in an already amplified sample (Figure 9-20). Single strands from the different alleles present in the amplification mix may mispair giving rise to novel bands on the gel. This phenomenon is generally seen only with too much input DNA and is manifest as two bands (one for each complementary strand mismatch) (see Figure 9-20). Even when present, the heteroduplex bands are so far out of the size range of normal alleles that they can be immediately recognized and excluded.

*iv*) shadow bands

Occasionally, D1S80 allelic bands are correlated with secondary weaker bands just below the primary bands. These "shadow bands" are not well understood, but have been variously explained as enzyme slippage during amplification and/or gel conditions during electrophoresis. Shadow bands rarely pose a problem in typing, as they are easily identified as artifacts.

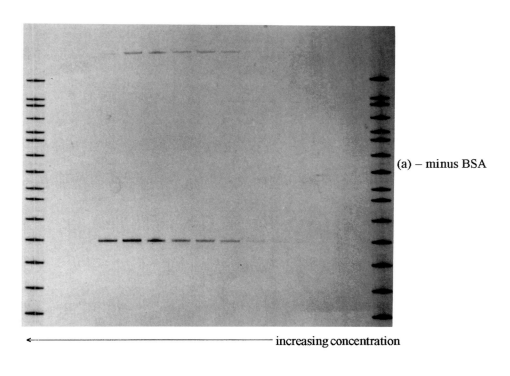

(a) – minus BSA

← ———————————————————— increasing concentration

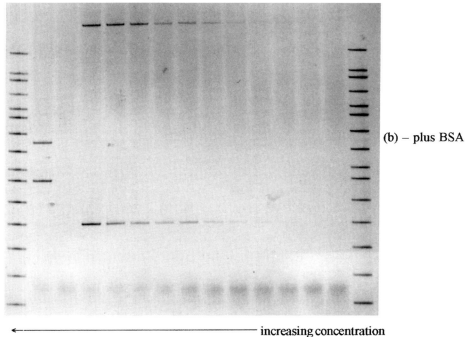

(b) – plus BSA

← ———————————————————— increasing concentration

**Figure 9-19. D1S80 silver-stained gel demonstrating preferential amplification.** A DNA sample containing alleles of disparate length was run in increasing concentration from left to right on the gels. It is clear that in Panel (a), without BSA, that particularly at higher concentrations, the smaller allele is preferentially amplified. Addition of the universal remedy, BSA, returns the band intensities to an equal level.

1  2  3  4  5  6  7  8  9  10

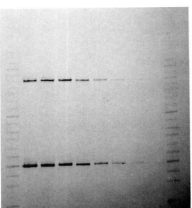

**Figure 9-20. A D1S80 silver-stained gel demonstrating heteroduplex formation after amplification.** Lanes 2 to 9 contain the same sample in decreasing concentration from left to right. Particularly in the more concentrated samples, two extra diffuse bands (indicated by arrows) are seen high above the range of the allelic ladder. These are due to mismatched heteroduplex fragments formed between single strands of the different alleles. A large portion of the middle part of the gel has been cropped for the purpose of this illustration.

*b. STRs*
Several overlapping strategies have been developed for amplifying and detecting STR markers, including multiplexing three or four markers in the same amplification tube, tagging the PCR primers with fluorescent labels, and the use of alternative detection technologies. Some interpretational issues are inherent in the STR marker system, while others are detection-specific.

*i*) doublets
In order to achieve the high resolution necessary for the separation of STR alleles, it is required to both separate (denature) the single DNA strands in the sample and to employ a denaturing gel system that prevents them from reannealing during electrophoresis. Because the complementary strands of each fragment have different nucleotide compositions, they migrate slightly differently on the high resolution gels employed in this system. Consequently, the smaller alleles are reproducibly resolved as doublets (Figure 9-21). When the gel is stained to detect the bands *after* electrophoresis (with silver or a fluorescent dye), both doublet strands of a single allele are stained equally. Because this phenomenon is completely understood, reproducible, and applies equally to samples and allelic ladders, it does not constitute an interpretational issue.

However, an advantage inherent in the automated detection systems using fluorescent PCR primers is that only one of the two DNA strands is labeled, and thus the other, although present, is invisible. Although primarily an aesthetic consideration, the presence of only one band per allele is easier for non-scientists (such as the jury) to comprehend.

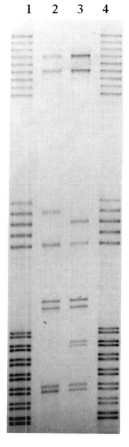

**Figure 9-21. An STR silver-stained gel demonstrating doublets.** The alleles falling in the bottom third of the gel are resolved as doublets. The sample and ladders can be directly compared.

*ii*) stutter

Stutter refers to the observed phenomenon of a minor band appearing one repeat unit larger or smaller than the primary STR band (Figure 9-22). Some STR loci are more prone to this occurrence than others, (this appears to be sequence related), and there tends to be a greater percentage of stutter in alleles with a greater number of repeats (i.e., a ten repeat allele shows more stutter than a three repeat allele at the same locus). A conclusive mechanism for this phenomenon has not yet been determined.

Stutter becomes an issue particularly in putative mixed samples, where a decision must be made as to whether a band is due to stutter (and therefore an artifact), or if it is a true allele from another DNA source. The threshold for stutter in forensic systems is generally about 5% to 15% of the primary band. In other words, any band or peak immediately adjacent to a primary allele that is less than 15% is interpreted as stutter; any band or peak comprising more that 15% of the primary allele may be interpreted as a true allele (depending, of course, on the specifics of the case).

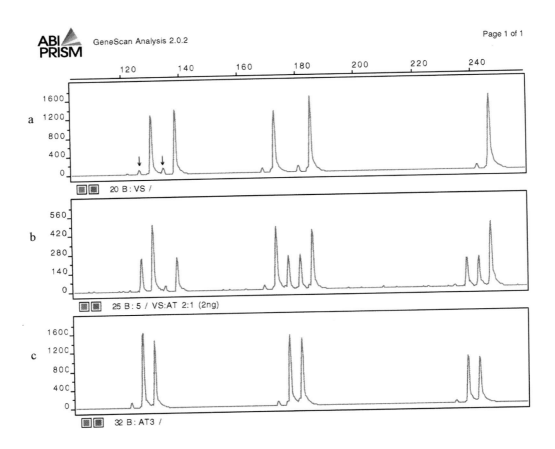

**Figure 9-22. STR printout of peaks demonstrating a mixture and stutter.** Each panel represents a DNA sample that has been amplified at three different loci (multiplexed) and run and detected on the Applied Biosystems (ABD) automated sequencer. Panels (a) and (c) each represent one individual, and Panel (b) contains a 2a:1c mix of the two. Notice that even in the lanes containing DNA from one individual, small peaks are present just before each main one (arrows). This is an example of stutter. Even in the mixed sample, however, the stutter doesn't interfere with discerning the types present in the sample. The peaks representing true alleles are clearly distinguishable. The peak heights representing the alleles belonging to each individual are proportional to their concentration in the mixture.

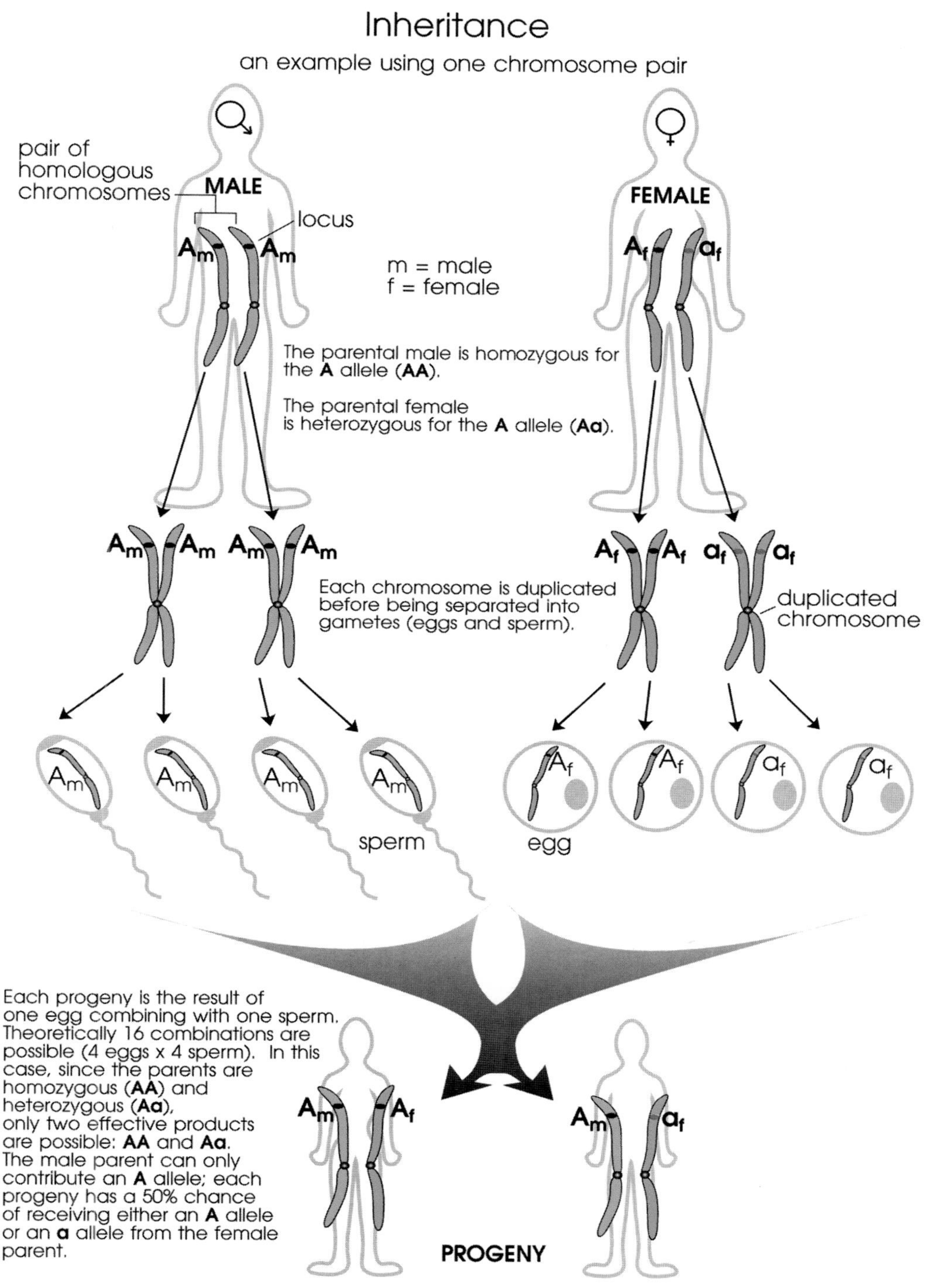

# Inheritance

## an example using one chromosome pair

**Plate 1.** Inheritance.

# The DNA Double Helix

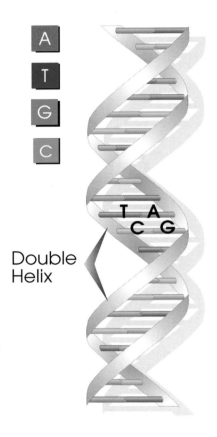

Double
Helix

**Plate 2.**  The DNA Helix.

# Length Polymorphisms

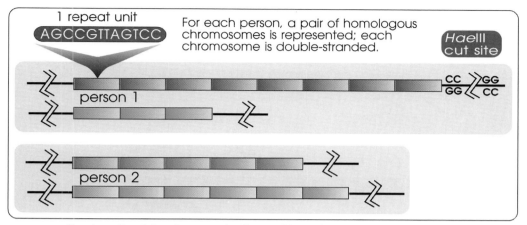

1 repeat unit

AGCCGTTAGTCC

For each person, a pair of homologous chromosomes is represented; each chromosome is double-stranded.

HaeIII cut site

$\begin{matrix} CC \\ GG \end{matrix}$ $\begin{matrix} GG \\ CC \end{matrix}$

person 1

person 2

The length of the fragment after cutting with HaeIII is determined by the number of repeat units at the locus.

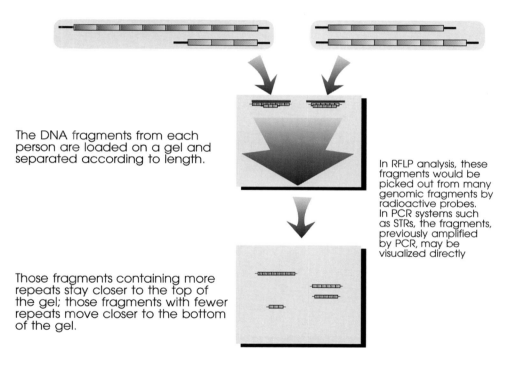

The DNA fragments from each person are loaded on a gel and separated according to length.

In RFLP analysis, these fragments would be picked out from many genomic fragments by radioactive probes. In PCR systems such as STRs, the fragments, previously amplified by PCR, may be visualized directly

Those fragments containing more repeats stay closer to the top of the gel; those fragments with fewer repeats move closer to the bottom of the gel.

**Plate 3.**   Length Polymorphisms.

# PCR Amplification - round 1

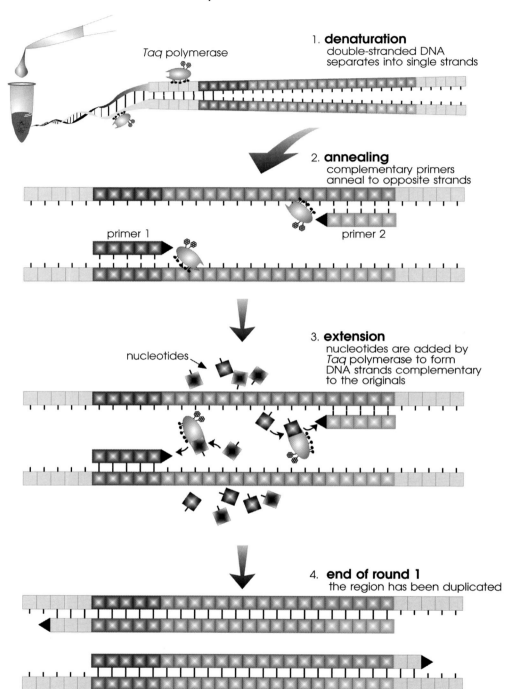

**Plate 4.** PCR - round 1.

# PCR Amplification - round 2

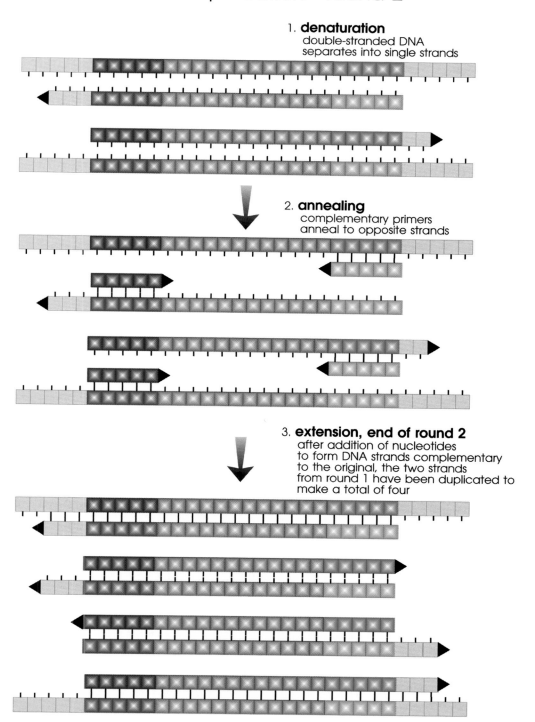

**1. denaturation**
double-stranded DNA
separates into single strands

**2. annealing**
complementary primers
anneal to opposite strands

**3. extension, end of round 2**
after addition of nucleotides
to form DNA strands complementary
to the original, the two strands
from round 1 have been duplicated to
make a total of four

**Plate 5.** PCR - round 2.

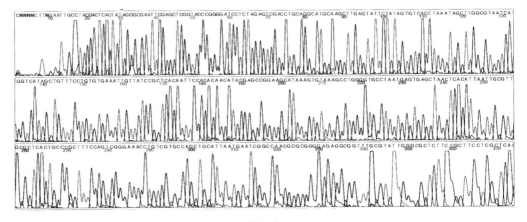

**Plate 6a**

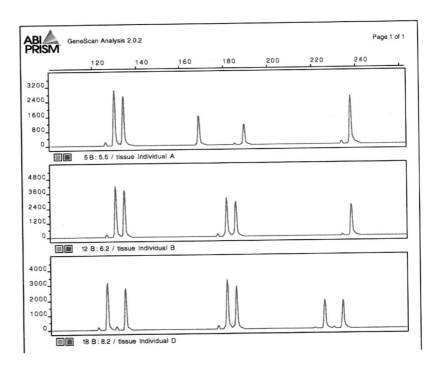

**Plate 6b**

**Plate 6a.  Automated DNA sequencing.**  An example of DNA sequencing on the Perkin Elmer Applied Biosystems Division (ABD) automated sequencer.  Detection of DNA sequencing products occurs during electrophoresis as each fluorescently tagged fragment passes a fixed laser beam.  Each of the four DNA bases is represented by a different color. The computer software calls the order of bases and prints each one above the corresponding peak of the histogram.  The DNA sequence is read from left to right starting in the upper left hand corner.  This is the type of result obtained from mitochondrial sequencing.

**Plate 6b.  Histogram of STR profiles.**  Lanes 5, 12, and 18 from the STR gel in Plate 8b depicted as histograms.  Each lane of the gel is viewed as a separate panel.  The bands appear as peaks along the time axis at the top of the figure.  The computer software makes it possible for any of the lanes to be displayed adjacent to any other, even if they are located on opposite sides of the gel.  This facilitates a direct visual comparison of any two fragments.

# STRs and GENDER ID

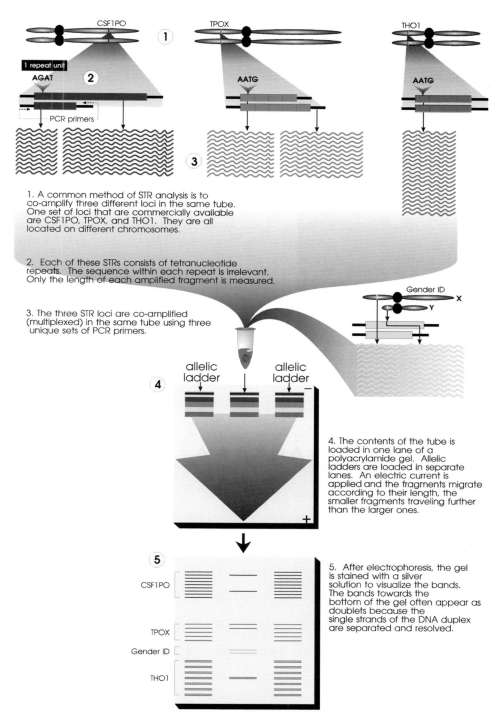

1 repeat unit
AGAT
PCR primers

1. A common method of STR analysis is to co-amplify three different loci in the same tube. One set of loci that are commercially available are CSF1PO, TPOX, and THO1. They are all located on different chromosomes.

2. Each of these STRs consists of tetranucleotide repeats. The sequence within each repeat is irrelevant. Only the length of each amplified fragment is measured.

3. The three STR loci are co-amplified (multiplexed) in the same tube using three unique sets of PCR primers.

allelic ladder    allelic ladder

4. The contents of the tube is loaded in one lane of a polyacrylamide gel. Allelic ladders are loaded in separate lanes. An electric current is applied and the fragments migrate according to their length, the smaller fragments traveling further than the larger ones.

5. After electrophoresis, the gel is stained with a silver solution to visualize the bands. The bands towards the bottom of the gel often appear as doublets because the single strands of the DNA duplex are separated and resolved.

CSF1PO
TPOX
Gender ID
THO1

**Plate 7.** **Diagram of the main steps in STR analysis with Gender ID.** PCR amplification, gel electrophoresis, and manual detection by silver staining of an STR triplex with gender ID (amelogenin). The same general process may be used for any amplified fragment length polymorphism including D1S80.

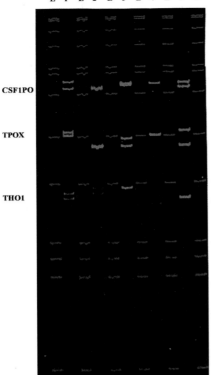

**Plate 8a**

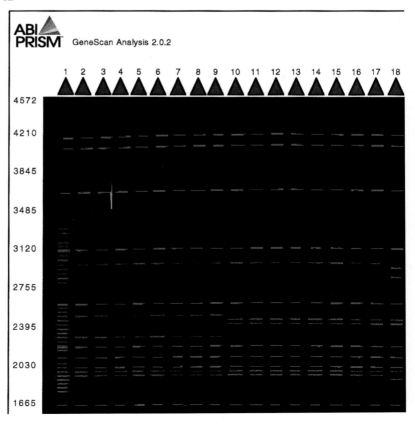

**Plate 8a. STR analysis on the Hitachi FMBIO 100.** An example of the STR Triplex CTT (CSF1PO, TPOX and THO1) analyzed on the Hitachi FMBIO 100 fluorescent scanner. Each of the five lanes where green bands are present contains an amplified sample from a different individual. The lanes with red bands contain molecular ladders used to size the amplified fragments. Fluorescently tagged PCR product fragments are detected after electrophoresis using a scanning laser.

**Plate 8b. STR analysis on the Perkin Elmer ABD automated sequencer with GeneScan software.** The loci amplified are an STR Triplex known as "AmpFlSTR Blue." Lane 1 contains both an allelic ladder (blue bands) and a molecular ladder (red bands). The remaining lanes contain amplified samples (blue bands) and the molecular ladder (red bands). Detection of PCR product fragments occurs during electrophoresis as fluorescently tagged fragments pass a fixed laser beam. Sizing with an in-lane ladder corrects for any electrophoretic inconsistencies and provides extremely precise estimates of fragment length. Histgrams of lanes 5, 12, and 18 are shown in Plate 6b.

**Plate 8b**

## ——— *FURTHER REFERENCES*———

**Akane, A., Matsubara, K., Nakamura, H., Takahashi, S., Kimura, K.,** Identification of the heme compound copurified with deoxyribonucleic acid (DNA) from bloodstains, a major inhibitor of polymerase chain reaction (PCR) amplification, *Journal of Forensic Sciences*, 39, 2, 362-72, 1994.

AmpliType User Guide for the HLA DQα Forensic DNA Amplification and Typing Kit, 1990, Section - Interpretation, Cetus Corporation, Emeryville, California.

**Baechtel, F.S., Presley, K.W., Smerick, J.B.,** D1S80 typing of DNA from simulated forensic specimens, *Journal of Forensic Sciences*, 40, 4, 536-45, 1995.

**Barnett, P.D., Blake, E.T., Super-Mihalovich, J., Harmor, G., Rawlinson, L., Wraxall, B.,** Discussion of "Effects of presumptive test reagents on the ability to obtain restriction fragment length polymorphism (RFLP) patterns from human blood and semen stains", *Journal of Forensic Sciences*, 37, 2, 69-70, 1992.

**Comey, C.T., Budowle, B., Adams, D.E., Baumstark, A.L., Lindsey, J.A., Presley, L.A.,** PCR amplification and typing of the HLA DQ alpha gene in forensic samples. *Journal of Forensic Sciences*, 38(2), 239-49, 1993.

**Cosso, S., Reynolds, R.,** Validation of the AmpliFLP D1S80 PCR Amplification Kit for forensic casework analysis according to TWGDAM guidelines, *Journal of Forensic Sciences*, 40, 3, 424-34, 1995.

**Cotton, R.W., Forman, L., Word, C.J.,** Research on DNA typing validated in the literature, *American Journal of Human Genetics*, 49, 4, 898-903, 1991.

**Crouse, C.A., Schumm, J.,** Investigation of species specificity using nine PCR-based human STR systems, *Journal of Forensic Sciences*, 40, 6, 952-6, 1995.

**Culliford, B.J.,** *The Examination and Typing of Blood Stains in the Crime Laboratory.* Washington, D.C., 1971.

**Duewer, D.L., Currie, L.A., Reeder, D.J., Leigh, S.D., Liu, H.K., Mudd, J.L.,** Interlaboratory comparison of autoradiographic DNA profiling measurements, 2, Measurement uncertainty and its propagation, *Analytical Chemistry*, 67, 7, 1220-31, 1995.

**Fildes, N., Reynolds, R.,** Consistency and reproducibility of AmpliType PM results between seven laboratories: field trial results, *Journal of Forensic Sciences*, 40, 2, 279-86, 1995.

**Hochmeister, M.N., Budowle, B., Borer, U.V., Dirnhofer, R.,** Effects of nonoxinol-9 on the ability to obtain DNA profiles from postcoital vaginal swabs, *Journal of Forensic Sciences*, 38, 2, 442-7, 1993.

**Kimpton, C., Gill, P., D'Aloja, E., Andersen, J.F., Bar, W., Holgersson, S., Jacobsen, S., Johnsson, V., Kloosterman, A. D., Lareu, M. V.,** *et al.,* Report on the second EDNAP collaborative STR exercise, European DNA Profiling Group, *Forensic Science International*, 71, 2, 137-52, 1995.

**Laber, T.L., Giese, S.A., Iverson, J.T., Liberty, J.A.,** Validation studies on the forensic analysis of restriction fragment length polymorphism (RFLP) on LE agarose gels without ethidium bromide: effects of contaminants, sunlight, and the electrophoresis of varying quantities of deoxyribonucleic acid (DNA), *Journal of Forensic Sciences*, 39, 3, 707-30, 1994.

**McNally, L., Shaler, R.C., Giusti, A.,** *et al.,* The effects of environment and substrata on deoxyribonucleic acid (DNA) isolated from human bloodstains exposed to ultraviolet light, heat, humidity, and soil contamination. *Journal of Forensic Sciences*, 32, 5, 1070-1077, 1989.

**Presley, L.A., Baumstark, A.L., Dixon A.,** The effects of specific latent fingerprint and questioned document examinations on the amplification and typing of the HLA DQ alpha gene region in forensic casework. *Journal of Forensic Sciences*, 38(5), 1028-36, 1993.

**Roy, R., Reynolds, R.,** AmpliType PM and HLA DQ alpha typing from pap smear, semen smear, and postcoital slides, *Journal of Forensic Sciences*, 40, 2, 266-9, 1995.

Schneider, P.M. Fimmers, R., Woodroffe, S., Werrett, D.J., Bar, W., Brinkmann, B., Eriksen, B., Jones, S., Kloosterman, A.D., Mevag, B., *et al.*, Report of a European collaborative exercise comparing DNA typing results using a single locus VNTR probe, *Forensic Science International*, 49, 1, 1-15, 1991.

Schwartz, T.R., Schwartz, E.A., Mieszerski, L., McNally, L., Kobilinsky, L., Characterization of deoxyribonucleic acid (DNA) obtained from teeth subjected to various environmental conditions, *Journal of Forensic Sciences*, 36, 4, 979-90, 1991.

Shipp, E., Roelofs, R., Togneri, E., Wright, R., Atkinson, D., Henry B., Effects of argon laser light, alternate source light, and cyanoacrylate fuming on DNA typing of human bloodstains, *Journal of Forensic Sciences*, 38, 1, 184-91, 1993.

Thomson, W.C., Ford, S., The meaning of a match: Sources of ambiguity in the interpretation of DNA prints. In: Farley M, Harrington, J., eds. *Forensic DNA technology*. Chelsea MI; Lewis Publishers. 1991.

Walsh, D.J., Corey, A.C., Cotton, R.W., Forman, L., Herrin, G.L. Jr., Word, C.J., Garner, D.D., Isolation of deoxyribonucleic acid (DNA) from saliva and forensic science samples containing saliva, *Journal of Forensic Sciences*, 37, 2, 387-95, 1992.

Waye, J.S., Fourney, R.M., Agarose gel electrophoresis of linear genomic DNA in the presence of ethidium bromide: band shifting and implications for forensic identity testing, Applied and Theoretical Electrophoresis, 1, 4, 193-6, 1990.

Waye, J.S., Michaud, D. Bowen, J.H. Fourney, R.M., Sensitive and specific quantification of human genomic deoxyribonucleic acid (DNA) in forensic science specimens: casework examples, *Journal of Forensic Sciences*, 36, 4, 1198-203, 1991.

Webb, M.B., Williams, N.J., Sutton, M.D., Microbial DNA challenge studies of variable number tandem repeat (VNTR) probes used for DNA profiling analysis, *Journal of Forensic Sciences*, 5, 1172-5, 1993.

Wilson, R.B., Ferrara, J.L., Baum, H.J., Shaler, R.C., Guidelines for internal validation of the HLA DQ alpha DNA typing system, *Forensic Science International*, 66, 1, 9-22, 1994.

Thompson, W.C., Subjective interpretation, laboratory error and the value of forensic DNA evidence: three case studies, *Genetica*, 96, 1-2, 153-68, 1995.

Wilson, M.R., DiZinno, J.A., Polanskey, D., Replogle, J., Budowle, B., Validation of mitochondrial DNA sequencing for forensic casework analysis, *International Journal of Legal Medicine*, 108, 2, 68-74, 1995.

# Chapter 10

## DNA AND THE DATABASE

 Direct comparison of a sample to a suspect utilizes only a small fraction of the potential of DNA typing. DNA is effective in confirming the suspicion that several crimes have been committed by the same person. If DNA profiles from convicted criminals were stored in a databank, it could be searched for possible perpetrators of suspectless and serial crimes. Most people are familiar with the data banks now in use to track latent fingerprints. The Automated Fingerprint Identification System (AFIS) contains millions of people's fingerprints in computer files. Tens of thousands of crimes have been solved by searching the databank with an unidentified latent fingerprint.

Legislation mandating the collection and analysis of samples for DNA databanks has already been passed and implemented by most states. Generally, samples are collected from convicted felons, particularly rapists upon release from prison. The reasoning for this is that a large number of violent crimes are committed by a relatively small number of people; some studies estimate recidivism rates at least as high as 50%. Forty-three states have passed legislation mandating and funding the establishment of a DNA database.[14] Samples are collected from convicted felons upon release from prison and are funneled to the state DNA laboratory for typing and storage.

**Figure 10-1. The computer screen that is generated when a potential cold hit is scored.** Each of the four vertical panels is a comparison of the alleles at one locus in the profile of interest to the equivalent alleles in a database profile. The computer calculates windows of uncertainty for the band sizes of both the profile entered, and the putative hit, then compares them for overlap. The middle band of each triplet is the actual band size; the lower and upper bands define the uncertainty window. (see *Chapter 8, Appendix G*).

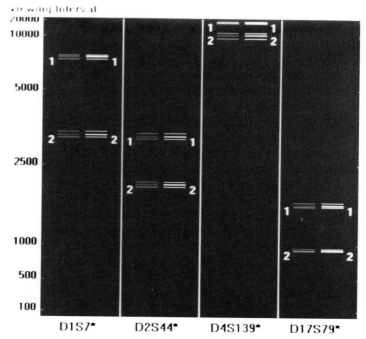

---

[14]As of October, 1995: Alabama, Alaska, Arizona, Arkansas, California, Colorado, Connecticut, Delaware, Florida, Georgia, Hawaii, Illinois, Indiana, Iowa, Kansas, Kentucky, Louisiana, Maine, Maryland, Michigan, Minnesota, Mississippi, Missouri, Montana, Nevada, New Jersey, New York, North Carolina, North Dakota, Ohio, Oklahoma, Oregon, Pennsylvania, South Carolina, South Dakota, Tennessee, Texas, Utah, Virginia, Washington, West Virginia, Wisconsin.

DNA profiles are particularly suited for computer storage and automated searches (see Figure 10-1) because information can be stored as a set of numbers, requiring very little in the way of sophisticated technology.  It is essential to realize that an initial "cold hit" in a database is usually only used as probable cause to obtain a sample from a suspect for further testing.  The markers used to identify the suspect are then retested, and the samples are compared further, using yet additional markers.  This system provides a safeguard against any clerical errors or sample switches that may have occurred in generating the data base.

In order for databanks to be most effective, especially on a national level, the DNA system used to create them must be standardized.  If California wants to check Nevada's database for a suspect who may have crossed state lines, at least some of the same markers must be tested in both cases.  The FBI is leading the effort to create a national database, to which states would all contribute information.  Pilot programs have, in fact, already been implemented.  Progress on the implementation of these programs continues, and newer, faster PCR-type systems that are just now coming on line, are beginning to be included.  These systems will greatly streamline the task of processing the tens of thousands of backlogged samples sitting in some state freezers.

Useful databanks may be created from groups of individuals other than crime suspects.  For example, a databank composed of voluntarily donated evidence samples from living victims would be used to track down the perpetrators of currently suspectless cases.  A databank containing DNA profiles from unidentified bodies would obviously be useful in identifying them as new information is uncovered.  The Armed Forces DNA Identification Laboratory (AFDIL) has already instituted a sample collection program from military personnel.  This will greatly assist in the identification of victims of war, particularly when extremities are missing.

DNA databanks have also been established in order to determine the frequencies with which forensic markers are found in different population groups.  A more in-depth discussion of this topic is found in *Chapters 5* and *8*.  The relevancy to this discussion is that population information must be maintained separately from any databank used to identify assailant in suspectless cases.  Privacy considerations in general are a larger issue for DNA testing than other personal identification methods.  Additional information pertaining to diseases, relatedness and physical traits are contained in the DNA sample.  These are not traits, however, that are tested in forensic labs, and any data stored in a computer would consist only of information about specific forensic markers.  Nevertheless, great care must be taken to protect the privacy of the individual, convict or not, as well as the security of the sample.  Recommendations to this effect have been made by national committees, such as the National Research Council (NRC), and are being followed.

## SIDEBAR 9

### The Botanical Witness
### (or, what the seed pod saw)

Over the last decade, the genomes of humans, as well as many animals, crop plants, and microorganisms have been well-characterized.  Since the DNA sequences, more specifically variable DNA sequences, are known in these cases, it has been possible to develop probes to these loci for the purpose of comparing individuals.  However, the majority of organisms have not necessarily been studied in this fashion, and little or no specific information is available about their DNA sequences. RAPD (random amplified polymorphic DNA) analysis uses 10 bp oligonucleotides of randomly generated sequence, that have the potential to act as primers in a PCR amplification. Under proper hybridization conditions, some of these primers will bind at many locations in the genomic DNA being tested. Because oligonucleotides complementing both strands are provided, some will anneal in an inverted orientation, forming primer pair combinations spanning a distance amenable to PCR amplification. This is different from a standard PCR amplification in that the size and location of the amplified regions are previously unknown to the investigator (and actually only their size is immediately obvious from the results). On average, about 50 different loci are amplified during a RAPD procedure. The PCR products are then separated by electrophoresis on an agarose gel, and usually visualized as ethidium bromide stained bands. Depending on the coefficient of inbreeding of the organism, the number of the bands that vary between individuals may be between about 5 and 30. A major caveat to the method is that the intensities of the bands vary both from each other, as well as between runs and laboratories; thus the interpretation is somewhat subjective, and reproducibility of the results can be problematic.

On May 3, 1992, the body of a black female was discovered under a Palo Verde tree in Phoenix, Arizona. In addition to the gouge in the tree, tire tracks and scrape marks in the surrounding dirt, a pager was found at the scene. The pager eventually led sheriff's deputies to Mark Bogen, who immediately became the prime suspect in the murder of Denise Johnson. The suspect, Mark Bogen, admitted to picking up the victim, and having sex with her, but denied any involvement in her death. The suspects truck was searched, and some seed pods from a Palo Verde tree collected. The seed pods from the truck were compared to the Palo Verde tree at the crime scene using RAPD analysis. In this case, the RAPD patterns between the seed pods recovered from the suspect's truck and those from the tree appeared to be an exact match even down to the band intensities. An important point to note is that the comparison had to be made using the seed pods, not the seeds. If the seeds (like human embryos) were a product of cross-pollination, half their genetic material would be from the other parent, and only half their band pattern would correlate with the maternal tree. The seed pods, on the other hand, are entirely derived from the maternal tissue of the tree.

Before the RAPD analysis could be admitted at trial, however, a Frye hearing had to be held; the State of Arizona did not at that time have a Supreme court ruling or statutory legislation upholding the admissibility of DNA evidence (a ruling is currently pending). Dr. Tim Helentjaris, then associate professor at the University of Arizona, had performed the work and testified for the prosecution; Dr. Paul Keim, a professor at Northern Arizona University testified as an expert for the defense. Although, in this case, the patterns of the tree and the pods appeared indistinguishable, Dr. Keim held that the procedure, as a rule, was not reliable and reproducible. He opined additionally that the population database of Palo Verde trees was too small (about 17 trees of the subspecies blue floridium), and the collection methods resulting in a total of 29 Palo Verde trees (i.e., by sheriffs deputies) were flawed. Based on this testimony, Judge Susan Bolton ruled that, for the first time, plant DNA profiles could be admitted as evidence in a criminal trial; however Dr. Helentjaris was not allowed to present a statistical probability regarding the significance of the pattern match. He testified that the DNA RAPD pattern of the seed pod was indistinguishable from the pattern obtained from the tree at the crime scene, and that it was his opinion that the pod came from the tree.

Based on the DNA profiles and a plethora of other physical evidence, in addition to an incriminating phone conversation and the testimony of the suspect and other court witnesses, Bogen was convicted of the murder of Denise Johnson. He was sentenced to life without the possibility of parole. Although the ruling was recently (1996) upheld by the Arizona State Court of appeals, a minority opinion argued that the DNA evidence should not have been introduced, but that its inclusion resulted only in "harmless error".

In a similar 1996 case in Santa Clara County, California, a bay leaf was associated with a particular tree using RAPD technology. In this case, however, the DNA evidence was not admitted to trial at all based on the lack of population data for bay trees.

**References:**

**Amato, I.,** Botanical Witness for the Prosecution, *Science* 260, 894-5, 1993.

**Clayton, B.,** Deputy County Attorney, Maricopa Co., *personal communication*, 1996

**Keim, P.,** Professor, Northern Arizona University, AZ, *personal communication*, 1996.

---

## SIDEBAR 10

### A Cold Hit in Minnesota
### (or, the database in winter)

On November 17, 1991, police were called to a first floor four bedroom apartment in South Minneapolis, where the body of Jean Broderick had been found in her bedroom. The cause of death was asphyxiation due to airway obstruction and strangulation and the medical examiner found evidence that Broderick had been sexually assaulted. This included a finding of semen on inner side of her buttocks. Several bloodstained items and a pubic hair were also collected at the crime scene. Although several eyewitnesses later identified the assailant, he was not immediately apprehended.

The Minnesota Bureau of Criminal Apprehension (BCA) received the evidence approximately two weeks later, and immediately began RFLP analysis of the semen swab, along with reference samples from the victim and her male roommate. The roommate was excluded immediately. However, since no suspect had yet been detained, there was no other reference sample to compare with the evidence. The one locus sample profile from the first autorad was entered into the Minnesota CSO database, and all but 6 of the 1700 individuals contained in the database were eliminated. A second locus was probed, and the two locus profile again compared to the 6 questioned profiles from the database.

Using only two probes, the lab was able to exclude all but one individual. A conventional blood marker, PGM, was also linked the evidence to the now suspect individual.

Based on the typing results, probable cause was established to obtain a fresh sample from the suspect, Martin Estrada Perez. He was immediately located by the Minneapolis Police Department. By December 23, BCA criminalists had received an early Christmas present: a known blood sample to compare to the evidence. DNA from the reference sample was extracted, along with fresh extractions of the evidentiary semen swab and the CSO sample. A total of 6 different loci were eventually tested, producing RFLP profiles that were indistinguishable between all three samples. Additionally, a bloody tan jacket yielded a mixture of types. The now defendant could not be excluded as a contributor to this mixture. The pubic hair found at the scene was also found to be indistinguishable from that of Mr. Perez.

The trial court admitted the DNA evidence, but excluded the introduction of statistics relating to the significance of the matching genetic profiles. In this, the court took judicial notice of the *Kim* ruling, based on a composite of several previous Minnesota Supreme Court rulings regarding the admissibility of statistics relating to scientific evidence (*State v. Carlson*, 1978, *State v. Boyd*, 1983, *State v. Kim*, 1987). The state's witnesses were permitted to testify that a six-locus pattern match is extremely rare, that there was not a significant chance that another person was the source of the evidence, and that to a reasonable medical/scientific certainty the defendant was the source of the unknown DNA samples found at the scene. The profile was also searched against a different database containing 3500 individuals, and no other sample was found that had the same profile at more than two loci. After considering the physical evidence as well as additional personal and eyewitness testimony, the trial court jury found Martin Perez guilty of first-degree murder. He was sentenced to life in prison without possibility of parole.

The defendant appealed his conviction and the case went before the appellate court in April, 1994. In the meantime, however, the Supreme court of Minnesota had reconsidered, jointly, the cases of *State v. Bloom, State v. Bauer* and *State v. Perez*, and partially reversed their decision regarding the admissibility of statistics. In fact, based on the NRC I report and their recommendation of the "interim ceiling method" for calculating composite genotype frequencies, the court made a specific exception for DNA evidence . In a decision filed April 29, 1994, the appellate court relied entirely on the new Supreme Court position and denied the appeal.

─────── *FURTHER REFERENCES* ─────────────────────

**Beck, Q., Shipley, B.,** Recidivism of Prisoners Released in 1983, *Bureau of Justice Statistics Special Report* NCJ-116261, Washington, D.C., 1989.

**de Gorgey, A.,** The advent of DNA databanks: implications for information privacy, *American Journal of Law and Medicine*, 16, 3, 381-98, 1990.

**Gill, P., Evett, I. W., Woodroffe, S., Lygo, J. E., Millican, E., Webster, M.,** Databases, quality control and interpretation of DNA profiling in the Home Office Forensic Science Service, *Electrophoresis*, 12, 2-3, 204-9, 1991.

**National Research Council,** *DNA Technology in Forensic Science*, National Academy Press, Washington D.C., 1992.

**McEwen, J. E.,** Forensic DNA data banking by state crime laboratories, *American Journal of Human Genetics*, 56, 6, 1487-92, 1995.

**McEwen, J.E., Reilly, P.R.,** A review of state legislation on DNA forensic data banking, *American Journal of Human Genetics*, 54, 6, 941-58, 1994.

**Scheck, B.,** DNA data banking: a cautionary tale, *American Journal of Human Genetics*, 54, 6, 931-3, 1994.

**Wilson, T.,** Automated Fingerprint Identification Systems, *Law Enforcement Technology*, 45-48, 1986.

## Chapter 11

## QUALITY CONTROL AND REGULATION

## CERTIFICATION AND ACCREDITATION

Formal external review of both a forensic laboratory and the individuals performing work in that venue is useful for a number of reasons. Internally, the results provide the laboratory and it's personnel with valuable information that can be used to correct deficiencies and improve performance. Of equal importance is the impartial assessment provided to judicial officers, the court, and other interested parties regarding the laboratory's credibility and fitness to reliably and accurately perform forensic testing.

### A. CERTIFICATION

Certification deals with the qualifications of an individual criminalist. In the U.S., certification is not currently required in order to perform forensic testing, but is regarded as highly favorable. The trend is toward encouraging certification in at least an analyst's field of specialization. Certification exams are provided by the American Board of Criminalistics (ABC), a group governed by a rotating quorum of qualified workers in the field that have an interest in upholding a self-imposed standard within their own ranks. Written examinations are offered in both general knowledge of forensic science, as well as in the various specialties. A passing score on the general knowledge exam qualifies the individual as a **diplomate** of the ABC. In order to obtain **fellow** status, the criminalist must pass a written specialty exam then submit the results of a hands-on proficiency test within one year and annually thereafter. A DNA specialist must pass both the general biology exam and DNA specialty examinations. If a fellow fails more than one proficiency test in a four year period, his status is temporarily revoked. It can only be reinstated when the deficiency is remedied to the satisfaction of the ABC review committee and a successful re-test completed.

### B. ACCREDITATION

Accreditation pertains to the qualification of a laboratory which provides forensic testing services. This service, provided by the American Society of Crime Laboratory Directors (ASCLD), is also at present voluntary and self-regulated. The program is managed and the standards established by the ASCLD Laboratory Accreditation Board (ASCLD/LAB), which is responsible to a delegate assembly composed of the directors of all accredited laboratories. Like individual certification, an outside review for accreditation serves to identify criteria which can be used by a laboratory to assess its level of performance and improve its operations. It is also an impartial means by which those that depend on the laboratory's services, as well as the general public, can ascertain that a particular lab meets established standards. In order to qualify for accreditation, the laboratory must demonstrate that they meet the standards for management, operations, personnel, procedures, equipment, physical plant, security, and health and safety procedures. The laboratory analysts must also participate in regular proficiency testing program. Accreditation is granted for five years, provided that a laboratory continues to meet the standard during this period. Both the initial accreditation and, reaccreditation on a five year cycle, require a full review of the laboratory including an on-site inspection.

## II. TWGDAM

TWGDAM, the technical working group on DNA analysis, was originally formed in 1988 at the behest of the FBI. Its self-assigned functions were to provide a forum for forensic DNA laboratories to discuss issues, to conduct studies, and to reach a consensus as to the DNA methodologies to be used in North American crime laboratories. TWGDAM also provides a medium for the different laboratories around the county to exchange DNA testing data, and has played a particularly important role in establishing guidelines for working forensic DNA laboratories. Members of TWGDAM include forensic scientists and experts in various fields from the academic community. Various subcommittees have been established to deal with specific issues, such quality control and quality assurance, database developments, and new systems as they are considered for use. Much of the internal policy for DNA testing has been promulgated by TWGDAM. To date, the group has completed the following:

- Established guidelines for a quality assurance program for DNA testing laboratories; including RFLP and PCR technologies (*Crime Laboratory Digest* 18, 44-75, 1995).
- Established guidelines for a Proficiency Testing Program for DNA analysis (*Crime Laboratory Digest* 17, 59-64, 1990).
- Established guidelines for conducting a DNA Quality Assurance Audit (*Crime Laboratory Digest* 20, 8-18, 1993).
- Established guidelines for DNA Proficiency Test Manufacturing and Reporting (*Crime Laboratory Digest* 21, 27-32, 1994).
- Sponsored a precision study for inter- and intra-laboratory variation of RFLP profiling data that resulted in 3 published studies.

TWGDAM has also issued several consensus statements on the validity and reliability of various DNA techniques and calculations, including statistical standards, the ceiling calculation, and responses to challenges to DNA testing. Although criticized by some as being too exclusive, particularly in the early stages of decision making, and also as potentially biased in developing standards in which it has a vested interest, TWGDAM has emerged as a nucleus around which the forensic community can assemble as the DNA typing explosion continues.

## III. NRC I AND II

DNA was first used in forensic casework in the United Kingdom in 1985. By 1986 it was instituted in commercial laboratories in the U.S., and in 1988 the FBI began testing. By the summer of 1989 important questions had begun to surface regarding scientific, legal, societal and ethical issues brought forth by this new technology. These questions had as much to do with public perception of the reliability and validity of DNA evidence as with the dependability of laboratory analyses.

The National Research Council (NRC) of the National Academy of Sciences volunteered to shoulder the difficult and capricious task of addressing the general applicability and appropriateness of DNA technology to forensic science, as well as issues of standardization, data management and legal, societal and ethical considerations. In January, 1990, the Committee on DNA Technology in Forensic Science held its first meeting, and in 1992 their report and recommendations were released and published.

Contrary to the news release printed by the New York Times on April 14, 1992, and retracted the next day, the committee recommended that the use of DNA analysis for forensic purposes be continued, during which time suggested improvements and changes were implemented. Their recommendations included many that were well-grounded in scientific principle and common sense. A few points, however, instigated even more controversy among the forensic and legal communities engendering a second gathering of experts under the further auspices of the NRC.

We will summarize the important, some of them controversial, points in the 1992 report then review and compare the report of the second committee, just published in 1996. The exact text of the specific recommendations of both committees is found in *Appendix I.*

## A. NRC I

The first NRC Committee on *DNA Technology in Forensic Science* put forth recommendations in six separate areas: technical considerations, statistical interpretation, laboratory standards, databanks and privacy, legal considerations, and societal and ethical issues.

The technical recommendations encompassed the basics of good scientific research and testing. Particular to forensics are the invocations to establish pattern identification and comparison criteria and to challenge and understand the limits of each particular typing system. Many of the technical concerns prevalent at that time have been remedied by both research and experience and have ceased to be issues even in court. The committee also suggested the establishment of a national committee on forensic DNA typing under the auspices of an appropriate government agency(s).

A hot item up for consideration was the statistical basis for interpretation of a DNA profile. The Committee's recommendation in this area sparked some heated discussion and generated the most compelling impetus for the formation of the second committee. A calculation, named the "ceiling principle" was invented, ostensibly to ensure that the rareness of any particular profile in the population was not underestimated. Unfortunately, the calculation was neither a principle, nor constituted a ceiling, and had no scientific basis. To further confuse the issue, an "interim ceiling principle", specifying even more conservative allele frequencies in the calculation was recommended until enough population sampling could be completed to provide a sound genetic and statistical basis for the use of actual allele frequencies.

The controversial issue of laboratory error rates was also addressed. Unfortunately, an "error" was never defined, nor was any specification for acceptable or unacceptable risks of error presented.

The committee called for standardization in the field and the assessment and assurance of quality in forensic DNA work. This challenge has been met by practicing laboratories and individuals in large part by voluntary submission to the accreditation and certification programs outlined above in *Section I.A.* The spotlight on DNA has, in fact, forced the entire forensic profession to move towards providing proof of quality services. This trend has served to not only improve actual laboratory operations and criminalist proficiency, but has given users of forensic laboratory services, as well as the courts, juries, and general public a higher confidence level in the validity and reliability of forensic testing in general and DNA analysis in particular.

The NRC I committee recommended that the courts take judicial notice of the basic underlying scientific validity of DNA typing and the fundamental soundness of the methods in use by the forensic community. They also supported the adjudication of DNA admissibility on a case-by-case basis, at least in the interim. This was a generally reasonable suggestion for that time, although many would argue that the specifics they suggested pertaining to methodology and standardization should more correctly be considered as to the weight of the evidence rather than its admissibility.

The creation of a national databank of DNA profiles was affirmed, along with an admonishment not to lock the format into technologies which are sure to become quickly outdated (see *Chapter 9*). Finally, cautions regarding the privacy of DNA information, the overselling of DNA evidence in court and the influence of parties with vested interests in the accreditation process or regulation of laboratories were enumerated.

During the process of organizing the national committee on forensic DNA typing and the same year NRC I were in session, an interesting sidelight emerged: who is qualified to render an opinion regarding DNA technology as applied to forensic analysis in general and about specific studies and cases? If the scientist is highly informed, involved in the field, and perhaps recognized as an outstanding contributor, is she necessarily biased and closed minded? On the other hand, is a "disinterested" expert in molecular biology, biotechnology or statistics with no forensic background really the appropriate person to render an opinion about a field with which he has no experience? On the surface, it might seem that an "outside opinion" from a "disinterested party" is more trustworthy. But if it is based on an incomplete body of knowledge, of what worth is it? Forensic scientists are uniquely qualified to render opinions on the reliability of a technology and on the interpretation of results. Because they routinely encounter evidence that comes from real world environments, they are able to devise experiments that will test the validity and reliability of new techniques that may have forensic utility under such conditions. They consult the literature and academic scientists in the process of understanding and testing new technologies.

Of the original 14 members on the NRC I committee, only two were working forensic scientists, and one had extensive academic knowledge of the subject. The others, although considered outstanding in their various related expertises in DNA technology, had no experience with forensic applications. Two others, who had just begun to venture into forensic DNA applications, were pressured to resign because of "vested interests". It is the opinion of the authors that judgments regarding the use of a technology best be rendered by those most familiar with its advantages, limitations and consequences. Although fresh ideas and critical review are always welcome and should be sought out, "disinterested outside experts" are just that, and their opinions should not be given undue weight in the misguided fear of bias.

## B. NRC II

In April 1993, Judge William Sessions, then Director of the FBI, requested that the NRC do a follow-up study to resolve, in particular, the statistical controversies generated by NRC I and also to incorporate new data on population substructure that had been accumulating. Dr. James Crow was asked to chair the second committee, and their first meeting was held in September 1994. A prepublication copy of the NRC II report, entitled *The Evaluation of Forensic DNA Evidence*, became available in the Spring of 1996 and the final published version is due out in November, 1996. The report is of a much narrower scope that the previous one and addresses primarily population statistic issues along with some additional consideration of laboratory operations and risk of lab errors.

The members of the new committee freely acknowledge the blunder incurred in the recommendation of both the "ceiling principle" and the "interim ceiling principle", and further submit that some of the supporting statements have been misinterpreted or misapplied in the courts.  They conclude that those calculations are not only unnecessary but, in fact, inadvisable.  In their place, they recommend standard statistical procedures based on population genetics, with suggestions for some of the special circumstances that arise in forensic applications.  In particular, they fully endorse the multiplication of allele frequencies from genetically independent loci (i.e., use of the **product rule**) when applied with the appropriate caveats and a modicum of common sense.

With regard to the estimation of risk of error, they severely discourage any attempt to adjust the estimation of a profile frequency by combining it with an "error rate".  Among other things, they recognize that the number of proficiency tests required to give an accurate estimate of an acceptable (by definition low) error rate would be outlandishly expensive and disruptive.  They suggest that such efforts would be better applied to raising laboratory standards.  Additionally, they emphasize that it is the current practice, not the past record of a laboratory that is relevant, particularly with rapidly evolving technology.  In order to address the ever-present issue of human error, the committee recommends the time-honored and reasonable practice of saving out a portion of the sample for a future independent test.

The NRC II committee concludes that overall "The technology for DNA profiling and the methods for estimating frequencies and related statistics have progressed to the point where the reliability and validity of properly collected and analyzed DNA data should not be in doubt."

## IV. FEDERAL DNA ADVISORY COMMITTEE

In 1994, the DNA Identification Act was passed by Congress, creating, among other things, a DNA advisory board (DAB).  Members are appointed by the FBI from nominations submitted by the National Academy of Sciences and other organizations.  It is expected that this board will provide guidelines to labs on a wide variety of issues, including standards for DNA testing and quality assurance.  The power of this new group is substantial, as any agency requesting federal development funds for DNA must demonstrate compliance with standards set by this group.  As with many TWGDAM guidelines, standards recommended by the DAB will become *de facto* for any lab providing DNA services to courts.  While several documents have been drafted for evaluation by the relevant communities, none have been adopted as this book goes to press.

———— *FURTHER REFERENCES*————————————————————————

DNA recommendations - 1994 report concerning further recommendations of the DNA Commission of the ISFH regarding PCR-based polymorphisms in STR (short tandem repeat) systems, *International Journal of Legal Medicine*, 107, 3, 159-60, 1994.

**Koehler, J.J.,** Error and exaggeration in the presentation of DNA evidence at trial, *Jurimetics*, J 34, 1993.

**Koehler, J.J., Chia, K., Lindsey, A.,** The random match probability (RMP) in DNA evidence: Irrelevant and prejudicial? *Jurimetics*, J 35, 1995.

Statement by DNA Commission of the International Society for Forensic Haemogenetics concerning the National Academy of Sciences report on DNA Technology in Forensic Science in the USA, *Forensic Science International*, 59, 1, 1-2, 1993.

Recommendations of the DNA Commission of the International Society for Forensic Haemogenetics relating to the use of PCR-based polymorphisms, *Forensic Science International*, 1, 1-3, 1992.

1991 Report concerning recommendations of the DNA Commission of the International Society for Forensic Haemogenetics relating to the use of DNA polymorphisms, *Forensic Science International*, 52, 2, 125-30, 1992.

DNA recommendations--1992 report concerning recommendations of the DNA Commission of the International Society for Forensic Haemogenetics relating to the use of PCR-based polymorphisms. *International Journal of Legal Medicine*, 105, 1, 63-4, 1992.

**Morton, N, E, Collins A.E.,** Statistical and genetic aspects of quality control for DNA identification, *Electrophoresis*, 16, 9, 1670-7, 1995.

**Technical Working Group on DNA Analysis Methods (TWGDAM),** Guidelines for a proficiency testing program for DNA Restriction Fragment Length Polymorphism Analysis, *Crime Lab Digest*, 17, 2, 50-60, 1990.

**Technical Working Group on DNA Analysis Methods (TWGDAM),** Guidelines for a quality assurance program for DNA Restriction Fragment Length Polymorphism Analysis, *Crime Lab Digest*, 16, 2, 40-59, 1989.

**Technical Working Group on DNA Analysis Methods (TWGDAM),** Statement of the Working Group on Statistical Standards for DNA Analysis, *Crime Lab Digest*, 17, 3, 53-58, 1990.

**National Research Council,** *DNA Technology in Forensic Science*, National Academy Press, Washington, D.C., 1992.

**National Research Council,** *The Evaluation of Forensic DNA Evidence*, National Academy Press, Washington, D.C., 1996.

# Chapter 12

## ADMISSIBILITY STANDARDS – SCIENCE ON TRIAL IN THE COURTROOM

### I. THE FRYE STANDARD AND THE FEDERAL RULES OF EVIDENCE

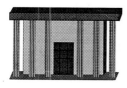 DNA evidence is not the first scientific evidence to be presented in a court of law, although it may well be the most highly scrutinized. Often, basic scientific procedures are adapted specifically for use in forensic science, or occasionally completely new techniques are developed to address a particular question. For all generally accepted testing procedures, there was once a first instance where a judge made the decision to allow a specific type of scientific evidence to be presented at trial. Generally, when a new technique is applied to criminal investigation an admissibility hearing is held by the trial court in order to determine if the evidence should be heard by the jury. If the ruling is confirmed by an appellate court and eventually by a supreme court, legal precedent is established for the admissibility (or inadmissibility) of a general category of scientific analysis. Lower courts may then take judicial notice of such a precedent and waive a pre-trial admissibility hearing.

One of the confusions that sometimes confounds the acceptance of scientific evidence is the existence of three different standards of admissibility at the federal level, one statutory and the other two grounded in case law. Individual states have generally adopted one of these three standards, often adding their own variations and restrictions. The oldest and most-often cited precedent relies on *Frye v. United States* (1923). The scientific evidence being presented in this case was the theory underlying lie-detector testing (polygraph). In *Frye*, it was ruled that

> "...the thing from which the deduction is made must be sufficiently established to have gained ***general acceptance*** in the particular field in which it belongs" (emphasis added)

The Polygraph test was ultimately not admitted and remains inadmissible to this day. This federal ruling, codifying the concept of *general acceptance*, has come to be known as the **Frye** **Standard**. And, in fact, with regards to DNA in particular, the majority of recent Federal decisions continue to rely on *Frye*. A majority of states (31) have adopted various iterations of it, and have contributed their own precedents as well.[1]

The corollary ruling to *Frye* on the admissibility of scientific evidence (voice prints) in California is *People v. Kelly* (1976), which consists of three parts:

1) Reliability must be established by experts
2) Experts must be properly qualified
3) Correct procedures must be used

---

[15]Alabama, Alaska, Arizona, California, Colorado, Connecticut, District of Columbia, Florida, Hawaii, Indiana, Kansas, Kentucky, Maryland, Massachusetts, Michigan, Minnesota, Mississippi, Missouri, Nebraska, New Hampshire, New Jersey, New Mexico, New York, North Dakota, Oklahoma, Pennsylvania, Rhode Island, South Carolina, South Dakota, Utah, Washington.

Several adjunct rulings are often quoted in the State of California.  In *People v. Guerra* (1984), *general acceptance* was equated with *consensus* or *clear majority*.  *People v. Reilly* (1987) defines the *field in which it belongs*, or *relevant scientific community* as:

1)  Forensic scientists
2)  Scientists in broader disciplines who are knowledgeable in the technique
3)  Well credentialed analysts

The states of Hawaii and Oregon also stand out as having specifically enumerated their guidelines for the admissibility of novel scientific evidence to the trial court.  The Hawaii Rules of Evidence, which are layered on top of *Frye* state that:

1)  The evidence will assist the trier of fact to understand the evidence or to determine a fact in issue.
2)  The evidence will add to the common understanding of the jury.
3)  The underlying theory is generally accepted as valid.
4)  The procedures used are generally accepted as reliable if performed properly.
5)  The procedures were applied and conducted properly in the present instance.

They then add that "The court should then consider whether admitting such evidence will be more probative than prejudicial", giving due to the Federal Rules of Evidence.

The state of Oregon also combines elements of both *Frye* and Relevancy.  *State v. Brown* (1984) reads:

"The salutary aspects of the *Frye general acceptance* test is retained, not as a prerequisite to admissibility, but as one of seven steps in the screening process.  To determine the relevance or probative value of proffered scientific evidence ...the following seven  factors are to be considered as guidelines:"

1)  The technique's general acceptance in the field
2)  The expert's qualifications and stature
3)  The use which has been made of the technique
4)  The potential rate of error
5)  The existence of specialized literature
6)  The novelty of the invention
7)  The extent to which the technique relies on subjective interpretation of the expert

The **Federal Rules of Evidence** were originally promulgated by the supreme court of the United States under its authority to proscribe the general rules for federal, civil and criminal proceedings.  They were enacted by Congress in 1975 and have been amended several times since.  These rules (specifically 702 and 403), may be summarized to say that if findings are reliable, relevant, and more probative than prejudicial, they may be admitted for the jury to consider.  The Federal Rules of Evidence are generally regarded as a somewhat looser standard than *Frye* and certainly relegate a wide berth of discretion to the court.  A number of states (14) have also coopted the **Relevancy Standard** based on the Federal Rules of Evidence, sometimes in addition to their own statutory Rules of Evidence.[16]  A couple of states have

---

[16]Arkansas, Delaware, Idaho, Louisiana, Maine, Montana, Nevada, Tennessee, Texas, Vermont, Virginia, West Virginia, Wisconsin, Wyoming.

drawn from both decisions.[17] and a few rely only on their own internal standards, often citing "reliability" and individual State Rules of Evidence.[18]

Most recently, a new federal decision, *Daubert et al. v. Merrell Dow* (1993), resulted in a ruling giving the trial judge even more discretion in determining the admissibility of scientific evidence. State courts have apparently paid this ruling little heed and continue to rely on *Frye* and to a lesser extent *Relevancy*. In a recent California Supreme Court decision (*People v. Leahy*, 1994), Chief Justice Malcolm Lucas held that California's standard for admissibility of new scientific evidence would continue to be the *Kelly-Frye* test, rather than the new federal standard adopted in *Daubert*. The case involved the horizontal gaze nystagmus test, a field sobriety test. Judge Lucas wrote "...*it may be preferable to let admissibility questions regarding new scientific techniques be settled by those persons most qualified to assess their validity*" (i.e., those with scientific rather than legal expertise).

Typically, an appellate decision regarding admissibility is regarded as precedent within the judicial system. A court might exercise its discretion to admit evidence without an evidentiary hearing through a process called judicial notice. At this writing there have been 147 reported state appellate decisions regarding DNA analysis; the vast majority (126) opined admission (*Appendix J*). A large number of these rulings represent RFLP cases (107/127), but PCR-based cases are becoming more common. No major decisions regarding the newer PCR tests such as polymarker, D1S80, STRs and mitochondrial sequencing have yet been rendered. As the rulings regarding DNA evidence work their way through the legal system, more and more State Supreme courts are taking under consideration several DNA cases from which to fashion a ruling. To date, 13 states have passed legislation mandating the admission of DNA evidence.[19] It is probable that, in the future, DNA testing will come to be as easily accepted as traditional fingerprints.

## .II. DNA - SOME LANDMARK CASES

### A. RFLP

The use of DNA typing in criminal cases in the U.S. got off to a somewhat inauspicious start. Virgin molecular biologists were running the show, and were unacquainted with, and uninitiated in, the intricacies and adversarial nature of the legal system. They were additionally naive in the nature of, and special problems presented by forensic evidence. Its first use in a criminal trial was in 1987 during the sexual assault case of *State of Florida v. Andrews* (see *Sidebar 11*). The first trial resulted in a hung jury, however a retrial resulted in a conviction for Andrews. Both the ruling and the conviction were upheld at the appellate level. For the next couple of years, DNA testing of forensic evidence in general, and RFLP analysis in particular, was admitted to trial almost without question. This sets the stage for the first case in which DNA was seriously challenged.

The year was 1987, the locale a New York State Trial Court, presided over by the Honorable Judge Gerald Sheindlin. Joseph Castro was accused of stabbing Vilma Ponce and her 2-year-old daughter to death. The evidence submitted for DNA analysis was a spot of blood, allegedly hers, on his watch. RFLP analysis was performed by a private company, Lifecodes, which had just entered into the forensic market. The autorads submitted would not

---

[17]Oregon, Vermont.
[18]Georgia, Iowa, North Carolina.
[19]State statutes on the admissibility of DNA testing as of October, 1995: Alabama, Alaska, Connecticut, Delaware, Indiana, Louisiana, Maryland, Minnesota, Nevada, North Dakota, Tennessee, Virginia, and Wisconsin.

have met today's critical standards. The lanes were dark with non-specific background, and a number of extra, unexplainable bands were present. As if this were not enough, the scientists chose to render an opinion that the blood on the watch came from the victim, even though the results were outside the match criteria established by their own lab.

In an unprecedented move, and to their credit, four of the expert witnesses, representing both prosecution and defense, met to review the scientific evidence after they had already testified. The result of this meeting was a two page consensus statement that addressed the inadequacy of the scientific evidence and the legal procedures for assessing scientific evidence. The court chose to render inadmissible the RFLP DNA evidence indicating that the blood on Castro's watch came from the victim; however, results were admitted to support an exclusion (it wasn't *his* blood). Judge Sheindlin later quipped that Joseph Castro and [the analyst] were the only two people in the courtroom who's opinion it was that it was her blood. Joseph Castro was convicted on the basis of other evidence and later confessed to the crime.

Thus, in *People v. Castro* (1989), the admissibility and reliability of DNA evidence was seriously challenged for the first time. In the process of considering its determination of the admissibility of the RFLP results, the court set out a three prong test criterion extending the *Frye* Standard.

1) Is there a sound theory behind DNA testing?
2) Are the techniques for testing capable of producing reliable results?
3) Were the tests performed properly in this case?

In *Castro*, concordant results linking the suspect to the crime were ultimately excluded from trial because they failed to meet the third prong, although an exclusionary result was admitted. While the inherent reliability of DNA typing was acknowledged, the inadequacy exhibited in this case prevented full admission of the DNA evidence. Since then, many courts have taken judicial notice of this decision and standard. This decision was a major factor in the focus on issues of accreditation, certification, quality control, and standardization which were already in progress in most forensic laboratories.

*United States v. Yee et al.* (1991) was the first case in which the FBI accepted evidence for RFLP analysis. On February 27, 1988, at approximately 9:30 p.m., David Hartlaub's body was found outside the night depository at a bank in Perkins Township, Ohio. Hartlaub had been shot in or near his van at least six times by gunmen who quickly fled the scene after completing the brutal and unprovoked murder (the crime was a murder for hire, and Hartlaub was mistaken for the intended victim). There were no eyewitnesses to the actual shooting, but fresh blood was found inside Hartlaub's van, that was driven from the scene by one of the group of Hell's Angels who had perpetrated the attack. It was this blood from the van that was submitted to the FBI lab for testing and subsequently showed the same genetic pattern as a sample obtained from the defendant, John Ray Bonds.

A contentious legal battle erupted between the scientific opponents and proponents of DNA testing. Richard Lewontin and Daniel Hartl led the attack on DNA in general, and the FBI analysis in particular, for the failure to account for possible population substructure which might have caused ambiguities in assessing the estimated frequency of the DNA profile in the population. Nevertheless, the judge in this federal trial court ruled in favor of the prosecution in allowing the DNA evidence into trial. This hearing called to the front issues regarding the interpretation of DNA results in the context of population genetics.

In *United States v. Jakobetz* (1992), a Federal appellate court upheld the admissibility of RFLP DNA evidence including statistical calculation to assess the significance of the results. The defendant had abducted a woman from an Interstate 91 rest area in Westminster, Vermont and forced her in the back of a tractor-trailer truck. She was then driven to an unknown location, raped, and ultimately released in the New York city area. Although RFLP DNA evidence was admitted and linked the defendant to the crime, Jakobetz was ultimately convicted only of kidnapping.

In *People v. Axell* (1991), Linda Axell was accused of killing the owner of a convenience store. Left behind in the grasp of the victim were several strands of hair containing roots. Depending on the number of hairs, and the amount and condition of cellular material attached to the root end, hairs can occasionally be analyzed by RFLP. In this case, the RFLP testing was successful and, in fact, concordance was demonstrated between the hair and Axell. A long term and long distance admissibility hearing was held, in which many experts from around the country testified (the testimony of some witnesses took place outside of court, usually in the experts' office or laboratory). The hearing focused on both the molecular biology and population issues. The judge allowed the DNA to be admitted, including the use of statistics.

The decision on *Axell* was filed in October of 1991. In December 1991, the beginnings of a controversy over the use of population statistics erupted in the pages of *Science*. At the heart of the debate was the effect of possible substructure in the population on the assumption of statistical independence of the genetic loci used for forensic analysis. The practical consequence of this assumption is that the frequencies for each allele can be multiplied together to give an estimate for the frequency of the composite DNA profile.

In 1992, the National Research Council (NRC) Committee on DNA Technology in Forensic Science published a set of recommendations addressing this topic and others. Their suggestion was to employ a calculation called the "ceiling principle" which put an artificial limit on the rareness of a particular genetic profile. The suggestion was intended as an interim solution (and in fact one iteration was called the "interim ceiling principle") only until a sufficient number of population groups could be empirically sampled. Once completed, the data from such a study would be used to determine if, in fact, significant substructuring existed and, more importantly, if it would preclude the multiplication of allele frequencies. Although the judicial system initially regarded the "ceiling principle" as a long-awaited solution, many scientists rebelled against it as an artificial construct with no scientific foundation. The original NRC committee itself was plagued with intrigue and dissent, so much so, that a new committee was convened (in 1994) in an attempt to clarify the many misunderstandings that resulted from the original document.

However, in the meantime, two more landmark cases came before the 1st Appellate District of California. In each of the cases, *People v. Barney* and *People v. Howard,* the county of Alameda superior court had ruled RFLP evidence admissible. In opposition to the *Axell* decision, the appellate court ruled that in the intervening time a controversy about the use of population statistics had surfaced in the scientific community. On the basis of this new information, the court barred the use of DNA until the controversy had been resolved. However, the error in admitting DNA was judged harmless, and both convictions were upheld based on other evidence. The irony of the situation can be summed up in a footnote of the decision: *"We recognize the irony in finding a frequency estimate of 1.2 in 1,000 (from conventional typing) to be significant while excluding DNA evidence which would have to be in error by five or six orders of magnitude—a degree of error not even claimed by Lewontin and Hartl—to approach a reduced equivalence...."*

In the face of apparent dissension and controversy, two more California appellate decisions on the admission of RFLP evidence followed in tracks of *Barney-Howard*. In *People v. Pizarro* (1992), the decision was remanded back to trial court for evidence on gene frequency estimates. Soon after, RFLP DNA analysis in *People v. Wallace* (1993) was rejected, also based on the perceived lack of consensus concerning the method for estimating gene frequencies. A 1994 decision from the fourth district Court of Appeals, *People v. Soto* reversed this trend. The case was an attempted rape of a 78 year old woman in Orange County which occurred in 1989. Sexual assault evidence was obtained and RFLP results associated Frank Soto with the crime scene. A *Kelly-Frye* hearing was held, and the Court of Appeals held that the procedures used to estimate the frequency of the DNA profile were considered reliable and valid by the relevant scientific community. Further, the judge's ruling stated that the DNA results were too relevant and probative to be ignored. Several other California Appellate courts have held DNA typing to be admissible. The California Supreme Court is currently considering a number of DNA cases with the intention of rendering a definative admissibility ruling.

Two states in particular have a history of admitting associative DNA testing results, while specifically barring any numerical statements regarding the significance of a pattern match. In Arizona this includes *State v. Hummert* and *State v. Hale* (1991), as well as a case dealing with analysis of plant DNA, *State v. Bogen* (see *Sidebar 9*). The Arizona Supreme Court is currently considering these cases, and in light of the most recent NRC report (see *Chapter 11*), it is expected that they will rule in favor of the admission of statistics used to estimate the significance of DNA results. Similarly, the Supreme Court of the State of Minnesota had, since the late 1970's, issued rulings precluding the introduction of statistics pertaining to any scientific evidence, not just DNA specifically. However, in 1994 while considering *State v. Bloom*, along with *State v. Bauer* and *State v. Perez*, they partially reversed themselves. In their decision they state that "National Research Council's adoption of a conservative *"interim ceiling method" for computation of probability that a randomly selected person would have same DNA profile as that of sample found at crime scene justifies creation of a **DNA exception** to the rule against admission of statistical probability evidence in criminal prosecution to prove identity; moreover, a properly qualified expert may, if the evidentiary foundation is sufficient, give an opinion that, to a reasonable degree of scientific certainty, the defendant is (or is not) the source of the bodily evidence found at the crime scene."*

## B. PCR

DNA evidence was first introduced in a United States civil trial in 1986 (*People v. Pestinikas*). PCR testing has enjoyed a higher success rate in the trial courts, even though it is a newer technique. Ironically, part of the reason is that the HLA DQα test, which was the only one available for many years, is not nearly as powerful as RFLP so the comfort level has been greater. Also, for DQα and also D1S80, only one locus is tested, so arguments about combining the results from several different loci do not come into play. This is already changing as more PCR markers come into use, in particular polymarker and multi-locus STR systems. Of the 20 PCR cases that have come before state appellate courts, only one has been remanded back to the trial court. There have been no major decisions as yet regarding the newer PCR tests, polymarker, D1S80, STRs and mitochondrial typing.

PCR DNA analysis has encountered different challenges than RFLP. While the issues in RFLP have focused on the population genetics, challenges to PCR have focused on the specific application of the methodology. *People v. Pestinikas* was the first U.S. case in which *any* DNA evidence was employed. Two autopsies were performed on the same body at different times. Formaldehyde-preserved tissues taken from each of the autopsies were compared by DNA typing to test the possibility that they were from different people. HLA DQα results were consistent with the notion that both sets of samples in question were from *Pestinikas*, and the evidence was accepted by the civil court.

PCR DNA testing, in particular HLA DQα, has garnered much public attention as a powerful tool to free men wrongly convicted of rape. In a number of these cases the victims had identified their alleged assailants in a line-up. Interestingly, no resistance has come from any corner concerning use of this technique.

One example of this use of DNA typing is *People v. Dotson*. In 1977 Gary Dotson was accused of raping Cathleen Webb. Although conventional serological typing was inconclusive, he was convicted in 1979 primarily on the basis of her eye witness identification. Eight years later, in 1985, the victim recanted her identification and admitted to having had consensual intercourse with her boyfriend. Eleven years later, HLA DQα typing clearly eliminated Dotson as the semen donor of the evidence; moreover, the boyfriend was included. The judge, however refused to believe either the victim's recantation or the corroborating DNA evidence and would not release Dotson. Ultimately, the governor of Illinois did not pardon but did grant clemency to Gary Dotson. *Dotson* is an example of a common use of HLA DQα – as an exclusionary tool. As with all genetic marker tests, exclusion is absolute.

In *People v. Martinez* (1989), one of a small number of early rejections of PCR evidence occurred. On post-conviction review, HLA DQα analysis showed a pair of panties from a child molestation victim to contain semen from someone other than the defendant. Testimony was offered by a single defense expert (the analyst who performed the test) whose results did not convince the judge to overturn the conviction. It seemed that the technique was simply too new at that time for the majority of forensic scientists to have had an opportunity to use it, much less endorse it. Dr. Edward Blake, a pioneer in the use of HLA DQα, was one of the few forensic scientists using the technique at the time, although PCR, in general, was already well-accepted in the general scientific community.

Another case in which HLA DQα evidence failed admissibility was *People v. Mack* (1990). This was a Sacramento, California case in which it was alleged that semen found on the panties of the decedent victim was from the defendant. As in *Martinez*, Judge Tochterman found that PCR had not yet achieved a reasonable level of acceptance in the forensic community, and that more validation was needed. An interesting aside is that Mack confessed on the stand to having had intercourse with the victim the last time she had been seen alive.

In *People v. Quintanilla* (1991) (see *Sidebar 3*), PCR typing was successfully advanced, and recently came before the appellate court of California. In this case, HLA DQα typing was used to both exclude the original suspect and subsequently include a different suspect. The evidence was admitted by the trial court and the second suspect was ultimately convicted. As in several other cases involving PCR in California, the appellate court refused to rule on the admissibility issue, saying any finding would constitute harmless error.

## III.  THE STATE OF THE DEBATE

In October of 1994, Eric Lander of the Whitehead Institute and Bruce Budowle of the FBI published a joint letter in the journal *Nature* in which they declared the DNA wars over. Lander had been one of the main detractors of the particular application of statistics to DNA analysis and was a member of the original NRC Committee.  Lander and Budowle wrote that the extensive scientific literature, existing quality control (QC) guidelines, and the NRC I Report had resolved all of the issues preventing the admissibility of DNA in court.  They further indicated that the NRC I report had been misinterpreted by the forensic community and legal system alike.  The "ceiling principle" had never been intended to replace an estimate obtained by multiplying the frequencies of alleles contained in a DNA profile; rather it was to provide a conservative limit value as a secondary alternative.  In the meantime, the data on substructuring has been accumulating; virtually everyone agrees that what little substructuring is present has little or no effect on the determination of the rareness of a particular DNA profile in the general population.

In Spring of this year (1996), the second committee gathered by the NRC issued a prepublication copy of its report (see *Chapter 11*).  It even more fully endorses DNA typing for forensic use.  Interestingly, the NRC II committee agreed with the dissenters regarding the lack of merit of the "ceiling principle", and has dropped support of its use in estimating profile frequencies.  Instead they suggest several alternative procedures, based on population genetics and statistics, for providing an estimate of the significance of indistinguishable genetic profiles.  In the Executive Summary of the NRC II report, they conclude that *"The technology for DNA profiling and the methods for estimating frequencies and related statistics have progressed to the point where the reliability and validity of properly collected and analyzed DNA should not be in doubt."*  Interestingly, a number of challenges to the admission of DNA evidence have been withdrawn since NRC II has issued it's report.  Although, as with all forensic evidence, each case must be considered on its own merits, it seems hopeful that a consensus regarding the general reliability of DNA analysis is at least within grasp.

---

### SIDEBAR 11

### The First RFLP Case
### (State of Florida v. Tommy Lee Andrews)

For the police in Orlando, Florida, the year of 1986 was marked by over 20 cases of prowling, breaking and entering, and attempted sexual assault.  In each case, the man would stalk his victim for weeks, prowling around her house, and peeping through windows.  When attacked, the assailant always managed to arrange things so that he was not directly observed for any length of time.  Tommy Lee Andrews was finally arrested, based mostly on composite drawings extracted from fleeting glimpses by his many victims.

Hal Uhrig, a private defense attorney was appointed council for Andrews.  Little did he know that he was about to become involved in the first criminal case in the United States where DNA evidence would be introduced. The prosecuting attorney had read an advertisement for DNA testing by Lifecodes Corp., and decided to employ their services.  RFLP testing was performed on some of the sexual assault evidence, and the first DNA admissibility hearing commenced.

Although the results from the Lifecodes tests were admitted, the trial ended in a hung jury.

Jeffrey Ashton was the prosecuting attorney for the retrial of Tommy Lee Andrews, and this time Andrews was convicted. Both the conviction and introduction of DNA evidence were upheld at the appellate level.

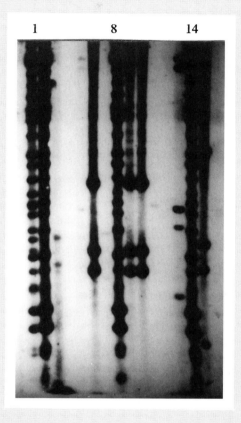

**One autorad from the case**. Lanes 1, 2, 8, and 14 contain a molecular ladder. Lane 3 contains a victim reference sample, Lane 5 contains the sexual assault evidence from a vaginal swab; the sperm and e. cell fractions were not separated in this case. Lane 13 contains the reference blood sample from Andrews. The other lanes contain various control samples. Bands from Andrews and the bands from the victim are both present in the mixed evidentiary sample..

*Addendum:* During the final editing of this book (October 1996) we became aware that mitochondrial DNA typing had been admitted at the trial court level in the U.S. The evidence consisted of several hairs that were ultimately associated with the suspect. Based on this evidence, a Chattanooga, Tennessee jury convicted a man of raping and murdering a 4-year-old girl.

─────── *FURTHER  REFERENCES*───────

*Andrews v. State*, 533 So. 2d 841, Fla. Dist. Ct. App, 1988.

**Blake, E., Mihalovich, J., Higuchi, R., Walsh, P.S., Erlich, H.**, Polymerase chain reaction (PCR) amplification and human leukocyte antigen (HLA)-DQ alpha oligonucleotide typing on biological evidence samples: casework experience, *Journal of Forensic Sciences*, 37, 3, 700-26, 1992.

**Budowle, B., Lander, E.S.**, DNA fingerprinting dispute laid to rest. *Nature*, 371, 735-738, 1994.

**Devlin, B., Risch, N., Roeder, K.**, Comments on the statistical aspects of the NRC's report on DNA typing, *Journal of Forensic Sciences*, 39, 1, 28-40, 1994.

**Devlin, B., Risch, N., Roeder K.**, Statistical evaluation of DNA fingerprinting: a critique of the NRC's report, *Science* 259, 748-750, 1993.

**Devlin, B.**, Technical Comments, *Science*, 253, 1039-1041, 1991.

**Evett, I.W., Buckleton, J.S., Raymond, A., Roberts, H.**, The evidential value of DNA profiles, *Journal - Forensic Science Society*, 33, 4 , 243-4, 1993.

*Frye v. United States*, 293 F. 1013, D.C. Circuit, 1923.

**Hartl, D.L.**, Forensic DNA typing dispute, *Nature*, 372, 6505, 398-9, 1994.

**Jeffreys, A.J.**, 1992 William Allan Award address, *American Journal of Human Genetics*, 53, 1, 1-5, 1993.

**Jeffreys, A.J.**, DNA typing: approaches and applications, *Journal - Forensic Science Society*, 33, 4, 204-11, 1993.

**Kisluik, B.**, Court spurns federal 'Junk Science' ruling, *The Recorder,* Oct. 1994.

**Lander, E.S.**, DNA fingerprinting on trial. *Nature*, 339, 501-505, 1989.

**Lewontin, R., Hartl, D.**, Population genetics in forensic DNA analysis, *Science*, 254, 1745-1750, 1991.

**Lewontin, R., Hartl, D.**, Statistical Evaluation of DNA Fingerprinting: a critique of the NRC's report, *Science*, 259, 748-750, 1993.

**Monckton, D.G., Jeffreys, A.J.**, DNA profiling, *Current Opinion in Biotechnology*, 4, 6, 660-4, 1993.

**National Research Council**, *DNA Technology in Forensic Science*, National Academy Press, Washington D.C., 1992.

**National Research Council**, *The Evaluation of Forensic DNA Evidence*, National Academy Press, Washington D.C., 1996.

*People of the State of California v. Daniel Leon Martinez*, No. A70932, Super. Ct., Los Angeles County, 1989.

*People of the State of California v. Mack*, No. 89-25, Super. Ct., Sacramento County, 1990.

*People v. Axell*, 235 Cal. App. 3d 836, 1991.

*People v. Barney*; Howard, 8 Cal. App. 4th 798, 1992.

*People v. Castro*, 144 Misc.2d 956, 545 N.Y.S. 2d 985, Sup. Ct. 1989.

*People v. Guerra*, 37 Cal. 3d. 385, 418, 1984.

*People v. Kelly*, 17 Cal. 3d 24, 1976.

*People v. Pizarro*, 10 Cal. App. 4th 57, 1992.

*People v. Soto*, 30 Cal. App. 4th 340 1994.

*People v. Wallace*, 14 Cal. App. 4th 651, 1993.

**Robertson, B., Vignaux, G. A.,** DNA evidence: wrong answers or wrong questions?, *Genetica*, 96, 1-2, 145-52, 1995.

**Rothwell, T. J.,** DNA profiling and crime investigation--the European context. *Journal - Forensic Science Society*, 33, 4, 226-7, 1993.

*State v. Bauer*, 516 N.W. 2d 174 (Minn. 1994) affirming 512 N.W.2d 11, Minn. Ct. App. 1994.

*State v. Bloom*, 516 N.W.2d 15, Minn. 1994.

*State v. Bogen*, 905 P.2d 515 (Ariz Ct. App. 1995).

*State v. Brown*, 297 Or. 404, 687 P.2d 751, 759, Or. 1984.

*State v. Hummert; Hale*, 905 P.2d 493 (Ariz. Ct. App. 1994)

*State v. Perez*, 516 N.W.2d 175, Minn. 1994, (See *State v. Bloom*).

**Technical Working Group on DNA Analysis Methods (TWGDAM)**, Guidelines for a proficiency testing program for DNA Restriction Fragment Length Polymorphism Analysis, *Crime Lab Digest* 17, 2, 50-60, 1990.

**Technical Working Group on DNA Analysis Methods (TWGDAM)**, Guidelines for a quality assurance program for DNA Restriction Fragment Length Polymorphism Analysis, *Crime Lab Dig.* 16, 2, 40-59, 1989.

**Technical Working Group on DNA Analysis Methods (TWGDAM)**, Statement of the Working Group on Statistical Standards for DNA Analysis, *Crime Lab Dig.* 17, 3, 53-58, 1990.

*United States v. Jakobetz*, 747 F. Supp 250, D. Vt. 1990.

*United States v. Yee*, ND, Ohio 129 FRD 692, 1990.

*William Daubert v. Merrell Dow*, 61 U.S.L.W., 4805, June 28, 1993.

**Wooley, J., Harmon, R.P.,** The forensic DNA brouhaha: science or debate?, *American Journal of Human Genetics*, 51, 5, 1164-5, 1992.

# Chapter 13

## EPILOGUE - MOVING INTO THE NEXT MILLENNIUM

Virtually every scientific paper published, whether critical or supportive of DNA typing in the forensic context, either starts or ends by stating that the technique is or will be a valuable tool in the crime lab. What does the future hold for DNA typing in the lab and in the courtroom?

In the lab, automation will become central. At least two forces will drive this movement. Felon databases have been enacted into law by many states, with the consequent collection of huge numbers of samples. For example, as of late 1994, the state of California had in excess of 50,000 samples from convicted violent offenders waiting for analysis. The Armed Forces are also instituting a complete DNA databank of all of their personnel, clearly a daunting project. Database samples are particularly amenable to automated methods because quantity and quality are much less of an issue than for casework samples. In addition, the increased acceptance of DNA in court will instigate the submission of an mounting volume of cases, forcing adaption of the current methodology to provide increased speed and efficiency. Since adding equipment is always less expensive than adding people, lab directors are looking for instruments and techniques that increase output by a factor of ten or more.

Progress has already been made with both RFLP-based and PCR-based methods in both these areas. A complete DNA profile using radioactive RFLP probes currently takes a minimum of 6 to 8 weeks. Non-isotopic labeling methods, such as chemiluminescence, are both safer and faster, reducing that time to about 1 1/2 to 2 weeks. The analysis of the newer STR systems incorporates multiplexing, a technique that amplifies and detects three or four different markers in one reaction run. In combination with fluorescent labeling, which greatly facilitates automated detection and data management, relatively high discrimination can be achieved with these methods in a matter of 2 to 4 days. Also on the horizon is capillary electrophoresis, another rapid, sensitive technique for the automated separation and detection of small DNA fragments. Human judgment is most critical during the initial steps of extracting and evaluating of DNA from evidence samples. But even in this arena, automation is making inroads. Perhaps that computer will testify to the source of the sample yet!

As population genetics issues become resolved, standard methods of expressing the significance of genetic concordance will be adopted. It is likely that labs will institute a predetermined set of markers with a combined $P_d$, such that an individualized profile is attained, no matter what types the profile contains. Alternatively, an analyst may sequentially test a set of markers until a population frequency estimate that has been determined to approach individuality is achieved; it would be redundant to continue the analysis past this point. As more loci and markers systems become available, labs can choose those that meet the particular needs of the lab or of the case.

There seems to be no end to the discovery of new DNA marker systems by researchers, many of which can be adapted for forensic use. A new technique called Minisatellite Variant Repeat (MVR) analysis is an example. This method approaches individualization with just one or two loci. An ideal use of MVRs would be to connect a series of rapes or to keep track of serial rapists who are still at large. Once a suspect is caught and his MVR profile confirmed, other, more common DNA markers could be used for court presentation.

Mitochondrial sequencing, which has been developed mostly for typing ancient DNA and anthropological samples, can be used to type hair shafts (no root is needed) providing a much greater level of discrimination than is now possible with conventional microscopic techniques. The ideal DNA laboratory will have a series of tools, each with different capabilities, available to solve the appropriate problem.

Quality control remains an area of contention surrounding forensic DNA typing. Issues of proficiency testing and risk of error continue to be raised by both the legal and scientific communities. Recent attention to self-regulation through accreditation and certification has succeeded in raising the general quality of work performed, but some insist that legislative regulation is necessary to ensure uniform quality. This issue promises to instigate the most volatile and vituperative DNA debate held yet .

DNA is clearly the most important type of evidence introduced to forensic science in many decades. It is subject to the same forensic framework as other types of evidence; it does not establish guilt; it must be performed by scientists who can think critically about the meaning of evidence in the context of the case; and it is used within the same confines of the legal arena. There will come a day when DNA analysis is just another part of the lab, and prosecutors and defense attorneys alike will automatically look for both the fingerprint *and* DNA reports.

────── *FURTHER REFERENCES* ──────

**Dimo-Simonin, N., Brandt-Casadevall, C., Gujer, H.R.,** Chemiluminescent DNA probes: evaluation and usefulness in forensic cases, *Forensic Science International*, 57, 2, 119-27, 1992.

**Gill, P., Ivanov, P. L., Kimpton, C., Piercy, R., Benson, N., Tully, G., Evett, I., Hagelberg, E., Sullivan, K.,** Identification of the remains of the Romanov family by DNA analysis. *Nature Genetics*, 6, 2, 130-5, 1994.

**Ginther, C., Issel-Tarver, L., Kin, M.C.,** Identifying individuals by sequencing mitochondrial DNA from teeth, *Nature Genetics*, 2, 2, 135-8, 1992.

**Hopkins, B., Williams, N.J., Webb, M. B., Debenham, P.G., Jeffreys, A.J.,** The use of minisatellite variant repeat-polymerase chain reaction (MVR-PCR) to determine the source of saliva on a used postage stamp, *Journal of Forensic Sciences*, 39, 2, 526-31, 1994.

**Jeffreys, A.J., MacLeod, A., Tamaki, K., Neil, D.L., Monckton, D.G.,** Minisatellite repeat coding as a digital approach to DNA typing, *Nature*, 354, 6350, 204-9, 1991.

**Jeffreys, A.J., Monckton, D.G., Tamaki, K., Neil, D.L., Armour, J.A., MacLeod, A., Collick, A., Allen, M., Jobling, M.,** Minisatellite variant repeat mapping: application to DNA typing and mutation analysis, *Exs*, 67, 125-39, 1993.

**Monckton, D.G., Tamaki, K., MacLeod, A., Neil, D.L., Jeffreys, A.J.,** Allele-specific MVR-PCR analysis at minisatellite D1S8, *Human Molecular Genetics*, 2, 5, 513-9, 1993.

**Neil, D.L., Jeffreys, A.J.,** Digital DNA typing at a second hypervariable locus by minisatellite variant repeat mapping, *Human Molecular Genetics*, Aug, 2, 8, 1129-35, 1993.

**Pearce, M.J., Watson, N.D.,** Rapid analysis of PCR components and products by acidic non-gel capillary electrophoresis, *Exs*, 67, 117-24, 1993.

**Skolnick, A.A.,** Mitochondrial DNA studies help identify lost victims of human rights,. *Jama*, 269, 15, 1911-3, 1993.

**Tamaki, K., Huang, X.L., Yamamoto, T., Uchihi, R., Nozawa, H., Katsumata, Y.,** Applications of minisatellite variant repeat (MVR) mapping for maternal identification from remains of an infant and placenta, *Journal of Forensic Sciences*, 40, 4, 695-700, 1995.

**Tamaki, K., Monckton, D.G., MacLeod, A., Allen, M., Jeffreys, A.J.,** Four-state MVR-PCR: increased discrimination of digital DNA typing by  simultaneous analysis of two polymorphic sites within minisatellite  variant repeats at D1S8, *Human Molecular Genetics*, 2, 10, 1629-32, 1993.

PCR: increased discrimination of digital DNA typing by simultaneous analysis of two polymorphic sites within minisatellite variant repeats at D1S8, *Human Molecular Genetics*, Oct., 2, 10, 1629-32, 1993.

**Yamamoto, T., Tamaki, K., Kojima, T., Uchihi, R., Katsumata, Y., Jeffrey, A.J.,** DNA typing of the D1S8 (MS32) locus by rapid detection minisatellite  variant repeat (MVR) mapping using polymerase chain reaction (PCR) assay, *Forensic Science International*, 66, 1, 69-75, 1994 .

**Yamamoto, T., Tamaki, K., Kojima, T., Uchihi, R., Katsumata, Y.,** Potential forensic applications of minisatellite variant repeat (MVR) mapping using the polymerase chain reaction (PCR) at D1S8, *Journal of Forensic Sciences*, 39, 3, 743-50, 1994.

# GLOSSARY

**A**  Single-letter designation of the base adenine; one of the four building blocks of DNA.

**ABC**  American Board of Criminalistics, the oversight body for certification of criminalists.

**Accreditation**  Crime Laboratories can be accredited for DNA testing. Accreditation of a Crime Laboratory means that the lab meets minimum professional standards for accurate and reliable testing.

**Acrylamide**  (see *polyacrylamide*)

**Adenine**  One of the four building blocks of DNA.

**AFIS**  Automated Fingerprint Identification System.

**Agarose**  Gel medium used for separation of DNA fragments in a variety of tests, including yield gels, digest gels, PCR product gels and RFLP analytical gel.

**Allele**  One of two or more alternative forms of a gene or genetic marker.

**Allele Frequency**  (see *Gene Frequency*)

**Amelogenin**  The locus at which gender may be determined in forensic typing systems.

**AMP-FLP, AFLP, AMFLP**  Amplified Fragment Length Polymorphism; a length polymorphism (VNTR) analyzed using PCR. D1S80 is analyzed as an AMP-FLP.

**ASCLD**  American Society of Crime Lab Directors.

**ASCLD/LAB**  American Society of Crime Lab Directors Laboratory Accreditation Board.

**ASO**  Allele specific oligonucleotide. A technically incorrect name for a short synthetic probe used to pinpoint a specific sequence using hybridization. (see **SSO**)

**Association**  Concept used in crime scene reconstruction; description of relationship between two objects, items, or people.

**Autoradiogram, Autoradiograph, Autorad**  An X-ray film on which radioactively or chemiluminescently labeled probes have left a mark determining the positions of particular DNA fragments; (see *Lumigraph*).

**Autosome**  Any chromosome other than the sex chromosomes, X and Y.

**Band**                    The visual image representing a particular DNA fragment on an autorad.

**Band Shift**              The phenomenon in which DNA fragments in one lane of a gel migrate at a rate different from that of identical fragments in other lanes of the same gel.

**Base**                    A subunit of nucleic acid. Technically, the base is the portion of a nucleotide that makes it an **A, G, T, C,** etc. The term is often used informally in discussing the nucleotide "residues" in a DNA or RNA molecule.

**Base Pair**               Two complementary bases held together by chemical bonds; complementary base pairing occurs between **A** and **T** and between **G** and **C.**

**Biallelic, Diallelic**    A locus at which only two alleles are found.

**Binning**                 A method used to assign allele frequencies in constructing a population database. All the alleles in a bin take on the frequency of the entire group.

**C**                       Single-letter designation of the base Cytosine; one of the four building blocks of DNA.

**CACLD**                   California Association of Crime Laboratory Directors.

**Ceiling Principle**       More properly a calculation, it is one of several which may be employed in multiplying allele frequencies to determine the significance of a genetic concordance. It states that for each allele in a product calculation, the highest frequency among the groups sampled, or 5%, must be used, whichever is larger.

**Cell**                    Basic building block of an organism.

**Centromere**              The central element of a chromosome.

**Certification**           Forensic scientists (criminalists) can be certified for DNA testing. Certification of a forensic scientist (criminalist) means that the analyst has demonstrated the minimum professional knowledge, skills, and abilities to perform DNA testing.

**Chelex**                  Chemical used in DNA extraction.

**Chelex Extraction**       One method of extracting DNA from cells.

**Chromosome**              The structure by which hereditary information is physically transmitted from one generation to the next; the organelle that carries the genes.

**Circumstantial Evidence** Any evidence in a case which is not observed by an eyewitness. All physical evidence is circumstantial.

| | |
|---|---|
| **Class Characteristic** | Term used in crime scene reconstruction. Characteristics of an item that put it in a class with other similar items. |
| **Coding** | A region of DNA that has the capability of producing a protein. |
| **CODIS** | Combined DNA Information System –a series of local, state and national computer applications and databases. |
| **Complementary Base Pairing** | (see *base Pairing*) |
| **Conservative Estimate** | An estimate that has factors incorporated into it that will deliberately overestimate the occurrence of any particular profile in the population. Depending on the circumstances of the case, this may or may not "favor the defendant". |
| **Controls** | Tests performed in parallel with experimental or evidence samples and designed to demonstrate that a procedure worked correctly. |
| **Cytosine** | One of the four building blocks of DNA. |
| **D1S80** | A VNTR locus used in forensic DNA typing. D1S80 is typed using PCR. |
| **D-loop** | A hypervariable region of DNA sequence located on mitochondrial DNA. |
| **Degradation** | The breaking down of DNA into smaller fragments by chemical or physical means. |
| **Denaturation** | The separation of double-stranded DNA into single-stranded DNA by heat or chemical means. |
| **Deoxynucleotides** | The specific type of nucleotides that comprise DNA. |
| **Deoxyribonucleic Acid (DNA)** | The genetic material of organisms composed of two complementary chains of nucleotides in the form of a double helix. |
| **Dideoxynucleotides** | A synthetic DNA nucleotide analogue. They are missing the portion that allows linkage to the next nucleotide in a chain, and therefore terminate DNA chains in which they become incorporated. |
| **Differential Extraction** | DNA extraction procedure in which sperm cells are separated from other cells before the DNA is purified. |
| **Digest Gel** | Diagnostic step in the RFLP DNA typing procedure; measures completeness of restriction enzyme digestion. |
| **Diploid** | Having two sets of chromosomes, in pairs; people are diploid organisms. |

| | |
|---|---|
| **Diplomate of the ABC** | A criminalist who has passed a general knowledge test in forensic science given by the American Board of Criminalistics. |
| **Discrete Alleles** | Any allele in a genetic typing system in which the detection method can clearly distinguish between the variants being tested. |
| **DNA** | Deoxyribonucleic acid. |
| **DNA Amplification** | Process of making multiple copies of DNA using the polymerase chain reaction (PCR). |
| **DNA band** | (*see Band*) |
| **DNA data bank (database)** | A collection of DNA typing profiles of selected or randomly chosen individuals. |
| **DNA Fingerprint** | A misnomer;  (see *DNA Profile, DNA Type*). |
| **DNA Polymerase** | An enzyme that synthesizes new DNA from an existing template. |
| **DNA Probe** | A short segment of DNA labeled with a radioactive or chemical tag that is used to detect the presence of a particular DNA sequence or fragment. |
| **DNA Replication** | The synthesis of new DNA from existing DNA. |
| **DNA Type, Genetic Type** | Profile compiled from the results of DNA testing of one or more genetic markers. |
| **DOJ** | Department of Justice. |
| **Double Helix** | Native form of DNA when single strands are held together by complementary base pairing and twined around each other in the form of a double helix. |
| **Double-Stranded DNA** | Form of DNA when single strands are held together by complementary base pairing. |
| **DQ$\alpha$** | (see *HLA DQ$\alpha$*) |
| **DQA1** | (see *HLA DQA1*) |
| **Electrophoresis** | A technique in which molecules are separated by their rate of movement in an electric field; in the case of DNA the fragments are separated according to size. |
| **Enzyme** | A protein that is capable of speeding up a specific biochemical reaction but which itself is not changed or consumed in the process; a biological catalyst. |
| **Epithelial Cells, E. Cells** | Cells such as skin cells, vaginal cells or other cells normally found on an inner or outer body surface. |

| | |
|---|---|
| **Error Rate** | The percentage of times that a laboratory or an analyst *reports* an incorrect inclusion or exclusion (genetic similarity or dissimilarity) between two samples. |
| **Ethidium Bromide** | Chemical dye that binds to double-stranded DNA and renders it visible in the presence of ultraviolet light. |
| **Eukaryote** | A type of cell that contains a nucleus and various organelles. |
| **Evidence Sample** | Sample taken from the crime scene or people or objects associated with it. |
| **Exclusion** | Term used in forensic analysis to describe a person or sample which could not have contributed a particular sample. |
| **Extension** | Term used in the polymerase chain reaction (PCR); the addition of nucleotides to form a new DNA strand from a primed template. |
| **FBI** | Federal Bureau of Investigation. |
| **Federal Rules of Evidence** | An admissibility standard for scientific evidence which relies on federal rules 702 and 403.  The criteria are reliability, relevancy, and more probative than prejudicial. |
| **Fellow of the ABC** | A criminalist who has passed a general knowledge test in forensic science, and also a specialty exam and hands-on proficiency test, given by the American Board of Criminalistics. |
| **Frye Standard** | An admissibility standard for scientific evidence which relies on the federal decision of *Frye vs. United States*. General acceptance in the relevant scientific community is the main criteria. |
| **G** | Single-letter designation of the base Guanine, one of the four building blocks of DNA. |
| **Gamete** | A haploid reproductive cell; sperm or egg. |
| **Gel** | Semisolid matrix (usually agarose or acrylamide) used in electrophoresis to separate molecules. |
| **Gene** | The basic unit of heredity; a sequence of DNA nucleotides on a chromosome. |
| **Gene Frequency** | The relative occurrence of a particular allele, or gene form, in a population. |
| **Genetic Concordance** | DNA profiles which appear indistinguishable in the tests conducted. |
| **Genetic Linkage, Linkage** | Used to describe genetic markers which are often inherited together. |

| | |
|---|---|
| **Genetic Marker, Marker** | A defined location on a chromosome having known genetic characteristics. |
| **Genetic Similarity** | DNA profiles which look similar in the tests conducted. |
| **Genome** | The total genetic makeup of an organism. |
| **Genotype** | The genetic makeup of an organism, as distinguished from its physical appearance or phenotype.  It may pertain to one locus or many. |
| **Guanine** | One of the four building blocks of DNA. |
| ***Hae*III** | A restriction enzyme used in RFLP analysis.  The standard enzyme used in the U.S. |
| **Haploid** | Having one set of chromosomes (compare *diploid*). |
| **Hardy-Weinberg Equilibrium** | The condition, for a particular genetic locus and a particular population, with the following properties: allele frequencies at the locus are constant in the population over time and there is no statistical correlation between the two alleles possessed by individuals in the population; such a condition is approached in large randomly mating populations in the absence of selection, migration, and mutation. |
| **Hemizygous** | The situation in which a chromosomal element has no complement.  This is normal for haploid organisms, and for some genetic elements, such as mtDNA in diploid organisms. |
| **Heredity** | The transmission of genetic characteristics from parent to offspring. |
| **Heteroplasmy** | In particular reference to mtDNA, the situation in which two populations of hemizygous molecules exist in an individual.  It is the exception to the norm. |
| **Heterozygote** | A diploid organism that carries different alleles at one or more genetic loci on each one of two paired chromosomes. |
| **Heterozygous** | Having different alleles at a particular locus; for most forensic DNA probes, the autorad generally displays two bands if the person is heterozygous at the locus. |
| **Heterozygosity ($h_o$)** | The proportion of the population that has two different alleles (heterozygous) at a particular locus.  It is preferable for loci used in forensic typing to exhibit a relatively high heterozygosity. |
| ***Hin*fI** | Restriction enzyme use in RFLP analysis.  Most European labs use this enzyme. |

| | |
|---|---|
| **HLA DQα** | The historical name for a locus used in forensic DNA typing. It also refers to the first iteration of the commercial kit available for its analysis; (see **HLA DQA1**). |
| **HLA DQA1** | The current name for a locus used in forensic DNA typing. It also refers to the second iteration of the commercial kit available for its analysis; (see **HLA DQα**). |
| **HMW, High Molecular Weight** | Use to describe DNA which is in large pieces, and has not been significantly broken down or degraded by physical or chemical means. |
| $h_o$ | (see *Heterozygosity*) |
| **Homozygous** | Having the same allele on both chromosomes at a particular locus; for most forensic DNA probes, the autoradiogram generally displays a single band if the person is homozygous at the locus. |
| **HRP, Horseradish Peroxidase** | Enzyme used in some forensic PCR typing systems; Produces a blue color marking the presence of a particular allele on a typing strip. |
| **Human Genome Project** | International project to decipher and catalogue all the information in the human genome. |
| **Human Leukocyte Antigen (HLA)** | Cell structures that differ among individuals and are important for acceptance or rejection of tissue grafts or organ transplants; the DNA locus of one particular class, HLA DQα, is used for forensic analysis with PCR. |
| **Hybridization** | Detection of particular DNA fragments or sequences by complementary base pairing of tagged probes. |
| **Hypervariable** | A DNA locus that shows extreme variation between people. |
| **Hypervariable Region I (HVI)** | In mtDNA, one of the two highly polymorphic areas in the control region. |
| **Hypervariable Region II (HVII)** | In mtDNA, one of the two highly polymorphic areas in the control region. |
| **In Vitro** | Literally "in glass", it refers to biochemical reactions which take place out of the body, usually in a test tube or other laboratory apparatus. |
| **Inclusion** | Term used in forensic analysis to describe a person or sample which could have produced a particular DNA type. |
| **Independent Segregation** | Offspring inherit one of each homologous chromosome from each parent, never two from the same parent. |
| **Individualization** | When an object or piece of evidence exhibits traits that are so unique we are convinced that only one of such a thing exists. |

**Interim Ceiling Principle**   More properly a calculation, it is one of several which may be employed in multiplying allele frequencies to determine the significance of a genetic concordance. It states that for each allele in a product calculation, the highest frequency among the groups sampled, or 10%, must be used, whichever is larger.

**Isotope**   An alternative form of a chemical element; used particularly in reference to the radioactive alternative forms, or radioisotopes.

**K562**   Name of standard sample used in forensic DNA analysis in the U.S.

**Kilobase Pair**   One thousand base pairs.

**Length Polymorphism**   Locus that exhibits variations in length when cut with restriction enzymes or amplified with PCR primers. In forensic DNA analysis, variable number tandem repeat (VNTR) loci and short tandem repeat (STR) loci are used. Polymorphism in the restriction enzyme site produces another kind of length polymorphism.

**Linkage Equilibrium**   When two or more genetic loci show no correlation of genotypes between them.

**Locus (pl. Loci)**   The specific physical location of a gene on a chromosome.

**Lumigraph**   An X-ray film on which chemiluminescently labeled probes have left a mark determining the positions of particular DNA fragments;  (see *Autoradiograph*).

**Match**   (see *Genetic Concordance, Genetic Similarity*)

**Match Criteria**   A set of empirically derived data which is used to set limits on the amount of difference within which two DNA fragments can be considered as the same size in RFLP analysis.

**Membrane**   The support (usually nylon) to which DNA is transferred during the Southern blotting procedure.

**Mitochondrion (pl. Mitochondria)**   An organelle found in the vast majority of cells in the human body. Its DNA (mtDNA) is of interest to forensic scientists.

**MO**   Modus operandus, pl. modus operandi. The behavioral elements of a crime.

**Molecular Weight**   Refers to the molecular mass of a molecule. In DNA analysis, "molecular weight" and "band size" are often used interchangeably.

**Molecular-weight size marker**   DNA fragments of known size, from which the size of an unknown DNA sample can be determined.

| | |
|---|---|
| **Monoclonal** | A group of chromosomes or cells derived respectively from one chromosome or cell, and thus are identical. |
| **Monomorphic Probe** | A probe that detects an allele that is the same in everyone, hence shows the same pattern. Used as a diagnostic standard in RFLP analysis to check for sample-to-sample variation due to causes other than genetic polymorphism, such as environmental and experimental factors. |
| **mtDNA** | Mitochondrial DNA. |
| **Multilocus Probe** | A DNA probe that detects genetic variation at multiple sites; an autoradiogram of a multilocus probe yields a complex, stripelike pattern of 30 or more bands per individual. This pattern was originally mis-called a "DNA fingerprint"; not currently in use in the U.S; (see *Single-Locus Probe*) |
| **MVR** | Minisatellite variant repeat. |
| **NIH** | National Institutes of Health. |
| **NIJ** | National Institute of Justice. |
| **NIST** | National Institute of Standards and Technology. |
| **Noncoding** | A region of DNA which lacks the capacity to produce a protein. |
| **Nuclear DNA** | The DNA contained within the nucleus of a cell. It constitutes the vast majority of the cell genome. |
| **Nucleic Acid** | A general class of molecules which are polymers of nucleotides. DNA is a nucleic acid. |
| **Nucleotide** | A unit of nucleic acid. Technically, nucleotides are the raw building blocks of DNA or RNA. The term is often used informally in discussing the nucleotide "residues" left after the molecule is strung together. |
| **Nucleus** | An organelle found in the vast majority of cells in the human body. It contains most of the cell's genome. |
| **Organelle** | Any of the subcellular structures found in eukaryotic cells. |
| **Organic Extraction** | One method of extracting DNA from cells. |
| **Partial, Partial Digest** | The result of incomplete digestion by restriction enzymes. In RFLP analysis, this may result in an inconclusive result. |
| **PCR** | Polymerase Chain Reaction. |

**PCR Product**

The DNA amplified as a result of the polymerase chain reaction (PCR).

$P_d$

(see *Power of Discrimination*)

**Phenotype**

The physical appearance or functional expression of a trait.

**Physical Evidence**

Any evidence in a case that can be subjected to physical analysis.  All physical evidence is circumstantial.

**Point Mutation**

An alteration of one complementary nucleotide pair in chromosomal DNA that consists of addition, deletion, or substitution of paired nucleotides.

**Polyacrylamide**

Polymer which is used to separate relatively small DNA fragments.  In forensic DNA analysis, used in AMP-FLP and STR analysis.

**Polymarker**

Common usage for a commercial kit called *AmpliType®* *PM*; group of five different bi- and tri-allelic loci exhibiting sequence variation.  Available as a kit for forensic DNA analysis.

**Polymerase**

Enzyme which catalyzes the addition of subunits into a polymer.  (see *DNA polymerase*)

**Polymerase Chain Reaction (PCR)**

A process mediated by a DNA polymerase, that yields millions of copies of a desired DNA fragment.

**Polymorphism**

The presence of multiple alleles of a gene in a population.

**Population**

A group of individuals occupying a given area at a given time.

**Population Substructure, Subpopulations**

The existence of smaller mating groups within a larger community.

**Power of Discrimination ($P_d$)**

Used in reference to a genetic marker or combination of markers.  Defines the potential power of a system to differentiate between any two people chosen at random.  This can be calculated from the allele frequencies in a defined population.

**Probe**

A short segment of synthetic, tagged DNA, that is used to detect a particular DNA fragment or sequence.

**Product Gel**

Diagnostic tool used in PCR analysis to determine if a DNA sample has been successfully amplified.

**Product Rule**

The calculation based on population genetics that allows individual allele frequencies and genotype frequencies to be multiplied together to generate a genetic profile.

| | |
|---|---|
| **Proficiency Tests** | Proficiency testing is the analysis of material provided by an outside agency or laboratory to determine whether a laboratory or analyst can accurately and reliably perform DNA typing; in open tests, the analysts are aware that they are being tested; in blind tests, they are unaware. Internal proficiency tests are conducted by the laboratory itself, and external tests are conducted by an independent agency. |
| **Prokaryote** | A cell lacking a nucleus or any other subcellular organelles. Prokaryotes are all bacteria. |
| **Protein** | A class of biological molecules made up of amino acids; proteins provide much of the body's structure and function; enzymes are a subclass of proteins that perform specific biochemical functions. |
| **Quality Assurance (QA)** | A program conducted by laboratory to ensure accuracy and reliability of tests performed. |
| **Quality Control (QC)** | Internal activities or activities according to externally established standards used to monitor the quality of DNA typing to meet and satisfy specified criteria. |
| **Random Assortment** | Describes the behavior of non-homologous chromosomes in the generation of gametes; any one of a homologous chromosome pair associates with any one of another pair randomly. |
| **Reannealing** | The process of complementary single strands of DNA binding together; (see *hybridization*). |
| **Reference Sample** | A sample, often blood, taken from a known person, against which the evidence sample is compared. |
| **Relevancy Standard** | (see *Federal Rules of Evidence*) |
| **Restriction Enzyme, Restriction Endonuclease** | An enzyme that cuts DNA at specific locations determined by the DNA sequence. |
| **Restriction Fragment Length Polymorphism (RFLP)** | Variation in the length of DNA fragments produced by a restriction endonuclease (an enzyme) that cuts at a polymorphic locus. The polymorphism may be either in the restriction enzyme site or in the number of tandem repeat between the cut points. Variable Number Tandem Repeat (VNTR) loci are used in forensic DNA analysis. |
| **Reverse Dot Blot** | Specific detection method used for DNA amplified by the polymerase chain reaction (PCR). The probe is bound to the typing strip, and the PCR product applied after. |
| **RFLP** | Restriction Fragment Length Polymorphism. |
| **RFLP Analysis** | Technique that uses probes to detect variation in a DNA sequence according to differences in the length of fragment created by cutting the DNA with a restriction enzyme |

**Sequence Polymorphism**  Variation in specific base pairs at a particular locus. May include addition, deletion or substitution of base pairs.

**Serology**  The discipline concerned with the immunologic study of the body fluids.

**Serum**  The liquid that separates from blood after coagulation.

**Sex Chromosomes ( X and Y Chromosomes)**  Chromosomes that are different in the two sexes; in humans, females are XX and males are XY.

**Single-Locus probe**  A DNA probe that detects genetic variation at only one site in the genome; an autorad that uses one single-locus probe usually displays one band in homozygotes and two bands in heterozygotes.

**Single-Stranded DNA**  A form of DNA where the two strands that normally make up the double helix are separated.

**Slot Blot**  A diagnostic tool used in DNA analysis to determine how much human DNA has been extracted from a sample. Useful in making decisions about how much sample to use various typing procedures.

**Southern Blot, Blot**  The technique for transferring DNA fragments that have been separated by electrophoresis from the gel to a nylon membrane.

**Sperm Fraction**  In a differential extraction, the portion of a sample containing sperm, which has been separated from the rest of the sample before releasing DNA from the cells.

**SSO**  Sequence specific oligonucleotide. A short synthetic probe used to pinpoint a specific sequence using hybridization. SSOs are sometimes incorrectly referred to as ASOs.

**Standards**  Criteria established for quality control and quality assurance; established or known test reagents, such as molecular-weight standards.

**State of the DNA**  Term used to describe the condition of a DNA sample, particularly after exposure to environmental conditions commonly encountered in crime scene samples.

**STR**  Short tandem repeat.

**Streptavidin**  Protein molecule used in the detection of amplified DNA on a reverse dot blot. Binds tightly to the protein biotin.

**Stringency**  Specific conditions used in the hybridization of DNA.

**Subpopulation, Substructure**  (see *Population Substructure*)

**T**  Single-letter designation of the base Thymine; one of the four building blocks of DNA.

| | |
|---|---|
| **Tandem Repeats** | Repeating units of an identical DNA sequence arranged in direct succession in a particular region of a chromosome. |
| *Taq* **DNA Polymerase** | The enzyme used to copy DNA in the polymerase chain reaction (PCR) technique. |
| *Taq* **Polymerase** | (see *Taq DNA Polymerase*) |
| **Thymine** | One of the four building blocks of DNA. |
| **Transfer Theory** | Theory regarding the transfer of trace evidence between two objects. |
| **TWGDAM** | Technical Working Group on DNA Analysis and Methods. |
| **Variable Number Tandem Repeat (VNTR)** | Repeating units of an identical DNA sequence, arranged in direct succession in a particular region of a chromosome, for which the number varies between individuals. |
| **VNTR** | Variable Number Tandem Repeat. |
| **Yield Gel** | Diagnostic tool in DNA analysis. Aids in determining the quality and quantity of DNA extracted from a sample. Affects decisions about how much to use in various typing procedures. |

## Appendix A

## DNA - SOME KEY PHRASES

- DNA is the genetic material that determines who we are.

- Every individual, with the exception of identical twins, has unique DNA.

- Siblings share the most genetic material; identical twins have exactly the same genetic material.

- The use of DNA for identification is called "DNA typing" or "DNA profiling".

- Several different kinds of DNA typing tests are available; they fall into two general categories called RFLP and PCR.

- Both RFLP and PCR-type methods are accurate, reliable and valid.

- RFLP loci, taken individually, currently exclude a greater number of people as potential donors of the sample.

- PCR loci, taken individually, currently exclude fewer people as potential donors of the sample.

- The power of both RFLP and PCR tests is increased by analyzing additional loci.

- RFLP requires a greater amount of sample and DNA of better quality.

- PCR results may often be obtained with a tiny sample of relatively poor quality.

- RFLP-type tests include *Hae*III and *Hin*fI.

- PCR-type tests include HLA DQα, polymarker and D1S80 and STRs.

- The final result in RFLP analysis looks like a simplified supermarket bar code.

- The final result in HLA DQα or polymarker is blue dots on a white strip.

- The final result in D1S80 looks like a simplified supermarket bar code.

- Similar patterns of bars or dots suggest with varying degrees of certainty that samples may have come from the same source.

- Poor quality DNA may be caused by exposure to sunlight, chemicals, soil, moisture.

- Poor-quality DNA may result from cells that have been outside of a living person for a long time.

- The significance of similar DNA types is usually expressed as how rare that type is in the population.

- Genetic similarity at three or more highly variable RFLP markers is considered strong evidence of a common source.

- The more genetic markers tested, the stronger the evidence of a common source for similar types.

- Usually 100 to 500 or more people are sampled from a population to see how common or rare the DNA types are.

- DNA can link a suspect or victim to the scene of a crime with varying degrees of certainty.

- Most body fluids and organs will give a DNA type.

- From one person, all body fluids and organs will show the same type.

- It is not possible to tell the race or ethnicity of a person by looking at the markers used in forensic DNA testing.

- A criminalist is an expert who examines and analyzes physical evidence used in criminal investigation.

- A forensic scientist is an expert who examines and analyzes physical evidence used in criminal investigation.

- A criminologist is an expert who analyzes sociological and psychological factors involved in criminal investigation.

- Crime laboratories can be accredited for DNA testing.

- Accreditation of a Crime Laboratory means that the lab meets minimum professional standards for accurate and reliable testing.

- Forensic scientists (Criminalists) can be certified for DNA testing.

- Certification of a Forensic Scientist (Criminalist) means that the analyst has the minimum professional knowledge, skills, and abilities to perform DNA testing.

- Proficiency testing is the analysis of material provided by an outside agency or laboratory to determine whether a laboratory or analyst can accurately and reliably perform DNA typing.

## Appendix B

## SLOT BLOT

The slot blot technique is used to obtain information about the quantity of human DNA recovered from a sample. A small portion of each sample is applied to a nylon membrane, similar to that used for RFLP analysis. A set of standard samples, for which the quantities are known, are also applied for comparison. After permanently fixing the samples to the membrane, they are probed with a small fragment of synthetic DNA that has been selected to hybridize only to primate DNA. This probe may also cross-react with horse and mouse DNA if they are present in large quantities. If the gorilla did it, you may be in trouble, but otherwise, this probe adequately detects DNA of human origin. Since bacterial DNA may often make up a significant portion of a forensic sample, it is critical to have this information in order to make appropriate decisions regarding subsequent analysis. A slot blot does not yield information regarding the state of degradation of DNA. The probe used in this case is tagged with an enzyme that causes a certain chemical to produce a discharge of light in its presence. This effect is called **chemiluminescence**. When the probed membrane is soaked in the chemical and exposed to X-ray film, a black band corresponding to the region detected by the probe is produced, just as with X-rays. This provides a permanent record and can be analyzed visually, as well as with computer-aided imaging systems.

**Walsh, P.S. Varlaro, J., Reynolds, R.,** A rapid chemiluminescent method for quantitation of human DNA, *Nucleic Acids Research*, 20, 19, 1992.

## slot blot

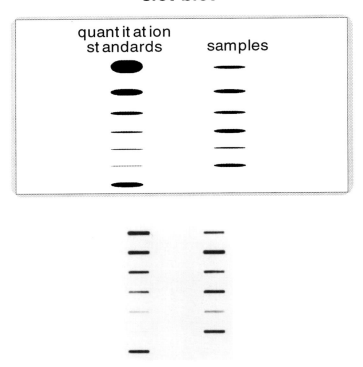

## YIELD GEL

A yield gel is a miniature version of an analytical RFLP gel. Its purpose is to aid in assessing the amount of total DNA recovered from a sample, as well as the state of degradation of the DNA. A miniature slab of agarose is prepared and a small portion of each sample loaded into separate wells. Standard samples of known quantity are run along side the questioned samples to provide a comparison. The run is complete in less than an hour and the gel is stained with the dye **ethidium bromide** which binds to double-stranded DNA. It binds to single-stranded DNA only poorly, so cannot be used to quantify Chelex-extracted DNA. The Ethidium bromide fluoresces under ultraviolet light and marks the place to where the DNA has migrated to in the gel. DNA viewed in this way is seen as a blob or smear, depending on it's state of degradation. Large, intact DNA molecules will form a compact band near the origin of the gel, similar in placement and shape to the standards. Degraded DNA will form more of a smear, and migrate further in the gel, depending on the average size of the pieces. Extremely degraded DNA may not be visible at all. Sometimes, but not always, evidence of bacterial DNA may be detected as a bright blob near the bottom of the yield gel. It is important to realize that staining with ethidium bromide dye detects all the DNA in the genome(s) present, and does not give any information about species or specific loci. The result is recorded using standard photographic techniques.

# yield gel

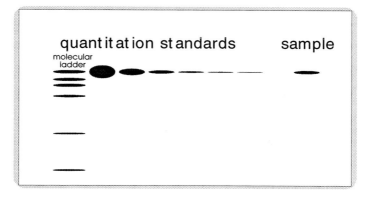

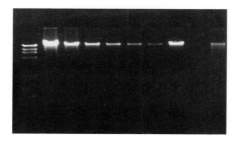

# Appendix D

## DIGEST GEL

The digest gel is prepared in the same way as a yield gel. it is used in assessing the completeness of restriction enzyme digestion before proceeding to a RFLP analytical gel. A small portion of DNA that is thought to be digested is removed and loaded into a well on the gel. Standards which are known to be either uncut or completely cut are loaded alongside for comparison. The gel is run for approximately an hour and stained with ethidium bromide like a yield gel. Uncut DNA will form a compact band near the origin of the gel, similar in placement and shape to the uncut standard. A complete digest is evidenced by a uniform smear made up of different size fragments running down the length of the lane, similar in placement and shape to the fully digested standard. The result is recorded using standard photographic techniques.

## digest gel

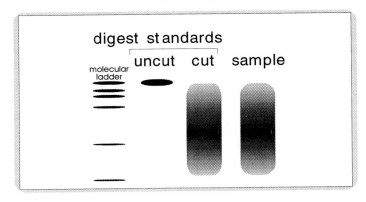

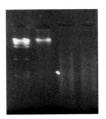

## Appendix E

## PRODUCT GEL

The product gel is used as a tool to assess the efficiency of amplification by *Taq* polymerase. It is prepared in much the same way as the yield and digest gels in RFLP analysis. After PCR amplification, a small sample is removed and loaded on the gel alongside a molecular ladder containing bands of known sizes. The gel is run for about an hour and stained with ethidium bromide. A band, or lack thereof, in a product lane gives an indication of the success of amplification. The bands are compared with the ladder to check that a band of the correct size has been generated; this is a check on the fidelity of the amplification. The result is recorded using standard photographic techniques.

# product gel

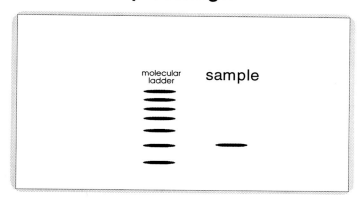

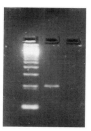

# Appendix F

## CHROMOSOMAL LOCATION OF SOME FORENSIC LOCI

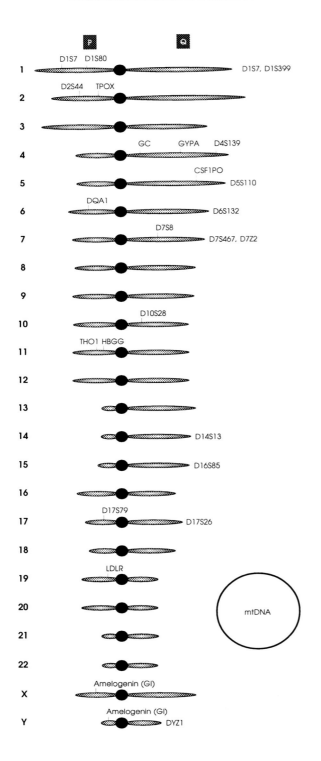

Note that each chromosome, identified by the number to its left, has two arms extending from a central element called a **centromere**. The shorter arm is conventionally called **P** and the longer arm is called **Q**. The locations of the loci in this diagram should not be considered accurate, and the order of some of the markers on the same chromosome arm may not be known. Loci for which the chromosomal locations could not be obtained are written next to the chromosome on which they are located. It is important to realize that even though two markers may be on the same chromosome, or even the same chromosome arm, the distances between them are still quite large when considered on a molecular level and the loci may be completely unlinked, that is show no tendency to be inherited together. See *Chapter 8* for further discussion of this topic. CSF1PO, THO1 and TPOX make up a common STR triplex and mtDNA represents the circular mitochondrial genome. GC, GYPA, LDLR, HBGG, and D7S8 comprise the polymarker typing set, along with DQA1. D1S80 is amplified individually. The other markers are all analyzed by RFLP. Additional RFLP markers that are currently in use are not indicated in this illustration.

# Appendix G

## SAMPLE FREQUENCY CALCULATION

In this example, we consider the results of a series of DNA tests performed on an evidence sample, and compare the results to reference samples taken from two individuals. We then estimate the frequency of the evidence DNA profile in a hypothetical population. Two RFLP loci, one sequence polymorphic locus (which will be referred to as an sequence specific oligonucleotide, or SSO) and one STR locus are used to illustrate various aspects of the procedures. For the purposes of this exercise, we will assume that the evidence sample represents only one individual.

DNA is first extracted from the evidence sample along with a series of control samples (these might include a substrate sample from the item on which the evidence sample was deposited, a reagent blank to test the chemicals used to perform the extraction, and an intralaboratory quality control sample; see *Chapter 7*). Next, the reference samples are extracted at a different time and or in a different space. A yield gel and/or a slot blot are used to estimate the state of the DNA and the amount present in each sample (see *Chapter 7*; *Appendices B, C*).

Lets assume that the sample is both of sufficient quality and quantity for RFLP analysis (see *Chapter 7*). A portion of the DNA from each sample is cut with a restriction enzyme, and each digested sample is placed into a separate lane on an electrophoretic gel. After running the gel, the fragments of DNA (which have now been separated according to their size) are transferred to a nylon membrane. The membrane is first probed at locus A, and the particular fragments to which the probe has bound are recorded as bands on a film, called the autorad. The probe from locus A is washed off, and a probe for locus B is applied. This results in another autorad, now with different bands marking the second locus . For the purpose of this example, we will stop with two loci, although typically many more are analyzed.

The analyst inspects the autorads to determine whether the evidence and either or both of the reference samples appear to be a visually concordant. If none of the band patterns are similar, both reference donors are excluded from having contributed to the evidence sample. If, in the analyst's trained judgment, the patterns are indistinguishable, the next step in determining the significance of the genetic concordance is to calculate the band sizes, usually with the aid of a computer.

The SSO locus is analyzed next. A separate portion of DNA is amplified using PCR and the resulting PCR product, containing the polymorphism of interest, is detected by the reverse dot blot procedure (*Chapter 7*). This results in a strip revealing the alleles present in the sample. Again, comparisons are made between the dot patterns in the evidence and reference samples (see *Chapter 8*) to determine if there is genetic concordance between any of them. If the patterns are clearly different, both the reference donors are excluded; if the patterns are similar, the significance must be determined.

In our example, an STR locus is analyzed next, using yet another portion of the DNA. The sample is amplified and the fragments are separated according to size by electrophoresis on a gel. This is followed by visualization using any of the various methods detailed in *Chapter 7*. Band patterns are compared between the evidence and reference samples; either the patterns are dissimilar, in which case analysis stops with an exclusion, or they are indistinguishable and the significance must be determined.  Alleles are assigned either by visual comparison to an appropriate ladder or by a computer algorithm.

The following results are obtained:

|  | Evidence stain | Individual 1 | Individual 2 |
|---|---|---|---|
| **RFLP Locus A** | 3500 bp | 3490 bp | 2750 bp |
|  | 2100 bp | 2050 bp | 1640 bp |
| **RFLP Locus B** | 6700 bp | 6620 bp | 3580 bp |
| **SSO Locus** | 3,3 | 3,3 | 3,5 |
| **STR Locus** | 2,5 | 2,5 | 3,7 |

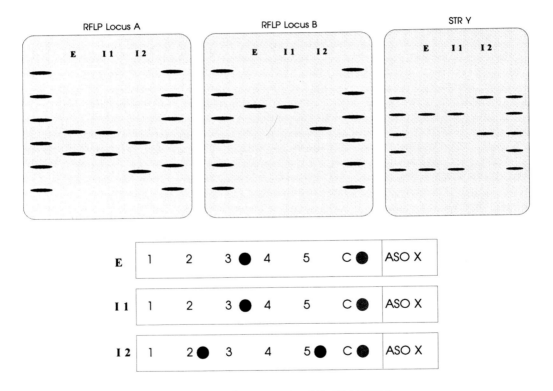

## I. DETERMINATION OF SIMILARITY

Notice that at one RFLP locus (locus B) the evidence shows a single-banded pattern. This could result from true homozygosity, or from technical failure to detect a second band (see *Chapter 9*).  Note also that the SSO locus shows a single allele in the evidence sample.

### A. DISCRETE ALLELE SYSTEMS

We first examine the discrete allele systems (the SSO and STR loci).  Individual 2 clearly shows different types than the evidence at both loci, so he is eliminated as a possible donor. However, the genotypes for Individual 1 and the evidence stain are the same (3,3; 2,5), so this individual is included as a possible donor of the evidence.

## B. CONTINUOUS ALLELE SYSTEMS

We next evaluate the RFLP loci. The elimination of Individual 2 by the other two systems is confirmed by the RFLP analysis. However, Individual 1 shows a band pattern that is visually indistinguishable from that of the evidence. In this situation it is necessary to perform a proscribed set of statistical calculations to either confirm or refute the visually established concordance.

Assume that laboratory experimentation has established that, when analyzed repeatedly, RFLP bands from the same source generally fall within ±1.8% of their combined average value. We must check the evidence and reference band sizes to see if they fit within this match criteria, or window of uncertainty. The measurment uncertainty for any band is calculated by adding and subtracting 1.8% of its measured size. For instance, the uncertainty window for band 1 of locus A spans the range from 3437 (−1.8%) below to 3563 (+1.8%) above the measured value. Similar calculations for band 1 of the reference sample produce an uncertainty window that measures from 3427 to 3553 bp. Notice that these two ranges overlap; when this occurs for all (usually both) bands in a profile, the samples are considered genetically indistinguishable. The following chart gives the values for the RFLP loci in this example:

| RFLP Locus A | | Size (bp) | Range of Uncertainty (bp) |
|---|---|---|---|
| Band 1 | Evidence | 3500 | 3437 - 3563 |
| | Individual 1 | 3490 | 3427 - 3553 |
| Band 2 | Evidence | 2100 | 2062 - 2137 |
| | Individual 1 | 2050 | 2013 - 2086 |
| **RFLP Locus B** | | | |
| Band 1 | Evidence | 6700 | 6579 - 6820 |
| | Individual 1 | 6620 | 6500 - 6739 |

All of the bands at both RFLP loci show an overlap in the range of uncertainty between the evidence sample and the reference sample from Individual 1. This leads to the conclusion that the samples are genetically similar (or show genetic concordance) at the RFLP loci tested, confirming our conclusion from analysis of the PCR-amplified loci. The results from both the continuous and discrete allele systems tested establish genetic concordance between the evidence profile and the profile from Individual 1.

## II. ESTIMATION OF THE PROFILE FREQUENCY

Having determined that the DNA profiles of the evidence stain and Individual 1 are indeed similar, we need to evaluate the probability of this match if someone other than Individual 1 is the donor. We will do this by estimating the frequency of this profile in a population, although other methods may be used.

A survey of the appropriate population is required to estimate profile frequencies. The usable form of this survey is a table of allele frequencies that are then used to calculate genotype frequencies for the profile of interest. As discussed in *Chapter 8*, all the alleles from each locus sampled in a population survey are grouped into arbitrarily designated "bins" down the length of the autorad; each bin contains a range of allele sizes. A hypothetical table of allele frequencies for use in this example is given here:

### RFLP Bin Table

| Bin # | Size Range | Locus A Allele Counts | Locus A Frequency | Locus B Allele Counts | Locus B Frequency |
|-------|------------|---------------|-----------|---------------|-----------|
| 1  | 0-500       | 0   | 0.000 | 3   | 0.004 |
| 2  | 501-1000    | 0   | 0.000 | 10  | 0.014 |
| 3  | 1001-1500   | 5   | 0.005 | 15  | 0.022 |
| 4  | 1501-2000   | 8   | 0.008 | 9   | 0.013 |
| 5  | 2001-2500   | 13  | 0.013 | 12  | 0.017 |
| 6  | 2501-3000   | 29  | 0.030 | 35  | 0.051 |
| 7  | 3001-3500   | 38  | 0.039 | 44  | 0.064 |
| 8  | 3501-4000   | 58  | 0.059 | 53  | 0.077 |
| 9  | 4001-4500   | 126 | 0.13  | 36  | 0.052 |
| 10 | 4501-5000   | 77  | 0.079 | 75  | 0.11  |
| 11 | 5001-5500   | 86  | 0.088 | 56  | 0.081 |
| 12 | 5501-6000   | 92  | 0.094 | 74  | 0.11  |
| 13 | 6001-6500   | 110 | 0.11  | 110 | 0.16  |
| 14 | 6501-7000   | 100 | 0.10  | 103 | 0.15  |
| 15 | 7001-7500   | 95  | 0.097 | 45  | 0.065 |
| 16 | 7501-8000   | 66  | 0.067 | 12  | 0.017 |
| 17 | 8001-8500   | 42  | 0.043 | 0   | 0.000 |
| 18 | 8501-9000   | 28  | 0.029 | 0   | 0.000 |
| 19 | 9001-9500   | 5   | 0.005 | 0   | 0.000 |
| 20 | 9501-10000  | 0   | 0.000 | 0   | 0.000 |

Allele frequencies in discrete allele systems, such as SSOs and STRs, may be used directly without any additional steps. Hypothetical tables for these systems are given below.

### SSO Allele Frequency Table

| Allele | Count | Frequency |
|--------|-------|-----------|
| 1 | 45 | 0.17 |
| 2 | 62 | 0.24 |
| 3 | 37 | 0.14 |
| 4 | 16 | 0.062 |
| 5 | 41 | 0.16 |
| 6 | 57 | 0.22 |

### STR Allele Frequency Table

| Allele | Count | Frequency |
|--------|-------|-----------|
| 2 | 34 | 0.13 |
| 3 | 53 | 0.21 |
| 4 | 26 | 0.10 |
| 5 | 13 | 0.05 |
| 6 | 5 | 0.02 |
| 7 | 78 | 0.30 |
| 8 | 34 | 0.13 |
| 9 | 15 | 0.058 |

**Note**: Assume that these population surveys have been tested for H-W and LE within and between loci and have been accepted for use in calculating profile frequencies.

## A. Continuous allele loci (RFLP)

For every band, we will determine the uncertainty of the size measurement, and compare the resulting size range to the bin frequency table. For RFLP locus A, we know that the uncertainty spans the range from 3437 to 3563 base pairs. Inspection of the bin table reveals that this range actually spans two allele bins: bin 7, which includes alleles ranging from 3001 to 3500 base pairs, and bin 8, which includes alleles ranging from 3501 to 4000 base pairs. When the potential size range of an evidence allele spans one of the arbitrarily designated bin boundaries, the bin that has the higher frequency is chosen for use in the frequency estimate. This potentially over-estimates the occurrence of the allele in the population, and is one of the devices used to ensure a conservative estimate. Bin 7 has a frequency of 0.039, and bin 8 has a frequency of 0.059. Therefore, the frequency of bin 8 (0.059) is chosen for use in the calculation. For the alleles at both locus A and locus B, the results are shown at the right.

| Locus A | Bin # | Frequency |
|---------|-------|-----------|
| Band 1 | Bin 8 | 0.059 |
| Band 2 | Bin 5 | 0.013 |
| **Locus B** | | |
| Band 1 | Bin 14 | 0.15 |

## 1. Calculating genotype frequencies

Now that we have decided which allele frequencies to use, we can calculate the genotype frequency for each locus by applying the following formulae:

For heterozygous loci (locus A), the genotype frequency is given by:

> **2 x (frequency of band 1) x (frequency of band 2)**

which, for locus A gives:

> **2 x 0.059 x 0.013 = 0.0015**

For homozygous loci (locus B), the genotype frequency is given by:

> **2 x (frequency of band 1)**

which, for locus B gives:

> **2 x 0.15 = 0.30**

The formula for homozygotes is basically a correction factor to Hardy-Weinberg proportions that, again, results in a conservative (not overstated) estimate of the genotype frequency.

## A. DISCRETE ALLELE LOCI (PCR)

The frequency tables for each locus are used to find the allele frequencies as follows: The SSO locus has two type 3 alleles.

**SSO Locus**

| allele | frequency |
|--------|-----------|
| 3 | 0.14 |

The frequency table for this SSO locus shows the frequency of the 3 allele to be 0.14.

**STR Locus**

| allele | frequency |
|--------|-----------|
| 2 | 0.13 |
| 5 | 0.05 |

The frequency table for this STR locus shows the frequency of the 2 allele to be 0.13 and the frequency of the 5 allele to be 0.05.

The following formulae are used to determine the genotype frequencies for discrete allele loci.

For heterozygous loci (locus A), the genotype frequency is given by:

**2 x (frequency of allele 1) x (Frequency of allele 2)**

which, for the STR locus, is

**2 x (0.13) x (0.05) = 0.013**

For homozygous loci (SSO locus), the genotype frequency is given by:

(Frequency of allele)$^2$ + correction factor ($p(1-p)\overline{\theta}$ ), where $\overline{\theta}$ helps to correct for any effect of population substructuring, recommended by NRC II as 0.01 for most U.S. populations.

For the SSO locus this is:

**$(0.14)^2$ + (0.14)(1-0.14)(0.01) = .021**

The last step is to estimate the frequency of the entire profile, incorporating the frequency estimates for each of the individual loci. Use of this formula is predicated on the assumption that the loci involved are in linkage equilibrium with each other in the population under consideration (see *Chapter 8*).

**RFLP locus A x RFLP locus B x SSO locus x STR locus**

which for this example gives:

**0.0015 x 0.30 x 0.013 x 0.021 = 1.2 x 10$^{-7}$**
**(about 1 in 8 million people)**

## Appendix H

**GUIDELINES FOR A QUALITY ASSURANCE PROGRAM FOR DNA ANALYSIS**

*Prepared by*

Technical Working Group on DNA Analysis Methods (TWGDAM)

CRIME LABORATORY DIGEST Vol. 22, No. 2, April 1995

---

The following is a reprint of the introductions that accompanied the 1989 and 1991 publications of the Technical Working Group on DNA Analysis Methods' "Guidelines for a Quality Assurance Program for DNA RFLP Analysis." The original quality assurance (QA) guidelines were intended to serve as a guide to laboratory managers in establishing their own QA program for RFLP DNA analysis laboratories. These introductions are being reprinted to preserve an historical perspective on the evolution of the original QA guidelines.

**Introduction to 1989 Guidelines:**

With the advent of DNA typing technology in the forensic laboratory, the forensic examiner now has the potential to individualize various body fluids and tissues. In addition, since the tests performed by crime laboratories can have a significant impact on the outcome of a trial, it is important that any test procedure used by the laboratory possess a high degree of accuracy and reproducibility. Consequently, the use of appropriate standards and controls is essential in order to ensure reliable results.

As any technology becomes more discriminating and precise, it is essential that the quality of the analytical data be more closely monitored. A detailed and flexible quality assurance program can assist in establishing a basis for scientifically sound and reliable forensic analysis.

Although often used interchangeably, quality assurance (QA) and quality control (QC) refer to different, specific quality functions (American National Standard ANSI/ASQC A3-1978; Kilshaw 1986, 1987a, b). The function of the QA program is to provide to all concerned the evidence needed to establish with confidence that the QC function is being performed adequately. This is accomplished in part through the use of proficiency tests and audits. The QC measures are employed by the DNA analysis laboratory to ensure that the quality of the product (DNA typing) will meet and satisfy specified criteria.

Although the application of formal QA programs in forensic laboratories is currently not widespread and little information has appeared in the forensic science literature (Bradford 1980; Brunelle *et al.* 1982; Pereira 1985), a great deal has been written on the application of QA programs to clinical and federally operated laboratories (Alwan and Bissell 1988; Box and Bisaard 1987; Bussolini *et al.* 1988; Ford 1988; Gautier and Gladney 1987; Hay 1988; Kenney 1987; Kidd 1987; Simpson 1983; Taylor 1985, 1987; Whitehead and Woodford 1981).

In November, 1988, the first meeting of the Technical Working Group on DNA Analysis Methods (TWGDAM) was hosted by the FBI Laboratory at the FBI Academy. This group consisted of 31 scientists representing 16 forensic laboratories in the United States and Canada and 2 research institutions. The purpose of this group is: (1) to pull together a select number of individuals from the forensic science community who are actively pursing the various DNA analysis methods; (2) to discuss the methods now being used; (3) to compare the work that has been done; (4) to share protocols; and (5) to establish guidelines where appropriate. During the first meeting, a subcommittee was established to formulate suggested guidelines for a QA program in crime laboratories conducting restriction fragment length polymorphism (RFLP) DNA analysis.

These guidelines represent the minimum QA requirements for DNA RFLP analysis and are intended to serve only as a guide to laboratory managers in establishing their own QA program for DNA RFLP analysis.

These QA guidelines were designed using established quality functions (American National Standard ANSI/ASQC CI-1968; ANSI/ASQC Z-1.15-1979, ANSI/ASQC Q90-1987a, b; Juran 1979; Ruzicka 1979) to follow systematically the DNA RFLP typing procedure and cover all significant aspects of the laboratory process. In addition, they provide the necessary documentation to ensure that the DNA analysis process is operating within the established performance criteria, and they provide a measure of the overall quality of the results.

These guidelines form the basis of a quality assurance program for RFLP analysis and are subject to future revisions as the state of the art and experience dictate.

**Introduction to 1991 Guidelines**

Quality assurance is a dynamic and ongoing process which requires periodic review. Following an extensive review of the original 1989 guidelines, these revised and expanded "Guidelines for a Quality Assurance Program for DNA Analysis", were jointly prepared by the Technical Working Group on DNA Analysis Methods (TWGDAM) and the California Association of Criminalists Ad Hoc Committee on DNA Quality Assurance. Reviews are warranted as new technologies are developed and implemented by crime laboratories and serve to clarify issues concerning laboratory quality.

Efforts toward establishing DNA testing standards were begun by TWGDAM in 1989 with publication of 'Guidelines for a Quality Assurance Program for DNA Restriction Fragment Length Polymorphism Analysis" in the April-July issue of the *Crime Laboratory Digest* (Vol. 16, No. 2, pp. 40-59).

The QA guidelines were supplemented in July 1990 by the publication of "Guidelines for a Proficiency Testing Program for DNA Restriction Fragment Length Polymorphism Analysis" (*Crime Laboratory Digest*, Vol. 17, No. 3, pp. 59-64).

The function of a QA program is to provide the evidence needed to establish with confidence that the quality control function is being performed adequately. These revised guidelines represent the QA requirements of DNA analysis that should be the goals of laboratory managers in establishing their own QA program. These are only guidelines and should be used as a model for laboratory managers to set up an appropriate QA program for their laboratory. This document should not be construed as a mandate; it does not mean that failure to comply with each and every guideline, or that the use of an alternative or equivalent method is insufficient or likely to produce incorrect or unreliable results.

The revised QA guidelines in this issue build on the foundation established by the original TWGDAM guidelines and address the technical issues related to the next generation of DNA typing methods based on the Polymerase Chain Reaction (PCR). Future changes to quality assurance standards for DNA testing will be necessary to accommodate evolving technology and laboratory practices.

### Introduction to 1995 Guidelines

As noted in the introduction to the 1991 edition of the *Guidelines for Quality Assurance Program for DNA Analysis*, published in the April issue of the *Crime Laboratory Digest* (Vol. 18, No. 2, pp. 44-75), it was recognized that changes in the quality assurance standards for DNA testing would be necessary to accommodate evolving technology and laboratory practices.

Since the publication of the 1991 guidelines, a number of proposed changes to the guidelines have been submitted to the Technical Working Group on DNA Analysis Methods (TWGDAM) Quality Assurance (QA) Subcommittee. As a result of evolving laboratory experience and practices, as well as the advent of mitochondrial DNA analysis technology, it was determined that a review of the current guidelines was necessary.

During the January 1995 meeting of TWGDAM, a number of proposed changes to the guidelines were evaluated by the QA Subcommittee. The proposed changes were submitted in writing and were accompanied by a justification for each change. Based on the evaluation of the proposed changes and the supporting justification the recommendations of the QA Subcommittee were forwarded to the entire TWGDAM committee for discussion. Following the discussion, each proposed change was voted upon the TWGDAM members.

A two-thirds majority was required for the adoption of each proposed change. As a result of this voting, revisions to the following sections of the 1991 guidelines were adopted: 4.1.3, 4.1.5.10, 4.4.2.1, 5.3.2, 7.2.2, 7.3, 7.5.1.3, 7.5.1.4 (deleted), and 10.1. The 1995 revised edition of the *Guidelines for a Quality Assurance Program for DNA Analysis* follows.

### 1. Planning and Organization

    1.1        Goals: It is the goal of the laboratory's program to:

            1.1.1     Provide the users of laboratory services access to DNA typing of selected biological materials associated with official investigations using DNA testing.

            1.1.2     Ensure the quality, integrity and reliability of the DNA typing data and its presentation through the implementation of a detailed Quality Assurance (QA) program.

    1.2        Objectives: It is the objective of the QA Program to ensure that:

            1.2.1     The analytical testing procedures and reporting of DNA typing are monitored by means of Quality Control (QC) standards, proficiency tests and audits on a routine basis.

1.2.2    The entire DNA typing procedure is operating within the established performance criteria and that the quality and validity of the analytical data are maintained.

1.2.3    Problems are noted and corrective action is taken and documented.

1.3    Authority and Accountability

1.3.1    Organization Structure: Defines the relationships within the laboratory between individuals, job responsibilities and operational units. It defines the relationship of the QA program to DNA analysis and related laboratory operations as well as to the laboratory management.

1.3.2    Functional Responsibilities: The job function and responsibility for each position within the laboratory should be clearly established. It should specify and describe the lines of responsibility for developing, implementing, recording and updating the QA program.

1.3.3    Levels of Authority: Clear lines of authority and accountability should be established between personnel responsible for the QA program and those assigned to manage and perform the DNA analysis. It should be established as to who may take what action, whether approval is required, and from whom approvals are needed.

## 2. Personnel

2.1    Job descriptions

The job descriptions for all DNA personnel should include responsibilities, duties and skills.

2.2    Qualifications

The education, training, experience and qualifying criteria of technical personnel within the DNA testing laboratory will be formally established by each laboratory. Supervisors or technical leaders and examiner/analysts must demonstrate the ability to critically evaluate and interpret the evidence, results and data. The minimum requirements for those individuals are specified as follows.

2.2.1    Qualifying Procedure

It is highly desirable that these persons undergo a formal qualifying procedure which reviews and documents that prerequisite criteria have been satisfied prior to the assumption of duties. These criteria should include:

2.2.1.1    Knowledge of the scientific principles, techniques and literature of DNA typing as demonstrated by course work and/or written or oral examination.

2.2.1.2    Practical laboratory skills in the performance of DNA analysis as demonstrated by observation and successful analytical results.

2.2.1.3 Competency of individuals engaged in DNA analysis as demonstrated by the successful completion of proficiency testing.

2.2.1.4 Competency of supervisors/technical leaders as demonstrated by the successful completion of proficiency testing–designed to evaluate interpretational skills.

2.2.2 Maintaining Qualification - There must be a procedure for the periodic review of continuing education, proficiency testing and performance of personnel.

2.2.3 Supervisor/Technical Leader

If the supervisor alone does not meet the following criteria, the laboratory must have a technical leader or employ a consultant who satisfies all the criteria or who, in combination with the qualifications of the supervisor, satisfies the criteria. The supervisor/technical leader, or other designated qualified individual, must regularly review the laboratory work product and must be available for consultation. It is highly desirable that at least one individual possess all of these qualifications.

2.2.3.1 Education–Must have a minimum of a BA/BS or its equivalent in a biological, chemical or forensic science and have received credit in courses in genetics, biochemistry and molecular biology (molecular genetics, recombinant DNA technology) or other subjects which provide a basic understanding of the foundation of forensic DNA analysis.

2.2.3.2 Training–Must have, at a minimum:

(a) Training in the fundamentals of forensic biology, and

(b) Documented training in DNA analysis with individuals, agencies, or other laboratories, in a program that includes the methods, procedures, equipment and materials used in forensic DNA analysis and their applications and limitations (ASCLD 1985).

2.2.3.3 Experience–Supervisor or technical leader must have a minimum of 2 years experience as a forensic biology examiner/analyst and meet all the requirements of Section 2.2.4.3.

2.2.3.4 Continuing Education - Must stay abreast of developments within the field of DNA typing by reading current scientific literature. Attendance at seminars, courses or professional meetings is highly desirable. Laboratory management must provide the opportunity to comply with the above requirements.

2.2.4 Examiner/Analyst

2.2.4.1 Education–Must have a minimum of a BA/BS degree or its equivalent in a biological, chemical or forensic science and have received credit in courses in genetics, biochemistry and molecular biology (molecular genetics, recombinant DNA technology) or other subjects which provide a basic understanding of the foundation of forensic DNA analysis.

2.2.4.2  Training–Must have, at a minimum:

(a)  Training in the fundamentals of forensic biology

(b)  Training in DNA analysis with individuals, agencies or other laboratories in a program that includes the methods, procedures, equipment and materials used in forensic DNA analysis and their applications and limitations (ASCLD 1985).

2.2.4.3  Experience–Must at a minimum include:

(a)  One year-forensic biology experience.

(b)  Prior to independent case work analysis using DNA technology, the examiner/analyst must have adequate forensic DNA laboratory experience including the successful analysis of a range of samples typically encountered in forensic case work.  This typically requires 6 months experience in a DNA laboratory.

2.2.4.4  Continuing Education–Must stay abreast of developments within the field of DNA typing by reading current scientific literature.  Attendance at seminars, courses or professional meetings is highly desirable.  Laboratory management must provide the opportunity to comply with these requirements.

2.2.5    Technicians

2.2.5.1  Technicians involved in performing analytical techniques related to DNA analysis should have a minimum of a BS/BA degree (or equivalent) and receive on-the-job training by a qualified analyst.  Technicians will not interpret DNA typing results, prepare final reports or provide testimony concerning such.

2.2.5.2  Technicians not performing analytical techniques should have the experience and education commensurate with the job description.

## 3. Documentation

The DNA laboratory must maintain documentation on all significant aspects of the DNA analysis procedure, as well as any related documents or laboratory records that are pertinent to the analysis or interpretation of results, so as to create a traceable audit trail.  This documentation will serve as an archive for retrospective scientific inspection, reevaluation of the data, and reconstruction of the DNA procedure. Documentation must exist for the following topic areas:

3.1    Test Methods and Procedures for DNA Typing

This document must describe in detail the protocol currently used for the analytical testing of DNA. This protocol must identify the standards and controls required, the date the procedure was adopted and the authorization for its use. Revisions must be clearly documented and appropriately authorized.

3.2    Population Data Base–To include number, source and ethnic and/or racial classification of samples.

3.3    Quality control of critical reagents (such as commercial supplies and kits which have expiration dates)–To include lot and batch numbers, manufacturer's specifications and internal evaluations.

3.4    Case files/case notes - Must provide foundation for results and conclusions contained in formal report.

3.5    Data analysis and reporting

3.6    Evidence handling protocols

3.7    Equipment calibration and maintenance logs

3.8    Proficiency testing

3.9    Personnel training and qualification records

3.10   Method validation records

3.11   Quality assurance and audit records

3.12   Quality assurance manual

3.13   Equipment inventory

3.14   Safety manuals

3.15   Material safety data sheets

3.16   Historical or archival records

3.17   Licenses and certificates

## 4. Validation

4.1    General Considerations for Developmental Validation of the DNA Analysis Procedure

4.1.1    Validation is the process used by the scientific community to acquire the necessary information to assess the ability of a procedure to reliably obtain a desired result, determine the conditions under which such results can be obtained and determine the limitations of the procedure. The validation process identifies the critical aspects of a procedure which must be carefully controlled and monitored.

4.1.2    Validation studies must have been conducted by the DNA laboratory or scientific community prior to the adoption of a procedure by the DNA laboratory.

4.1.3    Once an RFLP procedure has been validated, appropriate studies of limite scope (*e.g.*, population studies, human DNA control value determination) must be available for each new locus used. A similar standard should be maintained when adding new loci to the different PCR-based techniques (e.g., addition of a short tandem repeat (STR) locus to a validated STR procedure).

4.1.4    The DNA primers, probe(s) or oligonucleotides selected for use in the forensic DNA analysis must be readily available to the scientific community.

4.1.5    The validation process should include the following studies (*Report of a Symposium on the Practice of Forensic Serology* 1987, and Budowle *et al.* 1988):

4.1.5.1    Standard Specimens–The typing procedure should have been evaluated using fresh body tissues, and fluids obtained and stored in a controlled manner. DNA isolated from different tissues from the same individual should yield the same type.

4.1.5.2    Consistency–Using specimens obtained from donors of known type, evaluate the reproducibility of the technique both within the laboratory and among different laboratories.

4.1.5.3    Population Studies–establish population distribution data in different racial and/or ethnic groups.

4.1.5.4    Reproducibility–Prepare dried stains using body fluids from donors of known types and analyze to ensure that the stain specimens exhibit accurate, interpretable and reproducible DNA types or profiles that match those obtained on liquid specimens.

4.1.5.5    Mixed Specimen Studies–Investigate the ability of the system to detect the components of mixed specimens and define the limitations of the system.

4.1.5.6    Environmental Studies–Evaluate the method using known or previously characterized samples exposed to a variety of environmental conditions. The samples should be selected to represent the types of specimens to be routinely analyzed by the method. They should resemble actual evidence materials as closely as possible so that the effects of factors such as matrix, age and degradative environment (temperature, humidity, UV) of a sample are considered.

4.1.5.7    Matrix Studies–Examine prepared body fluids mixed with a variety of commonly encountered substances (e.g. dyes, soil) and deposited on commonly encountered substrates (e.g. leather, denim).

4.1.5.8    Nonprobative Evidence–Examine DNA profiles in nonprobative evidentiary stain materials. Compare the DNA profiles obtained for the known liquid blood versus questioned blood deposited on typical crime scene evidence.

4.1.5.9    Nonhuman Studies–Determine if DNA typing methods designed for use with human specimens detect DNA profiles in nonhuman source stains.

4.1.5.10    Minimum sample–Where appropriate, establish quantity of DNA needed to obtain a reliable typing result.

4.1.5.11    On-site Evaluation–Set up newly developed typing methods in the case working laboratory for on-site evaluation of the procedure.

4.1.5.12    It is essential that the results of the developmental validation studies be shared as soon as possible with the scientific community through presentations at scientific/professional meetings. It is imperative that details of these studies be available for peer review through timely publications in scientific journals.

4.2    Characterization of Loci

During the development of a DNA analysis system, basic characteristics of the loci must be determined and documented. (Baird 1989; AABB Standards Committee 1990).

4.2.1    Inheritance–DNA loci used in forensic testing shall have been validated by family studies to demonstrate the mode of inheritance. Those DNA loci used in parentage testing should have a low frequency of mutation and/or recombination.

4.2.2    Gene Mapping–The chromosomal location of the polymorphic loci used for forensic testing shall be submitted to or recorded in the Yale Gene Library or the International Human Gene Mapping Workshop.

4.2.3    Detection–The molecular basis for detecting the polymorphic loci shall be documented in the scientific or technical literature.

4.2.3.1    For RFLP this includes the restriction enzyme and the probes used.

4.2.3.2    For PCR this includes the primers and probes, if used.

4.2.4    Polymorphism–The type of polymorphism detected shall be known.

4.3    Specific Developmental Validation of RFLP Procedures

4.3.1    Restriction–The conditions and control(s) needed to ensure complete and specific restriction must be demonstrated.

4.3.2    Separation–Parameters for the reproducible separation of DNA fragments must be established.

4.3.3    Transfer–Parameters for the reproducible transfer of DNA fragments must be established.

4.3.4    Detection–The hybridization and stringency wash conditions necessary to provide the desired degree of specificity must be determined.

4.3.5    Sizing–The precision of the sizing procedure must be established.

4.4    Specific Developmental Validation of PCR Based DNA Procedures

4.4.1    Amplification

4.4.1.1  The PCR primers must be of known sequence.

4.4.1.2  Conditions and measures necessary to protect preamplification samples from contamination by post PCR materials should be determined. (See Section 7.5)

4.4.1.3  The reaction conditions such as thermocycling parameters and critical reagent concentrations (primers, polymerase and salts) needed to provide the required degree of specificity must be determined.

4.4.1.4  The number(s) of cycles necessary to produce reliable results must be determined.

4.4.1.5  Potential for differential amplification must be assessed and addressed.

4.4.1.6  Where more than one locus is amplified in one sample mixture, the effects of such amplification on each system (alleles) must be addressed and documented.

4.4.2    Detection of PCR Product

The validation process will identify the panel of positive and negative controls needed for each assay described as follows.

4.4.2.1  Characterization without hybridization

(a) When a PCR product is characterized directly, appropriate standards for assessing the alleles shall be established.

(b) When a PCR product is characterized by direct sequencing, appropriate standards for assessing the sequence shall be established.

4.4.2.2  Characterization with hybridization

(a) Hybridization and stringency wash conditions necessary to provide the desired degree of specificity must be determined.

(b) For assays in which the amplified target DNA is to be bound directly to a membrane, some mechanism should be employed to ensure that the DNA has been applied to the membrane.

(c) For assays in which the probe is bound to the membrane, some mechanism should be employed to show that adequate amplified DNA is present in the sample (*e.g.* a probe which reacts with any amplified allele or a product yield gel).

4.5     Internal Validation of Established Procedures (ASCLD 1986)

Prior to implementing a new DNA analysis procedure, or an existing DNA procedure developed by another laboratory that meets the developmental criteria described under Section 4.1, the forensic laboratory must first demonstrate the reliability of the procedure in-house. This internal validation must include the following:

4.5.1     The method must be tested using known samples.

4.5.2     If a modification which materially effects the results of an analysis has been made to an analytical procedure, the modified procedure must be compared to the original using identical samples.

4.5.3     Precision (*e.g.*, measurement of fragment lengths) must be determined by repetitive analyses to establish criteria for matching.

4.5.4     The laboratory must demonstrate that its procedures do not introduce contamination which would lead to errors in typing.

4.5.5     The method must be tested using proficiency test samples. The proficiency test may be administered in internally, externally or collaboratively.

## 5. Equipment, Materials and Facilities

5.1     Equipment

Only suitable and properly operating equipment should be employed. Where critical parameters of equipment operation are identified in the validation procedure, monitoring of those parameters should be conducted and documented in the manner necessary to maintain successful operation of the typing technique.

5.1.1     Inventory–A list of equipment requiring calibration and monitoring for DNA analysis, which includes the manufacturer, model, serial number, agency inventory number and acquisition dates should be maintained.

5.1.2     Operation Manual–The manufacturer's operation manual should be readily available.

5.1.3     Calibration, Maintenance Procedures and Logs–There should be written calibration and maintenance procedures and schedules. There should be a permanent log of calibration and maintenance of equipment essential for DNA typing (e.g. Thermal cyclers and water baths).

5.1.4     Dedicated Equipment–Dedicated equipment should be readily identifiable as such.

5.2     Materials and Reagents

Chemicals and reagents should be of suitable quality, correctly prepared, and demonstrated to be compatible with the methods employed.

5.2.1   Logs must be maintained of commercial supplies and kits which have expiration dates (e.g. amplification kits, probes or enzymes) as indicated in Section 3.3.

5.2.2   Formulation–There must be a written procedure for the formulation of reagents, standards and controls.

5.2.3   Labeling Requirements–Labels should include identity, concentration, date of preparation, identity of individual preparing reagents, special storage requirements and expiration date, where appropriate.

5.2.4   A current inventory of supplies and materials should be maintained to include information on supplier, catalog number, lot number, date received and storage location.

5.2.5   Dedicated Materials and Reagents - Dedicated materials and reagents should be readily identifiable as such.

5.2.6   Glassware and Plastic Supplies Preparation - There should be specific procedures for cleaning, preparation and sterilization.

5.3   Laboratory Facilities for PCR Analysis

A PCR laboratory will require special laboratory configuration and sample handling (*AmpliType Users Guide* 1990).

5.3.1   Examination work area - Area(s) for examination, photography and microscopy must be separated in time or spare from the extraction and amplification setup areas.

5.3.2   Extraction work area(s)–This area is for sample extraction, concentration and digestion. It must be physically separate from the amplified DNA work area and be separated in time or space from the PCR setup area. An extraction area for samples containing low DNA levels (*e.g.,* telogne hairs, old bone) should be separated in time or space from other DNA extraction areas.

5.3.3   PCR setup work area–This area is isolated from the extraction area by time or in space to ensure that the reaction mix cocktails are prepared in a clean environment. This area must be physically separated from the amplified DNA work area.

5.3.4   Amplified DNA work area–This area is separated physically in the laboratory for containment of amplified DNA product. This area includes the amplification area with the thermal cycler and space for all procedures utilizing the product for typing (i.e., gel electrophoresis, hybridization and washing). Amplified DNA should be stored and disposed of in this area. All equipment and reagents used in this area should be dedicated and should not be used in either the extraction or PCR setup areas.

5.3.5   Decontamination–There must be written procedures for the cleaning and decontamination of facilities and equipment from DNA and PCR product DNA.

## 6. Evidence Handling Procedures

Evidence and samples from evidence must be collected, received, handled, sampled and stored so as to preserve the identity, integrity, condition and security of the item.

6.1 Sample labeling–Each sample must be labeled with a unique identifier in accordance with agency policy.

6.2 Chain of custody–A clear, well-documented chain of custody must be maintained from the time the evidence is first received until it is released from the laboratory (ASCLD 1986).

6.3 Sample handling and storage–Each agency will prepare a written policy to ensure that evidence samples (including isolated DNA and membranes) will be handled, processed and preserved, so as to protect against loss, contamination and deleterious change. Disposition of evidence should be in accordance with law and agency regulations. Refer to Section 5.3 for PCR sample handling considerations.

## 7. Analytical Procedures

7.1    Sample Evaluation and Preparation

7.1.1    General characterization of the biological material should be Performed prior to DNA analysis. Evidence samples submitted should be evaluated to determine the appropriateness for DNA analysis.

7.1.2    When semen is identified, a method of differential extraction should be employed, and when appropriate, each of the DNA fractions typed (see Section 4.1.5.10).

7.1.3    Testing of evidence and evidence samples should be conducted to provide the maximum information with the least consumption of the sample. Whenever possible, a portion of the original sample should be retained or returned to the submitting agency as established by laboratory policy.

7.2    DNA Isolation

7.2.1    The DNA isolation procedure should protect against sample contamination.

7.2.2    The effectiveness of the DNA isolation procedure should be evaluated by regular use of an appropriate source of human DNA.

7.3    Procedures for Estimating DNA recovery

Where appropriate, a procedure should be used for estimating the quality (extent of DNA degradation) and quantity of DNA recovered from the specimens. One or more of the following procedures may be employed to evaluate the effectiveness of the DNA recovery.

7.3.1    Yield Gel–Yield gels must include a set of high molecular weight DNA calibration standards for quantitative estimate of yield.

7.3.2    UV absorbance–Absorbance and wavelength standards or a high molecular weight DNA calibration standard may be used.

7.3.3    Fluorescence–Approximate quantification of extracted DNA can be accomplished by comparison with known concentrations of high molecular weight DNA.

7.3.4    Hybridization–Quantitation with human/primate specific probes requires an appropriate set of human DNA standards.

7.4    Analytical Procedures for RFLP Analysis

7.4.1    Restriction Enzymes

7.4.1.1    Prior to its initial use, each lot of restriction enzyme should be tested against an appropriate viral, human or other DNA standard which produces an expected DNA fragment pattern under standard digestion conditions. The restriction enzyme should also be tested under conditions that will reveal contaminating nuclease activity.

7.4.1.2    Demonstration of Restriction Enzyme Digestion - Digestion of extracted DNA by the restriction enzyme should be demonstrated using a test gel which includes:

(a)    Size Marker–Determines approximate size range of digested DNA.

(b)    Human DNA Control - Measures the effectiveness of restriction enzyme digestion of genomic human DNA.

7.4.2    Analytical Gel–The analytical gel used to separate restriction fragments must include the following:

7.4.2.1    Visual Marker–Visual or fluorescent markers which are used to determine the end point of electrophoresis.

7.4.2.2    Molecular Weight Size Markers–Markers which span the RFLP size range and are used to determine the size of unknown restriction fragments. Case samples must be bracketed by molecular weight size marker lanes.

7.4.2.3    Human DNA Control–A documented positive human DNA control of known type which produces a known fragment pattern with each probe and serves as a systems check for the following functions:

(a)    Electrophoresis quality and resolution
(b)    Sizing process
(c)    Probe identity
(d)    Hybridization efficiency
(e)    Stripping, efficiency

7.4.2.4    A procedure should be available to interpret altered migration of DNA fragments.

7.4.3    Southern Blots/Hybridization–The efficiency of blotting, hybridizations and stringency washes are monitored by the human DNA control and size markers.

7.4.4 Autoradiography–The exposure intensity is monitored by the use of multiple X-ray films or by successive exposures in order to obtain films of the proper intensity for image analysis.

7.4.5 Image and Data Processing–The functioning of image and data processing is monitored by the human DNA control allelic values.

7.5 Analytical Procedures for PCR Based Techniques

7.5.1 Internal Controls and Standards

The laboratory's QC guidelines should contain specific protocols to assess critical parameters in normal operations which include the following:

7.5.1.1 Negative controls to be included with each sample set are:
(a) a reagent blank
(b) an amplification blank.

7.5.1.2 A human DNA known type must be introduced at the amplification step as a positive control and carried through the remainder of the typing.

7.5.1.3 Where appropriate, controls should be collected from the evidence and should be processed at the same time as evidence samples.

7.5.1.4 To characterize amplified fragment length polymorphisms, markers which span the allele size range must be used. Case samples must be bracketed by marker lanes.

## 8. Case Work Documentation Interpretation, Report Writing and Review

Laboratories should have policies, checks and balances in place which ensure the reliability and completeness of the documentation, data analysis, reports and review process.

8.1 Case Work Documentation

Documentation must be in such a form that a competent analyst or supervisor/ technical leader, in the absence of the primary analyst, would be able to evaluate what was done and to interpret the data.

Documentation must include, but is not limited to, data obtained through the analytical process. It should also include information regarding the packaging of the evidence upon receipt, and the condition of the evidence itself, paying particular attention to those factors which are relevant to the preservation of the biological material. All documentation of procedures, standards and controls used, observations made, results of the tests performed, charts, graphs, photographs, autoradiographs, communications, etc., which are used to support the analyst's conclusions, must be preserved as a record according to written laboratory policy. Results should be preserved by photography, autoradiography or other suitable means.

8.2 Interpretation of Data

Laboratories should have general guidelines for interpretation of data for each method of DNA analysis.

8.2.1    Evaluation of Controls

8.2.1.1    Guidelines for interpreting and acting upon positive and/or negative control results.

8.2.1.2    Guidelines for statistical monitoring of the human DNA control if appropriate to the procedure (ANSI/ASQC A1-1987, ANSI/ASQC Z1.1-1985, ANSI/AS Z1.2-1985, ANSI/ASQC ZI.3-1985; AT&T Technologies 1985; Westgard et al. 1981; Gryna 1979; Bicking and Gryna 1979; National Bureau of Standards 1966).

8.2.2    Evaluation of Samples

8.2.2.1    The basis for concluding when samples are, or are not the same type, or when the results of the analysis are inconclusive or uninterpretable should be established.

8.2.2.2    For RFLP analysis, confirmation of visual matches of the restriction fragment bands must be made by quantitative analysis based on tolerance limits.

8.2.2.3    Statistical Evaluation–The frequency of occurrence for the DNA profile should be calculated using a scientifically valid method from an established population data base.

8.3    Report Writing

Contents–It is highly desirable that reports contain the following:

8.3.1    Case identifier

8.3.2    Identity of examiner/analyst

8.3.3    Date of report

8.3.4    The DNA locus (defined by the Nomenclature Committee of the International Gene Workshop), as identified by particular probe(s) or sequence(s)

8.3.5    Restriction enzyme, primer pair or other descriptor of the methodology

8.3.6    Results

8.3.7    Conclusions

8.3.8    Statistical evaluation

8.3.9    Signature of the reporting analyst

8.4 Review

Data, documentation and reports must be reviewed independently by a second qualified individual. Prior to issuing a report, both individuals must agree on the interpretation of the data and the conclusions derived from that data.

## 9. Proficiency Testing

Proficiency testing is used periodically to demonstrate the quality performance of the DNA laboratory and serves as a mechanism for critical self evaluation. This will be accomplished by the analysis and reporting of results from appropriate biological specimens, submitted to the laboratory as open and/or blind case evidence.

All specimens submitted as part of an open or blind proficiency test must be analyzed and interpreted according to the DNA analysis protocol approved by the laboratory for use at the time of the proficiency test.

Participation in a proficiency testing program is a critical element of a successful QA program and is an essential requirement for any laboratory performing forensic DNA analysis. A forensic laboratory involved in DNA analysis may establish its own proficiency testing program or establish a program in cooperation with another forensic laboratory.

The DNA laboratory should participate in proficiency testing programs, conducted by outside institutions or provided by other reputable sources, which are appropriately designed for forensic DNA analysis.

9.1     Open Proficiency Testing

Open proficiency test specimens are presented to the laboratory and its staff as proficiency specimens and are used to demonstrate the reliability of the laboratory's analytical methods as well as the interpretive capability of the examiner/analyst. Participation in an open proficiency test program is the primary means by which the quality performance of the DNA laboratory is judged and is an essential requirement if a DNA laboratory is to perform case work.

9.1.1   Personnel

Open proficiency testing pertains to those laboratory examiners/analysts and technicians actively engaged in DNA testing.

9.1.2   Frequency

Open proficiency tests must be submitted to the DNA testing laboratory such that each examiner/analyst, as well as those technicians involved in performing analytical techniques related to DNA analysis, are tested at least twice a year.

9.1.3   Specimens

Each open proficiency test may consist of dried specimens of blood and/or other physiological fluids, either singly or as a mixture. Each sample to be tested should contain an amount sufficient so that a conclusion can be drawn from the results of the analysis.

For those DNA procedures which use electrophoretic analysis for identification of the DNA polymorphisms, the number of specimens included in the proficiency test should be such that all may be accommodated on a single analytical gel.

For those DNA analysis procedures which use PCR for DNA amplification, coupled with a nonelectrophoretic method for the identification of the DNA polymorphism, an equivalent number of samples should be tested.

Those samples which comprise proficiency tests intended for PCR based techniques must include the appropriate negative controls as specified in Section 7.5.1.3.

9.1.4     Sample preparation, Storage and Distribution

(a) All specimens and proficiency tests should be uniformly prepared using materials and methods that ensure their integrity and identity.

(b) All open proficiency test specimens will be prepared on washed cotton cloth, cotton swabs or other suitable material.

(c) Each specimen and set must be labeled with a unique identifier that should be independently verified by at least one other person to ensure proper assignment of the identifier.

(d) A portion of each specimen used to prepare the open proficiency test should be retained by the preparing laboratory for possible referee analysis and comparison if circumstances dictate.

(e) A person in the DNA laboratory, as designated by laboratory management, should acknowledge the receipt of each proficiency test and assign it to the DNA laboratory staff.

9.2     Blind Proficiency Testing

Ideally, blind proficiency test specimens should be presented to the testing laboratory through a second agency. These samples should appear to the examiner/analyst as routine evidence. The blind proficiency test serves to evaluate all aspects of the laboratory examination procedure, including evidence handling, examination/testing and reporting. It is highly desirable that the DNA laboratory participate in a blind proficiency test program, and every effort should be made to implement such a program.

9.2.1     Personnel

Blind proficiency testing pertains only to personnel previously qualified by their laboratory to conduct DNA testing.

9.2.2     Frequency

Those laboratories which have implemented a blind testing program, and are engaged in the analysis and interpretation of DNA profiles, should be tested by a blind proficiency test at least once a year.

9.2.3     Specimens

Each blind proficiency test will consist of liquid or dried specimens of blood and/or other physiological fluids, either singly or as a mixture. Each sample to be tested should contain an amount sufficient so that a conclusion can be drawn from the results of the analysis.

For those DNA procedures which use electrophoretic analysis for identification of the DNA polymorphisms, the number of specimens included in the proficiency test should be such that all may be accommodated on a single analytical gel.

For those DNA analysis procedures which use PCR for DNA amplification, coupled with a nonelectrophoretic method for the identification of the DNA polymorphism, an equivalent number of samples should be tested.

Those samples which comprise proficiency tests intended for PCR based techniques must include the appropriate negative controls as specified in Section 7.5.1.3.

9.2.4    Sample Preparation, Storage and Distribution

(a)    All specimens and proficiency tests should be uniformly prepared using materials and methods ensuring their integrity and identity.

(b)    All blind proficiency tests should be prepared so as to realistically simulate the characteristics of actual case work.

(c)    The identity of each specimen and set must be independently verified by at least one other person to ensure proper assignment of the identifier.

(d)    A portion of each specimen used to prepare the blind proficiency test should be retained by the preparing laboratory for possible referee analysis and comparison if circumstances dictate.

(e)    Once prepared, all samples must be packaged separately, and sets must be stored until submission to the testing agency so as to maintain their integrity and condition.

(f)    The QA coordinator, or other individual designated by the laboratory, will make all necessary arrangements for the covert submission of the blind proficiency test, including supporting documentation and agency contact.

(g)    Unless specifically authorized by the laboratory director or QA coordinator, prior to the analysis and reporting of the blind proficiency results, no person in the laboratory undergoing blind proficiency testing should be aware of the ongoing blind proficiency test or the personnel involved.

9.3    Documentation of Proficiency Test Results

9.3.1    Open Proficiency Tests

At a minimum, the following proficiency test data and information should be collected and submitted to the QA coordinator, or other designated individual, for evaluation:

1.    Open proficiency test set identifier
2.    Identity of examiner/analyst
3.    Dates of analysis and completion
4.    Copies of all data sheets and notes
5.    Photographs of yield, post restriction (digestion) test, and analytical gels and/or dot blots as appropriate

6.  Lot numbers of primers or probes and the sequence of use
7.  Lot numbers of commercially prepared supplies or kits
S.  Original or duplicate autorads where appropriate
9.  Computer imaging sizing data where appropriate
10. Likelihood estimates for samples
11. Results/conclusions

9.3.2    Blind Proficiency Tests

The report of the DNA laboratory will be sent to the submitting agency in the normal course of laboratory operations, and prior arrangements should be made for its immediate forwarding to the QA coordinator or other designated individual.

Upon receipt of the forwarded DNA report, the QA coordinator, or other designated individual will require that the DNA laboratory provide the data and documentation specified in 9.3.1. In addition, documentation on the receipt, storage, handling and chain of custody may also be requested for review. The blind proficiency test evidence may also be recovered from the testing or submitting agency and examined for proper documentation and handling. If the testing laboratory retains portions of the tested materials or products of its analysis, these should be examined for proper documentation and storage.

9.4    Review and Reporting of Proficiency Test Results

The QA coordinator, or other designated individual, will review all test materials and compare results to the information from the manufacturer of the test. The QA coordinator will provide a written summary report for each proficiency test to the examining examiner/analyst and other appropriate individuals as established by the laboratory policy. This review should be conducted in a timely manner. All original notes, records and other data pertaining to the open proficiency test results should be retained according to laboratory policy.

9.5    Corrective Action

The specific policies, procedures and criteria for any corrective action taken as a result of a discrepancy in a proficiency test should be clearly defined and approved by the appropriate individuals in accordance with established laboratory policies.

9.5.1    Authority and Accountability

It is the responsibility of the QA coordinator, or designated individual, to assure that discrepancies are acknowledged and that any corrective action is documented.

In the event of an unresolved disagreement between the designated QA individual and DNA laboratory, the matter should be referred to the laboratory director.

9.5.2    Administrative Error

Any significant discrepancy in a proficiency test determined to be the result of administrative error (*e.g.*, clerical error, sample confusion, improper storage, inaccurate documentation, etc.) will be corrected according to established laboratory policy.

9.5.3    Systematic Error

Any significant discrepancy in a proficiency test determined to be the result of a systematic error (*e.g.*, equipment, materials, environment) may require a review of all relevant case work since the DNA unit's or laboratory's last successfully completed proficiency test. Once the cause of the discrepancy has been identified and corrective action taken, all examiners/analysts should be made aware of the appropriate corrective action in order to minimize the recurrence of the discrepancy.

9.5.4    Analytical/interpretative Error

(a)  Any significant discrepancy in a blind or open proficiency test result determined to be the consequence of an analytical/interpretative discrepancy should prohibit the individual(s) involved in producing the discrepant result from further examination of case evidence until the cause of the problem is identified and corrected. The QA coordinator, or designated individual, will determine the need to audit prior cases, according to established laboratory policy.

(b)  Before resuming analysis or interpretation of case work, an additional set of open proficiency samples must be successfully completed by the individual responsible for the discrepancy.

9.6    Documentation

The results of all proficiency tests will be maintained by the DNA laboratory according to established laboratory policy.

## 10. Audits

Audits are an important aspect of the QA program. They are an independent review conducted to compare the various aspects of the DNA laboratory's performance with a standard for that performance (Mills 1989; Sayle 1988). The audits are not punitive in nature, but are intended to provide management with an evaluation of the laboratory's performance in meeting its quality policies and objectives.

10.1    Audits or inspections should be conducted at least once every two years by individuals separate from and independent of the DNA testing laboratory. It is highly desirable that at least one auditor be from an outside agency.

10.2    Records of each inspection should be maintained and should include the date of the inspection, area inspected, name of the person conducting the inspection, findings and problems, remedial actions taken to resolve existing problems, and schedule of next inspection.

## 11. Safety

11.1    Policy–The DNA testing laboratory shall operate in strict accordance with the regulations of the pertinent federal, state, and local health and safety authorities.

11.2     Written Manuals - Written general laboratory safety and radiation safety manuals shall be prepared by the laboratory and be made available to each member of the DNA analysis laboratory and/or other persons affected. (Code of Federal Regulations 1988 a,b; Bond 1987; Gibbs and Kasprisin 1987; Sax and Lewis 1987; National Fire Protection Association 1986; National Research Council 1981; Wang *et al.* 1975; Steere 1971).

11.3     Material Safety Data Sheets (MSDS)–There should be a file of MSDS received from the manufacturer for all chemicals used in the laboratory. These data sheets should be readily available to all laboratory personnel.

11.4     Storage and Disposal–All chemicals, supplies and radioactive materials must be stored, used and disposed of under conditions recommended by the manufacturer and in a manner conforming to established safety requirements.

## References

*AABB Standards Committee, (1990).*   P7.000 DNA Polymorphism Testing.   In: Standards for Parentage Testing Laboratories. 1st ed.   American Association of Blood Banks, Arlington, Virginia.

*Alwan, L. C. and Bissell, M. G. (1988).*   Time series modeling for quality control in clinical chemistry, Clin. Chem. 34:1396-1406.

*American National Standard ANSI/ASQC Q90-1987 (1987).*   Definitions, Symbols, Formulas, and Tables for Control Charts.  American Society for Quality Control, Milwaukee, Wisconsin.

*American National Standard ANSI/ASQC Q90-1987 (1987a).*   Quality Management and Quality Assurance Standards - Guidelines for Selection and Use.  American Society for Quality Control, Milwaukee, Wisconsin.

*American National Standard ANSI/ASQC Q90-1987 (1987b).*   Quality Management and Quality System Elements - Guidelines.  American Society for Quality Control, Milwaukee, Wisconsin.

*American National Standard ANSI/ASQC ZI.2-1985 (1985).*   Guide for Quality Control Charts.  American Society for Quality Control, Milwaukee, Wisconsin.

*American National Standard ANSI/ASQC ZI.2-1985 (1985).*   Control Chart Method of Analyzing Data.  American Society for Quality Control, Milwaukee, Wisconsin.

*American National Standard ANSI/ASQC ZI.3-1985 (1985).*   Control Chart Method of Controlling Quality During Production.  American Society for Quality Control, Milwaukee, Wisconsin.

*American National Standard ANSI/ASQC Z1.15-1979 (1979).*   Generic Guidelines for Quality Systems.  American Society for Quality Control, Milwaukee, Wisconsin.

*American National Standard ANSI/ASQC A3-1978 (1978).*   Quality Systems Terminology American Society for Quality Control, Milwaukee, Wisconsin.

*American National Standard ASQC Standard C1-1968 (1968).*   Specification of General Requirements of a Quality Program. American Society for Quality Control, Milwaukee, Wisconsin.

AmpliType User Guide for the HLA DQα Forensic DNA Amplification and Typing Kit, 1990, Section - Laboratory Setup, Cetus Corporation, Emeryville, California.

*ASCLD (1986).*  Guidelines for Forensic Laboratory Management Practices.  American Society of Crime Laboratory Directors, September.

*ASCLD (1985).* ASCLD Accreditation Manual. American Society of Crime Laboratory Directors, Laboratory Accreditation Board, February.

*AT&T Technologies (1985).* Statistical Quality Control Handbook. AT&T Technologies, Indianapolis, Indiana, May.

*Baird, M. (1989).* Quality Control and American Association of Blood Bank Standards. Presented at the American Association of Blood Banks National Conference, April 17-19, Leesburg, Virginia.

*Bicking, C. A. and Gryna, F. M. (1979).* Process Control by Statistical Methods. In: Quality Control Handbook. 3d ed. Edited by J. M. Juran. McGraw-Hill, New York.

*Bond, W. W. (1987).* Safety in the Forensic Immunology Laboratory. In: Proceedings of the International Symposium on Forensic Immunology, U. S. Government Printing Office, Washington, D. C.

*Box, G. E. P. and Bisaard, S. (1987).* The scientific context of quality improvement, Quality Progress 20(6):54-61.

*Bradford, L. W. (1980).* Barriers to quality achievement in crime laboratory operations, J. Forensic Sci. 25:902-907.

*Brunelle, R. L., Garner, D. D. and Wineman, P. L. (1982).* A quality assurance program for the laboratory examination of arson and explosive cases, J. Forensic Sci. 27:774-782.

*Budowle, B., Deadman, H. A., Murch, R. S. and Baechtel, F. S. (1988).* An introduction to the methods of DNA analysis under investigation in the FBI Laboratory, Crime Lab. Digest 15:8-21.

*Bussolini, P. L., Davis, A. H. and Geoffrion, R. R. (1988).* A new approach to quality for national research labs, Quality Progress 21(1):24-27.

*Code of Federal Regulations (1988a).* Title 10, Part 19 - Notices, Instructions, and Reports to Workers; Inspections. U. S. Government-Printing Office, Washington, D. C.

*Code of Federal Regulations (1988b).* Title 10, Part 20 - Standards for Protection Against Radiation. U. S. Government Printing Office, Washington, D. C.

*Ford, D. J. (1988).* Good laboratory practice, Lab. Practice, 37(9):29-33.

*Gautier, M. A. and Gladney, E. S. (1987).* A quality assurance program for health and environmental chemistry, Am. Lab., July, pp. 17-22.

*Gibbs, F. L. and Kasprisin, C. A. (1987).* Environmental Safety in the Blood Bank. American Association of Blood Banks, Arlington, Virginia.

*Gryna, F. M. (1979).* Basic Statistical Methods. In: Quality Control Handbook. 3d ed. Edited by J. M. Juran. McGraw-Hill, New York.

*Hay, R. J. (1988).* The seed stock concept and quality control for cell lines, Anal. Biochem. 171:225-237.

*Juran, J. M. (1979).* Quality Policies and Objectives. In: Quality Control Handbook, 3d ed. Edited by J. M. Juran. McGraw-Hill, New York.

*Kenney, M. L. (1987).* Quality assurance in changing times: proposals for reform and research in the clinical laboratory field, Clin. Chem. 33:328-336.

*Kidd, G. J. (1987).* What Quality Means to an R & D Organization. 41st Annual Quality Congress Transactions, May 4-6, American Society for Quality Control, Milwaukee, Wisconsin.

*Kilshaw, D. (1986).* Quality assurance. 1. Philosophy and basic principles, Med. Lab. Sci. 43:377-381.

*Kilshaw, D. (1987a).* Quality assurance. 2. Internal quality control, Med. Lab. Sci. 44:73-93.

*Kilshaw, D. (1987b).* Quality assurance. 3. External quality assessment, Med. Lab. Sci. 44:178-186.

*Mills, C. A. (1989).* The Quality Audit A Management Evaluation Tool. American Society for Quality Control, Milwaukee, Wisconsin.

*National Bureau of Standards (1966).* The Place of Control Charts in Experimental Work. In: Experimental Statistics. National Bureau of Standards Handbook 91. U. S. Government Printing Office, Washington, D. C.

*National Fire Protection Association (1986).* Standard on Fire Protection for Laboratories Using Chemicals. National Fire Protection Association. Batterymarch Park, Quincy, Massachusetts.

*National Research Council (1983).* Prudent Practices for Disposal of Chemicals from Laboratories. National Research Council's Committee on Hazardous Substances in the Laboratory, National Academy Press, Washington, D.C.

*National Research Council (1981).* Prudent Practices for Handling Hazardous Chemicals in Laboratories. National Research Council's Committee on Hazardous Substances in the Laboratory, National Academy Press, Washington, D. C.

*Pereira, M. (1985).* Quality assurance in forensic science, Forensic Sci. Int. 28:1-6.

Report of a Symposium on the Practice of Forensic Serology 1987, Method Evaluation (Topic 4), Sponsored by the California Department of Justice Bureau of Forensic Services, California Association of Criminalists, and the UNISYS Corporation.

*Ruzicka R. K. (1979).* Documentation: Configuration Management. In: Quality Control Handbook. 3d ed. Edited by J. M. Juran. McGraw-Hill, New York.

*Sax, N. I. and Lewis, R. J. (1987).* Hazardous Chemicals Desk Reference. Van Nostrand Reinhold, New York.

*Sayle, Allan J. (1988).* Management Audits: The Assessment of Quality Management Systems. 2d ed. American Society for Quality Control, Milwaukee, Wisconsin.

*Simpson, J. (1983).* National Bureau of Standards Approach to Quality, Test and Measurement World, December, p. 38.

*Steere, N. V., ed. (1971).* CRC Handbook of Laboratory Safety. 2d ed. The Chemical Rubber Co., Cleveland, Ohio.

*Taylor, J. K. (1987).* Quality Assurance of Chemical Measurements. Lewis Publishers, Chelsea, Michigan.

*Taylor. J. K. (1985).* The quest for quality assurance, Am. Lab., October, pp. 67-75.

*Wang, C. H., Willis, D. L. and Loveland, W. D. (1975).* Radiotracer Methodology in the Biological, Environmental and Physical Sciences. Prentice-Hall, Englewood Cliffs, New Jersey.

*Westgard, J. O., Barry, P. L., Hunt, M. R. and Groth, T. (1981).* A multi-rule Shewart chart for quality control in clinical chemistry, Clin. Chem. 27:493-501.

*Whitehead, T. P. and Woodford, F. P. (1981).* External quality assessment of clinical laboratories in the United Kingdom, J. Clin. Pathol. 34:947-957.

## NRC I AND NRC II RECOMMENDATIONS

**RECOMMENDATIONS OF NRC I**

### Technical Considerations

- Any new DNA typing method (or substantial variation of an existing method) must be rigorously characterized in both research and forensic settings, to determine the circumstances under which it will yield reliable results.

- DNA analysis in forensic science should be governed by the highest standards of scientific rigor, including the following requirements:

  — Each DNA typing procedure must be completely described in a detailed, written laboratory protocol.

  — Each DNA typing procedure requires objective and quantitative measures for identifying the pattern of a sample.

  — Each DNA typing procedure requires a precise and objective matching rule for declaring whether two samples match.

  — Potential artifacts should be identified by empirical testing, and scientific controls should be designed to serve as internal checks to test for the occurrence of artifacts

  — The limits of each DNA typing procedure should be understood, especially when the DNA sample is small, is a mixture of DNA from multiple sources, or if contaminated with interfering substances.

  — Empirical characterization of a DNA typing procedure must be published is appropriate scientific journals.

  — Before a new DNA typing procedure can be used, it must have not only a solid scientific foundation, but also a solid base of experience.

- The committee strongly recommends the establishment of a National Committee on Forensic DNA Typing (NCFDT) under the auspices of an appropriate government agency or agencies to provide expert advice primarily on scientific and technical issues concerning forensic DNA typing.

- Novel forms of variation in the genome that have the potential for increased power of discrimination between persons are being discovered. Furthermore, new ways to demonstrate variation in the genome are being developed. The current techniques are likely to be superseded by others that provide unambiguous individual identification and have such advantages as automatability and economy. Each new method should be evaluated by the NCFDT for use in the forensic setting, applying appropriate criteria to ensure that society derives maximal benefit from DNA typing technology.

### Statistical Basis for Interpretation

- As a basis for the interpretation of the statistical significance of DNA typing results, the committee recommends that blood samples be obtained from 100 randomly selected persons in each of 15-20 relatively homogeneous populations; that the DNA in lymphocytes form these blood samples be used to determine the frequencies of alleles currently tested in forensic applications; and that the lymphocytes be "immortalized" and preserved as a reference standard for determination of allele frequencies in tests applied in different laboratories or developed in the future. The collection of samples and their study should be overseen by a National Committee on Forensic DNA Typing.

- The ceiling principle should be used in applying the multiplication rule for estimating the frequency of particular DNA profile. For each allele in a person's DNA pattern, the highest allele frequency found in any of the 15-20 population or 5% (whichever is larger) should be used.

- In the interval (which should be short) while the reference blood samples are being collected, the significance of the findings of multilocus DNA typing should be presented in two ways: (1) If no match is found with any sample in a total databank of N persons (as will usually be the case), that should be stated, thus indicating the rate of a random match. (2) In applying the multiplication rule, the 95% upper confidence limit of the frequency of each allele should be calculated for separate U.S. "racial" groups and the highest of these values or 10% ( whichever is the larger) should be used. Data on at least three major "races" (e.g., Caucasians, Blacks, Hispanics, Asians, and Native Americans) should be analyzed.

- Any population databank used to support DNA typing should be openly available for scientific inspection by parties to a legal case and by the scientific community.

- Laboratory error rates should be measured with appropriate proficiency tests and should play a role in the interpretation of results of forensic DNA typing.

**Standards**

Although standardization of forensic practice is difficult because of the nature of the samples, DNA typing is such a powerful and complex technology that some degree of standardization is necessary to ensure high standards

- Each forensic science laboratory engaged in DNA typing must have a formal, detailed quality-assurance and quality-control program to monitor work, on both an individual and a laboratory-wide basis.

- The technical Working Group on DNA Analysis and Methods (TWGDAM) guidelines for a quality-assurance program for DNA RFLP analysis are an excellent starting point for a quality-assurance program, which should be supplemented by the additional technical recommendations of this committee.

- The TWGDAM group should continue to function, playing a role complementary to that of the National Committee on Forensic DNA Typing (NCFDT). To increase its effectiveness, TWGDAM should include additional technical experts from outside the forensic community who are not closely tied to any forensic laboratory.

- Quality-assurance programs in individual laboratories alone are insufficient to ensure high standards. External mechanisms are needed, to ensure adherence to the practices of quality assurance. Potential mechanisms included individual certification, laboratory accreditation, and state or federal regulation.

- One of the best guarantees of high quality is the presence of an active professional-organization committee that is able to enforce standards. Although professional societies in forensic science have historically not played an active role, the American Society of Crime Laboratory Directors (ASCLD) and the American Society of Crime Laboratory Director-Laboratory Accreditation Board (ASCLD-LAB) recently have shown substantial interest in enforcing quality by expanding the ASCLD-LAB accreditation program to include mandatory proficiency testing. ASCLD-LAB must demonstrate that it will actively discharge this role.

- Because private professional organizations lack the regulatory authority to require accreditation, further means are needed to ensure compliance with appropriate standards.

- Courts should require that laboratories providing DNA typing evidence have proper accreditation for each DNA typing method used. Any laboratory that is not formally accredited and that provides evidence to the courts - e.g., a nonforensic laboratory repeating the analysis of a forensic laboratory - should be expected to demonstrate that it is operating at the same level of standards as accredited laboratories.

- Establishing mandatory accreditation should be a responsibility of the Department of Health and Human Services (DHHS), in consultation with the Department of Justice (DOJ). DHHS is the appropriate agency, because it has extensive experience in the regulation of clinical laboratories through programs under the Clinical Laboratory Improvement Act and has extensive expertise in molecular genetics through the National Institutes of Health. DOJ must be involved, because the task is important for law enforcement.

- The National Institute of Justice (NIJ) does not appear to receive adequate funds to support proper education, training, and research in the field of forensic DNA typing. The level of funding should be re-evaluated and increased appropriately.

**Databanks and Privacy of Information**
- In the future, if pilot studies confirm its value, a national DNA profile databank should be created that contains information on felons convicted of particular violent crimes. Among crimes with high rates of recidivism, the case is strongest for rape, because perpetrators typically leave biological evidence (semen) that could allow them to be identified. Rape is the crime for which the databank will be of primary use. The case is somewhat weaker for violent offenders who are most likely to commit homicide as recidivist offense, because killers leave biological evidence only in a minority of cases.

- The databank should also contain DNA profiles of unidentified persons made from biological samples found at crime scenes. These would be samples known to be of human origin, but not matched with any known persons.

- Data banks containing DNA profiles of members of the general population (as exist for ordinary fingerprints for identification purpose) are not appropriate, for reasons of both privacy and economics.

- DNA profile databanks should be accessible only to legal authorized persons and should be stored in a secure information resource.

- Legal policy concerning access and use of both DNA samples and DNA databank information should be established before widespread proliferation of samples and information repositories. Interim protection and sanctions against misuse and abuse of information derived from DNA typing should be established immediately. Policies should explicitly define authorized uses and should provide for criminal penalties for abuses.

- Although the committee endorses the concept of a limited national DNA profile databank, it doubts that existing RFLP-based technology provides an appropriate wise long-term foundation for such a databank. We expect current methods to be replaced soon with techniques that are simpler, easier to automate, and less expensive - but incompatible with existing DNA profiles. Accordingly, the committee does not recommend establishing a comprehensive DNA profile databank yet.

- For the short term, we recommend the establishment of pilot projects that involve prototype databanks based on RFLP technology and consisting primarily of profiles of violent sex offenders. Such pilot projects could be worthwhile for identifying problems and issues in the creation of databanks. However, in the intermediate term more efficient methods will replace the current one, and the forensic community should not allow itself to become locked into an outdated method.

- State and federal laboratories, which have a long tradition and much experience in the management of other types of basic evidence, should be given primary responsibility , authority, and additional resources to handle forensic DNA testing and all the associated sample-handling and data-handling requirements.

- Private-sector firms should not be discouraged from continuing to prepare and analyze DNA samples for specific cases or for databank samples, but they must be held accountable for misuse and abuse to the same extent as government-funded laboratories and government authorities.

**DNA Information in the Legal System**
- Courts should take judicial notice of three scientific underpinnings of DNA typing:

  — The study of DNA polymorphism can, in principle, provide a reliable method for comparing samples.

  — Each person's DNA is unique (except that of identical twins), although the actual discriminatory power of any particular DNA test will depend on the sites of DNA variation examined.

  — The current laboratory procedure for detecting DNA variation (specifically, single-locus probes analyzed on Southern blots without evidence of band shifting) is fundamentally sound, although the validity of any particular implementation of the basic procedure will depend on proper characterization of the reproducibility of the system (e.g., measurement variation) and inclusion of all necessary scientific controls.

- The adequacy of the method used to acquire and analyze samples in a given case bears on the admissibility of the evidence and should, unless stipulated by opposing parties, be adjudicated case by case. In this adjudication, the accreditation and certification status of the laboratory performing the analysis should be taken into account.

- Because of the potential power of DNA evidence, authorities should make funds available to pay for expert witnesses, and the appropriate parties must be informed of the use of DNA evidence as soon as possible.

- DNA samples (and evidence likely to contain DNA) should be preserved whenever that is possible.

- All data and laboratory records generated by analysis of DNA samples should be made freely available to all parties. Such access is essential for evaluating the analysis.

- Protective orders should be used only to protect the privacy of individuals.

**DNA Typing and Society**
- In the forensic context as in the medical setting, DNA information is personal, and a person's privacy and need for confidentiality should be respected. The release of DNA information on a criminal population without the subjects' permission for purposes other than law enforcement should be considered a misuse of the information, and legal sanctions should be established to deter the unauthorized dissemination or procurement of DNA information that was obtained for forensic purposes.

- Prosecutors and defense counsel should not oversell DNA evidence. Presentations that suggest to a judge or jury that DNA typing is infallible are rarely justified and should be avoided.

- Mechanisms should be established to ensure accountability of laboratories and personnel involved in DNA typing and to make appropriate public scrutiny possible.

- Organizations that conduct accreditation or regulation of DNA technology for forensic purposes should not be subject to the influence of private companies, public laboratories or other organizations actually engaged in laboratory work.

- Private laboratories used for testing should not be permitted to withhold information from defendants on the ground that trade secrets are involved.

- The same standards and peer-review processes used to evaluate advances in biomedical science and technology should be used to evaluate forensic DNA methods and techniques.

- Efforts at international cooperation should be furthered, in order to ensure uniform international standards and the fullest possible exchange of scientific knowledge and technical expertise.

## RECOMMENDATIONS OF NRC II

### Admissibility of DNA Evidence (Chapter 2)

DNA analysis is one of the greatest technical achievements for criminal investigation since the discovery of fingerprints. Methods of DNA profiling are firmly grounded in molecular technology. When profiling is done with appropriate care, the results are highly reproducible. In particular, the methods are almost certain to exclude an innocent suspect. One of the most widely used techniques involves VNTRs. These loci are extremely variable, but individual alleles cannot be distinguished, because of intrinsic measurement variability, and the analysis requires statistical procedures. The laboratory procedure involves radioactivity and requires a month or more for full analysis. PCR-based methods are prompt, require only a small amount of material, and can yield unambiguous identification of individual alleles.

The state of the profiling technology and the methods for estimating frequencies and related statistics have progressed to the point where the admissibility of properly collected and analyzed DNA data should not be in doubt. We expect continued development of new and better methods and hope for their prompt validation, so that they can quickly be brought into use.

### Laboratory Errors

The occurrence of errors can be minimized by scrupulous care in evidence-collecting, sample-handling, laboratory procedures, and case review. Detailed guidelines for QC and QA (quality control and quality assurance), which are updated regularly, are produced by several organizations, including TWGDAM. ASCLD-LAB is established as an accrediting agency. The 1992 NRC report recommended that a National Committee on Forensic DNA Typing (NCFDT) be formed to oversee the setting of DNA-analysis standards. The DNA Identification Act of 1994 gives this responsibility to a DNA Advisory Board appointed by the FBI. We recognize the need for guidelines and standards, and for accreditation by appropriate organizations.

**Recommendation 3.1:** Laboratories should adhere to high quality standards (such as those defined by TWGDAM and the DNA Advisory Board) and make every effort to be accredited for DNA work (by such organizations as ASCLD-LAB).

### Proficiency Tests

Regular proficiency tests, both within the laboratory and by external examiners, are one of the best ways of assuring high standards. To the extent that it is feasible, some of the tests should be blind.

**Recommendation 3.2:** Laboratories should participate regularly in proficiency tests, and the results should be available for court proceedings.

## Duplicate Tests

We recognize that no amount of care and proficiency testing can eliminate the possibility of error. However, duplicate tests, performed as independently as possible, can reduce the risk of error enormously. The best protection that an innocent suspect has against an error that could lead to a false conviction is the opportunity for an independent retest.

**Recommendation 3.3:** Whenever feasible, forensic samples should be divided into two or more parts at the earliest practicable stage and the unused parts retained to permit additional tests. The used and saved portions should be stored and handled separately. Any additional tests should be performed independently of the first by personnel not involved in the first test and preferably in a different laboratory.

## Population Genetics

Sufficient data now exist for various groups and subgroups within the United States that analysts should present the best estimates for profile frequencies. For VNTRs, using the 2p rule for single bands and HW for double bands is generally conservative for an individual locus. For multiple loci, departures from linkage equilibrium are not great enough to cause errors comparable to those from uncertainty of allele frequencies estimated from databases.

With appropriate consideration of the data, the principles in this report can be applied to PCR-based tests. For those in which exact genotypes can be determined, the 2p rule should not be used. A conservative estimate is given by using the HW relation for heterozygotes and a conservative value of $\overline{\theta}$ in Equation 4.4a for homozygotes.

**Recommendation 4.1:** In general, the calculation of a profile frequency should be made with the product rule. If the race of the person who left the evidence-sample DNA is known, the database for the person's race should be used; if the race is not known, calculations for all racial groups to which possible suspects belong should be made. For systems such as VNTRs, in which a heterozygous locus can be mistaken for a homozygous one, if an upper bound on the genotypic frequency at an apparently homozygous locus (single band) is desired, then twice the allele (bin) frequency, 2p, should be used instead of p2. For systems in which exact genotypes can be determined, $p^2 + p(1 - p)\,\overline{\theta}$ should be used for the frequency at such a locus instead of $p^2$. A conservative value of $\theta$ for the US population is 0.01; for some small, isolated a populations, a value of 0.03 may be more appropriate. For both kinds of systems, $2p_ip_j$ should be used for heterozygotes.

A more conservative value of $\overline{\theta} = 0.03$ might be chosen for PCR-based systems in view of the greater uncertainty of calculations for such systems because of less extensive and less varied population data than for VNTRs.

## Evidence DNA and Suspect from the Same Subgroup

Sometimes there is evidence that the suspect and other possible sources of the sample belong to the same subgroup. That can happen, e.g., if they are all members of a an isolated village. In this case, a modification of the procedure is desirable.

Recommendation 4.2: If the particular subpopulation from which the evidence sample came is known, the allele frequencies for the specific subgroup should be used as described in Recommendation 4.1. If allele frequencies for the subgroup are not available, although data for the full population are, then the calculations should use the population structure equations 4.10 for each locus, and the resulting values should then be multiplied.

## Insufficient Data

For some groups—and several American Indian and Inuit tribes are in this category— there are insufficient data to estimate frequencies reliably, and even the overall average might be unreliable. In this case, data from other, related groups provide the best information. The groups chosen should be the most closely related for which adequate databases exist. These might be chosen because of geographical proximity, or a physical anthropologist might be consulted. There should be a limit on the number of such subgroups analyzed to prevent inclusion of more remote groups less relevant to the case.

**Recommendation 4.3:** If the person who contributed the evidence sample is from a group or tribe for which no adequate database exists, data from several other groups or tribes thought to be closely related to it should be used. The profile frequency should be calculated as described in Recommendation 4.1 for each group or tribe.

## Dealing with Relatives

In some instances, there is evidence that one or more relatives of the suspect are possible perpetrators.

**Recommendation 4.4:** If the possible contributors of the evidence sample include relatives of the suspect, DNA profiles of those relatives should be obtained. If these profiles cannot be obtained, the probability of finding the evidence profile in those relatives should be calculated with Formula 4.8 or 4.9.

## Statistical Issues (Chapter 5)

Confidence limits for profile probabilities, based on allele frequencies and the size of the database, can be calculated by methods explained in this report. We recognize, however, that confidence limits address only part of the uncertainty. For a more realistic estimate, we examined empirical data from the comparison of different subpopulations and of subpopulations within the whole. The empirical studies show that the differences between the frequencies of the individual profiles estimated by the product rule from different adequate subpopulation databases (at least several hundred persons) are within a factor of about 10 of each other, and that provides a guide to the uncertainty of the determination for a single profile. For very small estimated profile frequencies, the uncertainty can be greater, both because of the greater relative uncertainty of individually small probabilities and because more loci are likely to be multiplied. But with very small probabilities, even a larger relative error is not likely to change the conclusion.

## Database Searches

If the suspect is identified through a DNA database search, the interpretation of the match probability and likelihood ratio given in Chapter 4 should be modified.

**Recommendation 5.1:** When the suspect is found by a search of DNA databases, the random-match probability should be multiplied by N, the number of persons in the database.

If one wishes to describe the impact of the DNA evidence under the hypothesis that the source of the evidence sample is someone in the database, then the likelihood ratio should be divided by N. As databases become more extensive, another problem may arise. If the database searched includes a large proportion of the population, the analysis must take that into account.

In the extreme case, a search of the whole population should, of course, provide a definitive answer.

## Uniqueness

With an increasing number of loci available for forensic analysis, we are approaching the time when each person's profile is unique (except for identical twins and possibly other close relatives). Suppose that, in a population of N unrelated persons, a given DNA profile has probability P. The probability (before a suspect has been profiled) that the particular profile observed in the evidence sample is not unique is at most NP.

A lower bound on the probability that every person is unique depends on the population size, the number of loci, and the heterozygosity of the individual loci. Neglecting population structure and close relatives, 10 loci with a geometric mean heterozygosity of 95% give a probability greater than about 0.999 that no two unrelated persons in the world have the same profile. Once it is decided what level of probability constitutes uniqueness, appropriate calculations can readily be made.

We expect that the calculation in the first paragraph will be the one more often employed.

### Matching and Binning

VNTR data are essentially continuous, and, in principle, a continuous model should be used to analyze them. The methods generally used, however, involve taking measurement uncertainty into account by determining a match window. Two procedures for determining match probabilities are the floating-bin and the fixed-bin methods. The floating-bin method is statistically preferable but requires access to a computerized database. The fixed-bin method is more widely used and understood, and the necessary data tables are widely and readily available. When our fixed-bin recommendation is followed, the two methods lead to very similar results. Both methods are acceptable.

Recommendation 5.2: If floating bins are used to calculate the random-match probabilities, each bin should coincide with the corresponding match window. If fixed bins are employed, then the fixed bin that has the largest frequency among those overlapped by the match window should be used.

### Ceiling Principles

The abundance of data in different ethnic groups within the major races and the genetically and statistically sound methods recommended in this report imply that both the ceiling principle and the interim ceiling principle are unnecessary.

### Further Research

The rapid rate of discovery of new markers in connection with human gene-mapping should lead to many new markers that are highly polymorphic, mutable, and selectively neutral, but which, unlike VNTRs, can be amplified by PCR and for which individual alleles can usually be distinguished unambiguously with none of the statistical problems associated with matching and binning. Furthermore, radioactive probes need not be used with many other markers, so identification can be prompt and problems associated with using radioactive materials can be avoided. It should soon be possible to have systems so powerful that no statistical and population analyses will be needed, and (except possibly for close relatives) each person in a population can be uniquely identified.

Recommendation 5.3: Research into the identification and validation of more and better marker systems for forensic analysis should continue with a view to making each profile unique.

### Legal Issues

In assimilating, scientific developments, the legal system necessarily lags behind the scientific world. Before making use of evidence derived from scientific advances, courts must scrutinize the proposed testimony to determine its suitability for use at trial, and controversy within the scientific community often is regarded as grounds for the exclusion of the scientific evidence. Although some controversies that have come to closure in the scientific literature continue to limit the presentation of DNA evidence in some jurisdictions, courts are making more use of the ongoing research into the population genetics of DNA profiles. We hope that our review of the research will contribute to this process.

Our conclusions and recommendations for reducing the risk of laboratory error, for applying human population genetics to DNA profiles, and for handling uncertainties in estimates of profile frequencies and match probabilities might affect the application of the rules for the discovery and admission of evidence in court. Many suggestions can be offered to make our recommendations most effective: for example, that every jurisdiction should make it possible for all defendants to have broad discovery and independent experts; that accreditation, proficiency testing,, and the opportunity for independent testing (whenever feasible) should be prerequisites to the admission of laboratory findings; that in resolving disputes over the adequacy or interpretation of DNA tests, the power of the court to appoint its own experts should be exercised more frequently; and that experts should not be barred from presenting any scientifically acceptable estimate of a random-match probability. We have chosen, however, to make no formal recommendations on such matters of legal policy; we do, however, make a recommendation concerning scientific evidence—namely, the need for behavioral research that will assist legal decision makers in developing standards for communicating about DNA in the courtroom.

**Recommendation 6.1:** Behavioral research should be carried out to identify any conditions that might cause a trier of fact to misinterpret evidence on DNA profiling and to assess how well various ways of presenting expert testimony on DNA can reduce such misunderstandings.

The full texts of both NRC reports are available from:

National Academy Press, Washington D.C., 1-800-624-6242.

**Appendix J**

## STATE STATUTES AND LEGISLATION REGARDING THE ADMISSIBILITY OF DNA EVIDENCE
(October 1995)

1.  Alabama - ALA. CODE @ 36-18-30 (1994)

2.  Alaska - ALASKA STAT. @ 12.45 (1995)

3.  Connecticut - CONN. GEN. STAT. @ 54-86k (1994)

4.  Delaware - DEL. CODE ANN. tit. 11 § 3515 (1994)

5.  Indiana - IND. CODE @ 35-37-4-13 (1991)

6.  Louisiana - LA. REV. STAT. ANN. @ 15:441.1 (Supp. 1990)

7.  Maryland - MD. CTS & JUD. PROC. CODE ANN. @ 10-915 (Supp. 1991)

8.  Minnesota - MINN. STAT. ANN. @ 634.25-.26 (Supp. 1989)

9.  Nevada - NEV. REV. STAT. @ 56.020 (Supp. 1989)

10. New Hampshire - N.H. REV. STAT. 632-A:21 (1996)

11. North Dakota - N.D. CENT. CODE. @ 31-13-01 et. seq. (1995)

12. Tennessee - TENN. CODE ANN. @ 24-7-117 (July 1, 1991)

13. Virginia - VA. CODE ANN. @ 19.2-270.5 (Code of VA 1950 as amended, 1990)

14. Wisconsin - WISC. STAT. ANN. @ 972.11(5) (August 1993)

Assembled by:

American Prosecutors Research Institute (APRI)
99 Canal Center Plaza; Suite 510
Alexandria, Virginia 22314
Telephone: (703) 549-4253; Facsimile (703) 836-3195

# APPENDIX K

## STATUTES AND LEGISLATION REGARDING MANDATORY SUBMISSION OF BLOOD SAMPLES FOR DNA IDENTIFICATION
(October 1995)

1. Alabama - ALA. CODE @ 36-18-20 et. seq. (1994); 12-15-102 (1996)

2. Alaska - ALASKA STAT. @ 22.20 & 44.41.035 (1995)

3. Arizona - ARIZ. REV. STAT. ANN. @ 31-281 (1990) and ARIZ. REV. STAT. ANN. @ 13-4438 (1993)

4. Arkansas - HOUSE BILL NO. 1560 (April 5, 1995)

5. California - CAL. PENAL CODE @ 290.2 (1990); 3060.5; GOVERNMENT CODE @ 76104.5 (1989; amended 1993 and 1994)

6. Colorado - COLO. REV. STAT. @ 17-2-201 (5)(g)(I) (1990)

7. Connecticut - CON. GEN. STAT. @ 54-102g - 54-102l (1994)

8. Delaware - DEL. CODE ANN. tit. 29 § 4713 (1994)

9. Florida - FLA. STAT. ANN. @ 943.325 (1990)

10. Georgia - GA. CODE ANN. @ 24-4-60 (1992)

11. Hawaii - HAW. REV. STAT. @ 706-603 (1992)

12. Illinois - ILL. REV. STAT. ch. 730 para. 5-4-3 (1990)

13. Indiana - IND. CODE @ 20-12-34.5 et. seq. (1990)*; IND. CODE @ 10-1-9 (effective July 1, 1996)

14. Iowa - IOWA CODE ANN. @ 13.10 (1990) and @ 61-8.1(13) et. seq. (1990)

15. Kansas - KAN. STAT. ANN. @ 21-2511 (1991)

16. Kentucky - KY. REV. STAT. ANN. @ 17:170 and 17:175 (1992)

17. Louisiana - LA. REV. STAT. ANN. @ 15:535 (1995)

18. Maine - ME. REV. STAT. ANN. tit. 25, @ 1571 et. seq. (1995)

19. Maryland - MD. ANN. CODE , ART. 88B, @ 12A (1994)

20. Michigan - MICH. COMP. LAWS ANN. ß 750.520(m) (1994) AND M.C.L.A. 791.233d (1994)

21. Minnesota - MINN. STAT. ANN. @ 609.3461 (1990) and 299C.155 (1990)

22. Mississippi - MISS. CODE ANN. @ 45-33-15 (1994)

23. Missouri - MO. ANN. STAT. @ 650.050 and 650.055 (1994)

24. Montana - MONT. CODE ANN. @ 41-5-604 (1995)

25. Nevada - NEV. REV. STAT. @ 176.111 (1990)

26. New Hampshire - N.H. REV. STAT. @ 632-A:21 (1996)

27. New Jersey - N.J. STAT. ANN. @ 53:1-20.17 et. seq. (1995)

28. New York - Laws of N.Y. Chapter 737, ART. 49-B, § 995-C (1994)

29. North Carolina - N.C. GEN. STAT. @ 15A-266.1 et. seq. (1993)

30. North Dakota - N.D. CENT. CODE @ 31-13-01 et. seq. (1995)

31.    Ohio - OHIO REV. CODE @ 2901.07 (May 31, 1995); @ 109.57.3 (1995); @ 2151.31.5 (1995)

32.    Oklahoma - OKLA. STAT. ANN. @ 57.584 (1991) and OKLA. STAT. ANN. 74 § 150.27a (1995); OKLA. STAT. ANN. 22 @ 751.1 (1995)

33.    Oregon - OREGON REV. STAT. @ 181.085 (1991) and @ 137.076 (1991)

34.    Pennsylvania - 18 PA CONS. STAT. @ 9209 (1995)

35.    South Carolina - S.C. CODE ANN. @ 23-3-600 et. seq. (1995)

36.    South Dakota - S.D. CODIFIED LAWS. ANN. @ 23-5-14 et. seq. (1990)

37.    Tennessee - TENN. CODE ANN. @ 38-6-113   (1991) and @ 40-35-321 (1991); SENATE BILL NO. 1144 (February 6, 1995)

38.    Texas - TEX. CODE ANN. @ 411.141 et. seq. (1995)

39.    Utah - UTAH CODE ANN. @ 53.5-212.1 et. seq. (1994)

40.    Virginia - VA. CODE ANN. @ 19.2-310.2 (Code of 1950 as amended, 1990)

41.    Washington - WASH. REV. CODE @ 43.43.752 and 43.43.754 (1990)

42.    West Virginia - W. VA. CODE @ 15-2B-6 (1995)

43.    Wisconsin - WIS. STAT. ANN. @ 973.047 (August 1993) and 165.76 and 165.77 (August 1993)

*This statute merely establishes a statistical data bank by requiring that laboratories conducting DNA analysis submit all nonidentifying data concerning allele frequencies and demographics.

Assembled by:

American Prosecutors Research Institute (APRI)
99 Canal Center Plaza; Suite 510
Alexandria, Virginia  22314
Telephone:  (703) 549-4253; Facsimile (703) 836-3195

## Appendix L

## SUMMARY OF DNA DECISIONS [20]
May 21, 1996

| RFLP | Admitted | Without or With Limited Statistics | Remands and/or Exclusions | TOTAL |
|---|---|---|---|---|
| Federal Supreme Courts | 0 | 0 | 0 | 0 |
| Federal Appellate Courts | 10 | 0 | 1 | 11 |
| Federal Trial Courts[a] | 3 | 2 | 0 | 5 |
| State Courts of Last Resort | 57 | 16 | 12 | 85 |
| State Appellate Courts | 107 | 6 | 14 | 127 |
| State Trial Courts[a] | 4 | 2 | 2 | 8 |
| **Total RFLP Decisions** | **181** | **26** | **29** | **236** |
| PCR[c] | | | | |
| Federal Supreme Courts | 0 | 0 | 0 | 0 |
| Federal Appellate Courts | 1 | 0 | 0 | 1 |
| Federal Trial Courts[a] | 0 | 0 | 0 | 0 |
| State Courts of Last Resort | 12 | 0 | 2 | 14 |
| State Appellate Courts | 19 | 0 | 1 | 20 |
| State Trial Courts[a] | 3 | 0 | 0 | 3 |
| **Total PCR Decisions** | **35** | **0** | **3** | **38** |
| **Total DNA Decisions[b]** | **211** | **25** | **31** | **265** |

[a]Reported decisions only

[b]Decisions that address both RFLP and PCR are listed in both summaries, but only counted once in the Total DNA Decisions.

[c]The vast majority of these decisions relate to DQ$\alpha$, and few to polymarker, and D1S80.

[20]The information presented here was compiled from several sources, including the American Prosecutors Research Institute (APRI), and the Investigative Law Unit, DNA Legal Assistance Subnit (DNALAS) of the Federal Bureau of Investigation (FBI). The reporting and interpretation of legal decisions varies. This compilation is accurate to the best of our knowledge as of July 1996 and may vary from other reports.

# Appendix M

## REPORTED COURT DECISIONS ON FORENSIC DNA EVIDENCE
June 20, 1996
(listed by court)

### ALABAMA

#### State Courts of Last Resort:

*Ex Parte Hutcherson*, No. 1931660, 1996 WL 77600 (Ala. February 23, 1996) *withdrawing* No. 1931660, 1995 WL 728541 (Ala. December 8, 1995) *remanding* No. CR-92-925, 1994 WL 228861 (Ala. Crim. App. May 27, 1994) (RFLP *and* PCR analysis performed) *(SEE: Hutcherson v. State*, No. CR-92-925, 1996 WL 189233 (Ala. Crim. App. April 19, 1996)

*Ex Parte Perry*, 586 So. 2d 242 (Ala. 1991) *See Perry v. State*, 606 So.2d 224 (Ala. Crim. App. 1992)

#### State Intermediate Appellate Courts:

*Hutcherson v. State*, No. CR-92-925, 1996 WL 189233 (Ala. Crim. App. April 19, 1996) (See *Ex Parte Hutcherson*, ___ So.2d ___, 1996 WL 77600 (Ala. February 23, 1996) (RFLP *and* PCR analysis performed)

*Myers v. State*, No. CR-94-0645, 1995 WL 664621 (Ala. Crim. App. November 9, 1995)

*Padgett v. State*, 668 So.2d 78 (Ala. Ct. App. 1995)

*Snowden v. State*, 574 So.2d 960 (Ala. Crim. App. 1990)

*Turner v. State*, No. CR-93-1940, 1996 WL 187768 (Ala. Crim. App. April 19, 1996)

*Yelder v. State*, 630 So.2d 92 (Ala. Crim. App. 1991)

#### *State Intermediate Appellate Courts (PCR):*

*Payne v. State*, No. CR-93-1697, 1995 WL 316918 (Ala. Crim. App., May 26, 1995)

*Seritt v. State*, 647 So.2d 1 (Ala. Crim. App. 1994)

### ALASKA

#### State Intermediate Appellate Courts:

*Harmon v. State*, 908 P.2d 434 (Alaska Ct. App. 1995) (RFLP *and* PCR analysis performed)

#### *Unreported State Courts:*

*State v. Hartvigsen*, No. 3KN-S89-174 CR (Alaska Trial Ct. July 26, 1990)

### ARIZONA

#### State Courts of Last Resort:

*State v. Bible*, 62 USLW 2140, 858 P.2d 1152 (Ariz. 1993)

*State v. Gallegos*, 870 P.2d 1097 (Ariz. 1994)

#### State Intermediate Appellate Courts:

*State v. Boles*, 905 P.2d 572 (Ariz. Ct. App. 1995)

*State v. Clark*, No. 1 CA-CR 91-0673, 1 CA-CR 93-0533 PR, 1994 WL 178569 (Ariz. Ct. App May 12, 1994).

*State v. Hummert*, 905 P.2d 493 (Ariz. Ct. App. 1994)

*State v. Johnson*, 905 P.2d 1002 (Ariz. Ct. App. 1995)

**State Intermediate Appellate Courts (PCR):**

*State v. Bogan*, 905 P.2d 515 (Ariz. Ct. App. 1995) **\*\*NOTE:** *This case involves randomly amplified polymorphic DNA (RAPD) procedures.*

**Unreported State Courts:**

*State v. Despain*, No. 15589 (Ariz. Super. Ct., Yuma County, February 12, 1991)

*State v. Hale/Hummert*, No. CR 90-05559 (Hummert); No.CR 90-03684 (Hale) (Ariz. Super. Ct., Maricopa County, April 16, 1991)

*State v. McComb*, No. CR 90-06024 (Ariz. Super. Ct., Maricopa County, April 29, 1991)

**ARKANSAS**

**State Courts of Last Resort:**

*Prater v. State*, 307 Ark. 180, 820 S.W.2d 429, (Ark. 1991)

*Moore v. State*, 323 Ark. 529, 915 S.W.2d 284 (1996)

*Swanson v. State*, 308 Ark. 28, 823 S.W.2d 812 (Ark. 1992)

**CALIFORNIA**

**State Intermediate Appellate Courts:**

*People v. Amundson*, 34 Cal.App.4th 1151, 41 Cal.Rptr.2d 127 (Ct. App. 1995) **(Both RFLP and PCR analysis performed)**

*People v. Axell*, 235 Ca.App.3d 836, 1 Cal. Rptr. 2d 411, 60 U.S.L.W. 2311 (Ct. App. 1991)

*People v. Barney; Howard*, 8 Cal. App. 4th 798, 10 Cal. Rptr. 2d 731, 60 U.S.L.W. 2158 (Ct. App. 1992)

*People v. Littleton*, 7 Cal. App.4th 906, 9 Cal.Rptr. 2d 288, (Ct. App. 1992)

*People v. Marlow*, 34 Cal. App.4th 460, 41 Cal. Rptr.2d 5, (Ct. App. 1995) (April 25, 1995 decision modified on May 24, 1995)

*People v. Pizarro*, 12 Cal. Rptr. 2d 436, (Ct. App. 1992)

*People v. Smith*, 42 Cal. App.4th 204, 49 Cal. Rptr.2d 608 (Ct. App. 1996)

*People v. Soto*, 30 Cal.App. 4th 340, 35 Cal. Rptr.2d 846 (Ct. App. 1994)

*People v. Taylor*, 33 Cal.App.4th 262, 40 Cal.Rptr.2d 132 (Ct. App. 1995)

*People v. Venegas*, 36 Cal. Rptr.2d 856 (Ct. App. 1995)

*People v. Wallace*, 14 Cal. App. 4th 651, 17 Cal. Rptr.2d 721 (Cal. Ct. App. 1993)

*People v. Wilds*, 31 Cal.App.4th 636, 37 Cal.Rptr.2d 351 (Ct. App. 1995)

**State Intermediate Appellate Courts (PCR):**

*People v. Amundson*, 34 Cal.App.4th 1151, 41 Cal.Rptr.2d 127 (Ct. App. 1995) **(Both RFLP and PCR analysis performed)**

*People v. Morganti*, 43 Cal. App.4th 643, 50 Cal. Rptr.2d 837 (Ct. App. 1996)

**Unreported State Courts:**

*People v. Garcia*, No. 15883, (Cal. Super. Ct., San Luis Obispo County, March 22, 1991)

*People v. Gross*, No. C-75486, (Cal. Super. Ct., Orange County, April 4, 1991)

*People v. Halik*, No. VA 00843, (Cal. Super. Ct., Los Angeles County, September 26, 1991)

*People v. Walker*, No. C-72540 (Cal. Super. Ct., Orange County, January 21, 1990)

**Unreported State Courts (PCR):**

*People of the State of California v. Mack*, No. 89-257 (Super. Ct., Sacramento County, 1990)

*People of the State of California v. Daniel Leon Martinez*, No. A709321 (Super. Ct., Los Angeles County, 1989)

*People of the State of California v. Leonard James McSherry*, No. A040264-01 (Super. Ct., Los Angeles County, 1989)

*People of the State of California v. Mello*, No. 88-230 (Super. Ct., Riverside County, 1989)

*People of the State of California v. Jessie R. Moffett*, No. CR 103094 (Super. Ct., San Diego County, 1991)

*People of the State of California v. La Peer Edward Moore*, No. CR 106428 (Super. Ct., San Diego County, 1991)

*People of the State of California v. Armando Quintanilla*, No. C-23691 (Super. Ct., San Mateo County, 1991)

*People of the State of California v. Rudolph Jose Roybal*, No. CRN 20596 (Super. Ct., San Diego County, 1992)

*People of the State of California v. James David Tulk*, No. 90-5945 (Super. Ct., Shasta County, 1992)

## COLORADO

**State Courts of Last Resort:**

*Fishback v. People*, 851 P.2d 884 (Colo. 1993)

*Lindsey v. People*, 892 P.2d 281 (Colo. 1995) *affirming* 868 P.2d 1085 (Colo. Ct. App. 1993)

**State Intermediate Appellate Courts (PCR):**

*People v. Groves*, 854 P.2d 1310 (Colo. Ct. App. 1992) (RFLP Analysis May Also Have Been Performed)

## CONNECTICUT

**State Intermediate Appellate Courts:**

*State v. Sivri*, 231 Conn. 115, 646 A.2d 169 (1994)

*State v. Zollo*, 36 Conn.App. 718, 654 A.2d 359 (App. Ct. 1995)

## DELAWARE

**State Courts of Last Resort:**

*Nelson v. State*, 628 A.2d 69, (Del. 1993) *affirming* No. IK89-09-0882 to IK89-09-0884, 1991 WL 190308 (Del. Super. Ct. 1991)

**Reported State Trial Courts:**

*State v. Pennell*, 584 A.2d 513 (Del. Super. Ct., New Castle County, 1989) (Statistics not allowed in testimony)

## FLORIDA

**State Courts of Last Resort:**

*Hayes v. State*, 20 Fla. L. Weekly S296, 660 So.2d 257 (1995)

*Robinson v. State*, 17 Fla. L. Week. S389, 17 Fla. L. Week. S635, 610 So.2d 1288 (1992)

*State v. Vargas*, 20 Fla. L. Weekly S594, 667 So.2d 175 (1995) *affirming* 19 Fla. L. Weekly D1187,

*640 So.2d 1139 (Dist. Ct. App. 1994)*

*Wilding v. State, 21 Fla. L. Weekly S213, 1996 WL 266140 (May 16, 1996)*

*"Notice: This opinion has not been released for publication in the permanent law reports. Until released, it is subject to revision or withdrawal."*

*Wyatt v. State, 19 Fla. L. Weekly S437, 641 So.2d 1336 (1994)*

**State Intermediate Appellate Courts:**

*Andrews v. State, 533 So.2d 841 (Fla. Dist. Ct. App. 1988)*

*Brim v. State, 20 Fla. L. Weekly D932, 654 So.2d 184 (Dist. Ct. App. 1995) affirming Nos. 93-00860, 93-00863, 93-00864, 1995 WL 92712 (Fla. Dist. Ct. App. March 8, 1995)*

*Cade v. State, 20 Fla. L. Weekly D1335, 658 So.2d 550 (Dist. Ct. App. 1995)*

*Crews v. State, 19 Fla. L. Weekly D2299, 644 So.2d 338 (Dist. Ct. App. 1994)*

*Gibson v. State, 21 Fla. L. Weekly D358, 667 So.2d 884 (Dist. Ct. App. 1996)*

*Martinez v. State, 549 So.2d 694, (Fla. Dist. Ct. App. 1989)*

*State v. Olvera, 19 Fla. L. Weekly D1619, 641 So.2d 120 (Dist. Ct. App. 1994)*

*Toranzo v. State, 17 Fla. L. Week. D2450, 608 So.2d 83 (Dist. Ct. App. 1992)*

## GEORGIA

**State Courts of Last Resort:**

*Caldwell v. State, 260 Ga. 278, 393 S.E.2d 436, (1990) (statistics allowed but reduced)*

*Johnson v. State, 461 S.E.2d 209 (Ga. 1995) SEE: Johnson v. State, 448 S.E.2d 177 (Ga. 1994)*

*Smith v. State, 265 Ga. 570, 459 S.E.2d 420 (1995)*

**State Intermediate Appellate Courts:**

*Blige v. State, 221 Ga. App. 771, 440 S.E.2d 521 (Ct. App. 1994)*

*Greenway v. State, 207 Ga. App. 511, 428 S.E.2d 415 (Ga. Ct. App. 1993)*

*Hornsby v. State, 210 Ga. App. 571, 436 S.E.2d 767 (Ga. Ct. App. 1993)*

*Morris v. State, 212 Ga. App. 42, 441 S.E.2d 273 (Ct. App. 1994)*

*Nichols v. State, 435 S.E.2d 502 (Ga. Ct. App. 1993)*

*Redding v. State, 219 Ga. App. 182, 464 S.E.2d 824 (Ct. App. 1995) (Both RFLP and PCR analysis performed)*

**Unreported State Courts:**

*State v. Jefferson, No. 91-CR-7568 (Ga. Super. Ct. October 1991) (Irwin County)*

## HAWAII

**State Courts of Last Resort:**

*Hawaii v. Montalbo, 828 P.2d 1274 (Hawaii 1992)*

## IDAHO

**State Courts of Last Resort:**

*State v. Faught, 908 P.2d 566 (Idaho 1995)*

## ILLINOIS

**State Courts of Last Resort:**

*People v. Moore,* 171 Ill.2d 74, 662 N.E.2d 1215 (1996)

**State Intermediate Appellate Courts:**

*People v. Ehlert,* 211 Ill.Dec. 243, 654 N.E.2d 705 (Ct. App. 1995)

*People v. Heaton,* 203 Ill.Dec. 710, 640 N.E.2d 630 (App. Ct. 1994)

*People v. Johnson,* 199 Ill.Dec. 630, 634 N.E.2d 1285 (App. Ct. 1994) *superseding* 1994 WL 197386 *withdrawn* (Ill. App. Ct. May 20, 1994)

*People v. Lipscomb,* 215 Ill.App.3d 413, 158 Ill.Dec. 952, 574 N.E.2d 1345 (App. Ct. 1991)

*People v. Mehlberg,* 188 Ill. Dec. 598, 618 N.E.2d 1168 (App. Ct. 1993)

*People v. Miles,* 217 Ill.App.3d 393, 160 Ill.Dec. 347, 577 N.E.2d 477 (App. Ct. 1991)

*People v. Stremmel,* 197 Ill.Dec. 177, 630 N.E.2d 1301 (Ct. App. 1994)

*State v. Watson,* 196 Ill. Dec. 89, 629 N.E.2d 634 (Ct. App. 1994)

**Unreported State Courts:**

*People v. Watson/Fleming,* 90-CR-2716; 90-CR-5546 (Ill. Cir. Ct. March 12, 1991) (Cook County)

## INDIANA

**State Courts of Last Resort:**

*Davidson v. State,* 580 N.E.2d 238 (Ind. 1991)

*Hopkins v. State,* 579 N.E.2d 1297 (Ind. 1991)

*Jenkins v. State,* 627 N.E.2d 789 (Ind. 1993)

*Lockhart v. State,* 609 N.E.2d 1093 (Ind. 1993)

*Woodcox v. State,* 591 N.E.2d 1019 (Ind. 1992)

**State Courts of Last Resort:**

*Harrison v. State,* 644 N.E.2d 1243 (Ind. 1995)

**State Intermediate Appellate Courts**:

*McElroy v. State,* 592 N.E.2d 726 (Ind. Ct. App. 1992)

## IOWA

**State Courts of Last Resort:**

*State v. Brown,* 470 N.W.2d 30 (Iowa 1991)

**State Intermediate Appellate Courts**:

*State v. Ripperger,* 514 N.W.2d 740 (Iowa Ct. App. 1994)

**Unreported State Courts:**

*State v. Smith,* No. 41733, (Iowa Dist. Ct. November 1988) (Polk County)

## KANSAS

**State Courts of Last Resort:**

*State v. Colbert,* 896 P.2d 1089 (Kan. 1995)

*Smith v. Deppish; Smith,* 248 Kan. 271, 807 P.2d 144 (1991)

*State v. Dykes,* 847 P.2d 1208 (Kan. 1993)

**State Courts of Last Resort (PCR):**

*State v. Haddock*, 897 P.2d 152 (Kan. 1995)

*State v. Hill*, 895 P.2d 1238 (Kan. 1995)

**State Intermediate Appellate Courts:**

*State v. Wilson*, 817 P.2d 1136 (Table) *Unpublished disposition* *   see 1991 WL 188630 (Kan. Ct. App. 1991)

*\*Not designated for publication. See Supreme Court Rule 7.04 precluding as precedent except to support claims of res judicata, collateral estoppel, or law of the case. (Text in Westlaw)*

## KENTUCKY

**State Courts of Last Resort:**

*Harris v. Commonwealth*, 846 S.W.2d 678 (Ky. 1992)

*Mitchell v. Commonwealth*, 908 S.W.2d 100 (Ky. 1995)

**State Intermediate Appellate Courts:**

*Petrey v. Commonwealth*, No. 94-CA-000360-MR, 1995 WL 457212 (Ky. Ct. App. August 4, 1995)

## LOUISIANA

**State Court of Last Resort:**

*State v. Charles*, 617 So.2d 895 (La. 1993)

*State v. Quatrevingt*, 670 So.2d 197 (La. 1996) *affirming* 617 So.2d 484 (La. Ct. App. 1992) *(rehearing denied) [See also State v. Quatrevingt*, No. 90-KA-1169, 1993 WL 166806, (La. Ct. App. May 12, 1993)]

**State Intermediate Appellate Courts:**

*State v. Brossette*, 634 So.2d 1309 (La. Ct. App. 1994)

*State v. Quatrevingt*, 617 So.2d 484 (La. Ct. App. 1992). See also *State v. Quatrevingt*, No. 90-KA-1169, 1993 WL 166806, (La. Ct. App. May 12, 1993) *(rehearing denied)*

*State v. Stelly*, 645 So.2d 804 (La. Ct. App. 1994)

**State Intermediate Appellate Courts (PCR):**

*State v. Spencer*, 663 So.2d 271 (La. Ct. App. 1995)

**Unreported State Courts:**

*State v. Luckett*, No.91-K-1030 (La. Ct. App. May 24,1991)

## MAINE

**Unreported State Courts:**

*State v. Fleming*, Criminal Docket No. 93-144 (Me. Super. Ct. May 12, 1994) (Penobscot County)

*State v. McLeod*, No. CR-89-62, (Me. Super. Ct.) (Cumberland County)

## MARYLAND

**State Courts of Last Resort:**

*Armstead v. State*, 342 Md. 38, 673 A.2d 221 (1996)

**State Intermediate Appellate Courts:**

*Cobey v. State*, 80 Md. App. 31, 559 A.2d 391 (Ct. Spec. App. 1989)

*Jackson v. State*, 92 Md. App.3d 304, 608 A.2d 782 (Ct. Spec. App. 1992)

*Keirsey v. State*, 106 Md. App. 551, 665 A.2d 700 (Ct. Spec. App. 1995)

*Tapscott v. State*, 106 Md. App. 109, 664 A2d 42 (Ct. Spec. App. 1995)

*Wilson v. State*, 87 Md. App. 659, 591 A.2d 524 (Ct. Spec. App. 1991)

**Unreported State Courts:**

*State v. Stavrakas*, No. 1613, (Md. Ct. Spec. App. June 1, 1990)

## MASSACHUSETTS

**State Courts of Last Resort:**

*Commonwealth v. Curnin*, 409 Mass. 218, 565 N.E.2d 440 (1991)

*Commonwealth v. Daggett*, 416 Mass. 347, 622 N.E.2d 272 (1993)

*Commonwealth v. Lanigan*, 419 Mass. 15, 641 N.E.2d 1342 (1994) *modifying* 413 Mass. 154, 596 N.E.2d 311, 61 U.S.L.W. 2128 (1992)

**State Intermediate Appellate Courts:**

*Commonwealth v. Teixeira*, 40 Mass.App.Ct. 236, 662 N.E.2d 726, (1996)

*Commonwealth v. Vega*, 36 Mass.App.Ct. 636, 634 N.E.2d 149 (Mass. App. Ct. 1994) (Refer to *Curnin* and *Daggett* cases)

**Reported State Trial Courts:**

*Commonwealth v. Fowler*, 2 Mass. L. Rptr. 168, 1994 WL 87960 (Super. Ct. March 31, 1994)

## MICHIGAN

**State Intermediate Appellate Courts:**

*People v. Adams*, 195 Mich. App. 267, 489 N.W.2d 192 (Ct. App. 1992)

*People v. Chandler*, 211 Mich. App. 604, 536 N.W.2d 799 (Ct. App. 1995)

*People v. Courts*, 205 Mich. App. 326, 517 N.W.2d 785 (Ct. App. 1994)

*People v. Jackson*, 213 Mich. App. 245, 539 N.W.2d 758 (Ct. App. 1995)

**State Intermediate Appellate Courts (PCR):**

*People v. Lee*, 212 Mich. App. 228, 537 N.W.2d 233 (Ct. App. 1995)

*People v. McMillan*, 213 Mich. App. 134, 539 N.W.2d 553 (App. Ct. 1995)

**Unreported State Courts:**

*People v. Gregory Joseph Dujardine*, No. 121457 (Mich. Ct. App. April 14, 1992)

*People of the State of Michigan v. Alden Knopek/Chester Kelly*, File No. 91-45239-FC, 91-45124-FC, 91-45-27-FC (Mich. Cir. Ct. March 11, 1992) (Genesee County)

*People v. Adams, Perkins, & Szeman*, No. CR 88 89732 FC, (Mich. Cir. Ct. October 27, 1989) (Oakland County)

**Unreported State Courts (PCR):**

*People of the State of Michigan v. Lamont Waldron Marshall*, No. 90-51811-FC (Cir. Ct. 1990) (Kent County)

## MINNESOTA

**State Courts of Last Resort:**

*State v. Alt*, 505 N.W.2d 72 (Minn. 1993) *affirming* 504 N.W.2d 38 (Minn. App. Ct. 1993)

*State v. Bauer*, 516 N.W.2d 174 (Minn. 1994) *affirming* 512 N.W.2d 112 (Minn. Ct. App. 1994)

*State v. Bloom*, 516 N.W.2d 159 (Minn. 1994)

_State v. Jobe_, 486 N.W.2d 407 (Minn. 1992)

_State v. Johnson_, 498 N.W.2d 10 (Minn. 1993)

_State v. Nielson_, 467 N.W.2d 615 (Minn. 1991)

_State v. Perez_, 516 N.W.2d 175 (Minn. 1994) (See _State v. Bloom_)

_State v. Schwartz_, 447 N.W.2d 422 (Minn. 1989)

**State Intermediate Appellate Courts:**

_State v. Bloom_, No. C8-95-218, 1996 WL 33092 _unpublished_ (Minn. App. January 30, 1996) _affirming_ 516 N.W.2d 159 (Minn. 1994)

_State v. Johnson_, No. C0-95-844, 1996 WL 56515 _unpublished_ (Minn. App. February 13, 1996)

**Reported State Trial Courts (PCR):**

_State v. Grayson_, No. K2-94-1298, 1994 WL 670312 _unpublished_ (Minn. Dist. Ct. November 8, 1994)

**MISSISSIPPI**

**State Courts of Last Resort:**

_Polk v. State_, 612 So.2d 381 (Miss. 1992)

**MISSOURI**

**State Courts of Last Resort:**

_State v. Davis_, 814 S.W.2d 593 (Mo. 1991), _cert. denied_, 60 U.S. 3479, 112 S.Ct. 911, 116 L.Ed. 812

**State Intermediate Appellate Courts:**

_State v. Conaway_, 912 S.W.2d 92 (Mo. Ct. App. 1995)

_State v. Davis_, 860 S.W.2d 369 (Mo. App. Ct. 1993)

_State v. Funke_, 903 S.W.2d 240 (Mo. Ct. App. 1995)

_State v. Huchting/Huchting v. State_, Nos. 65861 & 68410, 1996 WL 310244 (Mo. Ct. App. June 11, 1996)

_"Notice: This opinion has not been released for publication in the permanent law reports. It may be subject to a motion for rehearing or transfer. It may be modified, superseded or withdrawn."_

**State Intermediate Appellate Courts (PCR):**

_State v. Hoff_, 904 S.W.2d 56 (Mo. Ct. App. 1995)

**Unreported State Courts:**

_State v. Ferguson_, Cause No. 591717A (Mo. Cir. Ct. July 16, 1992) (St. Louis County)

**MONTANA**

**State Courts of Last Resort:**

_State v. Moore_, 885 P.2d 457 (Montana 1994) (RFLP _and_ PCR analysis performed)

_State v. Weeks_, 891 P.2d 477 (Mont. 1995)

**NEBRASKA**

**State Courts of Last Resort:**

_State v. Carter_, 246 Neb. 953, 524 N.W.2d 763 (1994) (PCR)

_State v. Houser_, 241 Neb. 525, 490 N.W.2d 168 (Neb. 1992)

## NEW HAMPSHIRE

### State Courts of Last Resort:

*State v. Vandebogart*, 652 A.2d 671 (N.H. 1994) *modifying* 616 A.2d 483 (N.H. 1992)

## NEW JERSEY

### Reported State Trial Courts (PCR):

*State v. Williams*, 252 N.J.Super. 369, 599 A.2d 960, (Super. Ct. 1991)

### Unreported State Courts:

*State v. Harvey*, Indictment No. 1568-11-85 (N.J. Super. Ct. November 28, 1994) (polymarker)

## NEW MEXICO

### State Courts of Last Resort:

*State v. Anderson*, 115 N.M. 433, 881 P.2d 29 (1994) *reversing* 853 P.2d 135 (N.M. Ct. App. 1993)

*State v. Duran*, 881 P.2d 48 (N.M. August 25, 1994)

## NEW YORK

### State Courts of Last Resort:

*People v. Wesley*, 83 N.Y.2d 417, 611 N.Y.S.2d 97, 633 N.E.2d 451 (1994) *affirming* 183 A.D.2d 75,

589 N.Y.S.2d 197, 61 U.S.L.W. 2287 (App. Div. 1992)

### State Intermediate Appellate Courts:

*People v. Coit*, 621 N.Y.S.2d 1023 (App. Div. 1994)

*People v. English*, 634 N.Y.S.2d 599 (App. Div. 1995)

*People v. Giomundo*, 619 N.Y.S.2d 894 (App. Div. 1995)

*People v. Golub*, 601 N.Y.S.2d 502 (A.D. 1993)

*People v. Moore*, 604 N.Y.S.2d 976 (A.D. 1993)

*People v. Vann*, 627 N.Y.S.2d 473 (App. Div. 1995)

*People v. Vega*, 639 N.Y.S.2d 511 (App. Div. 1995)

*People v. White*, 621 N.Y.S.2d 728 (App. Div. 1995)

### Reported State Trial Courts:

*People v. Castro*, 545 N.Y.S.2d 985 (Sup. Ct. 1989)  (Bronx County)

*People v. Ladson*, 632 N.Y.S.2d 378 (Sup. Ct. 1995)

*People v. Mohit*, 579 N.Y.S.2d 990 (Westchester County Ct. 1992)

*People v. Rush*, 630 N.Y.S.2d 631 (New York County Crim. Ct. June 7, 1995)

*People v. Shi Fu Huang*, 546 N.Y.S.2d 920 (Sup. Ct. 1989)  (Nassau  County)

*People v. Watson*, 634 N.Y.S.2d 935 (Sup. Ct., Bronx County, September 11, 1995)

### State Intermediate Appellate Courts:

*People v. Morales*, ___ N.Y.S.2d ___, 1996 WL 290205 (App. Div. May 28, 1996) **polymarker analysis performed in this case.**

### Reported State Trial Courts (PCR):

*People v. Palumbo*, 618 N.Y.S.2d 197 (Sup. Ct. 1994)

**Unreported State Courts:**

*People v. Burton*, No. 1931-91 (Sullivan County Ct. October 6, 1992)

*People v. Greco*, 90-0122-S01 (N.Y. County Ct. October 23, 1992) (Erie County)

*People v. Hirsch*, No. 3286/89 (N.Y. Sup. Ct. June 26, 1990)

*People v. Ireland*, No. 90-815-1 (N.Y. County Ct. May 11, 1993) (Onondaga County)

*People v. Morales*, Ind. # 92-260 (N.Y. Rockland County Ct. October 7, 1994) (polymarker)

*People v. Rivera*, CC No. 379-91; IND. No. 259-91, (Suffolk County Ct. May 27, 1992)

## NORTH CAROLINA
**State Courts of Last Resort:**

*State v. Best*, 467 S.E.2d 45 (N.C. 1996)

*State v. Daughtry*, 459 S.E.2d 747 (N.C. 1995)

*State v. Pennington*, 327 N.C. 89, 393 S.E.2d 847 (1990)

**State Intermediate Appellate Courts:**

*State v. Bruno*, 424 S.E.2d 440 (N.C. Ct. App. 1993)

*State v. Futrell*, 436 S.E.2d 884 (N.C. Ct. App. 1993)

*State v. Hill*, 449 S.E.2d 573 (N.C. Ct. App. 1994)

*State v. McKenzie*, 468 S.E.2d 817 (N.C. Ct. App. 1996)

## OHIO
**State Courts of Last Resort:**

*State v. Kinley*, 72 Ohio St.3d 491, 651 N.E.2d 419 (1995) *affirming* 1993 WL 224496 *unpublished* (Ohio Ct. App. June 24, 1993)

*State v. Nicholas*, 66 Ohio St.3d 431, 613 N.E.2d 225 (1993)

*State v. Pierce*, 64 Ohio St.3d 490, 597 N.E.2d 107 (1992), *affirming* 568 N.E.2d 1228 (Ohio 1991) (Table) (See No. 89 CA-30, 1990 WL 97596, *unpublished*, [Ohio Ct. App. July 9, 1990])

**State Intermediate Appellate Courts:**

*State v. Blair*, 70 Ohio App.3d 774, 592 N.E.2d 854 (Ct. App. 1990)

*State v. Breeze*, No. 92AP-258, 1992 WL 365269 *unpublished* (Ohio Ct. App. November 24, 1992)

*State v. Crawford*, No. 65698, 1994 WL 326129 *unpublished* (Ohio Ct. App. July 7, 1994)

*State v. Dascenzo*, No. 11234, 1993 WL 79244 *unpublished* (Ohio Ct. App. March 16, 1993)

*State v. Drain*, No. 95APA03-351, 1995 WL 765169 *unpublished* (Ohio Ct. App. December 29, 1995)

*State v. Fontenette*, No. 59014, 1991 WL 184324 *unpublished* (Ohio Ct. App. Sept. 19, 1991) *cert. denied* 61 USLW 3264, 113 S.Ct. 301, 121 L.Ed.2d 225 (1994)

*State v. Honzu*, No. 94APA07-1011, 1995 WL 326214 *unpublished* (Ohio Ct. App. June 1, 1995)

*State v. Jackson*, No. L-91-178, 1992 WL 227455 *unpublished* (Ohio Ct. App. September 18, 1992)

*State v. Knight*, No. 59180, 1991 WL 243639 *unpublished* (Ohio Ct. App. November 21, 1991)

*State v. Lane*, No. C-940617, 1995 WL 734043 *unpublished* (Ohio Ct. App. December 13, 1995)

*State v. Lee*, No. 90CA004741, 1991 WL 197975 *unpublished* (Ohio Ct. App. December 5, 1990)

*State v. Owens*, 81 Ohio App.3d 412, 611 N.E.2d 369 (Ohio Ct. App. 1992)

*State v. Scudder*, No. 91AP-506, 1992 WL 302432, <u>*unpublished*</u> *(Ohio Ct. App. October 20, 1992) Motion to dismissed denied. (See 68 Ohio St.3d 1446, 626 N.E.2d 687 (1994) (Table)*

*State v. Thomas, 63 Ohio App.3d 501, 579 N.E.2d 290 (Ct. App. 1991)*

*State v. Tinch, 84 Ohio App.3d 111, 616 N.E.2d 529 (Ct. App. 1992)*

*State v. Walker, No. 4-CR-JAN-1993, 1993 WL 564235 <u>unpublished</u> (Ohio Ct. App. December 29, 1993)*

*State v. Williams, No. L-90-175, 1991 WL 156545 <u>unpublished</u> (Ohio Ct. App. August 16, 1991)*

**State Intermediate Appellate Courts (PCR):**

*State v. Penton, No. 9-91-25, 1993 WL 102507 <u>unpublished</u> (Ohio Ct. App. April 7, 1993) dismissed, jurisdictional motion overruled by 67 Ohio St.3d 1464, 619 N.E.2d 698 (Ohio 1993) (Table No. 93-1123) (**PCR**)*

## OKLAHOMA

**State Intermediate Appellate Courts:**

*Hale v. State, 888 P.2d 1027 (Okla. Crim. App. 1995)*

*Taylor v. State, 889 P.2d 319 (Okla. Crim. App. 1995)*

**State Intermediate Appellate Courts (PCR):**

*Mitchell v. State, No. F-92-678, 1994 WL 566973 (Okla. Crim. Ct. 1994)*

## OREGON

**State Intermediate Appellate Courts:**

*State v. Futch, 123 Or. App. 176, 860 P.2d 264 (Ct. App. 1993)*

*State v. Herzog, 125 Or. App. 10, 864 P.2d 1362 (Ct. App. 1993)*

**State Intermediate Appellate Courts (PCR):**

*State v. Lyons, 124 Or. App. 598, 863 P.2d 1303, (Ct. App. 1993)*

**Unreported State Courts:**

*State v. Wheeler, No. C89-0901CR, (Or. Cir. Ct. March 8, 1990) (Washington County)*

## PENNSYLVANIA

**State Courts of Last Resort:**

*Commonwealth v. Crews, 640 A.2d 395 (Pa. 1994)*

**State Intermediate Appellate Courts:**

*Commonwealth v. Rodgers, 413 Pa. Super. 498, 605 A.2d 1228 (Super. Ct. 1992)*

## RHODE ISLAND

**State Courts of Last Resort:**

*State v. Morel, A.2d , 1996 WL 285258 (R.I. May 30, 1996)*

## SOUTH CAROLINA

**State Courts of Last Resort:**

*State v. Dinkins, 462 S.E.2d 59 (S.C. 1995)*

*State v. Ford, 301 S.C. 485, 392 S.E.2d 781 (1990)*

**State Intermediate Appellate Courts:**

*State v. China*, 440 S.E.2d 382 (S.C. Ct. App. 1993)

*State v. Hyman*, No. 2513, 1996 WL 271493 (S.C. Ct. App. May 20, 1996)

*State v. McFadden*, 458 S.E.2d 61 (S.C. Ct. App. 1995)


**Unreported Cases:**

*State v. Dyar*, (S.C. Ct. of Gen. Sess. 1991) (Richland County)

**SOUTH DAKOTA**

**State Courts of Last Resort (PCR):**

*State v. Moeller*, 1996 SD 60, ___ N.W.2d ___, 1996 WL 271674 (S.D. May 22, 1996)

*State v. Schweitzer*, 533 N.W.2d 156 (1995)

*State v. Wimberly*, 467 N.W.2d 499 (S.D. 1991)


**TENNESSEE**

**State Intermediate Appellate Courts:**

*State v. Harris*, 866 S.W.2d 583 (Tenn. Ct. App. 1992). Appeal denied August 2, 1993.

*King v. State*, No. 01C01-9310-CR-00366, 1994 WL 406173 underlined(Tenn. Crim. App. August 4, 1994)

*State v. Myers*, No. 03C019108CR00255, 1992 WL 297626 underlined(Tenn. Crim. App. October 22, 1992)

*State v. Steele*, No. 03C01-9207-CR-233, 1993 WL 415836 underlined(Tenn. Crim. App. October 13, 1993)

**State Intermediate Appellate Courts (PCR):**

*State v. Begley*, No. 01C01-9411-CR-00381, 1996 WL 12152 underlined(Tenn. Ct. App. January 11, 1995)


**TEXAS**

**State Courts of Last Resort:**

*Bethune v. State*, 828 S.W.2d 14 (Tex. Crim. App. 1992) *affirming* 821 S.W.2d 222 (Tex. Ct. App. 1991)*

*Clarke v. State*, 839 S.W.2d 92 (Tex. Crim. App. 1992) *affirming* 813 S.W.2d 654 (Tex. Ct. App. 1991) **(PCR)***

*Flores v. State*, 871 S.W.2d 714 (Tex. Crim App. December 8, 1993) **rehearing denied** March 9, 1994

*Fuller v. State*, 827 S.W.2d 919 (Tex. Crim. App. 1992)

*Glover v. State*, 825 S.W.2d 127 (Tex. Crim. App. 1992) *affirming* 787 S.W.2d 544 (Tex. Ct. App. 1990)*

*Hicks v. State*, 860 S.W.2d 419 (Tex. Crim. App. 1993)

*Kelly v. State*, 824 S.W.2d 568, (Tex. Crim. App. 1992) *affirming* 792 S.W.2d 579,(Tex. Ct. App. 1990)*

*Trimboli v. State*, 826 S.W.2d 953 (Tex. Crim. App. 1992) *affirming* 817 S.W.2d 785 (Tex. Ct. App. 1991) **(Both RFLP and PCR Analysis Performed)**

**State Courts of Last Resort (PCR):**

*Campbell v. State*, 910 S.W.2d 475 (Tex. Crim. App. 1995)

*(Texas Court of Criminal Appeals is the highest appellate court of review for criminal cases)*

**State Intermediate Appellate Courts:**

*Barnes v. State*, 838 S.W.2d 118 (Tex. Ct. App. 1992)

*Brown v. State*, 881 S.W.2d 582 (Tex. Ct. App. August 11, 1994)

*Forte v. State*, No. 05-91-00809-CR, 1992 WL 297350 *unpublished* (Tex. Ct. App. October 8, 1992)

*King v. State*, No. 05-90-00905-CR, 1991 WL 122396, *unpublished* (Tex. Ct. App. July 8, 1991)

*Lopez v. State*, 793 S.W.2d 738 (Tex. Ct. App. 1990) (**PCR**)

*Mandujano v. State*, 799 S.W.2d 318 (Tex. Ct. App. 1990)

*McLaughlin v. State*, No. B14-91-00872-CR, 1193 WL 22050 *unpublished* (Tex. Ct. App. February 4, 1993) *affirming* No. B14-91-00872-CR, 1992 WL 370411 *unpublished* (Tex. Ct. App. December 17, 1992) (**PCR**)

*Perryman v. State*, 798 S.W.2d 326 (Tex. Ct. App.1990) (follows *Glover v. State*)

*Robertson v. State*, No. 14-93-00251-CR, 1996 WL 87189 *unpublished* (Tex. Ct. App. February 29, 1996)

*Ross v. State*, No. B14-90-00659-CR, 1992 WL 23575 *unpublished* (Tex. Ct. App. February 13, 1992)

*Turner v. State*, 886 S.W.2d 859 (Tex. Ct. App. 1994)

*Vickers v. State*, 801 S.W.2d 214 (Tex. Ct. App. 1990)

*Williams v. State*, 848 S.W.2d 915 (Tex. Ct. App. 1993)


**UTAH**

**State Courts of Last Resort:**

*State v. Smith*, 909 P.2d 236 (Utah 1995)


**VERMONT**

**State Courts of Last Resort:**

*State v. Streich*, 658 A.2d 38 (Vt. 1995)

**Unreported State Courts:**

*State v. Allain*, Docket Nos. 412/3-3-90Bcr, 150-2-91Bcr (Vt. Dist. Ct., Bennington County, January 12, 1993)

*State v. Passino*, No. 185-1-90, (Vt. Dist. Ct. May 13, 1991) (Franklin County)


**VIRGINIA**

**State Courts of Last Resort:**

*Satcher v. Commonwealth*, 421 S.E.2d 821, (Va. 1992)

*Spencer v. Commonwealth*, 238 Va. 563, 385 S.E.2d 850 (1989) (Spencer III) *cert. denied* 493 U.S. 1093, 110 S.Ct. 1171, 107 L.E.2d 1073 (1990)

*Spencer v. Commonwealth*, 238 Va. 295, 384 S.E.2d 785 (1989) (Spencer II), *cert. denied* 493 U.S. 1093, 110 S.Ct. 1171, 107 L.E.2d 1073 (1990)

**State Courts of Last Resort (PCR):**

*Spencer v. Commonwealth*, 240 Va. 78, 393 S.E.2d 609 (1990) (Spencer IV) *cert. denied* 111 S.Ct. 281, 112 L.Ed.2d 235 (1990)

**State Intermediate Appellate Courts:**

*Brown v. Commonwealth*, No. 0074-94-1, 1995 WL 378611 *unpublished (Va. App. Ct. June 27, 1995)*

*Commonwealth v. Brummett*, No. 0485-94-3, 1996 WL 10209 *unpublished (Va. App. January 11, 1996). NOTE: The trial court excluded the DNA evidence presented by the defendant citing the evidence as irrelevant. The appellate court disagreed with conclusions rendered in this case, as well as the exclusion of the DNA evidence, and reversed and remanded case for retrial. The appellate court ruled the evidence relevant and admissible.*

*State v. Husske*, 448 S.E.2d 331 (Va. Ct. App. 1994)

*Taylor v. Commonwealth*, No. 1767-93-1, 1995 WL 80189 *unpublished (Va. Ct. App. February 28, 1995)*

## WASHINGTON

### State Courts of Last Resort:

*State v. Buckner*, 125 Wash 2d. 915, 890 P.2d 460 (1995) *reversing* 876 P.2d 910 (Ct. App. 1994).

*State v. Cauthron*, 120 Wash.2d 879, 846 P.2d 502 (Wash. 1993)

*State v. Kalakosky*, 121 Wash.2d 525, 852 P.2d 1064 (1993)

### State Courts of Last Resort (PCR):

*State v. Gentry*, 125 Wash.2d 570, 888 P.2d 1105 (Ct. App. 1995) (PCR)

*State v. Russell*, 125 Wash.2d 24, 882 P.2d 747 (1994) (PCR)

### Unreported State Courts:

*State v. Dyer*, No. 93-1-00489-0 (Wash. Super. Ct. April 12, 1994) (King County)

## WEST VIRGINIA

### State Courts of Last Resort:

*State v. Woodall*, 182 W.Va. 15, 385 S.E.2d 253 (1989)

## WISCONSIN

### State Intermediate Appellate Courts:

*State v. Peters*, No. 94-1094-CR, 1995 WL 117027 (Wis. Ct. App. March 21, 1995)

## WYOMING

### State Courts of Last Resort:

*Rivera v. State*, 840 P.2d 933 (Wyo. 1992)

*Springfield v. State*, 820 P.2d 435 (Wyo. 1993)

## FEDERAL DECISIONS

### APPELLATE COURTS:

*People v. Atoigue*, 36 F.3d 1103 (Table) (9th Cir.) *unpublished* (**NOTE:** Text in Westlaw 1994 WL 477518 *affirming* DCA No. CR 91-95A, S.C. No. CF0023-91, 1992 WL 245628 (D. Guam App. Div. September 11, 1992)

*United States v. Bonds*, 12 F.3d 540 (6th Cir. 1993) *affirming* 134 F.R.D. 161 (N.D. Ohio 1991) *(formerly reported as, and more widely known as, United States v. Yee.)*

*United States v. Chischilly*, 30 F.3d 1144 (9th Cir. 1994)

*United States v. Davis/Reed*, 40 F.3d 1069 (10th Cir. 1994)

*United States v. Jakobetz*, 955 F.2d 786 (2d Cir. 1992), *cert. denied* 113 S.Ct. 104, 61 U.S.L.W. 3257 (U.S. 1992) *affirming* 747 F.Supp. 250 (D.Vt. 1990)

*United States v. Johnson*, 56 F.3d 947 (8th Cir. 1995)

*United States v. Martinez*, 3 F.3d 1191 (8th Cir. 1993)

*Spencer v. Murray*, 5 F.3d 758 (4th Cir. 1993). *Death sentence appeal from state convictions. See Commonwealth v. Spencer.*

*United States v. Parrish*, 83 F.3d 430 (Table) (9th Cir. 1996) *unpublished* (**NOTE:** Text in Westlaw 1996 WL 184457).

*United States v. Sanchez, Romero-Colato*, 932 F.2d 964 (E.D. Va. 1991) (Table) *unpublished disposition* (Text in Westlaw)

*United States v. Two Bulls*, 918 F.2d 56 (8th Cir.1990), *opinion vacated and reh'g en banc granted*, 925 F.2d 1127, *(appeal dismissed (Defendant died prior to rehearing.)*

**APPELLATE COURTS (PCR):**

*United States v. Thomas*, 43 M.J. 626 (A.F. Ct. Crim. App. 1995) **NOTE:** The Amp-FLP method of PCR analysis was used in this case. RFLP testing was also used in this case to identify the the remains of the victim, not to establish the identity of the defendant.

**TRIAL COURTS:**

*United States v. Coronado-Cervantes*, 912 F. Supp. 497 (D. N.M., 1996)

*United States v. Young*, 754 F.Supp. 739 (D. S.D. 1990).

*United States v. Youngberg*, 43 M.J.379 (A.F. Ct. App. 1995)

**District of Columbia:**

*United States v. Bridgett*, Crim. No. F-8544-90, (D.C. Super. Ct. May 29, 1991) ***Unreported***

*United States v. Porter*, Crim. No. F06277-89, 1994 WL 742297 (D.C. Super. Ct. November 17, 1994) *modifying* 618 A.2d 629 (D.C. 1992)

**Territory of the Virgin Islands:**

*Government of the Virgin Islands v. Penn*, 838 F.Supp. 1054 (D. Virgin Islands 1993).

**FEDERAL PCR DECISIONS:**

*United States v. Beasley*, Criminal No. 4-94-127(1)(2) (D. Minn. September 21, 1995)

Assembled by:

Investigative Law Unit
DNA Legal Assistance Subunit (DNALAS)
FBI Headquarters, Room 7879
10th Street and Pennsylvania Avenue, N.W.
Washington, D.C. 20535
Telephone: (202) 324-4419
Facsimile: (202) 324-1043

# AMICUS BRIEF PRESENTED TO THE SUPREME COURT OF THE STATE OF CALIFORNIA BY THE CALIFORNIA ASSOCIATION OF CRIMINALISTS

IN THE SUPREME COURT OF THE STATE OF CALIFORNIA

THE PEOPLE OF THE STATE OF CALIFORNIA,
Plaintiff-Respondent,

vs.

SERGIO VENEGAS,
Defendant-Appellant.

BRIEF AMICUS CURIAE OF

THE CALIFORNIA ASSOCIATION OF CRIMINALISTS

IN SUPPORT OF RESPONDENT

===================================================================

INTRODUCTION

The California Association of Criminalists (CAC) hereby submits its brief amicus curiae in support of Respondent, the People of the State of California. The brief is limited to a discussion of CAC's perspective relative to DNA typing analysis.

The CAC is an internationally recognized professional organization of forensic scientists with a membership representing a broad spectrum of law enforcement laboratories, private forensic laboratories, and academic institutions. It is emphasized that members have presented evidence for both the prosecution and defense in criminal and civil proceedings at all levels of the judicial system. The CAC is in a unique position to bring to the attention of the Court the perspective of forensic science as practiced in this country and abroad.

The CAC has long been involved in the development of professional standards for the practice of forensic science. Efforts include support for technical innovation, proficiency testing, quality assurance programs, and improvement of scientific procedures used in the examination of physical evidence. A pertinent example is the publication in 1987 of a consensus standard of practice on analysis and interpretation of biological evidence [Critical and Emerging Issues in Forensic Serology (1987) Bureau of Forensic Services California Department of Justice], a joint effort with the California Department of Justice. Additionally, CAC members have given presentations on the analysis and interpretation of DNA evidence for both the prosecution and defense bars. The CAC established a DNA Advisory Committee in 1989. This committee authored Guidelines for a Quality Assurance Program for Forensic DNA Analysis Using the Polymerase Chain Reaction (1990). Through this committee, and through it's members, the CAC has participated in the Technical Working Group on DNA Analytical Methods (TWGDAM) sponsored by the Federal Bureau of Investigation. This group has produced a series of documents to be used as guidelines for the implementation and use of DNA testing, beginning with "Guidelines for a Quality Assurance Program for DNA Restriction Fragment Length Polymorphism Analysis" (Crime Laboratory Digest, 16(2):40-54, 1989). CAC members serve on the TWGDAM Quality Assurance subcommittee which developed "A

Guide for Conducting a DNA Quality Assurance Audit" (Crime Laboratory Digest, 20(1):8-18, 1993).

A CAC member (Dr. George Sensabaugh) was the only forensic scientist to serve on both National Research Council Committee's on DNA Technology in Forensic Science (NRC DNA Committee) which published "DNA Technology in Forensic Science" (Washington, D.C. National Academy Press, 1992) and "The Evaluation of Forensic DNA Evidence" (Washington, D.C.: National Academy Press, May 1996) . The CAC was the only professional organization of forensic scientists represented at the public meeting of the second NRC DNA  Committee held November 18, 1994, at which the Committee solicited input prior to the publication of the second Report.

Members of the CAC hold leadership positions on committees of the Laboratory Accreditation Board of the American Society of Crime Laboratory Directors (ASCLD). This is the only organization that accredits forensic laboratories both in the United States and abroad.  The CAC developed and implemented the first certification examination for crime laboratory personnel. This certification effort evolved into national certification under the auspices of the American Board of Criminalistics (ABC). The CAC remains active in the continuing development and administration of certification examinations for Criminalists, including certification in the specialty of forensic DNA analysis.

Thus, the CAC has a depth of expertise and a breadth of experience which enables it to provide unique assistance to the Court with regard to scientific evidence, including DNA evidence.

**FACTUAL SUMMARY**

A summary of the facts and circumstances of the underlying case is contained in the briefs filed by Appellant and Respondent.

**BACKGROUND**

State Supreme Courts throughout the United States have found that DNA evidence is generally accepted by the scientific community and have allowed its introduction into evidence. (See: New Mexico v. Duran (1994) 881 P.2d 48; Pennsylvania v. Crews (1994) 640 A.2d 395; Fishback v. Colorado (1993) 851 P.2d 884; Springfield v. Wyoming (1993) 860 P.2d 435; Hawaii v. Montalbo (1992) 828 P.2d 1274; Prater v. Arkansas (1991) 8205 W.2d 429; South Dakota v. Wimberly (1991) 467 N.W.2d 499; Indiana v. Jenkins (1993) 627 N.E.2d 789; Kansas v. Dykes (1993) 847 P.2d 1214; Kentucky v. Harris (1990) 846 S.W.2d 678). Appellate courts in California have split with regard to the issue of general acceptance of forensic DNA testing. People v. Barney (1992) 8 Cal.App.4th 798 and later People v. Wallace (1993) 14 Cal.App.4th 651; People v. Pizarro (1992) 10 Cal.App.4th 57 held that the way in which population frequencies were determined did not enjoy a consensus of reliability by the scientific community. The Venegas court additionally held that the technology used in that case did not pass the Kelly test (People v. Kelly (1976) 17 Cal.3d 24). Later courts (People v. Soto (1994) 30 Cal.App.4th 340; People v. Wild (1995) 40 Cal.App.4th 166; People v. Amundson (1995) 39 Cal.App.4th 468; People v. Marlow (1995) 34 Cal.App.4th 460) disagreed, finding that DNA analysis was generally accepted by the scientific community, particularly with regard to the method of calculating frequency estimates of the DNA profile.

The CAC would like to point out that DNA typing is simply an extension of the well-recognized and widely accepted genetic testing. DNA typing extends conventional genetic testing by its power to discriminate between individuals. The CAC supports the consensus of the scientific community that the forensic application of DNA technology is sound. This consensus is reflected in the numerous published journal articles, book, manuals, and protocol collections . These and other sources attest to the wide-spread opinion of the validity and usefulness of forensic DNA analysis.

The CAC does recognize that there are critics of the forensic use of DNA analysis. Some of the criticism appears based on ideology (Lewontin RC. "The Dream of the Human Genome" New York Review May 28, 1992); others seem to focus on the application of DNA technology in particular cases. The existence of contrarian opinion is not unusual in the scientific community, but the voices of a few dissenting individuals should not be construed as fundamental or broad disagreement among the scientific community; nor should it dissuade the court from regarding DNA analysis as generally accepted in the scientific community. DNA technology is widely used in academic research, commercial development, and diagnostic medicine. A technology widely used in the diagnosis and treatment of life threatening disease has also been shown to be acceptable for forensic uses.

## ARGUMENT

DNA evidence conforms to the three prong criteria mandated by Kelly, supra. Each prong is reviewed below.

### First Prong: Admissibility of DNA Evidence.

This prong considers whether or not the scientific technique (DNA analysis) is generally accepted in the relevant scientific community as appropriate for forensic use. The analysis of forensic evidence can be divided generally into two components: the technical performance of the test and the interpretation of the results of the test.

Technology: DNA testing methods will not be described in detail here; many excellent descriptions are to be found in the literature. The key point to be made is that testing procedures, whether used in forensic science, medical diagnostics, or molecular biology research, rest on a well established generic technology. For example, the generic methodology in RFLP analysis calls for DNA purification, digestion with a specific restriction enzyme, separation of restriction fragments by electrophoresis (a technique which has passed first prong Kelly scrutiny [People v. Reilly (1987) 196 Cal.App.3d 1127; People v. Morris (1991) 53 Cal.3d 152]), and visualization of specific VNTR loci by characterized probes. Laboratories can vary details of an analytical protocol without any significant impact on the outcome of the test. The proof of the pudding, as they say, is in the eating. With regard to forensic DNA testing, the "eating" is the performance of the technology when subjected to extensive interlaboratory comparison studies. The data from these studies has been analyzed by the National Institute of Standards and Technology (NIST). The NIST analysis shows exceptional and undisputed concordance of results both within and between laboratories, even among laboratories using variations on the basic generic technology. This work has been published in Analytical Chemistry, a peer-reviewed journal. This is a reflection of the robustness of the technology.

Interpretation: Forensic scientists use genetic profiling as a tool to provide evidence of an association between victims, crime scenes, weapons, and suspects. The scientific weight to be accorded genetic profile match depends upon the likelihood of any other possible explanation that would account for the evidence. Normally, this alternative is that the evidence sample originates from another individual who by chance has the same genetic profile. Accordingly, it has long been standard practice to calculate the frequency with which the genetic profile occurs in an individual chosen at random from a relevant population. A relevant population defined as a particular racial group if independently known; or defined by geography. Although critics have argued that the structure of US populations is not strictly heterogeneous through completely random mating, and hence that population frequencies can not be reliably estimated, there is now a substantial body of data showing that population structure effects are minor except in special recognizable cases and that, in any case, its effects on frequency estimates are minor. These points are clearly expressed in the second NRC report which makes specific recommendations regarding the use of statistical methods for the evaluation of DNA results (supra Chapters 4 and 5). These recommendations are based upon a sound foundation of population genetics and statistics, and are designed to provide conservative estimates. The report elaborates several methods for determining frequency estimates of a profile. Different approaches may be appropriate for particular case circumstances, but as the report illustrates, even when different approaches are used, the frequency estimates still fall in the same ballpark. Ultimately, if enough genetic markers are tested, that chance of two unrelated individuals sharing the same profile is vanishingly small. All of these points and methods have been borne out through extensive testing, experimentation and evaluation by qualified individuals and organizations. With the support and guidance of the NRC reports, TWGDAM, and other agencies, DNA analysis has been accepted by the general scientific community.

**Second Prong: Qualifications and Interests of Experts Providing Testimony.**

The courts should seek the opinions of the forensic community in deciding the reliability and validity of any new technique. The Kelly court questioned the objectivity, and therefore opinions, of those who would directly benefit from the admissibility of a new technology. The professional community of forensic scientists is bound by its Code of Ethics and standards of professional practice to employ no technologies that do not rest on a sound scientific foundation and which have not been validated by experimentation. It is not in the interest of this professional community to besmirch its reputation through the use of unsound and invalid procedures. Forensic scientists have demonstrated a history of cautious testing and validation before wholesale adoption of a new technique. Three examples illustrate this point. MN blood group typing was proposed shortly after its discovery (in the 1920's) as a new marker to be used in the testing of blood stains. Medical geneticists of the era actually attempted to employ the test in casework. However validation studies by crime laboratories showed an unacceptable rate of wrong answers. As a result, the test was never implemented by crime labs. The development of Neutron Activation Analysis, a powerful new tool for trace element detection, in the early 1960's offered the promise of using trace element profiles for the individualization of many kinds of evidence, including hair. However, exhaustive study revealed that there were too many variables that could affect the profile to allow for a reliable interpretation of the elemental profile. Again, this analysis was not implemented by crime lab scientists. Finally, mention must be made of the dermal nitrate test for the detection of gunshot and explosives residues on the hands of people handling these items. Uncritical use of this test has long been laid at the door of forensic science [see for example, Neufeld PJ and Colman N, "When Science Takes the Witness Stand" Scientific American 262(5):46-53, 1990] as an example of the profession's failure to subject its methods to scientific scrutiny. Although this test has been inappropriately used (as in the example cited by Neufeld and Colman), the proposition that the professional forensic science community was unaware of the limitations of the test is a myth. As stated in the leading early text in the field,(Crime Investigation, Kirk, P. Wiley, NY, 1953 at p.711), "There is fairly general agreement that the test is not completely reliable inasmuch as a person may fire a gun and receive no nitrate on his hands whereas another person who has not fired a gun may have nitrate on his hands from other sources, such as cigarettes, chemicals, fertilizers, etc." When there has been uncritical use of the test, it has been most often by untrained law enforcement personnel or by chemists from outside forensic science. Forensic scientists are uniquely qualified to render opinions on the reliability of a technology, and on the interpretation of results. Because they routinely encounter evidence that comes from "real world" environments, they are able to devise experiments that will test the validity and reliability of new techniques that may have forensic utility under such conditions. They consult the literature and academics in understanding and testing new technologies. Numerous such validation studies incorporating these elements have been conducted using DNA technology (for example, see Laber TL, Giese SA, *et al.* (1994) "Validation studies on the forensic analysis of restriction fragment length polymorphism (RFLP) on LE agarose gels without ethidium bromide: effects of contaminants, sunlight, and the electrophoresis of varying quantities of deoxyribonucleic acid (DNA)." Journal of Forensic Sciences, 39:707-730); indeed TWGDAM has issued guidelines on appropriate validation studies to perform on DNA markers (Crime Laboratory Digest 1995 18:44-75 section 4; Validation). From these studies comes data for the cautious and appropriate interpretation of results. Other contributions made by forensic scientists to the validation and proper use of DNA technology are listed below in the footnote entitled "Resources for Forensic DNA Analysis."

For these reasons, the opinion of forensic scientists should be sought in determining the validity and reliability, as well as the acceptance of the scientific community, of new forensic tests.

### Third Prong: Appropriate and Accurate Performance of Protocols and Reporting of Results.

If the trial court has reason to suspect that the methodology employed in the performance of DNA analysis in a given case was inadequate or inappropriate, it may conduct a hearing at its discretion. However, it is worth noting that (TWGDAM/CODIS) has demonstrated excellent agreement between laboratories using a generic RFLP protocol (Mudd, supra; Duewer, supra; Stolorow, supra). This work demonstrates that as long as the general steps of RFLP are followed, lab-specific variations should be viewed as preferences, not deviations.

Accreditation and certification are more reasonable measures of a laboratory's or an analyst's ability to correctly apply the generic protocol. Forensic laboratories may be accredited under the aegis of the Laboratory Accreditation Board of ASCLD. This accreditation program is international in scope. It requires regular proficiency testing for DNA analysts, and regular audits of laboratory operations. The program is designed to support rigorous standards of quality control in laboratory testing. It also sets educational standards and requires documentation of all protocols. These requirements are commensurate with laboratory accreditation standards in other areas of scientific testing (e.g., clinical labs).

Still, in any one case an error may occur. It has long been a part of the Code of Ethics of the CAC that one member may review the work of another. This review may take the form of a record review, or of actual re-analysis of the evidence itself. The CAC welcomes and encourages the review of cases, and reiterates the conclusion of the second NRC report that samples be set aside for independent re-analysis. A suspicion of error is best resolved by re-testing, not speculative questioning.

### Conclusion

The CAC would like the Court to consider our perspective on forensic DNA testing, summarized as follows;

The scientific community believes that DNA testing on forensic evidence, including performance of the test and the expression of its significance by use of frequency estimates, is reliable, valid, and generally accepted. Application of DNA testing in any case must adhere to established standards and protocols. Errors are minimized by accreditation of labs and proficiency testing of analysts, and best identified by review and/or repeat testing.

Forensic science has much to contribute in assisting courts to understand new technologies and their application to forensic specimens.

Dated: May 24, 1996

Respectfully submitted,

---

KEITH E. PETERSEN INMAN
Chair, DNA Committee
California Association of Criminalists

---

Matthew P. Harrington
LEPPER, SCHAEFER & HARRINGTON
Attorneys for Amicus Curiae
The California Association of Criminalists (CAC)

## Appendix O

## FORENSIC SCIENCE INTERNET RESOURCES

The following is an incomplete listing of forensic science resources available through the Internet and the World Wide Web:

**Forensic science mailing list**: send e. mail to <mailserv@acc.fau.edu> with subscribe in subject and body.

**Expert witness mailing list**: send e. mail to <expert-L@lern.mv.com> with subscribe in subject and body.

**Zeno's forensic page**: http://www.bart.nl/~geradts/forensic.html
    (everything else can be found from here)

**Banerian's forensic page**: http://www.eskimo.com/~spban/forensic.html

**California Association of Criminalists (CAC)**: http://www.criminalistics.com/CAC/

**American Academy of Forensic Science**: http://www.aafs.org/

**American Board of Criminlistics (ABC)**: http://www.criminalistics.com/ABC/

**Association of Crime Laboratory Directors (ASCLAD)**:
    http://www.shadow.net/~datachem/ascld.html

**Forensic Science Society**: http://www.demon.co.uk/forensic/index.html

**National Fish and Wildlife forensic laboratory**: http://ash.lab.r1.fws.gov/index.html

**Legal Research Network (LERN)**: http://www.witness.net/

# Index

## A

A (adenine), 33, 161
ABC (American Board of Criminalistics), 139, 161, 164, 240
ABO blood group, 6–8
Accreditation, 139, 243
Acrylamide gel, 77–79, 161, 170
Adenine, 33, 161
Admissibility standards, 145–153
  California Association of Criminalists brief, 241–242
  court decisions, 223, 224–238
    PCR, 150–151
    RFLP, 147–150, 152–153
  current debate, 152
  Frye standard and Federal Rules of Evidence, 145–147
  NRC recommendations, 215
  state statutes and legislation, 220
AFDIL (Armed Forces DNA Identification Laboratory), 20, 134
AFIS (Automated Fingerprint Identification System), 133, 161
Agarose, 65, 68, 77, 161
Alabama, 220, 221, 224
Alaska, 220, 221, 224
Allele frequencies, calculating, 90–94, 143, 165, 181–186, see also Population frequency
Alleles
  continuous, 88, 108, 183
  defined, 31, 161
  discrete, 88, 164, 182–183
    degradation, 12
DQα, 42
  D1S80 analysis, 47, 124–125
  heterozygous, 31
  homozygous, 31
  independent segregation, 31
  PCR, interpreting results, 114
  STR analysis, 48
Allele specific oligonucleotide (ASO), 71, 161
Allelic dropout, 113
Allelic ladder, 47
Amelogenin, 50, 161
American Board of Criminalistics (ABC), 139, 161, 164, 240
American Prosecutors Research Institute (APRI), 220, 222

American Society of Crime Laboratory Directors (ASCLD), 139, 212, 240
American Society of Crime Laboratory Directors- Laboratory Accreditation Board (ASCLD-LAB), 212, 215
Amicus brief presented by California Association of Criminalists, 239–244
Amplified Fragment Length Polymorphisms, 47
AmpliType PM system, see Polymarker analysis
Analytical error, 207
Analytical gel, 200
Ancient history, 20
Anderson, Anna, 54
Andrews, T. L., 147, 152–153
Animal DNA, 20, 21–22, 195
Animal geneticists, breeding programs, 20
Annealing, 69, 114–115
Anthropology, 20
APRI (American Prosecutors Research Institute), 220, 222
Arizona, 134–136, 150, 221, 224–225
Arkansas, 221, 225
Armed Forces DNA Identification Laboratory (AFDIL), 20, 134
ASCLD (American Society of Crime Laboratory Directors), 139, 212, 240
ASCLD-LAB (American Society of Crime Laboratory Directors- Laboratory Accreditation Board), 212, 215
ASO (allele specific oligonucleotide), 71, 161
Association
  blood typing, 7
  defined, 161
  population frequency and, 90
  in reconstruction, 3, 5
Audits, 207
Automated Fingerprint Identification System (AFIS), 133, 161
Automation, 157
  DNA typing, 1–2
  sequencing, 76
  systems, 83–85
Autoradiogram, see Autorads
Autoradiograph, see Autorads
Autorads
  minisatellite variable repeat analysis, 80
  RFLP, 37, 38, 39, 65, 69, 102
    degradation, 111
    incomplete digestion, 106
    star activity, 107

Autosome, defined, 161
Axell, L., 149

**B**

Bacterial contamination, 12, 15–16, 104, 177
Band, defined, 162
Band shift, defined, 162
Base analogues, 75
Base pairing, 33, 70, 162
Base pairs
    defined, 33
    in mitochondrial DNA, 51
    required for DNA analysis, 11, 15
Bases
    defined, 162
    DNA, 33
Biallelic, defined, 162
Binning, 92, 162, 184–185, 218
Biotin, 71
Blind proficiency testing, 204–205
Blood typing, 6–8
Blue denim, 15
Breeding programs, 20
BSA protein, 114, 115, 125
Budowle, B., 152
Burglary, 39

**C**

California, 21–22, 39, 42–44, 117–120, 149–150, 151,
        221, 225–226
    admissibility standards, 145–147
California Association of Criminalists, 239–244
Capillary electrophoresis, 85, 157
Case work documentation, 201
Castro, Joseph, 147–148
Caucasians, ABO blood group system, 7–8
C (cytosine), 33, 35, 163
Ceiling principle, 92, 141, 143, 149, 152, 162, 218
Cell, defined, 162
Cell organelles, 50
Cells, 29, 30
Centromere, 162, 180
Certification, 139, 162
    diplomate, 139
    fellow, 139
Chelex extraction
    defined, 162
    procedure, 59–62
Chemiluminescence, see Fluorescence detection
Chromosomal location of loci, 180
Chromosomes, defined, 29, 162, see also
        Allele entries; Population frequency
Circumstantial evidence
    defined, 162
    physical evidence as, 3
Class characteristics, 3–5, 163
Codeine, 5
Coding, defined, 163
CODIS, defined, 163
Collection of evidence, 13–14

Colorado, 221, 226
Color tests, 14
Complementary base pairing, 33, 70, 162
Complicating factors
    contamination, 103–104
    degradation, 102–103
    differential extraction, 101–102
    multiple contributors, 101
Computer technology, see Automation
Connecticut, 220, 221, 226
Conservative estimate, 150, 152, 163
Consistency studies, 194
Contamination
    inhibition of test, 103
    nonhuman DNA, 104
    sources, 12–13, 103
Continous allele systems (PCR)
    closely spaced bands, 108
    RFLP markers, 88, 92–93
Controls, defined, 163
Cougar identification, 20, 21–22
Court decisions, 223, 227–238
    PCR, 150–151
    RFLP, 147–150, 152–153
Cross-hybridization, DQα/A1 analysis, 120
Crossing-over, 31
Culliford, Brian, 7
Cycle sequencing, 75
Cytosine, 33, 35, 163
Czar's bones, identification, 52–54

**D**

Databases, 133–137, 142, 157, 213–214, 217
    cold hit, 133, 134
    defined, 164
*Daubert et al. vs. Merrell Dow*, 147
Degradation
    vs. conventional genetic markers, 11
    defined, 163
    detecting, 109–111, 177
    D1S80 analysis, 126
    effect on analysis, 12, 102–103
    environmental factors, 11
    polymarker analysis, 124
    preventing, 12
Delaware, 220, 221, 226
Denaturation
    defined, 163
    incomplete, 114
    in PCR, 69
Deoxynucleotides, 75, 163
Deoxyribonucleic acid, see DNA
Department of Health and Human Services, 213
Department of Justice, 213
Dermatoglyphic fingerprints, 5, 6
Diallelic, defined, 162
Dideoxynucleotides, 75, 163
Differential extraction
    complications, 101–102
    defined, 163
    procedure, 62–63

Digest gel, 64–65, 68, 105–106, 163, 178
Diploid, defined, 163
Diplomate of the American Board of Criminalistics, 139, 164
Discrete alleles, 47, 164
Discrete allele systems (PCR), 88, 93, 192–183
D-loop in mitochondrial DNA, 51, 163
DNA
    databases, 133–137
    defined, 163
    double-stranded, 33
    environmental factors and type, 11
    molecular biology, 33
    polymorphisms, 34
    single-stranded, 33
    stability, 11
    state of, 172
    uniqueness, 29
DNA Advisory Board, 143
DNA amplification, defined, 164, see also PCR amplification
DNA databases, 133–137, 142, 157, 213–214, 217
    cold hit, 133, 134
    defined, 164
DNA evaluation, 14–16, 63–64, 176, 177, 199–200
DNA fingerprinting, see DNA typing
DNA Identification Act, 143
DNA isolation, 59–64
    Chelex extraction, 59–62
    differential extraction, 62–63
    organic extraction, 62
    quality assurance, 199
DNA polymerase, see Taq polymerase
DNA primers, 70, 128
DNA probes, see Probes
DNA replication, defined, 164
DNA sequencing, 74–76, 84, 158
DNA type, defined, 164
DNA typing
    admissibility standards, 145–153
    applications, 19–20
    vs. blood typing, 7–8
    vs. dermatoglyphic fingerprints, 6
    discovery, 19
    history of, 19–21
    interpretation of results, 101–130
        complicating factors, 101–104
        quality assurance, 201
        for specific systems, 104–130
    key concepts, 174–175
    overview
        PCR, 41–52
        RFLP, 37–40
        sample requirements, 52–55
    PCR amplification
        analysis of products, 70–83
        procedure, 69–70
    procedures, 59–85
        automated systems, 83–85
        isolation, 59–63, 199
        quality and quantity determination, 63–64

RFLP analysis, procedure, 64–69
scientific basis, 29–35
significance of results, 87–94
    frequency estimate calculations, 90–91
    genetic similarity, 87–89
    population substructure, 91–94
    possible conclusions, 87
validation, 193–197
Documentation, 192–193, 201–202, 205–206
Dotson, G., 151
Double helix, 19, 164
Double-stranded DNA, 33, 164
Doublets in Short Tandem Repeats (STRs), 128, 129
DQA1 analysis, see HLA DQA1 analysis
DQα, see HLA DQα
D1S80 analysis
    defined, 163
    interpreting results, 124–128
    legal issues, 150
    procedure, 47, 77–79
    vs. STR, 48
D1S7 locus, 108
Duplicate tests, 216
Dye contamination, 15


**E**

E cells (epithelial cells), 62, 164
Electrophoresis, 77–79, 85, 157, 164, 181
Endonucleases, see Restriction enzymes
England, 20
    blood typing, 7
    nature of crime, 7
Environmental studies, 194
Enzyme markers
    blood typing, 7
    stability, 11
Enzymes, see also Restriction enzymes
    defined, 164
    function, 34
Epithelial cells, 62, 164
Error rates, 141, 143, 165
Errors, 141, 143, 206–207, 215
Ethidium bromide, 65, 165, 177, 178
Ethnic groups
    databases, 212
    population frequencies and, 92–93
Eukaryote, defined, 165
Evidence, see Physical evidence
Evidence sample, defined, 165
Exclusion, 87, 151, 165
Expert witnesses, 142, 242–243
Extension
    defined, 165
    in PCR, 69
Extraction of DNA
    Chelex, 59–62
    differential, 62–63, 101–102, 163
    organic, 62, 169

**F**

Family members, 94, 217
Family reunification, 19–20
FBI, 140, 143
Federal court decisions, 145, 147, 148–149, 227–238, 237–238
Federal Rules of Evidence, 146–147, 165
Fellow of the American Board of Criminalistics, 139, 165
Fibers, class characteristics, 4
Fingerprints
    vs. DNA analysis, 6
    individualizing traits, 5
Fixed-bin method, 218
Floating-bin method, 218
Florida, 147, 152–153, 221, 226–227
Fluorescence detection
    advantages, 157
    Molecular Dynamics FluorImager, 85
    quality assurance, 200
    slot blot technique, 176
    of STR loci, 48, 49, 77–79
Forensic science
    history of DNA typing, 20–21
    public scrutiny, 1
Forensic scientists, NRC recommendations on testimony, 142, 242–243
Fragment length, in RFLP, 88
Frequency, see Population frequency
Frye Standard, 145–147, 148, 165

**G**

Gametes
    alleles, 31
    defined, 165
Gel, defined, 165
Gel electrophoresis, 77–79, 181
Gender determination, 31
Gender identification, PCR, 50, 77–79
Gene, defined, 165
Gene frequency, 143, 165, 181–186, see also Population frequency
Gene mapping, 195
General acceptance concept, 145–146
Genetic concordance, 32, 87, 165, see also Genetic similarity
Genetic linkage, 31, 165
    linkage equilibrium and disequilibrium, 31, 32, 91–93, 168
Genetic markers
    blood typing, 7
    conventional, stability, 11
    defined, 166
    frequency, 90
    random assortment, 31
Genetics
    alleles, 31
    in mitochondrial DNA inheritance, 51
    physical basis of heredity, 29–31
    population, 32–33
    rope analogy, 32

Genetic similarity
    continuous allele systems, 88
    defined, 87, 166
    discrete allele systems, 88
    evaluating evidence, 89
    sample determination, 182–183
    significance standards, 157
Genetic typing
    blood typing, 6–8
    DNA typing, 8
Genome, defined, 166
Genotype, defined, 166
Genotype frequencies, 90–94, 143, 165, 181–186, see also Population frequency
Georgia, 221, 227
G (guanine), 33, 35, 165, 166
Glass fragments, 109
Guanine, 33, 35
    defined, 165, 166
Guns, 5

**H**

*Hae*III restriction enzyme
    defined, 166
    location of cuts, 35
    partial digestion, 105
    in RFLP, 37
    star activity, 107
    three-banded patterns, 104
Hair, class characteristics, 4
Haploid, defined, 166
Hardy-Weinberg equilibrium, 32, 91–93, 166
Hawaii, 221, 227
Hawaii Rules of Evidence, 146
Hemizygous, defined, 51, 166
Heredity, defined, 166, see also Genetics
Heteroduplex formation, 114–115, 126, 128
Heteroplasmy, 53, 166
Heterozygosity, defined, 166
Heterozygotes/heterozygous
    defined, 31, 166
    PCR results, 112–113, 186
    RFLP results, 108–109, 185
High molecular weight, 63, 167
*Hinf*I restriction enzyme, 35
    defined, 166
    in RFLP, 37
History of DNA typing, 19–21
HLA DQA1 analysis
    defined, 167
    interpretation of results, 115–117, 120–121
    murder case sidebar, 73–74
    polymarker system, 45–46
    procedure, 41–42, 45, 70–73
    Simpson case, 117–120
    sperm identification, 122
HLA DQα analysis, 11
    defined, 167
    interpretation of results, 115–117, 120–121
    landmark cases, 150–151
    polymarker system, 45–46

procedure, 41–42, 45
  Simpson case, 117–120
  sperm identification, 122
HLA (human leukocyte antigen), defined, 167
Homozygotes/homozygous, 12
  defined, 31
  PCR results, 112–113, 186
  RFLP results, 108–112, 185–186
Horseradish peroxidase (HRP), 71, 167
HRP (horseradish peroxidase), 71, 167
Human genetics, see Genetics
Human Genome Project, 19, 167
Human leukocyte antigen (HLA), defined, 167
Human material in contamination, 12–13
HVI (hypervariable region I), 167
HVII (hypervariable region II), 76–77, 167
Hybridization, 196–197
  defined, 33, 167
  in RFLP, 65
Hypervariable
  defined, 34, 167
  frequency determination, 90
  mitochondrial DNA, 51, 76–77
Hypervariable region I (HVI), 167
Hypervariable region II (HVII), 76–77, 167

**I**

Idaho, 227
Identification, 3–5
Illinois, 151, 221, 227–228
Inclusion, defined, 167
Inconclusive evidence, 87
Independent segregation, defined, 167
Indiana, 220, 221, 228
Individualization, 3–5
  defined, 167
  vs. match, 87
Inheritance, see Genetics
Innocence Project, 21
Interim ceiling principle, 141, 143, 149, 150, 168
Internet resources, 245
Interpretation of results, 101–130
  complicating factors, 101–104
  quality assurance, 201
  for specific systems, 104–130
*In vitro*, defined, 167
Iowa, 221, 228
Isolation of DNA, see DNA isolation
Isotope, defined, 168
Isotope labeling, 108, 157

**J**

Jeffreys, Alec, 19, 20

**K**

Kansas, 221, 228–229
K562 cell line, 68, 168
Kentucky, 221, 229
Kilobase pairs, 15, 168

**L**

Laboratories, see Quality assurance, TWGDAM
    report
Laboratory accreditation, 139, 243
Lander, E., 152
Law Enforcement Assistance Administration (LEAA),
    7
LDLR (low density lipoprotein receptor), 123
Legal issues, 1–2
  admissibility standards, 145–153
    California Association of Criminalists brief,
      241–242
    court decisions, 223, 224–238
    state statutes and legislation, 220
  mandatory submission of blood samples, 221–222
  NRC recommendations, 214, 215, 218–219
  PCR evidence, 134–137
  physical evidence
    science in reconstruction, 3
    transfer theory, 5
  qualifications for rendering opinions, 142
Legislation
  admissibility standards, 220
  DNA database, 133
  mandatory submission of blood samples, 221–222
Length polymorphisms, 34
  defined, 168
  interpretation of PCR systems, 124–130
Lie-detector testing, 145
Linkage, 31, 165
Linkage equilibrium and disequilibrium, 31, 32, 91–93,
    168
Locard Transfer Theory, 5
Locus
  characterization, 195
  chromosomal location, 180
  defined, 31, 34, 168
Louisiana, 220, 221, 229
Low density lipoprotein receptor (LDLR), 123
Lumigraph, defined, 168

**M**

Maine, 221, 229
Markers, see Genetic markers
Maryland, 220, 221, 229–230
Massachusetts, 230
Match, see also Genetic concordance; Genetic
    similarity
  defined, 87
  in PCR, 88
  in RFLP, 88, 89
Match criteria, 88, 168
Matrix studies, 194
Membrane, defined, 168
Michigan, 221, 230
Microorganisms, contamination of DNA, 12, 15–16, 104,
    177
Minisatellite variable repeat analysis (MVR), 79–83,
    157
Minnesota, 136–137, 150, 220, 221, 230–231

Mississippi, 221, 231
Missouri, 221, 231
Mitochondria, defined, 168
Mitochondrial DNA analysis
    applications, 158
    identifying the Romanov's bodies, 52–54
    legal issues, 153
    procedure, 50–52, 74–77
    sequencing, 74–76
Mixed samples, 12, 101–102
    DQα/A1 analysis, 117
    PCR, 113
    quality assurance, 194
Modus operandus (MO), 168
Molecular Dynamics FluorImager, 85
Molecular weight
    assessment, 63
    defined, 167, 168
    required for DNA analysis, 11, 15
Molecular-weight size marker, defined, 168
MO (modus operandus), 168
Monoclonal, defined, 51, 169
Monomorphic probe, defined, 169
Montana, 221, 231
Mountain lion identification, 20, 21–22
mtDNA, see Mitochondrial DNA
Multilocus probe, defined, 169
Multiple donors
    DQα/A1 analysis, 117
    interpretation of results, 101–102
    polymarker analysis, 123
Multiplexing, 157
Mutation, point, 170
Mutation rate, in mitochondrial DNA, 51

**N**

National Institute of Justice (NIJ), 169, 213
National Institute of Standards and Technology (NIST),
        169, 241
National Institutes of Health (NIH), 169
National Research Council I and II (NRC I and II),
        140–143, 149, 150, 152, 211–219
    ceiling principles, 218
    databanks and privacy of information, 213–214,
        217
    duplicate tests, 216
    further research, 218
    laboratory errors, 215
    legal issues, 214, 215, 218–219
    matching and binning, 218
    population genetics, 216–217
    population substructure, 92
    proficiency tests, 215
    societal issues, 214–215
    standards, 212–213
    statistical issues, 211–212, 217
    technical considerations, 211
    uniqueness, 217–218
Nebraska, 231
Nevada, 220, 221
New Hampshire, 220, 221, 232

New Jersey, 221, 232
New Mexico, 232
New York State, 147–148, 221, 232–233
NIH (National Institutes of Health), 169
NIJ (National Institute of Justice), 169, 213
NIST (National Institute of Standards and Technology),
        169, 241
Noncoding, defined, 169
Nonhuman studies, 195
Nonprobative evidence, 194
North Carolina, 221, 233
North Dakota, 220, 221
NRC I and II, see National Research Council I
        and II
Nuclear DNA, 50, 169
Nucleic acid, defined, 169
Nucleotides, 33, 70, 169
Nucleus, 29
    defined, 169

**O**

Ohio, 222, 233–234
Oklahoma, 222, 234
On-site evaluation, 195
Oregon, 222, 234
Oregon Rules of Evidence, 146
Organelle, defined, 169
Organic extraction
    defined, 169
    procedure, 61, 62

**P**

Partial digestion by restriction enzyme, 64–65, 105–106,
        169, 178
Paternity cases, 19
PCR amplification
    admissibility of evidence, 215
    applications, 20
    complementary base pairing, 33
    contaminants, 15–16
    court decisions, 150–151, 223
    Czar's bones, identification, 52–54
    defined, 170
    D1S80 analysis, 47
    gender ID, 50
    HLA DQα/HLA DQA1, 41–42, 45
    interpretation of results, 112–130
        general considerations, 113–115
        length-based systems, 124–130
        sequence-based systems, 115–1–124
        Simpson case, 117–120
        sperm identification, 122
    invention, 19
    key concepts, 174–175
    loci-specific tests, 112–113
    match of samples, 88
    minimum amount of DNA required, 15, 55, 63
    mitochondrial DNA, 50–52
    overview, 40
    polymarker, 45–46